TEACHING CROWDS

Issues in Distance Education
Series editors: Terry Anderson and David Wiley

Distance education is the fastest-growing mode of both formal and informal teaching, training, and learning. It is multi-faceted in nature, encompassing e-learning and mobile learning, as well as immersive learning environments. Issues in Distance Education presents recent research results and offers informative and accessible overviews, analyses, and explorations of current topics and concerns and the technologies employed in distance education. Each volume focuses on critical questions and emerging trends, while also situating these developments within the historical evolution of distance education as a specialized mode of instruction. The series is aimed at a wide group of readers, including teachers, trainers, administrators, researchers, and students.

Series Titles

TEACHING CROWDS

LEARNING AND SOCIAL MEDIA

Jon Dron

Terry Anderson

AU PRESS

Published by AU Press, Athabasca University
1200, 10011 – 109 Street, Edmonton, AB T5J 3S8

ISBN 978-1-927356-80-7 (print)   978-1-927356-81-4 (PDF)   978-1-927356-82-1 (epub)
doi: 10.15215/aupress/9781927356807.01

A volume in Issues in Distance Education
ISSN 1919-4382 (print)   1919-4390 (digital)

Cover and interior design by Sergiy Kozakov
Printed and bound in Canada by Marquis Book Printers

Library and Archives Canada Cataloguing in Publication
Dron, Jon, 1961-, author
       Teaching crowds : learning and social media / Jon Dron and Terry Anderson.

(Issues in distance education series)
Includes bibliographical references and index.
Issued in print and electronic formats.

       1. Educational technology. 2. Education--Social aspects. 3. Social learning. 4. Social
media. 5. Group work in education. 6. Distance education. 7. Critical pedagogy. I.
Anderson, Terry, 1950-, author II. Title. III. Series: Issues in distance education series

LB1028.3.D76 2014   371.33   C2014-901074-5
                                           C2014-901075-3

We acknowledge the financial support of the Government of Canada through
the Canada Book Fund (CFB) for our publishing activities.

 Canadian   Patrimoine
Heritage   canadien

Assistance provided by the Government of Alberta, Alberta Multimedia
Development Fund.

Government

This text is dedicated to our lifelong friends and wives Kestra (Jon) and Susan (Terry), who have, on too many occasions, felt disconnected from us because we have been connecting with the crowd. We are learning.

CONTENTS

FIGURES AND TABLES

PREFACE

Learning is a remarkably social process. Social groups provide
the resources for their members to learn.
   John Seely Brown & Paul Duguid, The Social Life of Information

This book is about learning online with other people. Its title, *Teaching Crowds*, is deliberately ambiguous: the book is about how to teach crowds, but it is also about how crowds teach. What interests us are the ways in which people learn from and with one another in an online context while playing the roles of both learner and teacher—not always intentionally, and not always even as individuals. As we intend to show, there are ways in which the aggregated behaviours of crowds can teach.

Between the two of us, we have several decades of experience with using and creating social software for learning, and the time seems ripe to pull together some of what we have learned about learning. More than ever before, the crowd has become the teacher of the crowd, and, more than ever before, we have new tools and new methods with which to teach the crowd. This book is about how that vast cluster of connected individuals can learn together, within the context of institutions and beyond, and can begin to make sense of the torrent of useful and useless information that surrounds us all. In the pages to come, we will describe the theoretical foundations of the use of social software for learning and, building on those foundations, explore ways that such software can be used to support and enable learners to learn.

The book begins with an unashamed trumpeting of the potential value of social software for learning. In the opening chapter, we provide an overview of this software and describe the many advantages that may be gained through its effective employment. We hope that this introduction will tempt even skeptics to read on and learn more about the benefits, and the pitfalls, of social media as tools for learning.

In the second chapter, we present a range of theories—some mature, others still evolving—that have developed in tandem with social learning technologies over the past few decades. Our goal is to offer a theoretical foundation that both explains and predicts the value of different ways of understanding learning in a crowd. We make considerable use of our own three-generation model of distance learning pedagogies, describing the shift from early behaviourist and cognitivist models to the era of social constructivism and then on to the emerging connectivist age of distance learning. In addition, we explore a number of other theoretical constructs and approaches, such as the theory of transactional distance, complexity theory, the concept distributed cognition, and the notion of cooperative freedoms, that help to frame and illuminate many of the dynamics of social learning in both informal and formal contexts.

Having laid the theoretical groundwork for social learning and teaching, in chapter 3, we provide a framework for understanding the different ways in which people engage with one another in a learning situation. We introduce our model of social forms, which categorizes three broad and overlapping modes of social engagement used for learning: groups, networks (or nets), and sets. We also introduce the notion of collectives—emergent entities that result from social engagement in one or more of the three basic social forms. Until recently, most research into social learning in formal contexts has assumed the centrality of a traditional closed group, with hierarchies, roles, rules, and a strong sense of membership. The closed group is the social form characteristic of classrooms and tutorial groups, in schools and colleges the world over. Social media have, however, made it considerably easier to engage with people in other ways, notably through social networks (formed from direct connections between individuals) and social sets (loose communities defined by a particular interest, or by place, or by some other shared trait). As a result, the role of collective intelligence has become far more prominent than it was in pre-Internet times. Today, it is possible to learn not only from individuals but also from their collective behaviour and interactions. Our contention is that different social forms suggest and sometimes require different approaches to learning and teaching.

In chapters 4 to 7, we delve into the details of how learning and teaching happens in groups, networks, sets, and collectives. We describe methods, tools, pedagogies, and approaches that are of value in each of these four modalities, as well as their distinguishing features and points of overlaps, We also examine their relationship to transactional distance and the kinds of freedoms they provide and demand.

In chapter 8, to illustrate how our model applies in specific learning contexts, we share some of our discoveries as users and developers of social systems for learning. We describe our work on an Elgg-based system, Athabasca Landing, and the projects that led up to it, as well as providing examples of its integration into both formal and informal learning at Athabasca University. By translating the abstract ideas and models presented in previous chapters into concrete form, this chapter illustrates how the messiness of real-life settings provokes complex, and sometimes unanticipated, responses and evolving, rather than predetermined, outcomes.

Throughout the book, we acknowledge the many pitfalls and potential dangers associated with the use of social media for learning, ranging from loss of organizational control through to risks that pertain to the security, privacy, and comfort of individual users. In chapter 9, we accordingly examine the dark side of social software—the ways in which it can undermine or even jeopardize, rather than deepen and extend, the experience of learning. We present a series of overarching issues that warrant consideration by anyone who plans to use social software for learning. These include issues surrounding privacy, disclosure, and trust, cross-cultural dissonances, problems posed by the complexities of technology and by the digital divide, unpredictable systemic effects, and risks such as mob stupidity and filter bubbles. Where possible, we suggest ways of mitigating such risks. To the extent that risks are inherent, we describe the trade-offs—the benefits against which the risks must be weighed.

An underlying theme of the book is that learning and teaching involve a complex interplay of technologies, pedagogies, organizational structures, social bonds, and individual needs, with many interdependencies and systemic consequences. Changing one part of a learning system is seldom fully beneficial if one fails to consider that each part in a system affects, and is affected by, all the other parts. If the whole is not carefully analyzed and understood, changes can lead to unexpected, and often unwanted, outcomes. As we suggest in our penultimate chapter, "Issues and Challenges in Educational Uses of Social Software," a poorly considered strategy for using social media in learning may have calamitous consequences. At the same time, as we demonstrate throughout the book, social media have enormous potential value for learning, formal and informal. Our task is to find ways to make them work for us.

In concluding, we present our speculations on the implications of the changes wrought by the ever-increasing use of social media in distance learning and the various shifts that may or should occur across educational systems as a result. We offer a broad vision of a future in which parts that are now available might be fitted together to create a richer, more responsive, and more socially engaged culture, as well as a toolset for lifelong learning that is unfettered by path dependencies and academic structures and methods that date back to the Middle Ages. In mapping out this vision of learning, we go beyond institutional settings, although we also suggest some ways that institutions might adapt to cater to more flexible learning paths. We are under no illusions that our vision, taken as a whole, is likely to become reality any time soon, nor do we imagine that, in conceiving it, we have somehow broken free from our own backgrounds and personal and cultural orientations. We present it as one of many possible futures, in the hope that it will stimulate discussion and prompt movement toward a more human-centred, socially embedded educational system.

★ ★ ★

Like much discourse related to education, this book has a practical focus. For this focus, we offer no apologies but rather follow the lead of the American pragmatists, including William James and the great educational philosopher John Dewey. As James observed in a lecture delivered in 1906, pragmatism celebrates "the attitude of looking away from first things, principles, 'categories,' supposed necessities; and of looking toward last things, fruits, consequences and facts" (2000, p. 196). In the context of traditional education, these "last things" are the results of engaging in formal learning activities. In the broader setting of informal, lifelong learning, however, we have unprecedented opportunity to create new "last things" by engaging in global conversations that are, to a great extent, unmediated and uncontrolled by social and political elites. Our challenge as educators is to use this opportunity in ways that make significant differences in the lives our students, our communities, and our globe.

Social software both enables and encourages potentially disruptive patterns of social organization and interaction. Throughout the book, we highlight the manner in which these patterns of interaction support informal modes of learning—although, as a starting point, we focus on learning that occurs within the formal setting of an institution. As the book progresses, we will describe technologies and methods that apply equally in both formal and informal settings and may in fact tend to subvert traditional, institution-based approaches to learning. As will become clear, social software opens up possibilities for learning that do not sit neatly within a traditional educational context. Such unconventional learning, which often takes place far beyond institutional walls, in turn raises critically important questions surrounding equity and accreditation—how to recognize the legitimacy of such learning.

If we sometimes seem to paint a rosy picture of the potential of social software, remember that we are often describing what is possible given state-of-the-art tools and methods of systems design. We are also aware of the irony of discussing revolutionary changes in communications cyberspace in the form of a book, even though many readers will view this text on a computer screen or on a mobile device such as a tablet. Like the subjects we explore, this book is caught in the flux of shifting paradigms, rooted at once in the past, present, and future. At the same time, because Athabasca University Press is a fully open access publisher, this book will be available not only for purchase, in both print and epub format, but also as standard PDFs that can be downloaded for free at www.aupress.ca. We wanted to ensure that the book would be disseminated as widely as possible and that no one would be prevented from reading it by financial constraints, and we thank Athabasca University Press for providing us with this opportunity. We hope that, in the spirit of open scholarship, you will blog about, tweet, and otherwise share your reactions to the text with the online sets, nets, and groups to which you belong, and thus become a part of the crowd that teaches and a teacher of the crowd. To help support such social learning we encourage you to visit http://teachingcrowds.ca, where you will find further opportunities to explore, discuss, and develop the ideas presented here, as well as other resources that we hope you will find useful.

TEACHING CROWDS

ON THE NATURE AND VALUE OF SOCIAL SOFTWARE FOR LEARNING

In this chapter we define what social software is, and present a list of ways that it can be of use to learners, describing some of the potentially valuable functions and features that are available in these systems. The chapter is intended to establish a common understanding and vocabulary that provides a background to issues explored in greater depth throughout the rest of the book.

WHY LEARN ONLINE WITH OTHER PEOPLE?

The first reason to learn online with others is opportunity: what Stuart Kauffman (2000) calls the "adjacent possible." New technologies offer such an opportunity. There are more networked devices than people in the world, with around one-third of the world's population (2.26 billion people as of 2011) having access to the Internet, a figure projected to rise to around 40% by 2016 (Broadband Commission, 2012, p. 44). In Europe, over 60% of the population has regular access to the Internet, in North America, over 78% (Internet World Stats, 2012). In some countries, nearly the entire population has regular, personal Internet access. The digital traces this population leaves are vast. Google alone indexes over 30 trillion Web pages (Koetsier, 2013), which does not include countless others that are not indexed or contain dynamic, ever-changing content. The International Telecommunication Union (2012) reports that there were over 6 billion cellphone subscriptions worldwide by the end of 2011. Of those, over 30% (and rising) sold are smartphones, capable of connecting to the Internet. Nevertheless, there remain massive inequalities and barriers: only 24% of people in developing nations currently have Internet access and the number of countries that censor or prohibit the use of the Internet is rising. However, it is not unreasonable to suppose that, before very long, nearly every human on the planet may be able to connect with nearly every other in order to share information, knowledge, and ideas in a myriad of ways, virtually instantaneously. In our pockets we carry devices that can connect us not only to billions of living people but also with the digital traces they have left and the things they have shared, and with much of the accumulated knowledge of our forebears. Not only can we connect with people and their products but we can also connect with their aggregates—groups, organizations, companies, institutions, networks, communities, nations, and cultures. Social technologies for learning, from email to learning management systems, are ubiquitous in our schools and colleges.

The second reason for learning online with others is that, with every connection, direct and indirect, comes the opportunity to learn, and learning happens in many of these interactions. Almost every search on Google, visit to a page on Wikipedia or a how-to site is an act of intentional learning, one that is only possible because many people have, intentionally or otherwise, acted on our behalf as teachers. Meanwhile, a vast amount of intentional and unintentional learning is facilitated every day through posts on Twitter, Facebook, YouTube, LinkedIn, Pinterest, and countless other services. Smartphones and dumbphones (basic phones) are increasingly used more as information-finding devices than as simple communication tools. Large-scale courses and tutorials, often clumped together under the label of MOOCs (massive open online courses) are gathering millions of learners, eager and willing to learn.

LEARNING WITH TECHNOLOGIES IN CROWDS

In prehistoric times, knowledge spread through time and space by word of mouth and through example, stories and songs, apprenticeships, direct engagement, copying and observing others. The temporal and physical space between the original knowledge creator and knowledge constructor was sometimes very great, but the learner and teacher were physically and temporally adjacent. This is, of course, an oversimplification, even if we conveniently ignore things like cave paintings and other representations of knowledge such as sculpture and jewellery available to our ancestors. From the time we first started shaping tools, clothing, dwellings, and weapons, we have offloaded some of our cognitive processes into the spaces around us and shared in the intelligence of others as a result. In some cases, such as the carefully aligned stones of Stonehenge or cuneiform impressions in clay, the cognitive element of the artifacts we create is obvious: these are technologies at least partly intended to embody and enable thinking, though they may serve other functions as well. In the case of Stonehenge, the stones' alignment enabled prediction and calculation of solstices and other significant temporal events. Cuneiform impressions served many purposes that extended our cognition, including as an adjunct to memory, a means to record and manipulate numbers, and as a way of sharing our knowledge with those not occupying the same time and space. However, even the haft of a spear or the pressed clay of a drinking bowl makes a tool that we think with, a shared object of cognition from which our learning and thinking cannot be glibly separated (Saloman, 1993). These are shared objects that are innately social: they do not just perform tasks for individuals, but carry shared meanings, communicable purposes, and the memories of those who created, refined, and developed them over time. As S. Johnson (2012) observes about the skill of the pilot in a modern airplane, the pilot's success is only possible through a "duet" with the thousands of people whose learning is embodied in the systems, devices, and methods used to both create and sustain the aircraft.

Historically, learning was nearly always with and from a crowd: methods, tools, customs, dances, music and stories, whether prototypical or fully formed, all played a role in establishing a collective, learned culture. While the transmission of knowledge could be, and perhaps often was a one-to-one exchange, the innate physics of dance, music, and speech made much cultural transmission a crowd phenomenon, a sharable and shared performance.

In the past, written words conveyed and shared our insights and ideas beyond co-located groups, separate in both space and time. Writing is a technology that allows one individual to directly address another, whether separated by thousands of years, thousands of miles, or both. Artifacts like paintings and sculptures provide further examples of this mode of engagement, communicating facts, beliefs, and emotions over time and space. Similarly, once the skills of creating and reading have been mastered, writing seemingly requires no further interpretation or context to complete the connection between learner and teacher, though our familiarity belies much of the vast complexity of mastering the tools and sharing meaning in the most intricate and subtle of technologies. Writing is, in a sense, a one-to-one technology that may be replicated many times, the same one communicating with many other individuals, one at a time. Rarely, save in some limited contexts such as inscriptions on statues, shop signs, scoreboards at football games, or sacred texts read aloud in public gatherings, is writing a one-to-many technology like speech. Writing is ostensibly direct, a communication channel between writer and reader that seems unmediated and undistorted by the intercession of others. It thus serves to contract time and space. Even today, when writing is a medium that may be shared with billions of others both now and in the indeterminate future, it shares this interesting characteristic: it is at once the epitome of social technology and the most private of engagements since the reader is potentially unknown to the writer, and his or her context may be entirely different from that of the writer's.

The invention of printing changed the scale of this imbalance between the one and the many. Publication for the masses—without the need for an intermediary interpreter, or a creator of glosses—separated the writer (content creator) and the crowd almost entirely. This process continued in the nineteenth and twentieth centuries, which saw the emergence of mass, instantaneous, and global communications: sound and video recording, radio and television broadcasting, and a host of accompanying technologies and infrastructures combined with ever-more powerful tools for printing, and the dissemination of printed materials made one-to-many communication the predominant form of knowledge distribution. Though social in some important ways, this development made possible mass educational processes that were in many other ways asocial. Alongside that, first the telegraph and fax and later the telephone and mobile phone made it simple to engage in near instantaneous one-to-one communication across vast distances almost as easily as local conversations. A many-to-many gap had been created.

THE RISE OF CYBERSPACE

In recent decades we have witnessed the increasing convergence of all forms of communication, publication, and information-sharing onto networked digital platforms—mainly the Internet but also cellular networks, digital TV, gaming networks, satellite communication systems, personal area networks, and other networked digital media. Collectively, to emphasize that we are not always simply talking about the Internet, we will refer to this connected set of tools and the interactions they enable as "cyberspace," a term first coined by William Gibson (1984). Cyberspace may mimic other media, but it always carries with it far greater potential for two-or-more-way communication. In addition, its digital character makes the possibility of precise replication a simple task that, as often as not, needs little or no thought or effort to achieve. Even when there is no intention or facility for dialogue, the protocols and standards that underpin computer networking systems are seething with internal and hidden dialogues, exchanges, caches, and buffers that replicate and communicate between the devices we attach to our networks. Earlier forms of learning and teaching tools still exist but, increasingly, they are formatted first for cyberspace, and then placed in a secondary medium such as textbooks, classrooms, DVDs, or broadcast television.

This shift of both communication and content to cyberspace has profound implications for both lifelong learning and the formal education produced by our schools and universities. Clay Shirky (2008), in his insightful analysis of major communication innovations in history notes that cyberspace encompasses all previous innovations (print, video, radio, cinema, etc.) and supports one-to-one, one-to-many, and many-to-many communications at the same time, using the same low-cost tools. Beyond what is practical or possible in conventional human interaction, cyberspace supports dynamic collective knowledge generation. Our activities in cyberspace create traces and artifacts that, when aggregated, allow us to better understand the activities, ideas, and the nature of other individuals, along with the societies and communities they belong to; these activities can also provide novel insights into our own behaviours and interests.

All of these capabilities create new and very exciting opportunities for formal and informal learning. However, McCarthy, Miller, and Skidmore have argued that these "networks are the language of our times, but our institutions are not programmed to understand them" (2004, p. 11) . One major purpose of this book, therefore, is to explore these opportunities and provide both understanding and keys to action that can be used by educators and, as importantly, by learners.

As McLuhan (1994) and many others have observed, there is a rich interplay between the medium and the message it conveys. The media utilized by educators have very profound effects on the content taught, the organization of the learning process, and the range of available learning activities. The convergence of media in cyberspace has radically altered the conditions for teaching and learning, causing some to complain about the mismatch between the skills needed to operate effectively in a net-infused society, and the skills developed and information created in most of our industrial age schools and universities (Oliver, 2008). As W. Richardson notes,

> in an environment where it's easy to publish to the globe, it feels more and more hollow to ask students to "hand in" their homework to an audience of one . . . when many of our students are already building networks far beyond our classroom walls, forming communities around their passions and their talents, it's not hard to understand why rows of desks and time-constrained schedules and standardized tests are feeling more and more limiting and ineffective. (2006, p. 36)

The bulk of the applications introduced and discussed in this book can be classified as social learning technologies. The "social" attribute comes from the fact that
they acquire their value when used by two or more people. Many of these tools
are used to support sharing, annotating, discussing, editing, and cooperatively or
collaboratively constructing knowledge among collections of learners and "teachers" (a loose term for anyone, or ones, along with machinery or systems that make
learning more effective). Other social technologies connect people differently
and less directly—for instance, by aggregating their behaviours in order to recommend books (e.g., Amazon), movies (e.g., Netflix) or websites (e.g., Google or
Delicious). The size of the aggregations of people connected by social technologies can vary from two to many millions. The openness and potential for sharing
makes social technologies particularly useful for education and learning applications, since in many ways the vast majority of learning is a social activity. As we
shall see, many of our most powerful pedagogical theories and understandings of
learning processes assume that knowledge is both created and validated in social
contexts. Thus, developments in social technologies hold great promise to affect
teaching and learning.

While social software has existed for many decades, the term *social software*
is often attributed to Clay Shirky (2003), who defined it as "software that supports group interaction." This definition is so broad that it includes everything
from email to immersive, virtual worlds, so it has been qualified by a number of
authors. Allen (2004) noted the historical evolution of social software tools as the
Internet gained capacity to support human interaction, decision-making, planning, and other higher level activities across the boundaries of time and space,
and less adeptly those of culture and language. Levin (2004) noted the affordance
of the Web to support new patterns of interconnection that "facilitate new social
patterns: multi-scale social spaces, conversation discovery and group forming, personal and social decoration and collaborative folk art."

Coates (2002) describes the functional characteristics of social software to
extend human communication capabilities. He notes the enhanced communication capacity provided by social software over time and distance, which are the
traditional challenges of access addressed by distance education. He goes on to
point out that social software adds tools to help us deal with the complexities and
scale of online context such as collaborative filtering, spam control, recommendation, and authentication systems. He argues that social software supports the

efficacy of social interaction by alleviating challenges of group functioning such as decision-making, maintaining group memory, versioning, and documenting processes.

A useful addendum to the various definitions of social software was added by Mejias, who defined social software as "software that allows people to interact and collaborate online or *that aggregates the actions of networked users*" (2005; emphasis added). The benefits that accrue to learners from this aggregation of the ideas, behaviours, and attitudes of others are defining features for many of the forms of collective social software defined in this text. We are pleased that, unlike many others, this definition includes systems that are only obliquely "social" in the traditional sense that emerges from face-to-face interaction, such as Google Search, whose PageRank algorithm uses implicit recommendations supplied by the crowd, and Amazon's book recommendation feature, which employs similarities in user behaviour to help guide future choices. Social technologies extend the possibilities for us to help one another to learn in ways that were difficult or impossible in the past, and that is the focus of this book.

To further clarify the term in an educational context, we have in the past defined educational social software as "networked tools that support and encourage individuals to learn together while retaining individual control over their time, space, presence, activity, identity and relationship" (T. Anderson, 2005, p. 4). This definition speaks to the right of learners and teachers to retain control over the educational context in which they are engaged. It obviously resonates with distance educators who define their particular form of education by the increase in access in many dimensions to the educational process. However, social software is also being used on campus where it affords and encourages communication, collaboration, and social support within and outside of normal classroom learning, maintaining and building new social ties.

Beyond formal settings, social software has become one of the most central means enabling lifelong learning: Google Search and Wikipedia, both social technologies that benefit from extremely large crowds, are the first port of call for many learners seeking knowledge. Whereas learning with others in the past often meant giving up certain freedoms, such as those of place, time, or direction, increasingly our social technologies support networked individualism (Rainie & Wellman, 2012), where we interact with others but remain at the centre of our social worlds.

We also focus on the increasing rights and freedoms provided to learners by the advent of networked learning. Students now have options to choose the mode, the pace, the presentation format, the credential, and the degree of cooperative versus individual learning they wish to engage in, both in formal and informal learning contexts.

By definition, learning is associated with change. We change our ideas, actions, capacities and skills in response to challenges and opportunities. For most types of learning, the necessary knowledge or skills needed to solve our problem already exists in the mind of another person or resource. Our job as learners and educators is to provide tools, paths, and techniques by which this knowledge can be accessed, appropriated, constructed, and re-constructed so as to meet our individual and collective needs. Social software is designed to help in two fundamental ways. First, it creates a transparency by which we can locate individuals or groups of humans with the tools and means to help us learn. Second, it serves to effectively leverage the tacit knowledge contained in the minds of others and the myriad learning objects in ways that can easily be adapted to individual and collective needs. Like other Internet resources, it does this with an economy of scale that allows global access at an almost negligible cost. For the purposes of this book, we use the terms "social media" and "social software" interchangeably although, technically speaking, social software is the tool that enables social media to be embodied or enacted.

INTERACTIONS SUPPORTED BY SOCIAL SOFTWARE

Media used socially supports three obvious kinds of interaction:

1. One-to-one: a single person engaging with one other person
2. One-to-many: a single person or entity broadcasting to many people
3. Many-to-many: multi-way interaction between many people

A less obvious kind of interaction that is of particular significance in social media is many-to-one, in which the actions, judgments, or behaviours of many people are aggregated, transformed, and re-presented to an individual. A classic example of this is Google Search. Google's PageRank algorithm takes into account the number of links made to a page, and the number of links to the pages that link to the page, and so on, treating each as an implicit recommendation of the page that it links to. This is a form of latent human annotation (Kleinberg, 1998) where behaviours that may have occurred with other purposes in mind are mined and repurposed to serve the needs of individuals.

Social software tools may support synchronous interaction (real-time communication) and asynchronous interaction (communication that may be viewed, listened to, or read by the recipient at a different time than when it was posted), or both.

Social tools may afford direct or indirect forms of interaction: their purposes can vary from enabling communication to collaborative discovery, cooperative sharing, and more, often with layers of mediation that may either reveal or obscure the people who leave traces, intentional or otherwise, for others.

A vast number, perhaps the majority, of social software systems are aggregations of different forms, offering one-to-one, one-to-many, many-to-many, many-to-one, asynchronous, synchronous, direct and indirect interaction. Like all technologies, social technologies are assemblies and may be used with or as part of further assemblies (Arthur, 2009). In order to provide concrete and familiar examples, in table 1.1 we list a range of families of social software, broadly categorizing them by the predominant forms of social engagement that they involve.

Table 1.1 Examples of social software.

	Brief Description	Examples	One-to-one	One-to-many	Many-to-many	Many-to-one	Synchronous	Asynchronous	Direct	Indirect
Email	Uses SMTP protocol and IMAP or POP for inboxes, with dedicated clients	Gmail, Thunderbird, Outlook	•	•	•			•	•	
Instant messaging	Uses proprietary protocols and dedicated clients that typically run as background processes for a continuous connection at any time, enabling real-time or near-real-time text interaction	AIM, Skype, Jabber, SMS	•		•		•		•	
Chat	Similar to instant messaging, but uses protocols such as IRC or runs on the Web, typically with "rooms" or pages that must be explicitly visited rather than running in the background	Internet Relay Chat (IRC), Facebook chat, Google Talk	•		•		•		•	
Video/audio conferencing	Tools for connecting in real time using audio, and optionally, video	Phone, Skype, Google Hangouts, Viber	•		•		•		•	

	Brief Description	Examples	One-to-one	One-to-many	Many-to-many	Many-to-one	Synchronous	Asynchronous	Direct	Indirect
Social tagging	A feature rather than a tool for collectively categorizing resources. Distinct from the owner of a resource tagging an item, this is concerned with multiple people tagging the same resource	Del.icio.us		•	•	•		•		•
Social rating	Can be a feature or a standalone system, a means of sharing opinions and ratings	Epinions, rate-my-teacher		•	•	•		•		•
Screen sharing	A means of jointly sharing the same computer or other device	Skype, VNC, Google Hangouts	•							•
Shared whiteboard	A means of sharing a screen on which images, text, and drawings may be created by one or more people	Whiteboard.com, Adobe Connect	•	•	•		•			•
Webmeeting	Tools incorporating a range of features to support real-time meetings, typically includes embedded presentations, whiteboard, text chat, video/audio conferencing, telephone integration, polls, and online presence indicators	Adobe Connect, WebEx, Elluminate, Google hangouts	•	•	•		•	•		
Discussion forum	A range of methods for mainly text interactions, typically presented chronologically or threaded	Usenet News, Web forums, LMS forums, Listservs			•			•	•	
Microblog	Sharing very short messages with others	Twitter, Tumblr		•	•			•	•	
Social networking	A way to make connections with others, either reciprocally (typically called "friending") or asymmetrically (typically called "following"). Almost always associated with other tools, and usually involving the creation of personal profiles or pages representing an individual	Facebook, Google+, Orkut, MySpace, Bebo, Hi5	•	•	•	•	•	•	•	•

	Brief Description	Examples	One-to-one	One-to-many	Many-to-many	Many-to-one	Synchronous	Asynchronous	Direct	Indirect
Social curation	A means of sharing categorized content in the form of collections	Pinterest, Learnist	•	•	•			•		•
Social gaming	Any of a wide range of ways to play games with others	World of Warcraft, Farmville, SimCity	•		•		•	•	•	•
Social buying and selling	Ways of buying or selling in the company of others	eBay, Groupon	•	•	•			•		•
File sharing	Means to share files with others, typically using folders or other means of organizing files	Alfresco, Dropbox, Google Docs	•	•				•		•
Photo sharing	Means to share photos with others, typically with album and gallery functions	Flickr, Instagram, Picasa		•				•	•	•
Video sharing	Means to share rich media with others, usually incorporating ways to display them on a phone or in a browser	YouTube, TeacherTube		•				•	•	•
Presentation sharing	Means to share presentations with others, typically with an in-line slide display	SlideShare, Prezzi		•				•		•
Social bookmarking	Means to share bookmarks and links to sites and pages users find useful	Del.icio.us, Furl, Pinterest, Scoopit		•				•		•
Crowdsourcing, crowdfunding	Ways to employ the services of others either directly or indirectly	Kickstarter, Amazon Mechanical Turk, Innocentive, TopCoder	•	•			•	•		
Q&A systems	Places to pose questions and receive answers to questions	Quora, Yahoo Answers	•	•			•	•		
Reputation networks	Tools to demonstrate or establish a reputation in business or academia. Often a feature of other tools but occasionally the main purpose of a tool	LinkedIn, Academia.edu, eBay			•	•		•		•

	Brief Description	Examples	One-to-one	One-to-many	Many-to-many	Many-to-one	Synchronous	Asynchronous	Direct	Indirect
Collaborative filters and social recommenders	Systems that use the implicit or explicit preferences or behaviours of others to recommend resources or people that may be more appropriate to a user's needs or interests	Amazon Recommends, Google Search, Netflix				•		•		•
Publication	Tools to present information to other people, typically with the means for others to respond	Blogger, Facebook, LiveJournal		•	•		•	•		
Scheduling	Tools to arrange meetings and manage projects	Meeting Wizard, Outlook	•	•	•			•		•
Groupware/ content management	Multi-purpose tools designed to support the needs of groups of people working together, typically integrating messaging, file sharing, publication, discussion, blogs, and other tools, with a focus on supporting specific groups	Lotus Notes, Plone, Drupal	•	•	•			•	•	
Location-based systems	Social systems that connect people with others in their area, or that make use of location to provide information based on previous activities in that area	Foursquare, Google Latitude		•	•	•	•	•	•	•
Learning management systems	A particular form of content management system designed with education in mind, incorporating tools to manage the learning process including assessments, discussions, class management, and so on	Moodle, Blackboard, Desire2Learn	•	•	•			•	•	
Immersive environments	Tools that present (at least) a 3D space in which to interact with others, typically including voice and text chat as well as avatars that represent individuals and can interact with other avatars, usually in a simulacrum of a physical space	Second Life, ActiveWorlds, OpenSim	•	•	•	•	•	•	•	•

	Brief Description	Examples	One-to-one	One-to-many	Many-to-many	Many-to-one	Synchronous	Asynchronous	Direct	Indirect
MUDs and MOOs	Typically text-based interaction spaces, usually allowing users to create virtual rooms and objects around and within which interaction occurs	LambdaMOO, EduMOO	•	•	•	•	•	•	•	•
Reviews	Typically consumer or commercial sites with reviewing areas, also common in academic settings. May be linked with ratings	Amazon Books, Rate My Professors		•	•	•		•	•	•

We have broadly categorized a range of social tools to describe the predominant social features in terms of whether they are one–to–one, one–to–many, many–to–many, many–to–one, and direct or indirect, but many tools can be used for a range of purposes that could, at a stretch, allow them to fit into most categories. For example, in some cases email interactions *might* be almost as instantaneous as a text chat, yet we have characterized it as an asynchronous tool because that is its main use. A Skype system *could* be used to broadcast from one to many, but normally it is a two-way or multi-way conversation. It is also true that many tools are amalgams or mashups of different tools: YouTube, for example, not only includes options for discussing and rating videos but also allows social networking, social tagging, and more. Several tools fit into more than one category: for instance, immersive worlds usually incorporate text and video chat as well as other features.

THE VALUE OF SOCIAL SOFTWARE

In the same way that the definitions of social software are numerous, so are its functions and forms, and most importantly, the ways in which these tools are used to enhance teaching and learning. In this section we provide an overview of some of the major pedagogical contributions of social software for both formal and informal learning.

Social Software Helps Build Communities

The influential work of Etienne Wenger (1998) focuses on the value that community brings to professional practice and informal learning. Educators have applied these sociological insights to communities created during formal study, and have argued that "community is the vehicle through which online courses are most effectively delivered regardless of content" (Palloff & Pratt, 2005, p. 1). The creation of community is both an educational product and a process. Educational communities can extend beyond the time and place of study to become the tool that forms and cements values, attitudes, connections, and friendships. They thus become the crucibles within which the hidden curriculum of higher education is formed. This hidden curriculum can be used to propagate social and class advantages (Margolis, 2001), but also teaches learners to act as experts and professionals, and to play the educational game effectively (T. Anderson, 2002).

Community also creates social obligations and entitlements. Members of learning communities are empowered to both give and receive help from fellow members. Learning in formal education contexts is rarely easy, and many times the aid, encouragement, or obligation to or from community members provides a necessary motivation to persevere.

Social Software Helps Create Knowledge

Knowledge is information that has been contextualized, made relevant, and owned. Understanding and attending to context becomes more critical as information moves throughout our global community. Context both allows and constrains us from making sense of information and constructing a coherent framework in which to situate it. Of course, context includes language and the more subtle forms of cultural marking, but it also extends to relevance, applicability, and understandability. If information is obscure or incomprehensible to an individual or group, it will be discarded and remains outside of the context of understanding that allows it to be internally recreated as wisdom. Knowledge is also relevant to a real concern. We are bombarded with information in many formats delivered through numerous forms of media. We cannot and should not attend to it all, yet information we do wish to own must prove relevant to a real interest. Finally, knowledge is information that is owned by individuals and aggregations of individuals. This ownership is expressed in its capacity for recollection and application. Owned knowledge is valued, but unlike physical objects, knowledge gains value when it is given away, shared, replicated, and reapplied. Unlike rival goods, where possession by one person excludes ownership or use by others, knowledge is a non-rival good, which loses none of its original value to its possessor when it is shared (Benkler, 2006). Indeed, the act of sharing can enhance the knowledge of its possessor, because having to communicate an idea or skill to another is often reinforcing or even transformative: there is no better way to learn than to teach. Furthermore, knowledge gains in its capacity to be transformed and transforming as it is applied in different contexts, enabling its possessors to do new things and use it in new ways that its originators may not have imagined.

Social Software Engages, Motivates, and is Enjoyable

When social software becomes a component of formal education, students and teachers interact with one another in more meaningful ways, creating a variety of positive results. Ted Panitz (1997) details over 67 benefits from engaging in collective learning, arguing that collaborating reduces anxiety, builds self-esteem, enhances student satisfaction, and fosters positive relationships between students and faculty. Blog authors report feeling motivated by the opportunity to share their knowledge and expertise, experience pleasurable reactions to comments and the recognition of others, and positive reassurance about their own thinking and writing (Pedersen & Macafee, 2007). Engagement in the learning process is reflected in time spent studying, the level of enjoyment, and the quality of work and learning outcomes (Chickering & Gamson, 1987; Herrington, Oliver, & Reeves, 2003; Kearsley & Schneiderman, 1998; Richardson & Newby, 2006). Engagement is so critical to learning that Kearsley and Schneiderman have developed a whole theory of learning based upon it, and Shulman argues that engagement is both a critical process to learning development and an outcome of education itself: "[an] educator's responsibility is to make it possible for students to engage in experiences they would never otherwise have had" (2002, p.38).

Although it would be an exaggeration to suggest that all students enjoy working (and learning) with others, the opportunity to make new social contacts and build new networks of friends is an important reason why many engage in formal educational activities.

Social Software is Cost-effective

Unlike the development of computer-assisted instruction, tutorials, and other multimedia-enhanced forms of online learning, it is easy and very cost effective to include social networking in formal and informal learning. The content of educational social networking is, for the most part, created by the participants in the process of their learning. The most common networking activity is to make comments and engage in discussions relating to the subject of study. However, there are many other effective social learning activities, including the selection and annotation of learning resources (educational tagging), formal debates and guided discussion, collaboratively creating reports and presentations, individual and group reflections, and so on. All of these activities are created by participants in the process of learning. The archives of these activities become content for further study and reflection across course sections, years, and institutions.

The "conversant" forms of online learning have been criticized as not being scalable or cost effective—at least compared to more traditional, individual-based forms of distance education (Annand, 1999). Social software can, however, be used to enhance and focus on students responding to and helping one another as peers, thereby creating models of formal learning that may be more cost effective than those organized by teachers. While not denying the importance of "teacher presence" at some point in an educational transaction, there is a need for learning designs that are scalable and can meet the learning needs of the millions of learners who are currently unable to participate in more traditional forms of campus-based education (J. S. Daniel, 1996).

Social Software Encourages Active Learning

Active learning engages learners emotionally and cognitively in the education process. Although not without controversy in the educational world, active learning flows from constructivist ideals in which learners shape their own understandings, ideas, and mental models. Activities that induce active learning include debates, collaborative learning, problem-solving and, most recently, inquiry (Chang, Sung, & Lee, 2003). Active learning has been associated with ideas of discovery, as opposed to guided inquiry, but as Mayer (2004) notes, cognitive engagement is critical to all forms of learning. Social networking creates both motivations and obligations among learners to work together, or at least in harmony, through the learning process. Activities that draw out learners' interests, expertise, and individual gifts benefit not only the recipient of this expertise but also gives learners the thrill and expanded knowledge associated with helping or teaching another (B. Daniel, Schwier, & McCalla, 2003).

Social Software is Accountable and Transparent

Unlike many forms of communication, most types of social software leave persistent trails documenting the activities and conversations of participants. Although anonymous and fantasy-based approaches can be supported in social software contexts, in both formal and informal learning these are not the norm, and in most cases deception and anonymity are not acceptable social behaviours. The transparency and persistence of learning activities give rise to conditions that are ideal for the development of social capital. Individuals who have contributed the most to the community see their contributions giving them authority and prestige within that community and across their networks.

Social Software Spans the Gap Between Formal and Informal Learning

Social software, especially social networking, blurs the distinction between formal and informal learning. Research on learning often bifurcates learning into two often mutually hostile camps: formal education, with its institutional champions of accreditation, and informal learning, championed by advocates of community, workplace, informal and incidental learning. For example, Marsick and Watkins (2001, p. 28) conclude that informal learning is characterized as being:

- Integrated with daily routines—in contrast to formal education, which takes place at times and places defined by the educational institution.

- Triggered by an internal or external jolt. In formal education, the "jolt" almost always originates with requirements set by the teacher.

- Not highly conscious. Although formal education has also been criticized for putting learners to sleep in lecture theatres, the intent of the education is always made explicit in terms of expected learning outcomes.

- Haphazard and influenced by chance. In formal settings, the course outline ensures that curriculum is followed and certainly not influenced by chance.

- An inductive process of reflection and action. Although not excluded, reflection and action where ideas are validated in real-life contexts are rare in formal education.

- Linked to the learning of others. Formal education is almost always a contest among registered students for marks awarded by teachers, making the establishment of collaborative and supportive learning challenging, though not impossible.

Using Marsick and Watkins's criteria, we argue that social networking integrates formal and informal learning, since its tools and context are used to coordinate both formal learning, and workplace, family and community ideas, relations, and activities. Jolts or triggers arise both from formal learning interactions and occurrences in real life, and social networking provides a forum where these jolts can be discussed, assessed, and reflected upon. Reflection and the reactions of others in social networking contexts are most often stimulating and rewarding. Social networking spans across both formal education and learners' private and public lives. Thus, it is influenced both by chance and the requirements of formal education. Finally, social networking is, by definition and intense practice, linked to the learning of others. This linking may take place through formal collaborative tasks assigned by teachers, through reactions, feedback, and response to blogged reflections, or through spontaneous conversations in real time online or in face-to-face encounters.

Social Software Addresses both Individual and Social Needs

It has always been challenging to differentiate between the benefits and costs of education and how they are apportioned between the wider social community and the individual. John Dewey (1897) argued that "the school is primarily a social institution" and that "all education proceeds by the participation of an individual in the social consciousness of the race" (p.77), celebrating the role in which education is used to pass on to learners the benefits of socially derived knowledge. But the debate over education's cost also reveals that it benefits the individual, and this is readily verified by noting the earning gap between citizens with high and low education levels (although this is a circular argument—employers seek those with qualifications and, in the case of higher education, the weeding out of those with less innate capability by university admission procedures means that many of the differences may be put down to intelligence and aptitude, or in some cases, social class). But the benefits of schooling to either individuals or the state depend upon learners being able to work, collaborate, and engage in discussion and decision-making with others. Social networking both encourages and affords opportunities to practise these social skills in contexts that range from small groups to large and widely distributed networks.

Social Software Builds Identity, Expertise, and Social Capital

Generally the possession of social capital, like other forms of capital, allows individuals and groups to accomplish their goals because they can draw on the resources, support, and encouragement of these resources—in this case, human beings. Sandefur and Laumann (1988) argue that social capital confers three major benefits upon its owners: information, influence and control, and social solidarity. Social networking creates and enhances relationships among learners. These relationships can then be used by individuals and groups to achieve goals that are frequently beyond their individual capacity to attain (S. E. Page, 2008).

Social Software is Easy to Use

Most social software applications have very little functionality until they attract a significant number of users. In addition, their value to individual users increases as a function of other users. To attract high numbers of users, social software architects spend considerable effort in making interfaces friendly, intuitive, and easy to navigate. Social software has been built in an era dominated by "Net generation" learners who have adapted and adopted computer tools, but who are equally known for low attention thresholds—especially for confusing or difficult-to-understand applications. To be more precise, retaining such users requires rapid *learnability*. It is not the be-all and end-all: even those social tools that usability studies reveal as being very difficult to use may succeed due to their perceived value to the community. However, when all else is equal, learnability can mean the difference between success and failure in a social software system.

Social Software is Accessible

Social software is accessible in two senses of the word. First, the contributions of others in social software systems and tools are often not hidden behind passwords or closed classroom doors, nor are they archived in inaccessible libraries. Rather, social software has a tendency to meet the needs of a growing number of users. Failure to evolve results in the wreckage of empty and unused sites—a common sight on the changing twenty-first-century Web.

In a second sense, most social software is accessible to all learners, including those with physical or mental constraints. For example, being digital, social software can be reformatted into large print or audio formats to meet the needs of visually impaired users, or presented in alternative forms to those with dyslexia. It also makes no difference to social software users if input came from a voice, a keyboard, a Bliss board, or a drawing tablet. Social software can also be retrieved on many types of devices, ranging from home theatres to cell phones. This accessibility enables social software to be used for high-quality learning by anyone, anywhere. However, we do recognize that this is far from universally true, and there is a counter-trend to release early and often to appeal to the widest audience, sometimes making accessibility a secondary consideration.

Social Software Protects and Advances Current Models of Ownership and Identity

Social relationships are built on reputation and responsibility. Social software seeks to return the ownership of comments to their creator. Thus the persistence of contribution across formal and informal communities and the technical capacity for all participants to link, search, and archive contributions across these communities is critical. But social software also allows for new types of ownership. In pre-digital times, possession implied exclusive use—if I lost my possession, I was no longer able to use my property. Digital property, like the flame of a candle, is not diminished when shared with others. Indeed, the sharing of both candles and digital artifacts creates more light for the benefit of all.

Social Software is Persistent and Findable

Being digital and thus searchable, social contributions (with permission of the participants) can be used, referenced, researched, extracted, reused, and recycled across time and space (Erickson & Kellogg, 2000). The use of syndication, automatic and cooperative tagging, indexing, and spider tools allows social software contributions and information about their authors to be searched, harvested, and extracted.

Social Software Supports Multiple Media Formats

Although a powerful and expressive communication genre, and the one upon which most academic knowledge is inscribed, text is but one format for social expression. Social software supports audio (music, voice conversation, and podcasts), video (videoconferencing, videocasts), and graphics (photos, drawings, and animation displays). These can be combined to create immersive worlds, waves, VoiceThreads, and many other engaging media combinations.

Social Software Encourages Debate, Cognitive Conflict, and Discussion

Knowledge is built from active engagement with conflicting and confounding ideas that challenge older, pre-existing knowledge (Piaget, 1952). Given the capacity of online social learning to span the distance of both space and time, it is not surprising that learners become aware of the ideas of others. Since these ideas originate in different contexts, it is likely that some will be as divergent as they are convergent. Through this divergence, learners are forced to make explicit much of their implicit and pre-existing knowledge so that it can be communicated effectively to others. At the same time, the dissonance that arises when learners are exposed to divergent ideas forces them to defend, strengthen, alter, or abandon their existing ideas.

Social Software Leads to Emergence

Typically, social software contains elements that algorithmically combine the ideas, actions, or decisions of many to produce an unplanned result. For example, tag clouds form from the tagging behaviour of a system's users, with more popular tags being emphasized, typically displayed with a larger font. No one has decided which tags should be emphasized or not: the pattern emerges from the combined behaviours of many people.

Similarly, the buying behaviour of previous customers can be used to offer recommendations to future buyers who have exhibited similar purchase patterns, whether through explicit recommendation or simply by observing that people who bought a particular item also bought other items. As with tagging, no individual has decided that a particular book should be recommended: group behaviour dictates recommendations. There are many examples of such emergent patterns in social software systems, and we will discuss the implications of these at length later in this book.

Social Software is Soft

All technologies are assemblies of other technologies. That is how they evolve, and how they are built, through combination and recombination (Arthur, 2009). Some of those technologies in an assembly will be harder and more deterministic, some softer and open to change by end users. Softer technologies are those that incorporate humans in their design and enactment, allowing tools to be used in many different ways. Social technologies are inherently soft. Social technology applications are inseparable from the processes, rules, norms and techniques that are assembled with them. The technologies provide opportunities, and the users as individuals, groups, and networks determine how to best exploit them. Together they proceed in a dance (T. Anderson, 2009), intricately interwoven, mutually affective, and inseparable.

Social Software Supports Creativity

Being soft, social software is rich with assembling potential for human activities, and may be deeply interwoven with social and organizational processes. Unlike more specialized tools that are designed for particular purposes and have little flexibility, if any at all, for alternative uses, social software enables creative uses and purposes that its designers probably never dreamed of. It is thus a vehicle for change and creativity in learning and teaching.

Social Software Expands the Adjacent Possible

Every new technology that adds to those that came before extends what Kauffman (2000) refers to as the "adjacent possible:" the powerful driving force behind evolution and change in many aspects of the natural and built environment. Each time a new capacity evolves, it opens up avenues that were not there before. For example, it was necessary for light-sensitive cells to develop in animals before the potential existed for them to evolve into eyes. When we build a new technology, it opens up new paths for change. It is not just that we gain new capabilities, but that more potential capabilities consequently emerge. It would have been inconceivable for humans to reach the moon without a succession of earlier technologies, each building on and often incorporating the last, from the humblest rivet or metallurgical technique to the most sophisticated computational and propulsion devices.

In every way, not only do we, as Newton suggested, stand on the shoulders of giants, but everything that matters to us, from our bodies' cells to our television sets, emerges from the history of what came previously. Moreover, this expansion is increasing at an exponential rate (Kelly, 2010). The rapid proliferation of social software tools is opening up vast landscapes of possibility that were never there before and, because such technologies are soft and combinable, their affordances are far greater than more rigid or, as U. M. Franklin (1999) puts it, *prescriptive* technologies.

USERS OF EDUCATIONAL SOCIAL SOFTWARE

It is no exaggeration to claim that the number of users and applications of social software exploded during the first decade of the twenty-first century. The site Go2web20 provides links to over 3,000 unique Web 2.0 applications, most of which could also be classified as social software, and very few of which existed a decade ago. These networked applications have user numbers that range in size from very small to large country- or even continent-sized populations. The successful mega social software sites including Facebook, Twitter, Google+, YouTube, Tumblr, Pinterest, MySpace, SecondLife, Blogger, and Flickr number their user accounts in the tens of millions, and tabulations of monthly unique visitors in the millions or even billions. As we write this in early 2014, Facebook has over 1.3 billion user accounts (Statisticbrain, 2014a), Twitter over 645 million (Statisticbrain, 2014a), LinkedIn over 227 million (Linkedin, 2014), and Google+ has over 1.15 billion accounts, though the way this is designed to integrate far beyond the simple site-based approach used by Facebook means that only around a third of those are actively using the system (Wearsocial, 2014). WhatsApp, a fast growing mobile messaging system recently acquired by Facebook, has 450 million monthly users, growing at a rate of a million a day (Wearsocial, 2014). An astonishing 2 billion videos are watched on YouTube every day (Bullas, 2012) but this pales in comparison to users sharing content and links with Google +1 or Facebook shares. Searchmetrics predicts that, by May 2016, there will be 1096 billion Google +1s *every month*, and a further 849 billion via Facebook. Simple interactions such as sharing show not just passive interest in content but active social engagement with others.

A 2007 Canadian survey of a single social software application, Facebook, revealed that some cities had over 40% of the population as registered users (Feeley & Brooks, 2007). In 2011, the proportion of Canadian users had reached over 50%, a little below the global average. In Indonesia and the Philippines, social network use is well over 70%, and it is 60% in Russia and India (Broadband Commission, 2012, p. 9) Among Generation Y, social software use encompassed over 96% of the sampled population as early as 2007 (Grunwald Associates LLC, 2007). By 2010, the rate of growth for most social sites was still rapidly increasing, with Facebook experiencing a 7% increase in users year over year, and Twitter 11% (comScore, 2011). Perhaps the most interesting growth is seen in mobile social software. Though social media technology fit well with conventional mobile phones, broadband makes their data-intensive operation possible. With over 2 billion mobile broadband subscriptions worldwide compared to a mere 696 million fixed-line broadband subscriptions (Broadband Commission, 2013, p. 12), with broadband subscriptions in the third world now exceeding those in the developed world, and with anticipated growth to 7 billion mobile broadband subscriptions by 2017, it seems almost certain that mobile social media are bound to dominate (Broadband Commission, 2013, p. 14).

The largest growth in social software use is in older users, with a 36% increase in use between 2009 and 2010 for 55–64 year-old users and 34% for those 65+, though the majority are still in the 25–44 age range (comScore, 2012), and 98% of Americans in the 18-24 age range use social media of some kind (Statisticbrain, 2014 b). The demographic spread across different social software systems varies widely and reflects a maturing and ever more diverse range of systems and tools. It should be noted that many surveys do not consider tools such as YouTube, Wikipedia, and Google Search to be social media, despite the fact that they are entirely powered by the crowd and exist only because of user-generated content.

Social software includes a variety of types of networked applications offering different forms of social activity and focusing on different target audiences and interests. Social software is used to connect and reconnect people to families, past and current schoolmates, coworkers, local neighbours, and others sharing the same physical spaces. But it also links those separated by vast differences of geography and as importantly, differences of culture, age, income, and race. Besides supporting and enhancing existing relationships, social software also facilitates the discovery and building of new relationships through profiles, recommendations, observations, and charting of users with similar interests or activity patterns.

SOCIAL SOFTWARE IN FORMAL EDUCATION

The use of social software for personal reasons challenges educators used to having control over the tools used in their programs. Social software, unlike institutionally-based learning management systems (LMS), is often either not owned by the educational institution or incorporates elements that come from beyond it, is focused on individuals and their relationships rather than courses, and is under the control of these users, not teachers. In most current instances, social software applications have not been designed specifically for students enrolled in formal education programs. Rather, students join social networks for personal reasons, motivated by a desire to expand and enrich their social lives. Thus, a central challenge of this book is to help educators both understand social software use and equip them with the knowledge and skill to use educational software in formal courses and as doors to lifelong learning opportunities for themselves and their students.

To date, much social software use has focused on building communities in parallel or outside of formal education. For example, sites such as Facebook support communities of students enrolled or at least interested in a particular university or school. These groups often contain thousands of members and are used for discussions and announcements about special activities, providing a way to connect users who share a common interest in that particular institution—or at least its social life. We believe that these tools are too important and powerful to be excluded from the formal curriculum, that they can be used to support and encourage learning in all subject domains. In addition, the use of social software applications in formal education encourages and supports learners with lifelong learning skills that they will be able to apply beyond their graduation from any formal education program. Finally, social software develops "the kinds of skills needed to meet the challenge of earning a living in the twenty-first century—flexibility, adaptability, collaborativeness and problem-solving prowess—bear a one-to-one congruence with the constellation of skills and outlooks needed to engage in every other key participation opportunity related to human capacity development" (Levinger, 1996, Chapter 2, para. 16).

MOOCs

Recent years have seen a massive growth in MOOCs (Massive Open Online Courses), with courses from organizations like edX, Coursera, Udacity, and others gaining tens of thousands of participants. Their forebears, starting with CCK08—a connectivist course with a few thousand users (Downes, 2008b)—remain intensive in their use of social software, and could not run without extensive networked technologies such as Twitter, blogs, and social aggregation platforms. While many popular MOOCs employ predominantly instructivist approaches to teaching, they also provide tools for social interaction—as a result, a large ecosystem of social groups and networks has sprung up around them, with learners helping one another, exchanging ideas, and learning together in more or less formal groupings (Severance, 2012).

SOCIAL SOFTWARE IN INFORMAL LEARNING

Non-formal and informal intentional learning outstrips formal learning in both time spent on the activity and the number of people engaged in it many times over, and has always done so. Tough's research (1979) in the 1970s suggested that adults typically spent around 200 hours every year on intentional learning activities. In 2000, Livingstone found that Canadian adults spent considerably more time on informal learning than formal, in the area of 15 hours per week. Were these research studies to be repeated today, this amount of time may be considerably higher. Google's search engine is used by over 85% of Internet users (Pick, 2012) and whenever someone performs a search, it is usually in order to learn something or be reminded of something that they already know. Perhaps it would be more accurate to say that, in keeping with connectivist precepts, people know that the knowledge they seek resides in the network—even if they often do not need to retain it—but, in one way or another, they are seeking knowledge. In other words, Google Search is a learning technology and, by any measure, the most widely used distinct learning technology product in the world.

While language and books are undoubtedly more important learning technologies, there is no single book or language that reaches a wider audience than Google Search. Meanwhile, Wikipedia, its nearest competitor as a learning technology, receives close to 10 million visits an hour to its English-language site alone, with nearly 8 billion page views of over 4 million articles produced by tens of thousands of editors, over 33,000 articles described as "active", which means having had five or more edits per year (Wikimedia, 2014). Wikipedia gets further millions of visitors to its simplified English-language and Chinese sites, with billions of visitors to other sites using less commonplace languages. But Google Search and Wikipedia are just the tip of a massive iceberg of informal and non-formal learning that is enabled by the social web. Sites such as StackOverload, Answers.com, Lifehacker, How Stuff Works, Instructables, as well as millions of YouTube videos and thousands of less well-known sites provide more or less formal instruction to millions of people every day. Twitter, Facebook, and Google+ are rich sources of knowledge and information, providing simple questions and answers for study groups, reading groups, and collaborators. Despite the pointless trivia that often passes through it, the social web can be appreciated as a web of learning.

THE MANY PURPOSES OF EDUCATIONAL SOCIAL SOFTWARE

Social software functions in many ways and is as divergent in forms, systems, and software packages as it is in the interest and skills of users. However, Mejias (2005) argues that social software serves two purposes. The first is to manage ever-larger sets of social relationships, such that meaningful and functional social relationships can be built and effective communications can be maintained despite the numbers, distances, or time barriers that separate them. Second, social software affords us opportunity to create and support more intimate and authentic relationships between our closest friends, families, and colleagues. It also helps us to build social confidence, and sometimes, new relationships. Ellison, Steinfield, and Lampe (2007) have found that Facebook usage is associated with increased formation of social capital, especially for those with low self-esteem and lower life satisfaction. They also found that both bonding social capital (strengthening relationships with those whom one already has a primary relationship) and bridging social capital (weaker, more extended relationships with others) were associated with increased use of Facebook.

These direct social uses are important, but they are by no means the only ways that social software can provide value to learners. The social net creates an ecology "involving not only technologies but also other people, values, norms and social contexts" (Petrič, 2006, p. 293). This enables a learner to construct knowledge by seeing his or her place in the world, and hence grasping connections not just with other people but also with the world itself.

An obvious benefit that is not addressed by Mejias's classifications is that social software systems enable learners to create content, find answers to questions, make and receive challenges, and provide opportunities to see the world differently. A less obvious benefit is that social software can be used to aggregate the opinions, beliefs, and discoveries of many people in order to guide us through our learning journeys with little or no direct social interaction at all. Social software is not just social glue but an enabler of the creation, discovery, and presentation of new knowledge.

Other people have many roles to play in the learning process, not just in the construction of factual or procedural knowledge. From an educational perspective, social software can, for instance, enable users to:

- Provide helpful resources
- Help them move into the next zone of proximal development
- Solve problems
- Create more complex artifacts
- Present multiple perspectives and enrich connections
- Model different ways of thinking
- Explore ethical problems
- Learn to work with others
- Connect ideas from different perspectives and fill in gaps to connect existing ideas.

Uses for Social Software in Learning

We have already seen that there are many different forms of social software, which are becoming ubiquitous. However, though any exchange of information may instigate or enable learning, not all social software is suited to every learning task. In table 1.2 we present a few of the more obvious ways that social software can benefit the learner. Some of these functions overlap, and many of the same tools can be used for different purposes. The intention here is to give a sense of the range of ways that social software can support or enable learning to occur.

Table 1.2 Functions of educational social software.

Function	Education Use	Example
Connecting learners	User profiles indicate interests, locations, and courses learners are enrolled in and have completed, and other demographic data allow them to connect with one another.	Facebook or Elgg profile
Building and sustaining social capital	Allows learners to gain confidence and connections that are of use in learning.	Facebook, Twitter, LinkedIn, Academia.edu, CiteSeer
Enabling discussion	Allows learners to share reviews, insights, and questions related to course content, and to teach one another, hence learning and connecting in the process.	Moodle Forum, Elgg group discussions, Usenet News
Discovering knowledge and recommendations	Allows users to share and glean recommendations from others about articles, resources, images, video, or other digital resources.	Google Search, Amazon Recommends, eBay reputations, Slashdot Karma, Amazon bookshelf, CiteULike
Meeting support	Allows groups to meet, coordinate, and document face-to-face and online synchronous meetings, hence strengthening group processes and building learning communities more effectively.	MeetUp, Doodle, Outlook
Collaborative editing	Allows groups and networks to collaboratively author, annotate, and revise documents as part of the learning process.	Google Docs, wikis, Sharepoint, Etherpad
Collaborative resource evaluation	Allows learners to evaluate a resource and display collective results, hence giving them metacognitive skills (for the one rating), and helping others to learn through the results of those ratings.	CoFIND, SurveyShare
Simulated environments	Supports informal and structured synchronous interactions with avatar gesture enhancements, enabling learning in simulated spaces that may be expensive, dangerous, or impossible to access in real life, or to simulate social encounters in a safe and non-threatening manner.	SecondLife, Active Worlds, Habbohotel, Project Wonderland, Metaplace
Social games	Multiplayer simulations allow role-playing and collaborative problem-solving and improve motivation through the presence of others, providing achievable tasks and enabling the learner's control.	The Sims, World of Warcraft

Function	Education Use	Example
Self-publication	The means to share insights through text, audio, and video, and provide a space for others to comment, rate, engage in dialogue or recommend them, hence providing feedback as well as benefiting those for whom the work is published.	Blogs, vlogs/vodcasts, podcasts
Chatting	Real-time chat enables feedback when it is needed. Also a good motivator due to the presence of others.	Instant messaging, audio/video conferencing (Skype), web meetings (Elluminate, Adobe Connect, LiveMeeting)
Maintaining connections and social presence	Supports means of making others aware of our current activities and reduces loneliness in an online setting, hence improving motivation.	Microblogging (Twitter), presence indicators in instant messengers, Facebook status updates
Aggregating knowledge from multiple sources and benefiting from the aggregations of others	Enables users to gather information from multiple sources and organize it according to the interests and behaviour of the Many, fostering sense-making activities performed by the crowd or for the benefit of others. There are also metacognitive benefits in categorizing and assembling/curating content.	Digg, Slashdot, Mixx Pinterest, Learni.st
Discovering people and things in one's surroundings	Supports users' awareness of others within a physical locale, augmenting physical space with social tagging and annotation. Enriches face-to-face learning by increasing channels of engagement.	Foursquare, Facebook location sharing, Geotagging, Google Goggles
Resource discovery	Shares resources and discoveries with others, enables annotation and tagging of content, allows many to contribute and all to discover more than they would alone or with the aid of a single teacher.	Del.icio.us, Pinterest, Digg, Slashdot, CiteULike, Furl
Finding answers and solutions	Crowdsourced approaches to finding the answers to questions, helping learners over learning obstacles, and showing ways to move forward.	Amazon Mechanical Turk, Quora, Innocentive
Getting things done or made	A means of outsourcing work to others so that unnecessary tasks that do not benefit learning may be distributed to others.	Amazon Mechanical Turk, k68.cn
Crowdfunding	Enables individuals or groups to ask for funds to help a learning project.	Kickstarter

Function	Education Use	Example
Project coordination and workflow	Improves the ability of learners to work on a project with others or alone.	Github, Bugzilla, Microsoft Outlook, Microsoft Sharepoint
Social calendars	Helps manage the practical process of learning.	Doodle, Google Calendar, Zimbra
Crowdsourced knowledge creation	Provides answers to specific problems using the crowd.	SETI@home reCAPTCHA

ANYONE AND EVERYONE CAN BE A DEVELOPER

Building a social application is no longer the preserve of skilled experts. Anyone with a basic understanding of a web browser can now create a social application on Ning (ning.com) or set up a group on an Elgg system, Facebook, academia.edu, or LinkedIn. In the group-oriented institutional domain, many sites provide services that allow anyone to set up courses or even whole learning management systems. It takes little extra effort to use Microsoft's discontinued Popfly, and not much more for Yahoo Pipes, Google Gears, or Intel's Mash Maker. Users can make basic but highly useful mashups incorporating RSS feeds, interactive maps, discussions, podcasts, and more by using systems such as iGoogle, Netvibes, Sproutbuilder, or PageFlakes. For the more proficient computer user, a rapidly increasing assortment of tools is available to build applications for Facebook or OpenSocial that take advantage of the facilities, users, variables, and processes provided by such complex social software to extend or use their functionality in a new way. Mobile app builders are widely and, sometimes, freely available: ShoutEm, Mobile App Builder, MobinCube, and many more offer simple tools to create fairly sophisticated apps for iOS, Android, and other mobile platforms.

Given the ease with which new systems can be created and/or built on top of others, we are moving toward an era that is freer of the hegemony of technocrats and learning technologists, where any teacher or instructional designer can build, select, or aggregate the tools they need to create a new learning environment adapted to the needs of their learners. There are, of course, great risks in what are typically cloud-based tools: questions about the ownership of data, privacy and security concerns, and overall system reliability. Furthermore, such innovations exist within a structural and technological hierarchy that may hinder or restrict their development. The market for applications is a rapidly evolving and highly competitive space.

Perhaps more interestingly, the same tools can, in principle, be used by the learners themselves to take the pieces that they need in the form that they need them to create their own learning spaces. The notion of the Personal Learning Environment (PLE) has been gaining traction for some years: it is an aggregation of learning tools and environments that is built by and for the learner, often using some form of widget (Downes, 2007; S. Wilson et al., 2007). Specifications for widget standards are now reaching maturity through the efforts of the W3Consortium (W3C) and it is increasingly easy to combine these into a single, web-hosted space. Mature environments such as Elgg offer such capabilities out of the box, while other systems such as Wookie are built from the ground up to do nothing but serve widgets.

THE IMPORTANCE OF EFFECTIVE DESIGN

Though such tools can be very powerful learning aids, the corollary is that they are also potentially very dangerous: the greater the capabilities and flexibility of a system, the more it becomes an essential feature of our learning; and thus when it goes wrong, the more disastrous the effects. We have suffered enough over the years from the weaknesses of professionally designed software for education to know that there are many pitfalls and errors that can be made. Decisions that seem reasonable in one context may be inappropriate in another: we may inadvertently lock ourselves into technologies or approaches, build unusable interfaces, limit functionalities due to lack of time or skill, and so on. Just as limited options can lead us to poor choices, limitless options can make it hard to choose right from wrong for the learning environment.

The greater our capabilities, the easier it is to do things badly. Now that such systems are entering the toolsets of amateurs, the risks of poor design and inappropriate use have been magnified. It is too easy to forget that we are doing more than simply creating content, but embodying processes and patterns of learning and teaching that may tie us to systems that imprison rather than liberate us. If we are to become the creators of tools and environments rather than developing simple learning content, we must learn to do it right. In each chapter relating to sets, nets, groups, and collectives, we provide a set of design principles and guidelines as well as a framework for understanding social systems for learning that will hopefully reduce the capacity for error. In our "Stories From the Field" chapter, we present some stories and lessons that suggest useful ways to approach social systems for learning, and highlight some of the mistakes we have made on our journey.

CONCLUSION

We have painted what is mostly a very rosy picture of the potential and, in most cases, realized benefits of social software for learning. We have yet to spend much time on the dangers and disadvantages because we wish to present a *prima facie* compelling case that social software is worthy of investigation. As we shall see, all software comes with biases, embedded belief systems, risks, and pragmatic, pedagogical, and ethical pitfalls that can trap even wary designers. If we are to realize the potential value of social software for learning, it is therefore vital to understand how it works, how it does its job. That is the purpose of this book.

So far, we have presented no strong theoretical framework to help explain and inform how social software fits into a learning journey, and we have not examined the different ways it can work. These topics will be covered in the next few chapters, where we examine in turn the pedagogies of social learning, the social forms that are found in social software systems for learning, and the power and risks of the collective.

SOCIAL LEARNING
THEORIES

*He who loves practice without theory is like the sailor who boards ship
without a rudder and compass and never knows where he may cast.*

Leonardo da Vinci

In this chapter we provide an overview of the major learning theories that influence the development of social learning activity, culture, and research. For each theory we focus on the environment or the context in which learning takes place, and the constraints and facilities provided through that context. When this context is changed by pedagogical intervention, technological affordances, social expectations, or a host of other variables, one can expect change in learning effectiveness or efficiency. Social learning—especially in its cyber-enhanced forms—has evolved in a context of rapid change, and many of its proponents are champions of this. However, the formal institutional structures where most of these changes take place are noted more for their resistance to change and defence of tradition, than for the capacity for rapid or emergent adaptation (Bates, 2005; Winner, 1997). Thus online learning has long been engulfed in controversy, and there has been considerable jockeying among those with a vested interest in either change or the status quo. While this tension will and probably *should* never be fully resolved, we believe that dedicated educators often share underlying assumptions about teaching and learning. This section is designed to explicate the rationale for social learning and expose both its promises and shortcomings.

SOCIAL LEARNING

The defining component of social learning is the presence and participation of other learners and, at least in formal education, a teacher. In this section we will outline the theoretical and empirical evidence indicating how and why the presence of others makes a difference to both teaching and learning.

Until recently, most literature on social learning assumed that the interaction between participants takes place face-to-face, and often in a classroom, laboratory, or other structured context. However, recent pedagogical literature, especially from distance education and e-learning perspectives often assumes an electronically mediated context for teaching and learning. It is natural to wish to compare the online and face-to-face alternatives. When considered overall, studies reveal no significant difference in learning outcomes between activities and courses that are taken at a distance and those in the classroom (Russell, 2010). This is not too surprising because it is possible to use any learning technology well or badly, regardless of the type. It makes no more sense to ask whether people learn better at a distance or face-to-face than to ask whether pictures drawn in pencil are better than ones painted with oils. They are different technologies that can produce both excellent and atrocious results. That aside, the reliability of most studies that show the benefits of technology to learning are dubious, conflating many different factors (Oblinger & Hawkins, 2006; Russell, 2010). However, it is likely that the constraints and affordances of communication and information technologies, especially factors related to the limits of the media, scale, distance, and time, do effect how we learn from and with each other.

Different constraints and affordances will lead to different ways of doing things. Some methods will be difficult or impossible using certain media, but this is true in any setting. Just as it would not be wise to teach appreciation of music at a construction site or without the means to make music, it would not be sensible to teach programming without a computer. But the devil is, as always, in the details. Measuring the effects of teaching interventions and factoring in other contextual variables such as the nature and effectiveness of the technology, the users' experience and efficacy, their motivation and the nature of the subject is difficult when they combine to create very complex and multifaceted learning environments.

GENERATIONS OF DISTANCE LEARNING

There have been many attempts to examine the history of distance learning in terms of dominant technologies (e.g., Bates, 2005; Gunawardena & McIsaac, 2004). We have taken a slightly different tack, looking instead at the evolution of pedagogies in distance learning (T. Anderson & Dron, 2011). These perspectives are not totally at odds because there is a strong case to be made for treating pedagogies themselves as technologies that only bring about improvements in learning when used in combination with other technologies (Dron, 2012).

At the very least, pedagogies and technologies are intertwined in a dance, where the moves of one determine the moves of the other (T. Anderson, 2009). In our three-generation model, we have divided the generations of developments in distance learning into three distinct pedagogical eras; at the time of writing, the third generation is still emerging. We consider each generation to be partly determined by the communication and processing tools available, and partly by the popular pedagogies of the period, noting that changes in each one alters the adjacent possibilities and thus both the affordances and uses of the other. This co-dependency between tools and pedagogies is inevitable: until there are the means for cheap, rapid forms of many-to-many dialogue, for example, it is very hard to design distance learning experiences that require peer debate. Distance education was not a viable option at all until the advent of reliable and affordable technologies of production like the printing press, and communication systems such as a postal service.

Although we describe each generation as an historical sequence, this does not mean that previous generations have faded away or vanished. As Kelly (2010) has observed, technologies seldom, if ever, die. As new pedagogical models emerge, they do not replace what came before, though they may become more dominant than those they supersede. Not only is it possible to find large numbers of fairly pure examples of older approaches being used today, the newer generations incorporate the older ones in their assemblies so previous generations of pedagogy have become, if anything, more popular than they were when first adopted.

These are the three generations that we have identified as emerging so far:

1. Behaviourist/cognitivist: pedagogies of instruction
2. Social constructivist: pedagogies of construction
3. Connectivist: pedagogies of connection

We treat each of these in turn in the following sections.

THE INSTRUCTIVIST-ERA: COGNITIVIST/BEHAVIOURIST APPROACHES

Until fairly recently, there were very few alternatives to broadcast or distribute fixed media for distance learning. Mail, print, radio, TV, video or audio recordings made up the vast majority of media available to distance educators and students. Telephone, the postal service and, in some cases, two-way radio were about as good as it got if two-way communication was needed, which meant that communication was nearly always one-to-many or one-to-one. Before the advent of the postal service, distance education as we know it today was virtually impossible, so it is no coincidence that the first examples of the form date from the late eighteenth century when such systems became ubiquitous and reliable (Gunawardena & McIsaac, 2004).

It is almost inevitable, without much capacity to communicate, that an instructivist approach will become the dominant form of teaching. The notion that there is a body of knowledge that can be represented in written, spoken, or enacted form and communicated from the learned to the unlearned is a powerful one at the best of times, but when it is combined with a communication channel that limits dialogue in both quantity and pace, an instructivist approach is overwhelmingly likely to occur. There are exceptions: Piaget's constructivist pedagogies (1970), for example, focus on the construction of knowledge by an individual rather than simple conveyance of knowledge.

Instructivist teaching has, however, not historically been the dominant form of pedagogy, at least in Western culture. The Socratic form of pedagogic dialogue, for example, is inherently social. Apprenticeship models, while explicitly acknowledging that there are masters from whom to learn, are essentially conversational. Learning outside schoolrooms has almost always been a two-way flow of information. The "teacher" (whether a parent, peer, or formal pedagogue) imparts knowledge through telling and showing, but equally must pay attention to how and whether a learner is learning. With this in mind, and given that the focus of this book is on social learning, we briefly overview some of the main features of the cognitivist/behaviourist model of learning.

COGNITIVIST/BEHAVIOURIST PEDAGOGIES

Cognitivist/behaviourist pedagogies centre on the individual as an autonomous entity to which certain stimuli can be applied in order to achieve a certain measurable output. Behaviourist pedagogies deliberately go no further than these observable inputs and outputs (Skinner, 1974), whereas cognitivist approaches take into account the mental models and internal processes, building on a richer psychological understanding of learning and how it occurs (e.g., Bruner, 1966; Gagne, 1985; Gardner, 1993). In each case, however, the viewpoint is that of an individual, and the individual processes that are involved in learning. The cognitivist/behaviourist tradition is also predominantly instructivist, inasmuch as it is assumed there is a body of material or specified measurable skill to be learned that may be transmitted to the learner. This mould begins to be broken in the Piagetian branch of cognitivism: constructivism (Piaget, 1970).

For Piaget and his followers, knowledge occurs as a result of connecting and constructing ideas, feelings, and structures. In cognitivist-constructivist approaches, learning is seen as a process of construction, building models, and connecting old knowledge with new. Every individual constructs a view of the world for him- or herself. This epistemologically different understanding of learning leads naturally to pedagogies such as problem-based, enquiry-based, and constructionist (learning by creating) methods of learning, which assume that, though there may be measurable outcomes reached by all, every individual constructs knowledge differently: starting somewhere different, learning differently, with different meanings attached to what they learn.

However, though epistemologically more advanced, the emphasis of such approaches is very much on the learner as an autonomous agent, learning alone. Although the learner may learn from others, learning itself is seen as something internal to the individual. This perspective is important: it is vital to understanding how individuals learn as much as how they learn with others. Much modern research in the area draws on our increasing knowledge of the brain and how we process and store information, leading to a field of study under the name of "brain-based learning" (Jensen, 2008; Weiss, 2000). Cognitive behavioural pedagogical models dominate training programs and much computer-based training, and have shown consistently improving results when teaching individuals to accomplish pre-determined behavioural objectives (see, for example, Fletcher, 2009).

LEARNING AS AN INHERENTLY SOCIAL PROCESS

Processes of meaning-making, integrating new information, and creating knowledge are not only enhanced and stimulated through reaction, discussion, and argument with others but also much knowledge confirmation, interpretation, contextualization, and validation happens only through interaction with others.

In an interesting study, Okita, Bailenson, and Schwartz (2007) tested learning and the degree of arousal (associated with engagement) for learners who believed they were interacting with an avatar controlled by a human being, versus those who believed they were interacting with an animated but machine-controlled agent. They found that the belief that one was interacting with a human resulted in both better learning outcomes and more engagement with the learning task.

Further confirmation that we think and behave differently when we believe we are interacting with humans comes from a fascinating study by Krach et al., (2009), in which all subjects engaged in the same task (interacting with a computer to play the Prisoner's Dilemma), but showed significant differences in functional MRI scans depending on whether they believed they were interacting with a machine or a human. This does not mean that learning cannot or does not happen when an individual is studying on his or her own or interacting with simulations, tutorial systems, or other learning modalities, but it does highlight the increased attention of learners when they are, or believe they are, interacting with real human beings.

Humans have evolved for millions of years in contexts where shared support and cooperative activity has increased survival probabilities (E. O. Wilson, 2012). Thus we have evolutionary propensities for positively opening our social and learning selves to others who serve as models and sources of information, and who provide direct assistance in solving many types of problems. In our primordial past, and perhaps to a greater degree in our networked future, human beings *will* continue to exploit and benefit from the support and assistance of others. In the past these potential assistants shared common time and space—now they are available anytime and anyplace.

SOCIAL LEARNING THEORIES

The poet John Donne's proclamation that no man is an island suggests our deep interdependence with others. It is an interesting but perhaps irresolvable debate as to which came first—whether it was the emergence of self from the family or tribal origins, or whether society emerged from the aggregation of many selves. Even when we are working alone, our language, metaphors, thoughts, and feelings are guided and created through the use of signs, symbols, and expressions that we have acquired from others. John Dewey's colleague and fellow pragmatist George Herbert Mead is most remembered for his notions of how a sense of self can only arise through discourse with others. He notes how "we are in possession of selves just in so far as we can and do take the attitude of others towards ourselves and respond to those attitudes" (qtd. in Pfuetze, 1954, p.78). But Mead goes even further, arguing that in interaction and cooperative work with others, the giving and taking of directions and advice allows us to develop critical forms of empathy to create appropriate and viable images of ourselves. He argues that "in giving directions to others, he gives them to himself, and thus arouses a similar response in himself which is understood by himself" (Pfuetze, 1954, p.79). This lays the groundwork for responsibility and self-control.

Lave and Wenger argue, "activities, tasks, functions, and understandings do not exist in isolation; they are part of broader systems of relations in which they have meaning. These systems of relations arise out of and are reproduced and developed within social communities, which are in part systems of relations among persons" (1991, p. 53). For most early psychologists, this social development and growth of the self took place in wide varieties of face-to-face interaction and dialogue that has characterized human evolution from the earliest times. Now, however, face-to-face interaction is but one of many modes through which we see ourselves reflected in the response of others. Whether mediated interaction inevitably suffers due to social cues being filtered out or the media allows forms of hyper mediation (Walther, 1996) that affords more effective means of social interaction, is at present an unresolved issue. However, there can be no doubt that mediated interaction has come to form a major role in supporting cooperative work, collaborative understanding, discourse, and individual growth, as media use consumes an ever-greater proportion of our daily lives.

Much social learning theory developed in reaction to the behaviourist notions that learning resulted only from direct exposure to reinforcements and punishments, and further from cognitive notions of individual knowledge acquisition. Albert Bandura and others argued that people learn a great deal without experiencing rewards or punishments directly but through vicariously observing the effect of these on others. Bandura (1977) wrote, "learning would be exceedingly laborious, not to mention hazardous, if people had to rely solely on the effects of their own actions to inform them what to do. Fortunately, most human behaviour is learned observationally through modelling: from observing others one forms an idea of how new behaviours are performed, and on later occasions this coded information serves as a guide for action" (p. 27). Bandura further noted the necessity of opportunities for practice. This practice is best done in social contexts so that it can be refined through reaction and feedback from others.

Humans learn socially in many ways, and one of the oldest of these is imitation (Warnick, 2008). Aristotle argued, "To imitate is, even from childhood, part of man's nature (and man is different from the other animals in that he is extremely imitative and makes his first steps in learning through imitation)" (1997, p. 57). Imitative learning has most often been studied among infants, but models of technical and cognitive apprenticeship also celebrate the effectiveness and efficiency of learning by imitation. However, learning by imitation has historically been limited by both time and space. Geographic separation can be overcome to a limited degree by video and immersion, but time restrictions also occur in place-bound and traditional forms of imitation. Asynchronous imitation occurs when one models the behaviour, consciously or unconsciously assesses the means of expression, the rationale, or the arguments of others as displayed in their asynchronous uttering. This modelling often occurs when responding to discussion or problem sets, to which the answers of others already serve as visible models.

Social learning looks to the authentic clues that arise from interaction with others in a specific context. In the everyday interactions of individuals, problems arise and through negotiation, acquisition of information, and reflection, these problems are resolved (Dewey, 1916). Learning is not only the accumulation of facts and the understanding of concepts but also is both induced and confirmed through interaction and discussion with others. Even when one is alone, the shared use of language, cultural concepts, signs, and symbols both afford and constrain our understandings and creation of knowledge (Brown, Collins, & Duguid, 1989).

Social scientists have long struggled to match the predictability of their laws of human behaviour with those developed in the natural sciences. Cognitive and behavioural learning models have strong roots in empirical science, in which the discovery of generalized laws of learning that can be applied across contexts is a major goal. One of the popular attempts used in economics and game theory is to develop models where rational decision-making on the part of the individual is assumed. However, Buchanan (1985) notes that rational theories break down because people talk to one another, change their minds, and utilize both overt and covert efforts to change others. Thus the capacity to communicate with one another is an essential skill and, as we have discussed, has long been an important tool for learning. However, communication and learning (whether face-to-face or at a distance) are very complicated—influenced by a host of variables including context, skill, attitudes, and the form of mediation used to convey that communication. In later chapters we focus on ways that our conceptual model of social organization may reduce this confusion. We next turn to pedagogies that were specifically developed to benefit from our propensity and capacity to learn socially.

Social Constructivism

Constructivism of the non-social variety has deep philosophical and pedagogical roots, and has been associated in a learning context with the works of John Dewey, George Herbert Mead, and Jean Piaget. Like many popular theories, it has been defined and characterized by many, often with little consistency among authors. However, all forms of constructivism share a belief that individuals construct knowledge dependent upon their individual and collective understandings, backgrounds, and proclivities. Debate arises, however, over the degree to which individuals hold common understandings, and whether these are rooted in any single form of externally defined and objective reality (Kanuka & Anderson, 1999). Since much of constructivism is touted as driving the current educational discussion, it should be noted that it is a philosophy of learning and not one of teaching. Despite this incongruence, many authors have extracted tenets of constructivist learning, and from them developed principles or guidelines for the design of learning contexts and activities.

Drawing mainly from the work of Vygotsky and Dewey, social constructivist models of learning emerged in the early part of the twentieth century, though they were only adopted on a widespread basis by the academic community from the 1970s onward, after Vygotsky's work was discovered in the West, and Dewey's half-forgotten writings began to be reinterpreted in the light of a Vygotskian understanding (e.g. Popkewitz, 1998). From a social-constructivist perspective, knowledge and knowledge creation is a fundamentally social phenomenon. Not only are meanings negotiated and formed in a social context, the process of education is one where learners move from one zone of proximal development to the next, mediated by others who have already reached beyond where the learner wishes to go. In distance learning, social constructivist approaches were prohibitively expensive until the advent of affordable communications technologies. While there are many variants on the theme, social constructivist models share a number of common features that we outline in the following subsections.

Multiple Perspectives and Engagement that Includes Dialogue

Since knowledge is both individually and socially constructed, it follows that there must be opportunity, reason, and capacity for individuals to share, debate, and discuss their understandings. Individually, discussion is used to validate knowledge construction and to test its veracity against the understandings of others. Socially, groups of learners use one another to both amplify and dampen their understandings so as to construct understandings that are congruent—at least to the extent where cooperative action can be undertaken.

Learning in Authentic Contexts

If learning is to be meaningfully constructed, it must have worth for the individual learner. This value arises most easily if learning takes place in authentic contexts with genuine personal value that is perceived by the learner as both interesting and useful. Unfortunately, there are domains of knowledge that, in themselves, have little intrinsic meaning (at least for the majority of learners), but they are considered prerequisites for acquisition of more relevant knowledge to be studied at a later time. This focus on the prerequisite, regardless of its own authenticity or relevance, is typically over-valued by discipline-centred teachers, resulting in learners often being forced to ingest large quantities of information with little apparent value. Constructivist practitioners of authentic learning design activities that are wide-ranging enough so that their connection to the relevant "big picture" is apparent even at early stages of inquiry.

Inquiry and Problem-Solving

The inquiry and problem-solving features of constructivist learning emerge from the need for authentic contexts. Problems not only situate the learning in an authentic task-driven challenge but also provide motivation and focus to the learning process (Jonassen, 2002). This is especially important in collaborative learning where the diversity of interests, expertise, and aptitude may cause groups to move away from constructive problem-solving toward following the interests of dominating or particularly interesting diversions.

Learning is Open Ended and Ill-Structured

Most learning does not take place in classrooms, but in the real-life context of authentic problems situated in ill-structured environments (Spiro, Coulson, Feltovich, & Anderson, 1988). Thus constructivists prefer to situate learning problems in messier domains where there is no single comprehensive and correct answer. The ill-structured domain of the problem also stimulates discussion among learners as they attempt to construct a useful understanding of the domain and develop solutions to problems.

Cooperative and Collaborative Learning

Despite that fact most formal education takes place in group settings, very little of what goes on in traditional classrooms or online can be described as cooperative or collaborative. Rather, both teachers and learners usually conceive of learning as an internal cognitive process. Indeed, in many learning designs, students are set as competitors against one another, each striving for a limited number of high grades that will be allocated by the teacher.

Despite this individualistic orientation in current practice, there is a growing body of research demonstrating that cooperative and collaborative education not only results in greater learning but also is perceived by students as generally being more satisfying, and is associated with lower dropout rates. In a large meta-analysis of studies that included over 4,000 students comparing cooperative and collaborative learning to traditional individualized study, Springer, Stanne, and Donovan (1999) concluded that "students who learn in small groups generally demonstrate greater academic achievement, express more favourable attitudes toward learning and persist through science, mathematics, engineering and technology courses to a greater extent than their more traditionally taught counterparts" (p. 22).

There is an ongoing and generally inconclusive debate in the literature differentiating collaborative from cooperative learning. Generally, collaborative learning is considered to be less teacher-driven and more ill-defined than cooperative learning. Learners working collaboratively deliberately support one another's learning, negotiate the division of tasks, and help one another to learn by using and/or developing group processes in more or less formal ways to produce some common or individual outputs. Cooperative learning tends to be based on more structured sharing. For example, students may research topics independently, or focus on parts of a broad topic and share them with others in the class. Although many writers and teachers use the terms interchangeably, we will be fairly specific in defining collaborative learning as a process where learners deliberately work together to achieve outcomes of mutual benefit, and cooperative learning as a process where independent learners do work that benefits themselves and other students. Despite sometimes contested differences, there is a great deal of common theory and practice in both collaborative and cooperative learning. These similarities include:

- A teacher who is usually more a facilitator or guide than a "sage on the stage"
- Teaching and learning as shared experiences
- Students participating in small group activities
- Students taking responsibility for their own learning and that of their group
- Students stimulated to reflect on their own assumptions and thought processes; and
- Social and team skills developed through the give-and-take of consensus-building (adapted from Kreijns, Kirschner, & Jochems, 2003, p. 337).

In Springer et al.'s meta-analysis (1999), attempts to describe learning designs they investigated as either cooperative or collaborative and then comparing results revealed no significant differences in outcomes. However, the collaboration or cooperation reviewed in these studies took place in face-to-face interactions. In a smaller study comparing the two in online interactions, Rose (2004) found that groups characterized as cooperative achieved higher degrees of in-depth processing in a shorter period of time than those working collaboratively. This finding is consistent with our own experiences of online learning in which coordination, task clarification, assignment, and negotiation seems to take longer in online and especially asynchronous online contexts. Of course, such skills are themselves valuable, need to be learned, and may contribute to outcomes that are not intentionally measured.

Given the theoretical and empirical evidence supporting the use of collaborative and cooperative learning designs, one might reasonably ask why this model is not employed more often in formal education. The answers may lie in the social norms that privilege independence and individualism in many Western countries. However, there are also pedagogical, organizational, and technical problems that challenge collaborative design implementations. From a pedagogical perspective, many educators conceive of learning as an individual process, and assess it as such accordingly. The central role of assessment in institutional learning thus drives it toward patterns that emphasize the individual at the expense of the group.

Communities of Inquiry

Our final model of conventional social learning, Communities of Inquiry, is partly a systems theory and partly a model for analyzing learning transactions that both predicts and describes behaviours. It concerns the elements that are essential to the social educational experience. Explicitly concerned with group learning (see figure 2.1), it identifies three kinds of presence within a social learning transaction:

- *Cognitive presence.* The extent to which participants can construct meaning through reflection and discourse,

- *Social presence.* The extent of identification with a community and trusting inter-personal engagement, and

- *Teaching presence.* The design, facilitation, and direction of social and cognitive processes (Garrison, Anderson, & Archer, 2000, 2001).

We will return to the community of inquiry model in some detail later but, for now, note that it provides a way of understanding how learning occurs within a group setting, where a group of intentional learners and one or more teachers build knowledge together.

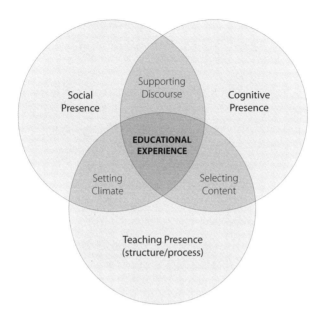

Figure 2.1 Community of Inquiry model (Garrison & Anderson 2003, p. 88).

We argue throughout this book that the affordances of cyberspace offer new ways to approach all forms of human interaction and communication, including education. It is thus not surprising that new pedagogies and theories of learning have arisen that attempt to both explain and provide guidance to educators when teaching in net-infused contexts. There are many related theories that help to explain and recommend approaches to learning in networked contexts, outside the classroom. Each addresses a set of related concepts:

- learning is and should be unfettered by formal boundaries and delimited groups;
- learning is not just a feature of individuals, but of communities;
- learning is distributed not just in the heads of humans but in the tools, conceptual and physical, that they use, the artifacts they create, and the environments they build and inhabit;
- knowledge exists in a social and physical context as well as a personal one;

- structure and meaning can be an emergent feature of the dynamic learning system in which many individuals, loosely joined, can play a role in creating;
- diversity has value to the whole learning community, and individual differences should be valorized.

Since the late twentieth century, these themes have emerged from multiple disciplinary areas and, in sum, add up to a new and different way of thinking about learning. In making this assertion, we distinguish Connectivism (a theory created by George Siemens (2005)) from connectivism with a small "c," which we use as a generic term for a family of network learning theories. Just as there are many different variations on social constructivism that share the unifying characteristics, so there are variations of connectivism that share the common properties of knowledge emerging from and within a network.

In the following subsections we explore some of the theories and models that have informed the connectivist era. While incomplete as theories of learning or teaching in themselves, they are woven into a fabric of ideas that informs the two most distinctive connectivist learning theories, communities of practice and Connectivism itself.

Heutagogy

The principles (and naming) of heutagogy were first articulated by Australian educators Stewart Hase and Chris Kenyon (2000). Heutagogy (derived from the Greek word for "self") is a direct result of self-determined learning theories and practice. Heutagogy brings these theories into a networked context by noting the ways in which the tools and resources for effective self-determined learning have been expanded exponentially through cyberspace. However, access to tools does not ensure that learners are capable of using them effectively. Thus, Hase and Kenyon also note the importance of *capability* in heutagogically based education. They write, "capability is a holistic attribute and concerns the capacity to use one's competence in novel situations rather than just the familiar, a justified level of self-efficacy for dealing with novel problems, having appropriate values, being able to work in teams, and knowing how to learn" (Hase & Kenyon, 2007, p. 113).

Heutagogy also stresses the need for learners to understand their own learning processes. This reflective capacity allows learners to direct their own learning when needed—even in the absence of a formal education structure. Interesting as well is Hase and Kenyon's (2007) distinction between *competencies* (the darling of many, especially vocational educators) and *capability*. Competencies are tested in known contexts and usually are focused backward on instruction already provided. Capability, however, looks to the future and celebrates the capacity to learn as contextually demanded. Increasingly, both workplaces and schools are changing rapidly, and thus the competencies acquired last year or last month may not provide the capacity to learn and apply that knowledge going forward in those environments.

Hase and Kenyon end their 2007 paper with a list of ways in which Heutagogical pedagogies are used to design learning processes applicable inside or outside of formal education. These capacities are magnified by the net-infused context in which collaboration, student input into content selection from vast open educational resources, self-reflection through tools like blogs, and greatly enhanced flexibility in where and when to learn are all afforded.

Distributed Cognition

The field of distributed cognition, originally developed by Edwin Hutchins (1995), is concerned with ways that the tools, methods, and objects we interact with may be seen as part of our thinking processes and extensions of our minds into the world. Rather than thinking of cognition as an internal process of thought, proponents of this perspective observe that memories, facts, and knowledge may be reified and embodied in objects and other people we interact with. In many cases, the environment places constraints on our thinking and behaviour, or influences us to think and behave in certain ways and, in many cases, is an integral part of thinking. Objects and spaces are participants in the cognitive process, not simply neutral things that we use, but an inextricable part of how we think and learn, both as individuals and as connected groups (Salmon & Perkins, 1998). S. Johnson provides a nice illustration of this: he talks of the successful landing of a plane damaged by geese as "a kind of duet between a single human being at the helm of the aircraft and the embedded knowledge of the thousands of human beings that had collaborated over the years to build the Airbus A320's fly-by-wire technology" (2012, Introduction, Section 2, para. 10). Knowledge is not just held within the artificial intelligence that guides the aircraft—although the subtle interactions with the autopilot do play a role—but in the design of controls, seats, and other artifacts through which pilots, co-pilots, and others interact with one another and the vehicle (Hutchins & Lintern, 1995; Norman, 1993). Similarly, we as individuals offload some of our cognition onto the objects around us—the organization of books on a bookshelf, the things we lay out on our desks, the pictures on our walls, and the cutlery in our kitchen drawers, all act as extensions of our minds that both reflect thinking and engender it. As Churchill (1943) said, "We shape our buildings and afterwards our buildings shape us."

Distribution not only applies to unthinking objects but also to us and the people around us: cognition is a social process where different people play different roles, leading to the distribution of knowledge within a group or network of people (Salmon & Perkins, 1998). A simple demonstration of this is the loss of cognitive capacity that occurs when couples split up or one partner dies. The remaining individual will have come to rely on their partner to remember things, perform activities from washing dishes to doing accounts, and vice versa, a process sometimes described as "socially distributed remembering" (Sutton, Harris, Keil, & Barnier, 2010). Whether in intentional organizations or looser networks, this socially distributed remembering allows us to do more and think further (S. E. Page, 2011).

Activity Theory

Most commonly associated with social constructivism but equally central to understanding connectivist models, activity theory emerged from the work of Soviet psychologists in the early-to-mid twentieth century such as Leontev and Vygotsky, who were attempting to find ways to explain how individuals and objects worked together as dynamic systems. The binding concept of an activity from which the name is derived is concerned with subjects doing things, typically together, engaging in activities through mediating objects or tools—be they physical or mental objects. It was elaborated on and brought to the West primarily by Engeström (1987) who added "community" to Leontev's individual and object as a fundamental unit of interaction.

One of Activity Theory's most distinctive features is its insistence that, in understanding the mental capabilities and learning of an individual, it makes no sense to treat an isolated person as a unit of analysis: the physical, cultural, and technical world that he or she inhabits is as much a player in any activity as the mental processes of the individual who engages in it. Activity Theory describes actions in a socio-technical system by considering six interdependent and related dimensions:

The object—the purpose of the activity

The subject—the individual actor

The community—the combination of all actors in the system

The tools—the artifacts used by actors

The division of labour—how work is divided and tools mediate the activity

The rules—things that regulate and guide the system

These interdependent parts are usually represented as a pyramid that illustrates their interactions (see figure 2.2).

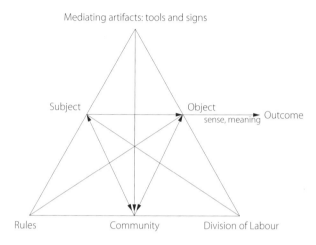

Figure 2.2 Activity theory view of a human activity system (Engeström, 1987, p. 78).

Activity Theory is not predictive, but provides a framework for understanding the complex ways that humans interact with the world and one another through mediating artifacts. The main lesson to take from its sometimes arcane perspective on the world is that, if we are to understand the ways individuals behave in a social context, it is important to consider not just their mental processes, but their interactions with the entire activity system including, importantly, the physical and mental tools and processes that they use. Combined, they provide a way of understanding consciousness as a social phenomenon that extends into and is inextricable from the world, the tools, and the signs (notably language) that people employ. In a very real sense, tools mediate between people and the world, not as simple channels, nor as a means of achieving ends, but actively affecting how the world is experienced and perceived. This makes it highly relevant to the context of networked learning, in which interactions are mediated and objects play not just a supportive role, but an architectural one in learning.

Actor Network Theory

Like Activity Theory, Actor Network Theory (ANT) is concerned with systemic interactions of people and the objects that they use in their interactions. While sharing some of the terminology and related conceptual models of activity theory, Actor Network Theory emerged from a very different tradition and has a complementary agenda. Conceived by Latour (1987, 2005) and elaborated by Law (1992), it was created in the context of social practices in science and technology, mainly in reaction to sociological and technologically determinist views of the role of technology in society. Latour, in particular, sought a "scientific" way of describing the behaviours of people that avoided self-referential explanations of the "social," therefore avoiding latent assumptions. His objective was to rebuild sociology from the bottom up without reference to what he saw as fuzzy or ill-defined terms that had bogged down the discipline, most notably eschewing use of the term "society" itself as a simple given.

Actors in an actor network may be human or non-human, with no special priority given to either. Instead, actors are constituted in heterogeneous relationships with one another: they form networks of related pieces that have no distinct edges. Given that such networks are continuous and unbounded, ANT helps educators to understand how some collections of actors may be thought of and considered as individual actors in their own right—for example, we can say things like "Athabasca University tops the league table of open universities," or "the US invaded Afghanistan." In the language of ANT, some networks may be black-boxed. In other words, we may choose to treat a complex network as a single entity, and to consider it in its relationships with others as a single actor.

Complexity Theory and Complex Adaptive Systems

Another notable feature of theories from the connectivist era is that they describe emergence and draw on the dynamics of complex systems. Complex systems are those where new and often unpredictable behaviour emerges out of multiple interactions of entities, where the interactions are known and follow fixed rules: the weather, for instance, is a good example of this, as are rainforests and eddies in flowing water. Complex *adaptive* systems (CASs) consist of interacting entities that adapt in response to changes often brought about by other entities: evolution, ecosystems, cities, economies, stock markets, and termite mounds are good examples of these (Kauffman, 1995).

Educational systems may be thought of as CASs: while they are typically constrained by top-down governance and rules that determine the range of behaviours that can occur, there are many parts which are complex and adaptive, including learning itself, where patterns and behaviours emerge as a consequence of individual actors and their interactions. Once we enter the world of informal learning, especially in the context of networks and sets, patterns that emerge are almost always complex and adaptive but, even in the most controlled institutional learning contexts, educational systems are open, unbounded, and connected to human and natural systems. This is the problem that confronts any educational researcher who attempts to analyze the effectiveness of a given intervention: it is never, in principle, possible to control all the variables that may affect any learning transaction.

Emergent behaviours arise when autonomous yet interdependent agents interact with one another within a context that partly determines the possibilities of interaction, and that is itself warped by the interactions of agents within it. This means that one of the most important defining characteristics of all complex systems is that they are, at least at some scales, unpredictable. While we can recognize patterns and broad tendencies, it is theoretically impossible to predict any particular event. The famous "butterfly effect," whereby the flap of a butterfly's wing in one part of the world might cause a storm in another, was a term originally coined by Edward Lorenz to describe his work (Lorenz, 1963) on what would later come to be known as chaotic systems. Lorenz (1963) showed conclusively that, though an entirely deterministic system, the weather at any given time is impossible to reliably and accurately predict from a previous known state. That a butterfly's or (in its original formulation) a seagull's wing flap can affect weather systems on the other side of the planet is a captivating, mathematically provable if empirically untestable image. Such sensitivity to initial conditions is observable in far more mundane and commonplace events that we can more easily observe, such as the movement of individuals in a crowd, the patterns of drips from a tap or the cascades of sand on a dune. But hand in hand with unpredictability come large-scale emergent patterns, in which higher levels of order emerge from small-scale interactions, such as can be seen in everything from ripples on a pond to life itself (Kauffman, 1995). In an educational context, theorists look for and attempt to predict "transformations or phase transitions that provide the markers for growth, change, or learning" (Horn, 2008, p. 133).

If systems are complex and unpredictable, they are not easily explained by positivist researchers and educators who attempt to eliminate or control all the variables that affect a learning transaction. Rather, those with a perspective based on recognizing complexity seek social structures that allow effective behaviour to emerge and evolve and ineffective ideas to be extinguished. Researchers in CASS seek to understand features of the environment, and especially social or structural norms or organizations that resist either overt or covert attempts at self-organization. Such attempts to stifle emergence may be impossible and involve a large expenditure of effort. Horn argues that "the management of social organizations of all types has been maintained by control measures that work to block the capacity of systems to operate autonomously" (2008, p. 133). These blocking mechanisms were designed for educational systems so that learners can operate in close proximity with one another without becoming mutually destructive or descending to chaos. But these same control mechanisms can thwart the emergence of adaptive behaviours and phase shifts that provide potential for rapid and profound learning.

Implications of complexity theory for learning and education operate on at least two levels. At the level of the individual learner, complexity theory, like constructivist theory, supports learners' acquisition of skills and power such that they can articulate and achieve personal learning goals. By noting the presence of agents and structures that both support and impede emergence of effective adaptive behaviour, individual learners are better able to influence and indeed survive in often threatening and always complex learning environments.

At the organization level of either formal or informal learning, complexity theory points to the social structures that we create to manage that learning. There is usually some level of self-organization going on in all complex systems, brought about by a combination of diverse learners with diverse backgrounds, needs, interests, and a wide range of ways to interact with one another, their surroundings, teachers, and learning resources. Any schoolteacher who has experienced a wasp or a thunderstorm in a classroom of children will be familiar with the way that small perturbations can have large effects on the learning behaviours and activities that are occurring, no matter how well planned they might have been in the first place. Even so, most of us can recall occasions when poor and stultifying approaches to teaching still resulted in good learning, often because of interactions with other learners or the chance discovery of interesting learning materials.

Good teachers adapt and change behaviours as the environment, context, and interactions between learners change. However, the self-organizing facets of a learning system can work against this, making it an uphill struggle. Complexity theorists (e.g., Kauffman, 1995, p. 233) talk of different levels of orderliness in self-organizing systems: the "Red Queen" and "Stalinist" regimes. When there is too much chaos and unpredictability, systems are always running to stay in the same place, like the Red Queen from *Alice Through the Looking Glass*. Conversely, if there is too little dynamism and change, then things settle down to a fixed and unchanging point or set of points—the Stalinist regime. Neither is helpful in learning. From the point at which these management functions begin to inhibit the emergence of positive adaptive behaviour or facilitate and sustain behaviours that are not conducive to deep learning, we can expect negative results. The emergence of complex self-organized behaviour occurs between the realms of chaos and order, for which Doyne Farmer coined the term "the edge of chaos" (Langton, 1990). Organizational structures should help us to surf the edge of chaos, not eliminate or constrain the creative potential of learners and teachers. Further, this understanding can guide us to create and manage these complex environments, not with a goal of controlling or even completely understanding learning, but instead with a goal of creating systems in which learning emerges rapidly and profoundly.

Complexity theory also encourages us to think of learning contexts—classrooms, online learning cohorts, and so on—as entities in themselves. These entities can be healthy or sick; emerging, growing, or dying. By thinking at the systems level, reformers search for interventions that promote healthy adaptation and the emergence of cultures, tools, and languages that produce healthy human beings.

Learning designers following complexity models eschew the linear processes associated with much instructional design theory. Rather, they situate learning in contexts that are characterized by fluidity and turbulence, located near the edge of chaos, with rich possibilities for diverse actions and reactions, in complex contexts, and the presence of strange attractors, where order emerges from chaos. Most importantly for our study of networked learning, high-quality learning contexts are marked by "interconnectedness of and intercommunications among all parts of the system" (Laroche, Nicol, & Mayer-Smith, 2007, p.72). Thus, individual learning is enmeshed in the complex social experience and context of group, network, and collective social activity and culture.

Complexity theorists have drawn examples from many contexts to show the power and usefulness of emergent organizations and their capacity to thrive without total understanding, much less control, of the context in which they exist. Connectivist-era models of learning embrace this uncertainty and seek ways to utilize complexity without the potential drift to chaos that a lack of top-down organization might entail.

Two connectivist theories have emerged as central and archetypal. The first, with the longest history, is that of communities of practice and its successor, networks of practice. The second is Connectivism, as propounded by its creator Siemens, with contributions from his collaborator Stephen Downes.

Communities of Practice

The theory of communities of practice was established in the work of Lave and Wenger (1991) and fully expounded in Wenger's seminal book, *Communities of Practice* (1998). Lave and Wenger sought to explain and improve upon learning that occurs outside of formal group-based courses, typically in the workplace or among co-located learners in communities. The theory describes primarily informal processes of community formation and growth, though much of Wenger's more recent work has focused on approaches to deliberate fostering of such learning communities. The concept, drawn from anthropological studies, relates to how newcomers to a collection of people, such as a department in a firm, a university, or a group of charity workers, learn the group's practices and become participants in the community. At first, Lave and Wenger used an all-encompassing notion of "legitimate peripheral participation" to describe the process of becoming a full member of the learning community, but Wenger's later work unpacked this in terms of

- mutual engagement—the group-like formation of shared norms and methods of collaboration,
- joint enterprise—a shared set of goals and purposes, also known as the community's domain, and
- shared repertoire—a set of resources, both physical and conceptual, that the community shares (Wenger, 1998, p. 73).

The concept of shared repertoire, in particular, echoes the notion of distributed cognition and sharply distinguishes this as a networked learning theory, in which both human and non-human actors in a network are mutually constitutive and joined together. Part of the value of the concept of a community of practice is that it treats learning as dynamic and situated, and describes ways that tacit knowledge spreads through a network, as opposed to the more formal methods of deliberate learning that may convey explicit and implicit knowledge, but do not (and, according to Polanyi (1966) *cannot*) succumb to explanation and formalization.

A particularly powerful aspect of the theory is its description and explanation of boundaries. In a conventional intentionally formed group, boundaries are defined easily: one either is or is not a member of the group, and there is usually a process involved in joining or leaving it. In the fuzzier realm of communities of practice, boundaries are typically emergent phenomena that arise out of shared practice, a bottom-up process resulting from the joint enterprise that naturally channels the community and separates it from others. Central to this idea is the importance of those who exist at or near the boundaries, and who cross them between communities of practice. Boundaries are spaces where learning is particularly likely to happen, because that is where different conceptual models are likely to clash or merge, where "competence and experience tend to diverge: a boundary interaction is usually an experience of being exposed to a foreign competence" (Wenger 1998, p. 233).

The divergence can be both creatively inspirational and a cause of conflict. Wenger's boundary-crossers may be networked individuals who move beyond and between closed communities, cross-fertilizing each community with ideas and practices of others. There may be more or less concrete boundary objects, including symbols and metaphors that are technological connectors like social software platforms and the processes enabled through them, which act as a means to bridge different communities. Communities thus become networked by boundary-crossing in order to play the role of one another's teachers, spread knowledge within the community, and also engender changes in knowledge in other communities.

Models and interventions based on communities of practice have been widely adopted in many sectors. The concept is not, however, without its problems. First, the term carries multiple terminology and disciplinary understandings associated with the word "community." Second, different researchers often understand the degree of formality of the "practice" differently. The "community of practice" label has been applied to emergent, informal, and spontaneous organizations of face-to-face professionals, but it has also been used to describe managed professional development activities which almost preclude only voluntary participation. Schlager & Fusco (2004) use the term extensively to define, and Wenger's theory to describe, online educators' forums (such as TappedIn); yet after years of studying this rather large community of practice, "the question of whether the users of the TappedIn environment collectively constitute a community or practice remains unresolved" (Schlager & Fusco, 2004, p. 121). In many ways, the blurring of the term has led to it being hijacked by those who are more fixed in a social-constructivist model of the world, so although communities of practice are, in the way Wenger first described them, in the vanguard of the connectivist era of learning theories, they still have one foot firmly planted in older models of learning.

Networks of Practice

Perhaps because of the fuzzy borders between networked and grouped ways of thinking of communities of practice, Wenger, Trayner, and Laat (2011) have extended the notion of communities of practice for the networked age, taking advantage of more recent work that treats networks and groups as distinct and separable social forms (e.g., Downes, 2007; Rainie & Wellman, 2012; Siemens, 2005). Although Wenger's earlier work did describe ways that knowledge spreads through a network, he did not explicitly distinguish between intentional groups and the broader, looser spread of network connections. In this more recent work, Wenger et al. make the distinction between communities (what we call "groups") and networks. Because networks do not have a specific domain or shared enterprise, they differ from communities of practice in some important ways:

> The learning value of a network derives from access to a rich web of information sources offering multiple perspectives and dialogues, responses to queries, and help from others—whether this access is initiated by the learner or by others. On the one hand, because of personal connections, networking enables access to learning resources to be very targeted—whether one sends an email query to a friend or decides to follow someone's Twitter feed. On the other hand, because information flows can be picked up, interpreted, and propagated in unexpected ways, they traverse networks with a high level of spontaneity and unpredictability. This potential for spontaneous connections and serendipity—and the resulting potential for collective exploration without collective intention or design—is a key aspect of the value of networks for learning. (Wenger et al., 2011, p.12)

While communities/groups are concerned with building a shared identity and fostering trust and commitment, networks, if they can be said to be concerned with anything at all, are about fostering and optimizing connectivity. Because networks are emergent features of connections with others, this concept is far more blurred and hard to grasp than it is in the context of groups, especially as those who are part of a network may not even be able to see the network, let alone view or affect aspects of its structure. Nonetheless, Wenger et al. identify a wide range of indicators to identify value within networks and make tentative steps toward identifying how such value may be reified through structured storytelling. This approach carries with it an underlying assumption that the networked learner is concerned with meaning-making in a constantly shifting, dynamic context. It is a process in which the creation of value is linked to the creation of content; the process of navigating a network and interacting with others in it is a process of learning in and of itself.

Connectivism

George Siemens coined the term *Connectivism*. In his 2006 book, *Knowing Knowledge*, he described it as "the integration of principles explored by chaos, network, and complexity and self-organization theories" (Siemens, 2006, p.30) Like Heutagogy, and drawing on the conceptual underpinnings of distributed cognition, actor-network theory, and communities of practice, connectivism assumes a context connected through pervasive networks that link not only individuals but also machines and resources as well. Siemens (2005) articulated eight oft-quoted principles of connectivism:

- Learning and knowledge rests in a diversity of opinions.
- Learning is a process of connecting specialized nodes or information sources.
- Learning may reside in non-human appliances.
- Capacity to know more is more critical than what is currently known.
- Nurturing and maintaining connections is needed to facilitate continual learning.
- The ability to see connections between fields, ideas, and concepts is a core skill.
- Currency (accurate, up-to-date knowledge) is the intent of all connectivist learning activities.
- Decision-making is itself a learning process. Choosing what to learn and the meaning of incoming information is seen through the lens of a shifting reality.

Connectivism shares many of the attributes of constructivism, notably in its valorization of diversity and a philosophical basis that knowledge is constructed in a social context. Like Heutagogy, Connectivism values capacity over what is currently known and proposes students learn how and what to learn and have input into this process.

Connectivism draws heavily from distributed cognition and actor-network theory in its view of learning in non-human appliances. This is about the traces that we leave in our networked lives, the artifacts through which we build and share knowledge and create new ideas, the tools and objects we offload cognitive functions to and think with. From the first time humans scrawled signs and images on cave walls or in the dirt, they were offloading part of their intellect into external space. Like those who rail against Wikipedianism and the Googlization of society today, Socrates saw this as problematic, as Plato relates in *Phaedrus* on the subject of the invention of writing:

> The specific which you have discovered is an aid not to memory, but to reminiscence, and you give your disciples not truth, but only the semblance of truth; they will be hearers of many things and will have learned nothing; they will appear to be omniscient and will generally know nothing; they will be tiresome company, having the show of wisdom without the reality. (Plato, trans. 1993, pp. 87-88)

Notwithstanding these dangers, this offloading enables us not only to stand more easily on the shoulders of giants but also on the shoulders of our peers, and to enable them to stand on ours.

Connectivism also acknowledges the speed with which knowledge expands and changes in net-infused societies. By being connected to both other humans and knowledge resources, we retain currency and benefit from the diversity of ideas and cultures that abound. Through our awareness and maintenance of these connections, we become able to create new connections, resolve problems for ourselves and others, and thus become truly networked lifelong learners.

There are some aspects of Connectivism—the theory itself, rather than the family of theories—that we remain unconvinced by. Siemens and particularly Downes have taken it to be a complete theory of learning, following from connectionist views of psychological reality, in which networks like the Internet and our social networks of knowledge are directly analogous to connections that we make in our brains and, ultimately, the synapses of which they are comprised (Downes, 2008a). While there are some strong topological similarities between these networks, there are also strong topological similarities between them and the patterns of flu virus epidemics and song charts (Watts, 2003), but this does not make them qualitatively similar. Connectivism presents one of the most compelling theories of the networked era of education, but it is, as its authors are happy to admit, a work in progress that provides a blueprint for others to follow, rather than a bible that must be adhered to in every respect.

No single generation of learning has ever superseded the last. Like all technologies, learning technologies evolve by assembly (Arthur, 2009) and incorporate and extend what came before. One does not need to look far to discover plentiful examples of each generation, often coexisting in the same course or set of learning transactions.

Connectivism as a theory in itself, as opposed to a collection of related theories, has been criticized on many fronts. Some suggest that it is not a theory at all (Ireland, 2007) but the more substantive critiques mostly relate to its notable inefficiencies (Kop, 2011; Kop & Hill, 2008; Mackness, Mak, & Wiliams, 2010). The vast majority of people who start out taking explicitly Connectivist courses, typically run as MOOCs, fail to finish them. However, the concept of "finishing" is itself not entirely relevant to connectivist learning. Its explicit emphasis on emergence rather than planned learning means that it is hard to measure whether targets have been reached at all, much less with efficacy, and perhaps more disconcertingly, it is far from clear whether the resulting learning might have been more effectively or efficiently achieved in some other way. In response to these and other criticisms as well as opportunities afforded by new technologies, there has been an evolution toward a more holistic model that incorporates all earlier models of learning, including connectivist models. We have christened this the 'holistic generation,' in recognition of the fact that it encompasses all earlier models.

Holistic approaches to learning are agnostic as to method. Drawing from connectivist and older models, they valorize diversity and the socially distributed cognition afforded by the read-write Web and other publishing models, accepting that every learning experience is unique, and every learner's needs are different. Connectivist approaches, for all their extensive reliance on networks of people engaging socially, are at heart focused on the individual—specifically, the individual's learning. Holistic models embrace the fact that it is sometimes more important that a group learns, rather than an individual, especially in collectivist cultures (Potgieter et al., 2006). Holistic models recognize that, sometimes, guidance is what is most needed, that people can learn without direct engagement with others and, even that transmittive instructionist models of teaching have a place.

The current generation of large-scale MOOCs provide a good example of this. Courses from the likes of Coursera and Udacity tend to follow a highly instructivist model but, because of their size, spawn networks and study groups of learners who meet face-to-face, and through various social media such as Facebook, to enhance and support one another using quite different and more connectivist approaches. To support diversity and maintain the right amount of coherence for any given learner, holistic approaches are, like connectivist methods, heavily reliant on technologies. In particular, they make use of tools that can aggregate the actions and behaviours of many people in order to help make sense of a topic for those that follow. Social and learning analytics, collaborative filters, recommender systems, reputation management tools, and social adaptation systems are used to counter the torrential flow of information and plethora of connections that characterize the connectivist process. We will discuss most of these in greater detail later in this book, but for now, note that one of the main features of such systems is that they use, directly or indirectly, the diverse knowledge and actions of a crowd.

THEORY OF TRANSACTIONAL DISTANCE

Beyond broad families of learning theories, the theory of transactional distance has been highly influential in distance learning teaching and research. It is a theory of instruction rather than learning, and it was developed within the specific context of distance education programming. Like activity theory, ANT, and complexity theory, it is a systems theory that looks at the interactions of agents and the effects that those interactions have on the behaviour of the system. As noted previously, social learning takes place in both formal and informal settings and in distance, classroom, and blended contexts. Nonetheless, it is perhaps most powerfully apparent when it operates beyond the limitations of time and space as a means of supporting distance education and distributed learning.

Moore (1993) attempted to develop a theoretical model that addresses both structured instructivist and dialogic social-constructivist models of distance education, and provides guidelines for creating mixtures of the two. Moore argues that the "distance" in "distance education" should be considered not in either geographic or temporal terms, but as a psychological and communications gulf between learner and teacher, measured on a continuum of structure and dialogue. The basic tenet of the theory is that a negative, "transactional distance" separates learners and instructors from one another and learners from the content they wish to master. This is not to suggest that high transactional distance necessarily leads to poor learning outcomes, but merely that there is greater transactional separation between learner and teacher.

Moore (1993) postulated that there are three dimensions of transactional distance—structure, dialogue, and autonomy. Structure refers to the degree of activity, learning outcome, media, and content selection that is prescribed by the instructor or delivery institution. Dialogue is the interaction between and among students and teachers, determined by factors such as the number of students in a given class, the degree of familiarity and cultural understanding among participants, the nature of learning activities engaged in, the immediacy of the technologies employed, and the sense of integration and identification with the educational institution, content, and other participants (Tinto, 1975). Autonomy is "the extent to which, in the teaching/learning relationship, it is the learner rather than the teacher who determines the goals, the learning experiences, and the evaluation decisions of the learning programme" (Moore, 1993, p. 28). Autonomy is dependent upon the self-discipline, existing knowledge, and self-motivation needed by learners to thrive in contexts that are not completely prescribed by external agents (teachers and rigid curriculum). As Candy (1991) observes, self-direction is a variable quantity that shifts in different contexts and is influenced heavily by external stimuli.

The educational designer has an opportunity to manipulate the structure and amount of dialogue in the learning sequence. High and low levels of each variable present educational opportunities in four quadrants, measured according to the degree of structure and dialogue found within them (Kawachi, 2009).

Figure 2.3 Transactional distance quadrants (adapted from Kawachi, 2009).

As illustrated in figure 2.3, there are many potential classic forms of formal and informal study that are associated with each of the quadrants. However, each learning context results in more or fewer restrictions on student freedoms, and each is associated with different degrees of scalability, speed of production, direct and indirect costs, and other variables. Rather than dispute the value of intense interaction as advocated by proponents of collaborative and cohort models of distance education (Garrison, 2000) or celebrating the autonomy offered by individual study (Holmberg, 1986), Moore's transactional distance theory (1993) helps us create models that trade off the advantages of both. Anderson has argued for an equivalency theory that postulates "deep and meaningful formal learning is supported as long as one of the three forms of interaction—student–teacher; student–student; student–content—is at a high level. The other two may be offered at minimal levels, or even eliminated, without degrading the educational experience" (2003, p.4). Thus, tension exists between developing formal learning programs that decrease transactional distance by increasing interaction and decreasing prescriptive activity, and providing access to educational experience that is of both high quality and affordable cost.

This accords with Moore's own view (1993) that effective learning may occur whether transactional distance is high or low: structure or dialogue may be used effectively to improve learning. However, Saba and Shearer (1994) have demonstrated a system dependency that implies the more there is of one, the less there is of the other. As structure increases, it reduces the opportunities for dialogue, and as dialogue increases, it breaks up any intended structure. For example, a broadcast video lecture, one of the most highly structured forms of teaching, offers no opportunities at all for dialogue, at least while the lecture is playing. Conversely, a web meeting equivalent of the same lecture, if chat or audio are enabled for participants, allows participants to interrupt, ask questions, seek clarification, and change the pace or direction of the speaker. As a consequence, the event becomes less structured. At its most extreme, a dialogue between multiple participants may exhibit nothing but emergent structure.

Transactional Distance in Crowds

While Moore's theory (1993) applies well within a traditional formal distance learning setting and has been verified and applied many times (e.g., Chen & Willits, 1998; Lowe, 2000; Stein, Wanstreet, Calvin, Overtoom, & Wheaton, 2005; Zhang, 2003), its applicability outside this setting, especially when social forms beyond the traditional dyadic or group modes of engagement are in play, is less clear. Transactional distance in social spaces that are not tightly controlled by a teacher is a complex phenomenon, whereby the teaching role may be distributed, anonymous, or emergent as a consequence of behaviours in a crowd, where the learner may be a contributor and active shaper of activities and content. We will be arguing that the concept applies differently under such circumstances and that, though the dynamic between an individual learner and teacher strictly obeys the inverse relationship between structure and dialogue, there are ways to bypass the problem when the teaching role is embodied in a crowd.

Moore (1993) does not distinguish between the communications gulf and psychological distance in their roles as definers of transactional distance, but as we have explored the range of ways that transactional distance operates within our typology of social forms, we have come to realize that the two aspects, communication and psychological gulf, are entirely separable. In some forms and tools used within new social media, it is possible to be in close and constant two-way communication without significant psychological attachment, without closeness to another human being. Less commonly, there may be a sense of closeness without significant two-way communication. Both psychological connection and communication are important aspects of what creates distance. For minimal transactional distance, negotiable control, rich communication, and a feeling of closeness (in a psychological sense) are all important. Reducing any one of these increases transactional distance, and each variable is potentially independent of the others.

Transactional Control

Like author Anderson, author Dron (2007b) has also examined Moore's theory of transactional distance (1993) and found equivalences: most notably, that the "distance" of which Moore speaks is actually composed of two distinct and largely independent variables. On the one hand, transactional distance is a mental phenomenon, a measure of the psychological and communications gulf between learner and teacher. On the other, it is a systems phenomenon that may be more precisely defined as an issue of control, which explains much of the negative correlation between dialogue and structure observed by Saba and Shearer. Both psychological/communication and control aspects are important, but they operate independently from each other.

From a systems perspective, when transactional distance is high, learner control over the learning transaction is lower and teacher control is higher, the teacher or teaching presence largely determining the learning trajectory. Through dialogue it is possible to negotiate control, and thus lower the transactional distance. The more dialogue there is, the more control is distributed among the participants. For example, learners can ask questions, seek clarification, express confusion, boredom, or interest, thus changing the path of the learning trajectory. The third dimension of Moore's model (1993), autonomy, equates to the learner having control over his or her learning trajectory, requiring neither structure nor dialogue. Dron's theory thus unifies the three variables identified by Moore in transactional distance theory by treating all as part of a continuum of control, from autonomous learner control through negotiated control via dialogue, to teacher control through structure (Figure 2.4).

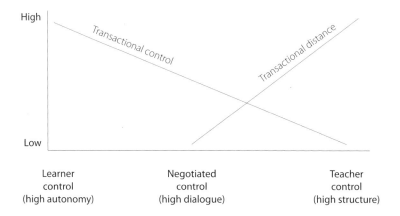

Figure 2.4 The relationship between transactional control and transactional distance (adapted from Dron, 2007, p.32).

Most real-life learning transactions occur at some point along the continuum of complete learner control through to complete teacher control, and they seldom if ever occur at the extremes. Even in the most regulated transactions learners may choose to tune out, switch off, and will always reinterpret or construct their own understandings; conversely, even the most autonomous of learners will usually allow some of their control to be taken away by narratives provided by the author of a book, director of a video, or creator of a website.

Cooperative Freedoms

It is valuable to unpack the notion of control a little further, as it is of some significance in all forms of learning, especially in a social context. Garrison and Baynton (1987) provide the important insight that control is not simply a question of choice. In order to make effective learning choices, the learner needs *independence*—which, as Candy (1991) shows, is a highly situated and context-sensitive variable—*power* (the capacity to exercise that independence), and *support* (the tools, people, and processes needed to implement that power). However, for the idea to have any meaning at all, it is necessary to know some of the constraints and factors over which learners may exercise control. If control is an important aspect of an educational transaction, we need to understand the nature of what can be controlled in a learning process. Morten Paulsen's theory of cooperative freedom (2003) describes a range of possible freedoms that might be available to a learner in a formal learning setting. His hexagon of cooperative freedoms (see figure 2.5) describes six dimensions:

- Place: freedom to choose where one learns
- Time: freedom to choose when one learns
- Pace: freedom to choose how fast or slow one learns
- Medium: freedom to choose the media used for learning
- Access: freedom to learn regardless of qualifications or extrinsic obstacles
- Content: freedom to choose what one learns

Figure 2.5 Paulsen's model of cooperative freedoms (adapted from Paulsen, 2003).

Paulsen's cooperative freedoms provide a fairly complete picture of freedoms in a formal, institutional learning context. However, there are gaps, and it does not describe well the different models of formal learning, such as those in connectivist transactions, or less formal learning environments. To Paulsen's list of six dimensions, T. Anderson (2005) added the freedom of *relationship*, that describes the ability to choose with whom and how one engages with others, an essential freedom if we are concerned with social learning. Related to freedom of relationship but distinct from it is the freedom of *disclosure*: deciding to whom one discloses one's communications. This is concerned with privacy and is of some significance to learners who may be fearful of displaying their ignorance. Disclosure is a more pronounced problem when entering the public realm rather than a closed group, although the commonplace requirement for students to engage with others in a group can also greatly limit this freedom.

In addition to these freedoms, Dron (2007a) has observed that there is also a meta-freedom to choosing whether or not and when to choose: the freedom of *delegation*. To be in control of one's learning, it is essential to be able to submit to the control of others when we do not ourselves have sufficient knowledge, experience, or time to decide what and how to learn next. Another freedom that is not quite addressed by Paulsen's "medium" is the *technology* used to present content. There is a world of difference between text presented on a mobile phone and text presented on a tablet or large screen, even though the medium may be considered the same. It is useful and, from a learner's perspective, valuable to distinguish between media and the technologies used to deliver them. We therefore add "technology" to the list of freedoms. We might use the word "tool" instead, but the popular term "technology" makes it more easily understood in this context.

While our newly added freedom of technology might be comfortably stretched to cover the pedagogies and processes of learning, it may also be valuable to consider the freedom of *method* as a separate category. This requires a little justification. There are many ways that method is inseparable from technology. Indeed, a full definition of any technology must include both the methods and any tools it may employ, and in some cases, the method is the technology. There are strong arguments suggesting that pedagogies, for example, should be treated as technologies (Dron, 2012). However, especially in a learning context, it remains valuable to think of methods separately, especially when we are talking about pedagogies, particularly as populist definitions of technologies tend to focus on the physical tools such as whiteboards, desks, cellphones, and computers, rather than what makes them into technologies. So, although we believe that any full definition of a technology must include both the tools of which it is comprised and the ways they are used, the two are often separable in popular understanding. One can, for instance, use the same tool in many different ways, employing different methods.

Of all Paulsen's freedoms, "access" stands out as being beyond the potential control of an individual or teacher. Access may be denied, for example, due to a lack of qualifications, but can be equally due to limited experience and prior knowledge. This is not a matter of personal choice, or if it is, it is at an entirely different scale from the other freedoms, sometimes relating back to choices made years or even decades ago. Access is not only about prior learning, it also relates to the availability of technology and the ability to use it. However, these are both covered by other freedoms—the freedom to choose an appropriate technology or medium, and the choice of method. Thus, while access is a very important issue, especially in formal learning, it is of a different kind and/or scale to the other freedoms and is not easily controlled by the learner; we therefore exclude it from the list.

This leads us to our own decagon of cooperative freedoms, extending and adapting those identified by Paulsen, illustrated in figure 2.6:

- Place: freedom to choose where one learns
- Time: freedom to choose when one learns
- Pace: freedom to choose how fast or slow one learns
- Medium: freedom to choose the media used for learning
- Content: freedom to choose what one learns, from what source
- Technology: freedom to choose the tools with which one learns
- Method: freedom to choose the approach and pattern of learning
- Relationship: freedom to choose with whom one learns and how to engage with them
- Delegation: freedom to choose whether and when to choose
- Disclosure: the freedom to decide what and to whom it is revealed

Figure 2.6 Decagon of cooperative freedoms (adapted from Paulsen, 2003).

Mirroring Moore's theory of transaction distance, cooperative freedoms are, in many cases, inversely related to one another, though due to the number of freedoms under consideration and the ways they can interrelate, the relationships are more complex. Of particular note, many forms of social learning and freedoms of relationship affect and are deeply affected by pace. If we are learning in direct dialogue with others, then the pace of interaction is strongly related to the pace of learning: we have to wait for responses, to work in synchronization with others. Similarly, social interaction may place limits on the potential times and places that learning transactions can occur, as well as the medium, technology, and method used. Likewise, if constraints are placed on relationships, then this may affect freedom of disclosure: for example, if engagement is required as a classroom activity. There is a constant and ever-shifting interplay between constraints and affordances in any sequence of learning transactions, in which technologies, pedagogies, physical and temporal constraints, financial imperatives, prior learning, future needs, methods, and media all help to determine the actual learning path that will be most useful or practical.

CONCLUSION

Social learning mediated and enhanced on digital networks has much in common with other models of learning, teaching, and associated instructional designs and pedagogies. Ideas and learning activities can be extracted from these other contexts and applied effectively in networked contexts; thus, there is value in extracting ideas and testing their efficacy in them.

In this chapter, however, we have focused on the main families of learning and educational theories that we believe are most directly relevant to the emergent context of networked learning. None of these are exclusive: the most rigidly behaviourist methods of learning have a social context and application, and may be found within learning trajectories that use social constructivist and connectivist models without negating the benefits of either. Connectivist learning often blurs into social constructivist modes as part of the emergent whole, and transactional distance provides a useful way to measure the varying quantities of control and social engagement at any point along the journey.

A TYPOLOGY
OF SOCIAL FORMS
FOR LEARNING

The beginning of wisdom is to call things by their right names.
Chinese proverb

The Internet era forces each of us to deal with an often bewildering and continuous set of technology-induced changes. When an infrastructure of powerful
computational and communications tools is matched with a ubiquitous communication network, the stage is set for rapid innovation. Some of these innovations are sustaining and help us to communicate, play, and learn more effectively
using familiar ideas and behaviours. Other innovations are disruptive—forcing
users to go outside the economic and social boundaries set by previous technologies and pedagogies to use them effectively (Christensen, 2008; C. Christensen,
Horn, & Johnson, 2008). Learning, however, is universal, and thus humans invent
means and applications to use both disruptive and sustaining technologies to
enhance their lives and those of others on the planet. In this chapter we introduce
an organizational scheme, or heuristic, designed to create a conceptual home for
both sustaining and disruptive networked technologies—and those with elements
of both when applied in particular contexts.

We developed this guiding heuristic for learning and education in 2007 (Dron
& Anderson, 2007) and it has been used in our work, and by others, to help make
sense of the changing social patterns in learning that cyberspace has engendered
(e.g., Buus, Georgsen, Ryberg, Glud, & Davidsen, 2010; Conole, 2010; Dalsgaard
& Paulsen, 2009; Gray, Annabell, & Kennedy, 2010; Kop, 2011; Ryberg, Dirckinck-
Holmfeld, & Jones, 2010; Thompson, 2011).

Though it proved to be of some value in its original form, we have since modified and refined our model for clarity and explanatory power. In brief, the evolved form illustrates three kinds of aggregation of learners in either formal or informal learning: *groups*, *networks*, and *sets*. We originally conflated sets with a further emergent entity that is not a social form as such, which we have referred to as the *collective*. The collective is an embodiment of collective intelligence, and it plays a binding and, in many cases, extremely active role in enabling social software systems to do things that were difficult or impossible in the past. Collectives are not a social form, but an emergent actor that arises from actions taken by people in a crowd.

To distinguish these forms, it may help to think of an example drawn from everyday life. Imagine that you are sitting in a café in the square of a busy city. Around you is a teeming multitude of people—the set of people in this part of the city. You do not know who they are, and they are not part of your social network though you may be learning things from them, such as whether it is raining or not: you might, for example, note how many are carrying unfurled umbrellas. As you look around, you see subsets of this set: men, women, children, people dressed in red coats, people running, people going to work. Some of these people come in groups—families, friends, classes of schoolchildren—that share a purpose and are, in some way, coordinated in their movements and activities. They may be there for the purpose of learning together: children on field trips, surveyors mapping out the land, or tourists being shown the sights of the city. Every now and then you see people running into friends, colleagues, and people they know. Strung between the people in the crowd are networks, exchanging information and co-constructing knowledge. Then you notice a cluster of people forming, gathering around a street entertainer performing in the middle of the square. No one has organized the gathering—a small crowd seems to attract more members, as though there were an invisible force pulling them together, a leaderless form of coordination, an emergent order: a collective. The crowd is acting as a signal for others to join it, playing a role not unlike that of a teacher telling a class to pay attention to some reading or performance.

Figure 3.1 illustrates the three social forms for learning, representing the fact that there is a continuum between the forms, each blurring into the next.

All of these social forms are bound by common attributes of sharing and communication that can contribute to the learning of others. Collectives, a particular form of collective intelligence, can emerge from any or all of these social forms and are characterized by algorithmic aggregation, filtering, data mining, clustering, and pattern-matching. These algorithmic processes may be internal to crowd members (e.g., responding to others in a crowd) and/or externally imposed, typically by computers (e.g., recommender systems) but sometimes by individuals (e.g., people who count votes in an election).

Figure 3.1 Social forms for learning: Sets, nets, and groups.

Our model is derived from our observations about collections of *learners* and how they benefit from one another's knowledge and actions. While these social forms can and do exist in contexts other than learning, it is not our intention to provide a complete model of human society, or to suggest that the model would be useful in all other contexts. This model is useful because, as we will demonstrate in the ensuing chapters, it helps to make sense of not only how social learning occurs in traditional educational settings but also how the different ways that we can connect using cyberspace technologies may contribute to our learning trajectories in informal and personal settings. These social forms can and do exist in many circumstances beyond learning, and we will from time to time provide examples of their use in other contexts in order to help illustrate what we mean, but it is not our intention to tread outside the boundaries of a learning context in applying this model.

Individuals

Before we move into the realm of truly social forms that involve multiple participants, it is important to observe that much learning involves only the most tenuous links between people. When we as individuals read a book, paper, web page, or news feed, transactional distance is extremely high. However, even for the most solitary of learners, other people are necessarily involved in the learning transaction as authors and creators of content. In many cases, this involves a form of guided didactic conversation (Holmberg, 1986) in which the learner engages in internalized dialogue with the very distant tutor. Even where this is not the case, the author's voice may be apparent and there is a strong sense that almost every learning process involves, at one or more steps removed, another human being. At a small scale, all textual communication and many that use voice, video, or avatars include a process of turn-taking in which we read/absorb and, potentially, respond. The difference for the individual learner is that the possibility of an ongoing exchange is not available.

Dyads

In 1984, B. S. Bloom famously posed the 2-sigma problem, referring to the finding that an average student tutored one-to-one performed two standard deviations better than an average student tutored using conventional one-to-many instructional methods. We are a little skeptical about the validity of the assessment used to take this measurement, since such objective-driven testing does not reveal all of the learning that may have occurred in a transaction, and does not look at creative gains or serendipitous discoveries that may have been made in larger groups or with different methods of learning and teaching.

However, the general point is hard to ignore: when compared to traditional institutional educational forms, where the goal is to transfer replicable knowledge, one-to-one tutoring works extremely well. Since Bloom's original challenge, one-to-one tutoring (assuming appropriate methods are applied) has remained the gold standard for effective instruction, and no other teaching model has consistently reached or bettered the same 2-sigma improvement that results from it. Unfortunately, one-to-one tutoring is very expensive and, in formal learning, only common in a limited range of situations such as Ph.D. mentoring, project work, and personal tutoring. More than that, there are gains to be had from a diversity of perspectives, heuristics, interpretations, and predictive models that may be found in a large number of people (S. E. Page, 2008).

Though a pair of people communicating may be seen, in some ways, as a very small network or group, one-to-one conversation is different from other forms of learning conducted with more than one person. Rainie and Wellman (2012) observe that as soon as a third person is introduced, the potential for coalitions arises, and the persistence of the group no longer stands or falls on the actions of a single individual: if one leaves, interaction does not necessarily cease. Greater numbers have many other benefits that differ from dyadic communication in scale, if not in kind. Diversity increases with more people, allowing greater types

and levels of interaction to occur, providing multiple perspectives, different interpretations, heuristics, and predictive models (S. E. Page, 2008), all of which can
contribute to learning: more possibilities mean greater breadth and depth of discourse, more creative opportunities, and better problem-solving capacity.

For all the benefits of many individuals learning together, from a learning perspective dyadic communication typically affords the greatest possible level of freedom of delegation for the learner: the tutor can respond directly to questions, adapt
teaching to the learner's stated or implied reactions, and the learner can choose
whether to intervene in the course of his or her own tuition without contest with
others (Dron, 2007a). Although it may occur in the context of a large group, a great
deal of dyadic communication underpins most forms of social learning, from email
exchanges to telephone conversations, face-to-face mentoring to instant messages. While the title of this book makes it clear that we are mostly concerned with
learning in larger groups, one-to-one dialogue represents an "ideal" form of guided
learning, at least where there is a teacher who knows more than the learner and is
able to apply methods and techniques to help that learner to learn. It continues to
play an important role in network forms of sociality because of the essentially one-
to-one edges between nodes that lead to what Rainie and Wellman (2012) refer to
as "networked individualism"—a focus on an individual and their many one-to-
one connections with others. It is also an important form in sets, where we may
interact with an unknown other in the same direct way.

GROUPS

The most familiar social form in an educational context is the group. In a formal
educational context, these are just a few of the common forms that groups may take:

Classes	Schools	Administrative
Tutorial groups	Colleges	departments
Seminar groups	Committees	Panels
Cohorts	Working groups	Special Interest Groups
Divisions	Workshops	Study groups
Centres	Conferences	Sports teams
Faculties	Project teams	Playground gangs
Universities	Academic departments	Houses
Learning technology	Research groups	Year groups
groups	Senior management	
Boards of governors	teams	

Each of these groups may be more or less formally constituted, and each can play a role in the learning experience for anyone affected by them. Groups are cohesive: they are identifiable as distinct entities with existences of their own that are, in principle, independent of their members. However, one of their defining characteristics is that their members are, in principle and often in practice, list-able. Groups often have formal lines of authority and roles, such as a designated chairperson, team leader or teacher, enrolled student, and so on, with implicit and/or explicit rules that govern behaviour and structure. They are structured around particular tasks or activities that may be term-based or ongoing, and institute various levels of access control to restrict participation, review of group artifacts, or transcripts to members, providing a less public domain. Groups often have schedules: members frequently use and create opportunities to meet face-to-face or online through synchronous activities, and their modes of interaction are typically many-to-many or one-to-many.

NETS

Our second major social form is the network. The distinction between groups and networks that we employ is a common one, used by many researchers in the field as well as in fields like community studies, sociology, and community informatics (e.g., Downes, 2007; Rainie & Wellman, 2012; Sloep et al., 2007; Wenger et al., 2011). Networks consist of nodes—such as people, objects, or ideas—and edges, the connections between them. In the social form of a network, networks connect distributed individuals and groups of individuals, one node and edge at a time. They are not designed from the top down, though we may create channels that make their emergence more likely. Instead, they evolve through our many and varied interactions with others. Entry and exit to networks is usually simple— we connect in some way with another person, or we don't: although we might occasionally cut our ties with other individuals, for the most part it is enough to simply not engage with someone for them to drift out of our network. Every individual's network is different from those of others because it is defined by social connections and therefore it matters whose perspective and connections are being observed. People may drift in and out of network activity and participation based on relevance, time availability, context, needs, and other personal constraints.

Networks have always been channels of knowledge diffusion and discovery: we learn from and with the people we know, whether connected via networked technologies or in person. Online, net forms are typically enabled by technologies incorporating social networking systems. Learners can be connected to other learners either directly or indirectly, and may not even be aware of all those who form part of the wider network to which they belong.

Many social networking sites such as Facebook, LinkedIn, and MySpace provide network support and facilitation tools, yet the form has been used by distance learners for much longer: earlier email lists and threaded discussions also support networked learning and physical social networks, and have long been important channels of knowledge diffusion.

It is important to distinguish some shifting notions in the concept of a network: the Internet, for example, is as much a physical network of machines and connections between them, as it is a network of people. Indeed, that physical network is the means through which people can come together. It is also important to recognize that, quite apart from a means of transport, a network can include or be entirely composed of things (physical and conceptual), not just people. Indeed, it is possible to view the entire universe as a network. Our concern here is not with the abstract topological form of networks in general, but with the *social* form of the network. Physical networks may be fundamentally required to connect people in a group, for example, but the group social form is different from the net social form even though both are, in several meaningful ways, describable as networks. Net modes of interaction can be one-to-one, one-to-many, and many-to-many.

SETS

Our final social form is the set. Sets are made up of people who are bound together by commonalities or shared interests. People may be unaware that they are part of a set (e.g., people with a particular genetic marker), or they may identify with it (e.g., people who are fans of football or constructivist teaching methods). Sets involve interactions with others, but typically these are impersonal or even anonymous. When an author publishes a textbook, he or she is writing for a set—an unknown number of people with a particular shared interest. Library books are categorized with metadata that puts them into sets, allowing individuals to seek items of interest.

In the past, the social interaction in most sets tended to be one-way, with a few exceptions such as a speaker's engagement with crowds in lecture theatres, for example. Online, the set form has become more significant. A blog post or public tweet (especially when tagged or given a subject line to indicate its content) is not usually aimed at an individual, a group, or a network of friends (though they may be included), but at others who share that interest. While learners seeking information about a topic may well take individuals and networks into account when choosing a blog post to read or article in an online journal, it is more often than not the topic that attracts them, not the network. Much of the time there will be no expectation of engagement, no new network formed, no group joined. When individuals browse YouTube videos, networks may well play a role but, for the most part, discovery is based on content similarity and shared keywords. When we pick curated items or those that have been highly rated, the network is simply the underlying infrastructure: what matters are the metadata that classify and organize social content. This does not make the social ties of sets unimportant: sets can be central to our identity and we may feel closeness with and trust others simply because they share attributes with us: people with the same religious beliefs, who like the same kind of music, or who support the same football team, for instance. Set modes of interaction are typically one-to-many and many-to one, though they can enable many-to-many engagement.

SOCIAL SOFTWARE SUPPORT FOR SOCIAL FORMS

Different kinds of social software support various social forms in diverse ways. Group-oriented systems tend to provide features like variable roles, restricted membership, and role-based permissions. Network-oriented systems tend to provide features like friending, linking, and commenting. Set-oriented systems tend to provide tools like topic- or location-based selections, tags, and categories. Very few substantial systems are limited to any single mode, but most have varying strengths or emphases in different areas. The more complex or multi-featured the system, the more likely it will be to support different modes, and most can, with sufficient effort, be cajoled into performing different roles even though their intended purpose may be at odds with a particular use. Table 3.1 provides a few examples of popular social systems categorized according to what we perceive to be the predominant forms they support at the time of writing: but the reader must bear in mind that this is a shifting arena where changes and enhancements are constantly being introduced and that our perceptions may differ from those of others that use them in different ways. These are all soft technologies composed not just of tools but of the methods, processes, and intentions of their users. Almost any tool can be ben to support almost any social form, even if the fit is poor.

Table 3.1 Support for social forms in some common social software.

System	Group	Net	Set
Facebook	*Medium*	*Very high*	*Medium*
	Facebook provides groups and group areas	This is Facebook's raison d'être	Facebook offers pages that people may set up for specific topics
Twitter	*Very low*	*High*	*Very high*
	There are third-party tools and ways to organize around sets, but Twitter does not support explicit groups	The "following" function in Twitter supports strong two-way links as well as (more commonly) one-way links	Twitter's hashtags provide a powerful means of clustering around a single topic
Pinterest	*Low*	*Medium*	*Very high*
	There is no explicit support for groups	Social networking is a feature, but seldom the main means of discovery of content on the site	As the name implies, Pinterest's most significant feature is that it relates to shared interests
LinkedIn	*Medium*	*Very high*	*High*
	LinkedIn offers closed interest groups that are quite widely used	This is LinkedIn's raison d'être	It is common to seek people based on categories of skills and interests that they supply
Moodle, Blackboard, and other LMS systems	*Very high*	*Very low*	*Low*
	Moodle courses are archetypal group support tools with strong roles, controlled membership, and tools to support collaboration in teams	Use of cross-system blogs and profiles allow for very minimal social networking, though we note these are rarely used	Courses, especially open ones, provide an anchor for subject-based interest, though the act of joining one makes this largely a group-support system

Many, if not most, social sites and software systems incorporate facilities to support and/or gain benefit from each social form. For instance, Facebook is primarily a social networking platform, yet it supports the formation of closed groups, individual-to-individual communication, and a host of collective aggregations such as voting systems, data mining to identify people you may know but have not connected to already, and add-in applications such as music/movie/book recommenders. An archetypal group such as a face-to-face class may contain many networks of friends that extend beyond and within the group, its members may be categorized in sets relating to, say, ability, interests, or opinions, and collectives may occur in many ways, such as a teacher counting a show of hands or collating the results of clicker presses.

There are many hybrid types of each of the main social structures we have identified that are as significant as the pure forms themselves. The "pure" forms of sets, nets, and groups may be mixed in different proportions to combine their features, producing some of the social organizational forms we are familiar with.

Group-Net: The Community of Practice

The classic intersection of a group and network is a community of practice (CoP). CoPs emerge, typically in workplace contexts, as networks of people who are within a group or groups. The notion of legitimate peripheral participation attests to the network-like features of a CoP, and yet there are many ways that members might regard them as cohesive units. It is helpful to think of these as clusters: a number of people in a network who share a purpose, practice, and often location, but without the explicit hierarchies, exclusions, and roles of a more defined group.

Group-Set: The Tribe/Community of Interest

Shifting from the pure group toward the set, communities of interest gather due to shared interests, and typically engage in more or less formal ways. They are often bound by interest in a topic more than by the group itself, though this may change over time. Some communities of interest occur at boundaries between sets and nets as well, if there are no formal kinds of engagement. When there is a shift beyond communities of interest toward more set-like engagement, we define this blurred category between groups and sets at the "set" end of the continuum as "tribes," a label that applies not just to actual tribes but also to a range of forms that share some characteristics of sets and some of groups: these include companies, universities, nations, and academic groupings.

Like groups, many tribes have hierarchies, social norms, explicit and implicit rules, and shared purposes. In a learning context, unlike groups, they are seldom time-limited, and few individuals know everyone in the tribe. They are bound by one distinct shared attribute, but this always comes with a range of other attributes, otherwise they would be pure sets. For example, those who share the same religion will also be bound by moral codes, belief systems, and expectations of behaviour, or other features that mark them as members of the tribe. As they become more set-like—for example, Goths, fans of a hockey team, learning technology researchers—the deliberate hierarchies disappear, becoming more diffuse and abstract, though the characteristics that make them a set may still be firmly associated with their sense of identity.

Set-Net: The Circle

It is commonplace to divide networks into more or less arbitrary categories that are often described as 'circles,' such as in 'my circle of friends.' We might, say, think of sets of people we know who live nearby and those who don't, or those who are friends and those we work with. Technologies such as Google+ Circles, Facebook Lists, and Elgg Collections are explicitly designed to allow us to classify people in multiple ways, reflecting the differences in how we relate to them, what we reveal about ourselves to them, and what we hide. Communities of interest may also occupy this blurred line between nets and sets, where the shared interest is the set attribute but where there are no formal or informal norms, rules, exclusions or inclusions. For example, followers of a particular band may come to know one another and cluster together at band concerts, without any formal, group-like constitution.

KINDS OF COLLECTIONS OF PEOPLE

As E. O. Wilson observed, "every person is a compulsive group-seeker" (2012, Chapter 24, Para. 10), a statement that is embodied in the phenomenal range of words that we have in the English language to distinguish different aggregations of people. In analyzing existing social forms to test our model, we came up with over 120 different words commonly used to refer to a collection of people, from alliances to workforces, without taking into account any of the millions of distinct proper nouns used to refer to specific groupings like banks, cities, countries, or scout troops. In our analysis, we discovered a few interesting things of note about this very incomplete example list. In the first place, many formal words relate to distinct organizational forms, especially those that occur in military, religious, business, and scholarly contexts—squads, sororities, flocks, federations, and the like. Bearing in mind that language has evolved slowly, this speaks to an important feature of many human groupings: they are technologized.

Many social groupings come with associated processes, methods, rules, legislations, procedures, rites of passage, rituals of entry and leaving, and are such an embedded feature that they have acquired their own vocabularies. Others categorize people according to things they share in common or that others perceive them as sharing in common such as race, class, dwelling place and so on, sometimes with implications that relate to other characteristics. Words like "tribe," "nation," "race," "working class," and "neighbours," for instance, indicate set-like characteristics that are used to fit people into slots.

IDENTIFYING SOCIAL FORMS

In determining the dominant social forms, the distinctions we have made are:

- Sets are social forms where people may have no knowledge of others in the set but are clustered by commonalities between them. This may lead to strong identification and trust in some cases, but not typically.

- Groups are social forms where individuals deliberately join others with shared goals and identify with group norms and behaviours.

- Nets are social forms where the connections between individuals and sometimes clusters of individuals are what bind them together.

While sometimes it can be hard to identify whether one collection of people is a group, net, or set, there are rules of thumb to follow. In brief:

- If the social entity persists even if there are no participants, likely it is a group.

- If there is little consequence to knowing who is involved and the topic is the most significant aspect, it is likely to be a set.

- If identifiable people are recognized by one another, it is probably a net.

In many cases, it is possible for all three to be true. It is helpful to visualize the typology as a Venn diagram of overlapping sets, the overlap indicating not only that we choose to see a particular social form within a collection of people and this does not exclude us from having other perspectives—all groups are both sets and nets, for instance—but also that there are often overlaps and fuzzy borders between them. Figure 3.2 shows the typology with some examples of the kinds of social entities relevant to learning found within them. Alternatively, you could see it as a continuum (see figure 3.3).

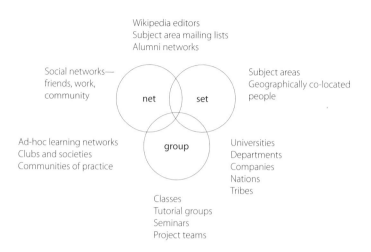

Wikipedia editors
Subject area mailing lists
Alumni networks

Social networks—
friends, work,
community

net   set

Subject areas
Geographically co-located
people

Ad-hoc learning networks
Clubs and societies
Communities of practice

group

Universities
Departments
Companies
Nations
Tribes

Classes
Tutorial groups
Seminars
Project teams

Figure 3.2 Venn diagram view of the typology.

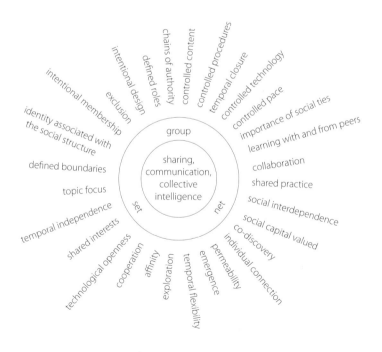

Figure 3.3 View of the typology as a continuum.

Each social form blends into the next. For example, many tribal forms such as affinity groups like hockey fans, Goths, or actor network theorists, are closer to sets than groups; others, like universities, nations, and international conferences are more group-like. Communities of practice exist somewhere on the continuum between groups and nets, often with limited or non-existent power structures but showing greater intentional cohesiveness than a simple network. The notion of blending is useful as it suggests an analogy to colours: an infinite variety of different shades and hues can be created by combining the three primary colours.

COLLECTIVES

Having defined the three social forms, we now turn our attention to collectives, which are perhaps the most intriguing of entities enabled by social software. Collectives, as we use the term, make the crowd behave as a single actor. They are not social forms like groups, nets, and sets, but are the machine- and/or human-aggregated results of the *activities* of a collection of individuals. Collectives achieve value by extracting information from the individual, group, set, and network activities of people, and then using that information to perform some action. Typically in cyberspace, these activities are aggregated by software and the results presented through computer interfaces, but humans can intentionally perform the aggregation role too. However, there need be no external agent involved for a collective to form: the individuals who form the crowd may themselves perform the aggregation, leading to emergent behaviours of the crowd.

Prior to the advent of the Internet, intentional collectives were used in, for instance, voting in elections or shows of hands in a classroom, but unintentional collectives occur in a more widespread manner, such as the formation of distinct footpaths in forests, the gathering of crowds around a street entertainer, and the movements of the stock market.

On the Internet, there are perhaps millions of applications that create value through aggregation, analysis, processing, and re-presentation of crowd activities, collecting user actions such as links placed on web pages (e.g., Google PageRank), photo and video tags, annotations and downloads (e.g., Flickr, YouTube, Instagram), article or solution evaluations (e.g., Digg, Mixx, Slashdot, StackOverflow), recommendations (e.g., Amazon, ratemyteacher.ca), and those that employ individuals' reputations for some other purpose (e.g., eBay). Crowd behaviour can be mined from implicit choices or contributions made at the individual, group, or network levels, from explicit behaviours such as rating or tagging, or by combinations of each approach. Collectives generally improve in value as the size of the group's/ network's/ set's sampled actions grows. When large numbers of resources are sorted, annotated, and rated by many, for example, the resultant resource listing can gain considerable collective value compared to a list rated by a single unknown individual.

Collectives behave as active agents within a system in ways that are analogous to the agency of human beings: in fairly predictable ways they make choices, value statements, expressions of belief, and act to bring about changes in the behaviour of others. This is of great importance in the context of learning in networks and sets because, in the absence of a formal teaching or cognitive presence, collectives often play that role. Collectives may sometimes act as mirrors of the group mind, or aspects of network consciousness that system designers or members of the crowd have chosen as significant. Because they represent chosen aspects of group, set, or network activity, the reflection of the collective mind is always shown through a distorting mirror that may be aggregating, refining, concentrating, selecting, filtering, averaging or otherwise processing aspects of crowd behaviour.

Typically, but not exclusively, collectives affect their own members in an iterative and self-organizing cycle. For instance, in social navigation, cues are often emphasized or de-emphasized as a result of individuals within a group or network moving around a system, which in turn affects the later navigation of that same group or network. However, this does not have to be the case. For example, the results of voting for a candidate by one group may influence the voting behaviour of another, or the tagging of photos within a system such as Flickr may influence the behaviour of outsiders and visitors to that system's resources.

SIZE OF GROUPS, NETWORKS, AND SETS

E.O. Wilson notes that "to form groups, drawing visceral comfort and pride from familiar fellowship, and to defend the group enthusiastically against rival group— these are among the absolute universals of human nature and hence of culture" (2012, Chapter 7, Para. 1). Groups in early human societies reached practical limits that were related to their function as humans evolved. The limits were constrained by available food sources to support communities, difficulties of coordination and allocation of work, and the laws of physics. Family-sized groups and workgroups are not viable persistent units in evolutionary terms because there are insufficient gains to be had from the division of labour and spread of innovation (Ridley,

2010). However, to extend beyond a certain size in the past required complex structures that evolved quite late in our species development, such as macrodemes and trade.

Moreover, with limited means of communicating over long distances, interactions were, of necessity, local: physics places limits on how far a voice can carry or the distance at which a person can be seen. While large herds are possible in many species, they emerge through individuals' coordination with others in the vicinity (Miller, 2010). For coordination of the kind seen in human communities, large sizes posed distinct limits.

British psychologist Robin Dunbar (1993) examined the size of groups among many primate species. He noted that the size of the group is related to the amount of social grooming engaged in by that species. Humans, however, have much larger brains than most primates, and limiting our interactions to those with whom we could be mutually engaged in social hair grooming would be both costly in time and likely very boring. Dunbar used statistical mapping techniques to suggest that our brains allow us to expand the size of groups with which we can interact and "can have a genuinely social relationship, the kind of relationship that goes without knowing who they are and how they relate to us" (1996, p. 77). Based on the size of our brains and validated by observations of both primitive and modern communities, online groups, army units, businesses, and other groups, Dunbar estimated this size is 150 persons, often referred to as *Dunbar's Number*. Interestingly, this coincides broadly with what Caporael (1997) distinguished as "macrodemes": originally seasonal gatherings of bands (demes of around 30 individuals that could sustainably hunt together) and later instantiated as the typical size of villages for around 15,000 years.

In reality, we operate in groups of significantly greater size than Dunbar's number suggests, though we may not, and in many cases cannot have a personal relationship with all the people in them. Companies, towns, universities, countries, religions, and many other group forms have developed primarily through the use of hierarchies and processes, methods and technologies that facilitate the exchange of knowledge between them. As Dunbar (1993) himself notes, language makes it possible for us to form groups with hierarchies and divisions of labour, so the actual size of human groups is considerably larger than what our brain capacity alone would suggest is possible (p. 689).

But what of broader networks in a technologically mediated age? Dunbar's notion of relationships in virtual spaces in the mid-1990s was decidedly jaded. He felt deception and fraud by "shadowy ciphers" would result in such an excess of deceit that face-to-face interaction would be necessary to restore trust, resulting in the number of trustworthy acquaintances conforming to earlier norms of around 150. However, technology changes that, and he was probably wrong in the first place. Apart from anything else, the definition of a "genuinely social relationship" that he uses is neither clear nor precise. Moreover, far from reducing genuine human interaction, it appears that the connections formed online strengthen and increase those that are face-to-face. As a probable result of improved Internet and mobile contact, the average number of friends whom American adults see in person grew 20% in the five years between 2002 and 2007 (Rainie & Wellman, 2012). More recent research suggests that the number of networked ties maintained by individuals in present-day developed societies tends to be closer to 600 (DiPrete, Gelman, McCormick, Teitler, & Zheng, 2011; T. H. McCormick, Salganick, & Zheng, 2010) and Dunbar himself explains close ties as only one of a series of layers of embedded relationships (Rainie & Wellman, 2012).

Donath (2007) brought the arguments on group size in virtual space to bear on popular social networks such as MySpace and LinkedIn. Using signalling theory, she notes the means by which individuals signal to each other using fashion, linguistic shortcuts, and public displays of "friendships" to build and maintain social networks and trust. Her speculations appear to explain the ways that sets can transition into networks and groups. Sets are, however, unbound by intrinsic size restrictions. They can be as small as an individual or as large as the population of the universe: we are all in the set of physical things, for example. All that is required for a set of unlimited size is the capacity to identify and present it. Modern search engines, classification schemes, aggregation tools, and filters make it possible to engage with enormous sets of people.

There is a loose correlation between size and the levels of our social typology. Most groups are smaller than most networks; many networks are smaller than many sets. However, technological mediation can make groups, nets, and sets of any size a possibility.

Aggregation and the "wisdom of crowds" arise at many levels, but the results generally become more useful as numbers increase and the benefits of large aggregation among otherwise non-related choices become apparent. This is the power of the long tail (C. Anderson, 2004), whereby even very small tendencies and interests arise in significant enough numbers to be of value. More is nearly always better. A classic example of a collective is the fairground game of guessing the number of candies in a jar. In this collective, a number of independent decisions which are, when considered individually likely to be wrong, are usually, when averaged together, very close to correct (Surowiecki, 2004). However, when there are only two people guessing, it is far less likely to be accurate than when there are a hundred, and the accuracy rises when there are a thousand. In the online world, Amazon's success at predicting books you will like is, in large measure, due to the number of people's independent choices that are available. If there were fewer people than books, to take an extreme example, it is quite unlikely that the results would be valuable.

SUMMARY OF THE VALUES OF DIFFERENT SOCIAL FORMS AND COLLECTIVES

When designing a social system to support learning, it is important to bear in mind what kinds of activities and what goals are intended, and to choose approaches and social forms that best serve the needs identified. To summarize the main strengths and weaknesses of each form:

- Groups offer the greatest value when the object of knowing is known and the process of knowing is complex. They are especially helpful when a sustained effort is needed. Groups are powerful motivators, exploiting our innate need for belonging and the ways that we have grown up and/ or evolved to live in hierarchies. However, groups require commitment and come with a large overhead of design and management; they are also expensive. Tools built to support groups should normally provide support for roles, processes, and procedures.

- Networks are embedded in practice, extend beyond the specifiable, and allow us to benefit from diversity and knowledge that transcends boundaries and easily specified objectives. Networks are great for topical, just-in-time learning, and expose us to serendipity and change. Networks, like groups, exploit social capital for both contribution and motivation. However, networks take effort to be exploited for learning. Without structure and guidance, we have to make decisions for ourselves. Generally speaking, network tools should help manage and sustain relationships, make and break connections, and deal with the organization of subsets of the network, with discretionary access and privacy controls.

- Sets are most useful when the knowledge we seek cannot be easily found in our groups and networks, when we need to know something but do not know who to ask. They are also a valuable means of gaining diverse insights and knowledge about a subject. However, like networks, they demand effort from us to decide what to learn in the first place and then to make decisions about reliability, relevance, and truthfulness. Sets need tools for organization and, on the whole, benefit most from the availability of collectives to support them.

- Collectives provide the means for us to make sense of, in particular, sets, to a lesser extent nets, and occasionally, groups. Like teachers, collectives tell us what to do, who to trust, what is interesting, and how to approach a subject. However, collectives are only as smart as the crowd, the means by which the crowd is selected, defined by the algorithms and presentations that perform the work. The learning needs, rather than simply the preferences, of their users should be supported.

The form or forms that an individual learner may make use of in his or her learning journey will always depend upon context and needs, but these will be codetermined by external structures like the need for assessment and accreditation, the formal and informal rules of behaviour in a given context, as well as other financial, personal, ethical, and social constraints.

Table 3.2 summarizes a range of attributes and their typical values of groups, nets, sets, and collectives so that the reader may match them with the needs of their own communities with which they are concerned.

Table 3.2 Groups, nets, sets, and collectives compared.

	Group	Net	Set	Collective
Metaphor	virtual classroom	virtual communities of practice	anonymous crowd	wisdom of crowds
Typical Activities	collaborative Projects	discussion, inquiry, exploration	knowledge-sharing, questions and answers, focused discovery	discovery, filtering
Typical Tools	threaded discussion, LMS (VLEs); video, web, Audio, and text conferencing (Blackboard, Moodle, Desire2Learn, etc.)	mailing lists, blog syndication, social networks (Facebook, LinkedIn, etc.)	Wikis, Q&A sites, social interest sites, (Twitter, Pinterest, Learni. st, etc.)	search engines, recommender systems, rating system, reputation systems (Amazon, Google, Slashdot, Stackoverflow, etc.)

	Group	Net	Set	Collective
Goals	accreditation, formal learning, task completion	knowledge generation, expanding social capital	finding answers, discovering networks and groups, exploring subject areas	knowledge extraction, knowledge discovery, knowledge organization
Pedagogies	social constructivist	connectivist	connectivist, instructivist	any
Time Frame	usually bound by semester, synchronous or asynchronous	short to long term—as beneficial to individual synchronous or asynchronous	asynchronous, on-demand, transient	long-term, asynchronous
Organization	hierarchical, predetermined	emergent, flexible, temporary	relational (set-based)	impersonal, market forces
Commitment to participate	High often assessed	Medium as needed or requested	Very low	Low often passive
Motivation to Contribute	external, required for credit, social capital, process value	social capital, altruism, professional reputation	altruism, money	passive (as a product of individual use), active (to improve value)
Expectation for Help	High often mutual dependence	Medium "share and share alike" ethos	Low	Low/none unconscious aggregation
Scalability	Low usually limited to 25–30 persons	Medium expands as potential membership grows	High	Very High
Operational sizes	can be effective at low numbers from 3–30, after which efficient operation requires increasing organization and segmentation	typically 30–50 active connections are needed to sustain network operation	any size	provides maximum value when very large numbers of users participate
Social Capital	bonding	bridging	exposing	free, as in beer
Mode	one-to-many, many-to-many	one-to-one, one-to-many	many-to-many, one-to-many, many-to-one	many-to-one

In many cases, the lines between the different social forms may be blurred or shifting. It is common, for example, to encourage communities of practice that share emergent properties with networks and, at least in their early stages of formation, have weak structures and limited hierarchies. Similarly, a tribal group may often be more set-like than group-like in terms of the interactions between people. For example, we may know no one in a large organization beyond our own groups, and so interactions beyond the group share many commonalities with interactions between strangers in a set. It is also, as we have observed, common for there to be blends of forms in any given community. There can be people that we know within an anonymous set, for instance, and we may have many cross-cutting networks within and beyond the groups we are members of.

CONCLUSION

We have presented a typology of the kinds of aggregation that social software can support and of collectives that can emerge from them. It is not the only possible means of categorizing such things, but it makes sense of the different ways that social software systems can support a social learning process, and helps us to unpack the sometimes subtle differences between ways of teaching and learning on the Net. We hope to show, as the book progresses, that the differences (though sometimes blurred or mixed) are profound, and failure to recognize the kind of entity with which we are dealing can, at best, lead to lost opportunities and, at worst, can undermine the educational endeavour.

Choosing names is an important task, and getting the right name matters. As the British philosopher J.L. Austin put it, "Words are our tools, and, as a minimum, we should use clean tools: we should know what we mean and what we do not, and we must forearm ourselves against the traps that language sets us" (1979, p. 182). The names we have chosen were the result of much debate and cogitation, but they may not fit with your own understanding of the words. If that is so, then we ask that you suspend your existing preconceptions for a while and, if you wish, substitute words that you find more appropriate. It is not the words we use that are important here, but what they signify.

4

LEARNING IN GROUPS

An impressive collection of studies has shown that participation in well-functioning cooperative groups leads students to feel more positive about themselves, about each other, and about the subject they're studying. Students also learn more effectively on a variety of measures when they can learn with each other instead of against each other or apart from each other.

Alfie Kohn, **Punished by Rewards**

In this chapter, we delve into the most commonly used form of social aggregation in campus-based, workplace, and distance-based forms of education. The group has a history that began with our primal ancestors as the most practical aggregation of individuals for survival and necessary social cooperation (Caporael, 1997; Ridley, 2010; E. O. Wilson, 2012). It has survived and flourishes today as, among many other things, the standard social form used in face-to-face classes, as the cohort and hierarchical organizational form that commonly characterizes education. The vast majority of research into social learning in formal education has focused on the group form because that has, until recently, been the only social option available to most face-to-face and distance institutional learners. In this chapter we examine the strengths and weaknesses of groups, and the typical evolution of educational groups as they form, perform, and dissolve. We also look at research on the development and support of social, teaching, and cognitive presence that defines quality online learning groups.

DEFINING THE GROUP

Webster's online dictionary defines a group as "(a) a number of individuals assembled together or having some unifying relationship; (b) an assemblage of objects regarded as a unit" ("Group," n.d.). These definitions alert us to the most important characteristic of groups, whether online or face-to-face. First, groups are gathered together and exist for some purpose. Second, group members regard themselves and are regarded by others as having some unifying purpose. However, the dictionary definition allows for a wide variety of interpretations and connotations, and does not capture its distinctiveness in formal learning. We need something more precise. With that in mind, we note the following characteristics of groups used in formal and non-formal learning.

Hierarchical Structure and Leadership in Groups

In order to define the purpose and activities that are central to the definition and function of a group, members develop organization and leadership roles. In education, this function is normally assigned to the teacher, who often articulates the structure of the group's activities in the ubiquitous course syllabus. Many courses also create smaller group activities—one of the challenges of this is that individuals must determine their own sense of structure and leadership—though often teachers fill this void as well by pre-determining group membership and even leadership roles. The same applies as we work our way up the organizational hierarchy: teachers report to department heads, principals, deans, vice-chancellors, presidents, and so on up the chain, often ending at regional or national government levels.

Groups Have Rules

The fact that teachers assign and structure groups reveals perhaps their most significant feature: they are designed. Groups exist largely as a set of implicit and/ or explicit rules that govern their constitution, their activities, and expected behaviours of their members. These may be strongly stated as laws, regulations, or procedures, or be vaguer or less tangible expectations, norms and patterns associated with group membership. The rules can shift between formal and non-formal manifestations as the group persists through time. This further implies that many of the characteristics of groups are designed to foster or enhance a sense of identity, and this is often created at the cost of individual freedom.

Groups are Purposeful

Ridgeway (1983) argues that groups are formed for two possible reasons: support or task accomplishment. Primary groups are formed to provide support for their members, while task groups are formed to reach some goal or to accomplish a task.

In the process of working together to meet either or both of these needs, the group creates a set of norms or an evolving culture that strengthens the sense of group commitment.

Groups are Technologically Driven

Groups are more than labels applied to a particular collection of individuals. In many cases, groups are invented devices designed to orchestrate phenomena to a purpose: they are thus technologies (Arthur, 2009). They have forms, processes, and functions that are distinct and not emergent from the members and their interactions. Groups are deliberately bound together as an assembly of processes and structural forms to achieve some purpose or set of purposes. They utilize a range of processes that relate to group function and construction. Frequently, these processes are made explicit: technologies such as scheduling, formalized processes such as lectures, seminars, or guided discussions, regulations for behaviour, and so on are the engine of many groups in an academic setting. Implicit group norms, tacit process structures, and hierarchical process management also contribute the technological assembly that enables and channels group behaviours and activities. In the language of actor network theory, they are black-boxed (Latour, 2005), and translated into punctualized actors (Law, 1992). The technologizing of the group form is perhaps its most distinctive feature when compared to network and set social forms, neither of which incorporates such formal structures and processes.

Groups Exist Independently of Members

Groups celebrate the stability and comprehensibility of form and function. This is not to suggest that groups do not change as they develop over time—a field of study often referred to as "group development"—but that the process of development is constrained within the structures and norms established by the group's founders and/or owners. In other words, groups exist as something distinct from their members. It is notable that some groups—companies, organizations, clubs, and societies, for example—have persisted for hundreds or even thousands of years with recognizable identities despite constantly shifting membership. While we might identify distinct cohorts and classes of students, the course they are enrolled in and its surrounding relationships with other technologies and structures remains a unitary object. The teacher, the location, the students, even the topics taught and means by which they are assessed may change over time, but a course can seemingly persist through all of this, like the Ship of Theseus, or a river that remains the same, though everything in it constantly changes.

Members Aware of Membership

Members of a group invariably know that they are members. There may appear to be some very rare exceptions, such as a native tribe not knowing that its members are part of a country, or non-Mormons not realizing they have been included as honourary Mormons in genealogical records but, in all cases, such membership is, from the point of view of the member, that of the set (we will have more to say about this later). Most of the time we join groups intentionally, though in some cases other actions, such as being born in a particular country, the merger of two companies or departments, living in a particular city, or being enrolled in a course because we are working in a program, can make us members without our assent. Once we are members, we become obligated to behave as the group's regulations require, or risk exclusion and possibly expulsion.

Groups are Exclusionary

Wilson, Ludwig-Hardman, Thornam, and Dunlap (2004) refer to groups that are formed in formal education contexts as "bounded communities." They erect barriers that separate members from non-members. Shirky (2008) observes that groups are as dependent for their existence on who they exclude as much as who they include. Most groups involve rites of admission such as filling in forms, pledges, initiations, formal introductions, rituals, admission to buildings, et cetera. They typically place restrictions on who can and who cannot join. Interestingly, restrictions are commonly defined by set-based characteristics—race, creed, gender, academic qualifications, job, location, marital status, family, et cetera— sometimes supplemented with network characteristics: whether they are known to or recommended by an existing member, for instance. There are often rules that determine how, whether, and when people might leave a group. Many groups set time limits, especially in an educational setting, have rituals for exit such as award ceremonies, retirement events, or farewell parties, and may include processes for deliberate expulsion.

DISTINCTIVE EDUCATIONAL GROUP FEATURES

While there are many common features for all groups, whether intended as vehicles for learning or not, some features are distinctive in a teaching setting.

Participation Often Required to Obtain a Desired End

Group membership in an educational context carries with it a commitment to share time and knowledge with group members. How to assess this participation remains a contentious issue. Some teachers track attendance—reminiscent of the all-too-familiar daily ritual of elementary schools. Others use tools and rubrics to assess the quantity and quality of students' contribution to online discussion forums. More innovative assessments include those where students produce learning artifacts, and assess themselves and their peers for attendance and participation.

Group Members do not Select Classmates or Instructor

Although larger institutions can offer greater choice for students, and students can and do enrol in courses with close friends, admission to a program and the assignment of teachers is a task jealously guarded by administrators. Despite the exclusion of student control at this level, students as stakeholders are being increasingly welcomed onto advisory and even governance committees in many institutions.

Group Members must Commit to a Fixed Length of Time

Course organization in batches, where cohorts proceed through a course of studies together, defines the vast majority of higher education learning systems. The groups that form using this organizational model provide a ready group of collaborators for social and cooperative forms of learning.

Group Members must make an Explicit Effort to Connect with Others

By coming together online or face-to-face, synchronously or asynchronously, group members enact the technology of the group. Groups do not meet unintentionally.

Groups Restrict Pace

If students are learning together as a group, there is nearly always some constraint on the speed at which they learn. Typically, they must attend the same lectures, or engage within a fixed period in a discussion forum, or submit assignments at the same time.

WHY GROUPS ARE WORTHWHILE

As a result of all these constraints, one might assume that groups are an unattractive form of learning organization, but this could hardly be further from the truth.

The vast majority of formal education takes place in group contexts. The group is a familiar and comfortable aggregation for both learners and teachers. The agricultural-based notions of pacing study to allow students freedom to work on the farm in the summer, and the flow of cohorts into evenly spaced and paced fall and spring terms has become synonymous with institutional learning, and is matched with promotions, catalogues, and advertising for even informal and non-credit forms of education.

The rationale for organizing formal learning in bounded communities is often defended, as the resulting security allows for the creation of a safe and supportive environment. Within this protected harbour, learners and teachers are free to explore ideas, make new friends, challenge one another's interpretations, and place obligations of cooperation and support upon one another. From the earliest days of formal education, security for scholars and scholarship to evolve outside of the constraints of ideological or theological hegemony has been a dominant component of academic freedom, necessary for the development of innovative solutions to solve the complex problems facing society. Thus, there remains a strong case for the provision of group-based learning.

COOPERATIVE FREEDOMS IN GROUPS

In an educational context, grouped modes of learning share a number of distinctive characteristics, some are simply a result of physics, and others are the product of the nature of group social forms. While there are uses for groups in self-paced models of learning that we will refer to later, by far the most common model used in institutional and organizational learning is that of the paced group, which we will focus on here. We present a spider chart indicating the typical notional freedoms available to learners working at a distance in paced groups in Figure 4.1, noting that such groups in face-to-face learning are significantly more constrained.

Place
Although home situations or the need to visit cafés or libraries for Internet access may occasionally impose some limits on the freedom of where learning occurs, as in all distance learning, there is in principle virtually no limit on freedom of place in a group-based distance learning context.

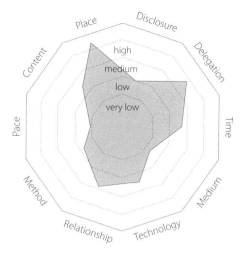

Figure 4.1 Notional levels of control in a typical paced course.

Content

Choosing or creating content has long been a defining role for teachers in group-based learning. Despite the large and growing quantities of learning resources available in cyberspace, many of which are freely accessible, students expect teachers to filter and annotate the content, so as to create a structured path through learning activities and content. It is interesting to note the widening gap between the learning that occurs in formal courses—where students are expected to consume content selected by teachers—and common behaviour in informal learning, where students turn to search engines, trusted friends, answer systems, or libraries when they want to learn something.

Pace

The fact that groups tend to work in lockstep makes control over pace relatively low in a group-based setting. Like time, it is a question of scale. In asynchronous mode, though a student may have to perform activities within a time period, he or she may vary the pace within those constraints. This is especially valuable when it comes to the much-lauded benefit of asynchronous discussion, because technologies provide students with time to reflect on contributions before posting them, with pedagogically beneficial results. Even when the primary mode of teaching is synchronous, the primary mode of learning may not be. It is, for example, common for readings or activities to be set so that the learner can choose to address at any time between synchronous sessions. This illustrates the important point that, though a method can be described as a social constructivist mode of learning, it will nearly always include some elements that are behaviourist/cognitivist in nature.

At the smallest scale, the way that messages are phrased in a social-constructivist dialogue will usually take into account some model of learning, implicit or explicit. We may, for instance, phrase something as simply as possible, make connections, or draw analogies, all of which assume some model of how individual people think and learn.

Method

While a teacher may determine the general pedagogies used in a group-based learning environment, there are some opportunities for learners to negotiate the method. For example, if a student in a group has difficulties with a particular issue, the teacher or other learners can reformulate a discussion, provide a different presentation, or an alternative perspective that is pedagogically different from what was originally planned. As with other freedoms in group contexts, however, the freedom of an individual may be constrained by the needs of others in the group.

Relationship

If the teacher has decided that a particular form of interaction is required, there may be relatively little control afforded to the learners in a group as to how and with whom engagement occurs. Indeed, it is commonplace in formal learning for engagement to be assessed, whether directly or indirectly, placing strong constraints on how and whether learners engage with one another or their tutors.

Technology

Most Internet-based solutions allow some control over the devices and software used to access them. This can, however, lead to problems such as inequalities between learners, and support for a preferred technology may be limited or non-existent. Particularly commonplace examples of this include when a textbook is only provided in either paper or electronic form, or a particular web browser must be used, or mobile devices are not supported.

Medium

Group-based approaches seldom offer much choice over the media used for learning. Normally the institution or the individual teacher makes a decision about the type of media used both for disseminating content and supporting interaction within the group. This decision has become much more challenging for both teachers and students with the development of very low cost so-called Web 2.0 applications, providing hundreds of additional choices beyond the text-book and face-to-face interaction that have defined classroom groups or the Learning Management Systems (LMSs) supporting the vast majority of online learning groups. Technical and end-user based support for large numbers of web-based programs present a large and growing challenge for learning organizations that, while attempting to provide up-to-date alternatives, are constrained by the need to protect group confidentiality and security, and ensure performance.

Time

Choice of time for learning engagement depends on whether communication is synchronous or asynchronous. In most group-based classes, it is common for asynchronous tools like email and discussion forums to be used for interactions. These provide a certain amount of freedom of time for engagement, albeit usually with constraints. It is typical to require responses within a period of days, or sometimes, hours. Synchronous tools, of course, provide no freedom of time at all.

Delegation

The ability to ask for clarification, change the direction of discussion, seek help and so on, makes freedom of delegation in a group-based learning context quite high. Though the hierarchical nature of group-based approaches to learning means that teachers may play a very large role in determining how and when interactions and learning transactions occur, there are often plentiful opportunities for learners to ask for more guidance. There are some dependencies, however, on other learners. While a single individual may seek further guidance or a change in direction, the needs of one typically need to be balanced with the needs of the many. If people are learning together, then outliers who wish to take a different direction may not always be heard.

Disclosure

There is seldom a great deal of control over what and how things are disclosed in a traditional institutional group setting. It is nearly always determined by the teacher, and represents one of the more technological aspects of groups: disclosure is designed into group interactions. A teacher may, for example, decide that sharing is bad for final assignments, but necessary for collaborative work. Commonly, the teacher may require students to engage in discussion forums or, less obviously controlling but equally coercive, may provide a discussion forum where every message is seen by all members of the group that is the only formal means of engagement for a course.

TRANSACTIONAL DISTANCE AND CONTROL IN GROUP LEARNING

Moore formulated his theory of transactional distance (1993) in an era when it was assumed that the teaching presence might be mediated through structured resources or more immediate communication between a student and his or her teacher via phone or letter. However, it provides a useful lens for exploring dynamics within groups. In a group, leaners and peers may also participate as teaching presences, leading to a more complex dynamic of distance. It is certainly true in most learning based on social constructivist models that the communication distance between teacher and learner is much lower than it is in an instructivist setting. This puts the learner in a more powerful position when negotiating control, where he or she is able to challenge and change the path of learning.

However, this occurs in a group setting in the company of other learners, each likewise engaged in negotiation for control, and each who may become the teaching presence in a learning transaction. The communication and psychological distance is thus very low, thanks to the effects of distribution within the group. However, transactional control is affected by competition. For example, if a learner seeks clarification from a teacher, though this increases control for him or her, from the point of view of others in the group their control is diminished, at least until they contribute and take back the reins themselves.

Group Size

Different patterns and methods work differently in various sizes of groups. In most cases, this is not due to the nature of groups as a social form so much as it is to the constraints of physics. For example, a teaching method that involves each member of the group sharing what they have learned with the rest may be effective among five to ten learners, but would require more hours than there are in the day with a group of 200, and would lead to massive decreases in attention and engagement after the first few students had shared their findings.

The technological nature of groups means that pedagogies for them must be engineered with due consideration for the exigencies and constraints of the group context, including its size. In the example above, one might use a different pedagogy altogether, or if one were set on the pedagogy, one could split the larger group into smaller ones, pick some students to present to the rest, or use a pyramiding process so that small groups selected the best and presented these to larger groups. While most size limitations are amenable to common sense, there are some differences in various kinds of groups that are worth mentioning.

Dyads

The basic dyad consisting of two individuals is common in, for example, supervisor-supervisee relationships, such as Socratic dialogue, master-apprentice models of learning, and personal tutelage. This is, as we observed in Chapter 2, a highly effective but generally too costly method of learning. While a group of two may be the smallest social group form from a logical perspective, there is normally little to distinguish a group of two from a set or net of two: individuals will establish roles and rules according to their needs. An exception exists in the supervisory relationship, where there may be rules and procedures that govern the nature of the interaction.

Work/Family Groups

It is not uncommon for study groups, tutorial groups, and small breakout groups to contain around five members, corresponding to the archetypal work/family group identified by Caporael (1997). Such small groups make the coordination and allocation of tasks simple to perform, even in the absence of particularly strong roles. In an online setting, a small group often communicates with nothing more than email or teleconferencing, modes of communication that, in larger groups, become very unwieldy.

Demes

The typical class in a school, and in many adult learning classes, is the rough size of what Caporael (1997) called a deme (from the Greek *dēmos*, or "people"), like the hunter/gatherer bands of our distant ancestors, consisting of around 30 members. It is at least a plausible hypothesis that we have evolved through group-level selection such that the deme is a manageable size of group that can work face-to-face in a coordinated way, assuming some leadership role to organize its actions.

Tribes

Identified by Caporael (1997) as the "macrodeme," some group forms drift toward the set in their constitution, typically when they approach or exceed around 150 members. As we have previously noted this is significant in an educational context because tribal groups such as universities, schools, and colleges have the features of closed membership, rules, roles, and hierarchies that are common to all groups but typically lack the close connections, time, and pace restrictions of things like classes, tutorial groups, and workgroups. In these cases, as well as in more time-constrained settings such as lectures given to large groups of students who do not know one another, it may be more useful to think of the group as being a set. Unlike a true set, a tribal group's hierarchies and rules mean the form of learning that occurs is typically very much dominated by the teacher or other group leader. This is not the self-directed, topic-driven process that characterizes set-based learning: the teacher not only determines content and activities but also can act as arbiter and judge of what the set shares. This latter feature of tribal learning is particularly valuable, as the teacher can guide the learner down the desired learning path. Also, as suggested by our example, the teacher is able to manage the group processes so that larger tribes can be split into smaller groups, with all the benefits they bring.

LEARNING IN GROUPS

Since group learning has been such a dominant form in institutional and organizational education, there is plenty of literature on how groups work in that context. Groups are as much machines for social action as they are social binders, and they are replete with repeatable processes that enable their construction and maintenance. In the following sections we explore some of the features of this semi-mechanical nature.

Online Group Formation

As groups in education are temporally bound, with pacing and scheduling limited by constraints on time for their formation and dissolution, it is important to pay attention to the way they evolve over time. A large number of researchers have studied the way groups form and develop. Here we present some of the more well-founded models.

Dimensions of Change

Many kinds of group development show great similarity among cyclical, linear, and recurring models. J.D. Smith (2001) argue that groups develop in three dimensions. The first is the social dimension, and occurs most often at the early stages of group formation when members come to know one another and the roles they are playing in the task. The second dimension relates to task development, in which the task that the group sets for itself evolves over time as component parts are completed and new assignments are accepted. The third, as Smith notes, is the dimension of group culture that develops with norms, values, and standards of behaviour. Even when assessment is criteria-based, student perceptions can lead to a competitive rather than cooperative environment. This interplay between dimensions provides a useful way to understand the growth of groups.

Forming, Storming, Norming, Performing, and Adjourning

Perhaps the most commonly known and easily remembered model of group development is Tuckman and Jensen's five-stage model of forming, storming, norming, performing, and adjourning (1977). This model adapts well to online learning groups.

> *Forming.* The formation stage is often set by the educational institution and is quite normalized by the familiar roles that teachers (assertive and taking charge) and students (passive) easily fall into. Once a course has begun subgroups may form, but they are typically guided in their inception by the teacher.

> *Storming.* The storming phase is also often constrained in formal education by the expectations and compliance of group members. Although aggressive and flaming behaviours in online groups have been widely studied (N. McCormick & McCormick, 1992; Schrage, 2003) formal education groups note the almost complete absence of such behaviour, and even an excess of what our colleague Walter Archer, cited in Garrison and Anderson (2003), refers to as "pathological politeness." Fabro and Garrison (1998) reported that the cohort they studied was "generally conditioned in many ways to be polite" and disagreement was taken "as either a personal affront or they were open and a very few people were open" (p. 48). This group appeared to be "quite timid" and "polite" and "began to just agree with each other rather than challenge each other's ideas" (Fabro & Garrison, 1998, p. 48). It should be noted however that

these observations were made on Canadian students, who may have distinct national problems with pathological politeness! Thus, for groups to form effectively in formal education, teachers might be advised to stimulate rather than repress "storming" behaviour; this might explain the popularity of online debates (Fox & MacKeough, 2003; Jeong, 2003).

Norming. Norming refers to the comfort level that members of groups develop with one another as they come to have both their social and task expectations confirmed in their interactions with others in group meetings. The group stage is now set for the production and accomplishment of tasks. In some cases, the norming stage may be formalized into rules, procedures, and perhaps even a social contract that specifies expectations (Kort, Reilly, & Williams, 2002).

Performing. Once the previous stages of group development have been accomplished, the group can get on with doing what it is supposed to do.

Adjournment. Finally the group prepares for adjournment, with such rituals as the end of class party, completion of course evaluation forms, and fretting and extensive questions related to final examinations and term paper requirements.

Despite the linear nature of Tuckman and Jensen's model (1977), many researchers have noted that group development also proceeds cyclically, revisiting earlier stages, or even progresses swinging like a pendulum, with "storming, norming, and performing" being visited in succession as the group develops over time.

Salmon's Five-stage Model

Most of the interest in and study of groups occurred during the last half of the twentieth century before online groups were common. Perhaps the most influential model of group development for online groups—and especially those within educational context—was developed by Gilly Salmon (2000). Her five-stage model has been particularly popular and successful in recent years as a means of developing learning communities. Emerging from her research into online communities, the model is both descriptive of successful learning communities and prescriptive as to how they evolve, particularly with regard to the role of the moderator in facilitating their development. The model works in Maslowian hierarchical style. The five stages are:

Access and motivation. At this stage, the moderator's role is to ensure that learners are able to use the relevant technologies, are enrolled as group members, and feel welcomed on arrival.

Online socialization. Learners engage in non-threatening message sending, typically greeting others, saying something about themselves, and getting to know people in the group. Salmon suggests that the moderator should help students become familiar with the norms and behaviours expected, offering bridges between this and prior experience in online and offline communities.

Information exchange. Learners begin to share ideas and knowledge with one another. The moderator now acts as a facilitator, establishing tasks and sharing learning materials and processes.

Knowledge construction. Learners begin to engage in meaningful dialogue, exploring and challenging ideas. The moderator facilitates this process with probing questions, challenging ideas, summarizing, channelling, and modelling good practices.

Development. At this stage, not reached by all groups, learners take responsibility for their own learning, challenging not just ideas but the process itself, taking the learning beyond the moderator's prescribed limits. When this occurs, the moderator becomes an almost equal participant, supporting the independence of learners and dealing with problems as they arise. The model seems to fit well with our experience of online groups up to this point. However, it is not entirely clear what is being developed at this stage. We would have expected to see "learning application" or at least "integration" with relevant and authentic aspects of the real world contained within this phase.

Salmon's model has proved useful in many online learning communities, and appears to describe what tends to happen in a well-moderated learning community, offering good advice for those hoping to facilitate such a process. There are complexities, however. In many cases, a cohort of learners will have gone through this process before, and may not need to do so again. Author Dron instituted Salmon's model across a distance-taught program, applying the pattern mindfully in every course, and found that the first two or three stages were of little or no further value once they had been addressed in the first course taken by a given cohort (Dron, Seidel, & Litten, 2004). Students in a cohort were already familiar with the tools and one another, so they were able to start a new course at stage 3 or even 4 of the model. The intentionally scaffolded process thus got in the way of efficient learner-centred learning. As with any framework, the context of application needs to be taken into account and the framework modified to suit the needs, subject area, and learning history of the group concerned.

POWER AND TRUST RELATIONSHIPS IN GROUPS

Roberts (2006) notes the problems with power in groups that are referred to as "oppressed group behaviour." Power relationships that define the organization often infuse thinking and constrain creativity within the group. The accountable nature of group interactions means that members act under the power constraints that define their lives, and these often exist outside the relationships within the group. This is especially relevant in the rigid hierarchy that differentiates teacher from student identity, power, and specific contributions in group contexts.

Trust is also problematic in groups. While group members need trust in order to freely elicit honest contributions from everyone, the unbalanced power dynamics noted above and the competition among students both limit its development. Formal education is marked by the assessment of student accomplishment. This has many downsides, not least of which is the enormously demotivating effects it has for both high and low achievers (Kohn, 1999), but is particularly pronounced when assessment is norm- rather than criteria-based, such that one excels based on their accomplishment and learning compared to other students, not from absolute knowledge of content or individual learning accomplishment. This was most dramatically evident during author Anderson's first-year calculus class at a university where rather inept teaching, coupled with low motivation and a very large class resulted in a pass mark being calculated at 19%! This curve-graded score allowed all (teacher included) to feel good about their learning and themselves, even though most were failing to achieve the objectives of the class. It relates back to the problem of power relationships: competitive grading is less a way of enabling students to learn, and more a way of emphasizing and enacting the power of the teacher to control the process (Kohn, 1999). It is difficult to develop trust in competitive environments, thus explaining in part the distrust many teachers and students have for collaborative and cooperative learning models, despite the proven efficacy of these approaches (D. Johnson & Johnson, 1994).

In 1999 author Anderson with colleagues Randy Garrison and Walter Archer at the University of Alberta devised a conceptual model for online education, which they named the Community of Inquiry model. They developed it to provide both practical guidelines for teachers and designers, and as a research model for what was then asynchronous, text-based models of online education that were the norm for online education. During the last decade many other researchers have employed this model, and it is likely the most frequently cited tool used to evaluate formal distance education. Google Scholar (2013) lists over 1,000 citations for each of the four major papers and the book written by the original COI authors. The seminal articles associated with this model, as well as links to the work of numerous researchers referencing and extending it are available at (www.communitiesofinquiry.com).

Foundations

The COI model has its roots in Dewey's (1933) pragmatic model of practical inquiry, in which ideas must be tested in the crucible of real application to establish and hone their accuracy. Lipman's (1991) community of inquiry provided the model with both its name and the notions of reflective learning in a formal education, which he characterizes as follows:

- Education is the outcome of participation in a teacher-guided community of inquiry;
- Teachers stir students to think about the world when they reveal knowledge to be ambiguous, equivocal, and mysterious;
- Knowledge disciplines are overlapping and are therefore problematic;
- Teachers are ready to concede fallibility;
- Students are expected to be reflective and increasingly reasonable and judicious;
- The educational process is not information acquisition, but a grasp of relationships among disciplines (Lipman, 1991, pp. 18–19).

Note especially the essential role of the teacher in Lipman's description, which fuelled the desire of Anderson, Rourke, Garrison, & Archer (2001) to explicate the role of the teacher and teaching presence created in formal education transactions. Lipman (1991) notes that within the community of inquiry members question one another, demand reasons for beliefs, and point out the consequences of one another's ideas, thus creating a self-guiding and emergent community when adequate levels of social, cognitive, and teacher presence are present. To round the process off, Garrison's (1991) model of critical thinking was used to develop stages and processes of reflection and decision-making that define critical thinking.

These theoretical works were used to provide conceptual order and a practical heuristic model to assess the teaching and learning context in the online community of inquiry. The model consists of three elements deemed essential to successful educational transactions: cognitive presence, teaching presence, and social presence. Garrison, Anderson, and Archer developed tools and techniques to reliably measure each of these three presences in text-based, asynchronous computer conferencing transcripts. In this section we expand and apply the ideas from the COI model to online group-based learning in both synchronous and asynchronous modes.

Community of Inquiry and Cognitive Presence

Cognitive presence differentiates social interaction in a group-based community of inquiry from casual interaction in the pub or on the street. Some have argued critical thinking most clearly defines quality in higher education contexts (Candy, 2000). We thus built on models and ideals of critical thinking to create our notion of cognitive presence.

Despite almost universal adoption of the notions of the importance of critical thinking in higher education, it is quite difficult to gain a consensus from the literature or practice on what it actually means. The confusion is related to the fact that critical thinking is both a process and a product (Garrison, Anderson, & Archer, 2000). Teachers in group contexts are expected to develop learning activities, model the process of critical thinking, and assess the outcomes of cognitive presence in the products of study—projects, papers, and test results—designed to provide evidence of the successful completion of critical thinking. In the Community of Inquiry model, we focused on gathering evidence of the process of critical thinking, and postulated it could be found in the activities of teachers and learners, as demonstrated by their contributions to the threaded discussions that serve as the main communication tool for much online group-based learning.

The first of four phases of cognitive presence is some sort of triggering event. This is often provided as an opening, question, or invitation for comment by the teacher's post to the group. But additional triggers arise when participants reflect upon or challenge one another. To be effective, triggering messages must be meaningful, must spring from the experience of the group, and must be accessible and within conceptual understanding of the group's members. Poscente and Fahy

(2003) empirically defined triggering statements by the numbers of responding posts learners generated and, as expected, found that teacher triggers were most heavily responded to. However, student triggering statements were also observed on a regular basis in threaded online discussion.

The second phase of cognitive presence is "exploration," within which group members iterate between individual reflection and group questioning, probing, and extension of their ideas and solutions to the triggering idea. This exploration is a divergent phase characterized by brainstorming, questioning, clarifications, and exchange of information.

During the third "integration phase" of the group-based development of cognition presence, focus shifts from exploring meaning to constructing it, and the integration of ideas into robust conceptual models. The leadership of the group is important at this stage, as group members often feel more comfortable "exploring" a problem until interest wanes without making the serious effort needed to arrive at a conceptually whole and integrated solution.

In the final "resolution phase," the group focuses on ways to apply the knowledge generated in the three previous phases. This resolution may take the form of application and testing in a real-life context. However, often in educational applications, the resolution is a well-argued and detailed answer to a triggering problem.

Cognitive presence has been measured through surveys of participants' qualitative interviews, automated neural network analysis of key words, and the transcript analysis method developed by the original COI team. In nearly all studies, evidence of the fourth and final resolution phase has been minimal, indicating that perhaps true resolution and critical thinking rarely occurs in the closed and often artificial groups or classes that define most forms of higher education.

Community of Inquiry and Social Presence

The second critical component of the Community of Inquiry is social presence, defined as "the ability of participants in a community of inquiry to project themselves socially and emotionally, as 'real' people (i.e., their full personality), through the medium of communication being used" (Garrison et al., 2000, p. 94). This definition was later expanded to include a sense of other group members as well as self and common commitment to a task. We identified three broad categories of social presence indicators: affective, open communication, and cohesive communicative responses. Thus development of a group and individual sense of social comfort is evidenced by use of affective interactions such as humour, self-disclosure, and changes in media use such as employing bold text, or the use of emoticons in group discussion. Open communication is shown by timely responses to member posts, quoting and referring to others, asking questions and complimenting or thanking other group members for their contributions. Finally, cohesive comments such as addressing group members by name, using inclusive pronouns to describe the group, and informal salutations indicate a sense of group cohesion and commitment that we defined as a component of social presence. Once again, through transcript analysis we were able to quantify the extent of social presence evidenced in the group, and this was correlated with satisfaction and perception of learning in a number of later studies.

Community of Inquiry and Teaching Presence

The final component of an effective group-based Community of Inquiry in formal education is Teaching Presence. Teaching presence begins with the instructional design and organization of tasks that are necessary to construct a context in which social and especially cognitive presence arises. In group activities within formal education contexts, both students and teachers have accumulated expectations about these organizational issues that often lead students to a role of passive reaction to the learning agenda specified by the teacher. The second component of teaching presence is the active facilitation of group discussion or other learning activities. Good teachers find opportunities to question, drill down and challenge learners to thoroughly explore, integrate, and apply the knowledge generated by the group. They also nurture the development of social presence by insuring appropriate levels of contribution by group members, and help establish a climate of trust and acceptance within the group. Finally, teaching presence includes direct instruction where the teacher or other group participants contribute their specialized knowledge to the group, diagnose misunderstandings, and otherwise provide leadership in the attainment of deep and meaningful learning experiences.

Applying the Lessons of the Community of Inquiry Model

The COI model has been widely used by both researchers and instructional designers. The designers validated and compared it to contexts beyond asynchronous online learning to show its relevance in comparison to face-to-face learning (Heckman & Annabi, 2005). Methodologically, the COI model was validated through student survey responses (Rourke & Anderson, 2002) and factor analysis of survey results (Arbaugh, 2007). Work has continued to develop a standardized instrument for measuring the extent of community of inquiry formation through student survey assessment (Swan et al., 2008).

We conclude this overview of COI's contribution to the design and function of group-based learning with the series of recommendations that Randy Garrison made for designers and teachers. He advises them to

- Establish a climate that will create a community of inquiry;
- Establish critical reflection and discourse that will support systematic inquiry;
- Sustain community through the expression of group cohesion;
- Encourage and support the progression of inquiry through to resolution;
- Foster the evolution of collaborative relationships where students are
- supported in assuming increasing responsibility for their learning;
- Ensure that there is resolution and metacognitive development.

As these recommendations demonstrate, the community of inquiry model has strong implications for process, and emphasizes the deeply technological nature of traditional groups in formal learning: this is about repeatable methods and techniques that carry with them assumptions of structure and architecture that are designed and enacted.

THE CRITICAL ROLE OF TASKS ON GROUPS

Collaborative behaviour is not a function of the group, but of the learning activities assigned or undertaken by that group. The task sets the context, the goals, and in most cases the appropriate organizational structure for the group. Townsend, DeMarie, and Hendrickson define virtual teams as "groups of geographically and/or organizationally dispersed coworkers that are assembled using a combination of telecommunications and information technologies to accomplish an organizational task" (1998, p. 18). The role of the task is highlighted as having major significance in the function, organization, and success of virtual and face-bound groups. Bell and Kozolowski (2002) observe that task complexity is an especially salient factor. However it is not only the task but also its treatment by the group that affects its complexity. Tasks used by educators with learners vary widely in a number of ways.

Van de Ven, Delbecq, & Koenig (1976) described four types of organizational structure of increasing complexity that a group may develop to accomplish a task. The first was termed polled or additive: group members simply combined their work to accomplish the task. The second requires group members to work on some part of the task before moving the incomplete work to another (often differentially specialized group member) for additional work. The third follows a less structured back-and-forth movement of task artifacts, with group members adding value at various times as the product moves through production stages to completion. The final and most complex structure was termed "intensive," and is characterized by continuous discussion, debate, evaluation, and contribution among team members at all stages of task function.

Virtual groups, because of the reduction in proximal clues, tend to need greater and more explicit amounts of external direction (teaching presence), and more structured forms of organization. They also tend to both rely upon and nurture more self-direction among learners than teacher-dominated groups characteristic of campus education. Learners have many more responsibilities than merely arriving at the designated teaching location at the correct time each week. These include technical competencies so that they can effectively utilize the various communication and information technologies necessary to complete of group tasks. They also must be able to monitor and effectively manage their time—being focused and committed enough to attend to assigned group tasks, while at the same time able to resist time-wasting activities such as unfocused web browsing.

TRUST, COHESION, AND GROUPTHINK

Groups or "teams" (as they are often referred to in business contexts), have long been the focus of study by business sociologists. Groups function as the primary means to increase trust, alignment, cohesion, and ultimately efficiency in the workplace (Burt, 2009). Group members, through exposure to one another and common social norms and behaviours, come to share common ideas, create local-ized jargon, and develop and share "similar views of proper opinion and practice and similar views of how to go forward into the future" (Burt, 2009, p. 4). This commonality leads to integration, the development of trust within the group, and the expectation of support and help when needed from individual group members. Further, increased communications within a tightly defined group cre-ates efficiencies, and perhaps just as important, an inhibiting relational cost for bad behaviour. All of this is positive and is used by effective group-based teachers and campus administrators in education to foster bonding and integration within classrooms, which in turn leads to increased engagement and academic success (Kuh, 2001).

However, cohesion in groups, like most social variables, has both positive and negative consequences. The American sociologist Irving Janis is credited with coining the term "groupthink," which he defined as "a mode of thinking that people engage in when they are deeply involved in a cohesive in-group, when the members' strivings for unanimity override their motivation to realistically appraise alternative courses of action" (1972, p. 9). Groupthink is a popular concept intuitively understood (at least in part) by academics from many disciplines and the general public. However, the antecedent conditions necessary for the emergence and symptoms of groupthink have not always been substantiated by rigorous experimental study (see, for example, Turner & Pratkanis, 1998). Nonetheless, some recent scholars have argued that the groupthink phenomenon is even more ubiquitous than Janis thought, and arises even in the absence of many of his critical antecedents.

Janis identified two groups of antecedent conditions leading to groupthink. The first are of a structural nature:

- Insulation of the group: Insulation is a cherished characteristic found behind the closed classroom door, gated campus, and password-protected discussions common in educational groups. Though originally designed as a way to protect dissenting scholarly views, the closed group now serves as much to isolate as it does to protect group members. As S. E. Page observes, this can lead to a lack of diversity, as well as reduced creativity and problem-solving capacity (2008).

- Lack of a tradition of impartial leadership: Educational contexts have a strong tradition of leadership exerted by the teacher and school administrators. While we do not suggest that this leadership inevitably lacks impartiality, the leadership is often authoritarian, and at best carries a bias toward scholarship and at worst one that favours conformity.

- Lack of norms requiring methodological procedures: School groups seldom lack methodological procedures for getting things done, but again these procedures are rarely critically examined by either students or teachers.

- Homogeneity of members' social background and ideology: Despite the desire of many advocates of liberal democracy for schools to serve as a great equalizer, there is considerable evidence that schools and the groups within them are one of the main conduits for the transmission of dominant social values with accompanying class divisions and capital moving only between generations of the privileged.

Janis's second set of antecedents of negative groupthink is associated with emergent social conditions that are characterized by

- High stress from external threats: The life of a student is often a very stressful one. Examinations are frequent, and the recent trend to require more group and collaborative work adds additional stress to many students forced to be dependent upon others and deal with exploitation by freeloaders and social loafers (Piezon & Ferree, 2008).

- Recent failures: The external threat imposed by numerous tests and examinations of course also gives rise (at least occasionally) to failures by both groups and individuals.

- Excessive difficulties on the decision-making task: When groups move online, there is evidence that group decision-making, though not impossible, is slower and usually less efficient (Walther, 1994); online groups "are more prone toward conflict, and, most importantly, have more difficulty achieving consensus" (Farnham, Chesley, McGhee, Kawal, & Landau, 2000, p. 299).

- Moral dilemmas: Formal education rarely struggles with ethical dilemmas, except through removed academic lenses. Nonetheless, educational groups have their own set of issues related to plagiarism, cheating, and other forms of ethical dilemmas (Demiray & Sharma, 2009).

From the above description of antecedents, one can see that there is high potential for groupthink and its associated negative outcomes in group-based models of formal education. Indeed, one could wonder—given the prevalence of these antecedents in formal education groups—if anything but impaired forms of groupthink ever arise. Confronting the lack of direct causal relationship between antecedents and groupthink outcomes, and the knowledge that groupthink impairments exist to some degree in almost all groups, Baron (2005) developed a ubiquity model of groupthink in which he identified three broader antecedents: shared social identity; salient norms; and low group self-efficacy.

Our own most vivid experience of groupthink in online groups was evident in the "pathological politeness" exhibited by many students in our online discussion groups (Garrison & Anderson, 2003). The literature from the earliest days of the Internet has documented examples of "flaming" and other disruptive behaviour (Lee, 2005; Sproull & Kiesler, 1986). However, in our classes and the transcripts of others we examined, we found just the opposite—many instances in which learners refused to engage in healthy debate or challenge one another's ideas or assertions. This excessive politeness is likely an indicator that groupthink is lurking, ready to muzzle ideas that potentially strain group cohesion or challenge established authority and ideas—not an atmosphere we were hoping to develop in our graduate courses.

This brief overview of the extensive literature on groupthink underscores the potential negative consequences of facilitating education in group contexts. These are to some degree balanced by the pedagogical value associated with collaboration and productive learning in a community of inquiry. Nonetheless, groupthink lurks, ready to emerge in any group context, and both learners and teachers are advised to guard against the social forces that attract us to familiar solutions that produce less stress and conflict among group members.

SOCIAL CAPITAL IN GROUPS

These group connections often persist beyond the course of studies and are a prime mechanism by which the "hidden curriculum" is propagated. The hidden curriculum is often associated with classism and dissemination of dominant ideologies (Margolis, 2001). It is worth repeating that, in education contexts, especially those operating at a distance, cohesive groups also are the primary mechanism for more positive applications of the "hidden curriculum," including help in "learning to play the game" and learn how to learn in often unfamiliar mediated contexts (T. Anderson, 2001).

THE TOOLS OF GROUPS

A variety of tools has been developed to support groups of learners, the most ubiquitous of which are learning management systems (LMSs), or as they are referred in the UK and some other places, Virtual or Managed Learning Environments (VLES or MLES).

Learning Management Systems

Learning management systems were developed to make online course creation and management possible for teachers with minimal Internet expertise. They offer a suite of tools matched to the needs and current classroom practice for average educators and trainers working with adults or high school-level students. Prior to the development of LMS, web course authorship was accessible only to those with considerable Internet and page creation skills, supplemented with unintegrated discussion tools such as newsgroups and email. Many early examples of web-based courses consisted of pages of text, with a few of the presentation, assessment, record-keeping or monitoring tools developed over the years for campus-based instruction. Thus, the arrival of effective and relatively easy-to-use LMSs proved instrumental for the rapid adoption of web technologies both in campus instruction as blended learning and for distance education applications.

A central binding feature of almost all LMSs and related systems is that of roles: there is nearly always at least a teacher role, with the power to control the environment to a far greater extent than a student role. In many systems, roles may be assigned for different features and aspects, and complex organizational forms may be embedded, with different roles for tutors, course coordinators, course designers, systems administrators, teaching assistants, evaluators, and of course, students. This deep structural embedding not only reflects the existing hierarchies but also reinforces them, preventing serendipitous ad hoc role reversals or shifts within hierarchies that might occur in a traditional classroom. The online teacher wishing to turn over control of a class to his or her students may face technical obstacles that make it difficult, awkward, or for some systems, impossible to achieve.

At the heart of the LMS is a system of security, authorization, and access control that allows learners only to enter into course spaces in which they are enrolled, and in many cases links to other components of an institution's student information system. Most LMS systems create an opening page that links students directly to the courses they are registered in, as well as to a variety of other student services such as the registrar, libraries, student clubs, and so on. Thus, the LMS becomes a sort of personalized portal to the services provided by the institution.

In the early days of online learning, there was a proliferation of homemade and/or unintegrated systems, sometimes composed of repurposed groupware such as Lotus Notes. While several of these were well tailored to the needs of their communities, lack of integration across courses and programs, a disjointed user experience, and above all, the difficulties of maintaining, developing, and sustaining such systems led many to ossify or degenerate into disuse. Nowadays, many institutions support only a single, centrally managed LMS system, to minimize technical support issues, so that both learners and students can become familiar and competent users throughout their time of enrolment with that institution. Similarly, to enhance ease of use, most LMS systems use single login systems so that users need to remember only one username and password to access all of the institutions' services.

LMS systems continue to increase the number and variety of modules available to instructors, in a "Swiss Army knife" approach that is designed to meet as many teaching needs as possible, while maintaining complexity and choice at manageable levels. Key components of modern LMS systems include organization and display tools with options for printing content on demand, calendars with important dates, quiz creation and administration, asynchronous text conferences, real-time text chats, group space for collaborative work, and drop boxes and grade books for assignment. All of these tools are integrated, and most are equipped with push capabilities such that new activity triggers notification by email or Rich Site Syndication (RSS). In the competitive drive to entice more customers, LMS developers are adding tools regularly, including ones more commonly associated with network learning such as blogs, wikis, and e-portfolios.

One particular developer, Blackboard, has captured a significant portion of the commercial LMS market, especially since acquiring competitors such as WebCT and ANGEL. There is intense competition from smaller companies and products such as Desire2Learn and GlobalScholar, but it is hard for them to make inroads where Blackboard is already incumbent. To some extent Blackboard's commercial success is inevitable: once an institution chooses an LMS vendor it tends to lock into using it, since the costs of transition, training, and content migration inhibit subsequent movement to rival brands. This means that being first comes with a lot of "stickability," and Blackboard has—understandably enough for a commercial company with a strong interest in keeping the cash flowing in—not gone far out of its way to enable migration and export.

The main competition for Blackboard comes from outside of the commercial sector. The open source movement has been very active in developing and delivering LMS products, and recent studies are showing that in the higher education applications, they may even be surpassing commercial LMS products in terms of the number of installations (see, for example, the market penetration statistics at Zacker.org [2014]). The growing number of users of open source LMS systems such as Moodle, Sakai, Canvas, and aTutor (to note just a few larger systems of hundreds available), bear evidence that some learning organizations are attracted to the lower initial cost, volunteer support community, and security of code ownership afforded by open source products.

Early fears that such systems would not be scalable have been put to rest by large-scale adoptions made by institutions like the Open University of the United Kingdom (which uses Moodle), who have also contributed generously to the system's development, as Athabasca University in Canada has done, and many others. Similar to other successful open source software, a variety of companies are now offering training, support, and integration services for these products, in an attempt to meet the needs of institutions that do not wish to develop these services in-house. Interestingly, as Dawson's (2012) article details, even Blackboard has absorbed companies providing Moodle hosting in a move that surprised many industry followers.

A quick look at the many orphaned applications distributed on the SourceForge repository of open source products reveals that it is much easier to create and release the first version of an open source software package than it is to gather and sustain a community of active developers. Nonetheless, examples such as Apache, Linux, and the LMS systems mentioned earlier prove that it is possible to develop and maintain very sophisticated products over extended periods of time using open source development tools and ideals. Many institutions either making the leap into learning management systems for the first time or fed up with the high costs and lack of flexibility of commercial systems are moving to open source environments. However, while they offer many advantages, like all such systems, portability of data remains an issue. Moving from one system to another, even when both support standards such as SCORM, is often a painful experience, and lock-in, whether deliberate or unintended, is a feature of almost any centralized environment.

An alternative model of hosting in the Cloud has developed in recent years and has been enthusiastically taken up by many smaller institutions, especially schools that do not have sufficient resources of their own to manage the complex software and hardware typically needed for self-hosting. In some cases, governments or consortia that work on behalf of a collection of schools or colleges manage such systems, in others they are directly paid for commercial services, and in others still they are supported by advertising or, occasionally, are free. The risk of such services is primarily in their reliability—terms of service may change, or companies may become bankrupt. However, there are other concerns: ensuring the privacy of their users is especially important where data protection laws are not strong (such as in the US), and they will sometimes be slower than campus-based alternatives. Even if their performance, reliability, security and privacy are sufficient, data portability is a significant concern. If users and their content are bound up with a particular system, the difficulties of moving to another platform are potentially much greater than even a locally hosted server may present. This is particularly significant if the interface plays an important role: even if data are portable, they may still be unusable outside the original platform without the means to present them effectively.

Synchronous Group Tools

> *The need for virtual teams to operate in real time (vs. distributed time) is expected to become more critical as tasks become more complex.*
> Bradford S. Bell and Steve W. J. Kozlowski, "A Typology of Virtual Teams"

Synchronous activities raise the visibility of all group members, especially those who use the media more effectively. Moreland and Levine (1982) argue that visibility is a key determinant of group participation, and thus group performance. Early forms of group-based online learning used audio or text chats, which were augmented by video to become ubiquitous web conferencing software (Skype, Collaborate, Connect, etc.) used in formal education, business, and personal applications. These synchronous tools have evolved into immersive environments that have attracted much interest from early adopters and researchers, but few sustained educational programs or courses make extensive use of them.

Synchronous activities bring a sense of immediacy and efficiency to group processes. Although we remain appreciative of the increased freedom, choice, and reflection affordance of asynchronous groups, we are aware that many students and teachers prefer the increased sense of camaraderie that often develops quickly through engagement in synchronous activity. In a comparison of asynchronous and synchronous courses, Somenarain, Akkaraju, and Gharbaran (2010) found increased student learning, perceptions of learning, motivation and effectiveness of communications among synchronous groups.

Effective group processes are based on trust, immediacy, and a sense of the presence. Although examples from courtship by mail to the development of social presence in asynchronous text discussion demonstrate that it is possible to develop effective educational groups through asynchronous communication, synchronous communication has many advantages.

First and most important is the sense of immediacy provided by real-time or synchronous communications. Albert Mehrabian defines immediacy as communication behaviours that "enhance closeness to and nonverbal interaction with another" (1969, p. 213). He focused on non-verbal cues that are greatly restricted in many forms of online behaviour—notably those that are text-based. But immediacy also carries a sense of immediate reactions, ones that are rich in body language, voice intonation, and facial expression.

Many researchers have studied the link between educational goals and teacher immediacy (J. Anderson, 1979; Frymier, 1993; Gorham, 1988). Generally these studies find that teacher immediacy increases student motivation to learn, student enjoyment and persistence, and to a more limited degree, cognitive outcomes. Teacher behaviours associated with immediacy include use of humour, self-disclosure, addressing students by name, and asking and answering student questions. Finkelstein (2006) argues that synchronous teaching, with implied increases in immediacy, is associated with each of Chickering and Gamson's (1987) oft-cited Principles for Good Practice in Undergraduate Education—notably increasing student–faculty contact, student cooperation time on task, feedback, and increasing diverse ways of knowing.

Despite these endorsements, synchronous learning activities are also associated with diminishing accessibility. Not all participants may be available at any given time, and the necessity for participants to gather in a single virtual place or have access to particular and often expensive equipment cannot always be met—especially if full-screen video is demanded to maximize the visibility of subtle non-verbal communication and body language. In our experience of online teaching, we have found that occasional use of synchronous technologies allows for quick bursts of immediacy that help forge group cohesiveness and serves to pace and synchronize the group, but it is best to make restrained use of the tools. Increased pacing leads to reduced learner control (Dron, 2007a, pp. 81-82).

Another drawback of synchronous activities is that they can and often are used to support regressive mimicking of classroom-based and lecture format teaching that not only bores learners but also fails to take advantage of new pedagogies and learning activities afforded in cyberspace. The familiar experience of teacher-led instruction can be transported online with regular video conferencing sessions. However, our experience has shown that the increase in complexity from dealing with off-site issues as well as impairments to clear visualization and auditory interaction create frustrations for those expecting "the same, only at a distance." For such sessions to work there is a need to provide plenty of support and a thorough grounding in protocols to avoid confusion and failure, like ensuring an adequate gap between asking a question and expecting a response, avoiding talking at the same time, avoiding real-world distractions, and the appropriate use of text chat. It is also often a good idea, especially in large groups of novice users, to allocate a second moderator to help manage technical issues. Effective groups therefore tend to make use of synchronous technologies judiciously and ensure that the convenience cost is warranted by collaborative interaction.

Synchronous learning activities come in a wide variety of formats and media. Both audio- and videoconferencing were used extensively in distance education formats for many years before their migration to cost-effective web technology. Text chat was the first and still the most common form of synchronous online interaction, and was even used as the primary tool in the earliest forms of immersive interaction (for example MOOs, MUDs, and Palaces). Text chat is, however, dependent upon typing skills and therefore is associated with the development of shorthand forms and lingo that can exclude new users from group interaction.

We are most impressed with web conferencing software as cost-effective and accessible group educational technologies (for example, Elluminate, Adobe Connect, WebEx, LiveMeeting, DimDim, etc.). Web conferencing supports multiple forms of synchronous interaction, including voice, text, low-resolution video, and presentation support. In addition, most systems support drawing on whiteboards, breakout rooms, application sharing, polling, and group excursions in cyberspace. From an accessibility perspective, web conferencing allows very easy recording and later playback for group members who are not able to attend real-time sessions. Recently, student response systems have been used in classrooms, and early results are showing increases in enjoyment, attendance, and even learning outcomes (Radosevich, Salomon, & Kahn, 2008). Student response through polling is a standard feature of most web conferencing systems for online use, thus providing a tool that enhances learning at a cost that is much lower than that associated with distributing "clickers" to campus-based students.

The use of synchronous interaction is also related to the complexity of group tasks. Simple dissemination of content (as in a lecture, or a reading in a textbook or article) likely gains little from synchronous interaction. But as the need for negotiation and collaboration increases, so does the need for real-time interaction (Bell & Kozlowski, 2002).

In our work, we have evaluated the effectiveness of extending groups across multiple schools to teach high school courses to rural students via videoconferencing technology. We found that although the videoconferencing has value, especially in terms of enrichment, along with professional and administrative value for teachers, as a primary tool for distance education it creates a rather impoverished and teacher-centric learning environment (T. Anderson, 2008).

Immersive Worlds

What for decades has promised to provide the most engaging form of synchronous activity is that which takes place in immersive environments such as SecondLife,

Project Wonderland, or Active Worlds. We have studied early examples of formal educational encounters in immersive environments, and conclude that group-enhancing forms of cognitive and teaching presence can be developed in these environments and that opportunities for greatly enhanced social presence abound. McKerlich and Anderson argue that "as the tasks a virtual team is required to perform become more complex and challenging, requiring greater levels of expertise and specialization, a higher premium is expected to be placed on synchronous workflow arrangements and the roles of individual team members will be more likely to be clearly defined, fixed, and singular" (2007, p. 34).

However, at the time of writing, there were numerous hurdles to overcome before such systems enter the mainstream. It is hard to learn to use them, with different controls and capabilities from one system to the next, and complexity in even simple tasks such as moving around. Although touted by their creators as the "3D web," nothing could be further from the truth. Only the most primitive of steps have been taken to enable a truly distributed and open environment like the World Wide Web in 3D immersive spaces. It was something of a breakthrough when, in 2008, IBM technologists were able to teleport an individual (without clothes or distinguishing features) from one immersive environment to another, but little mainstream development has occurred since then. Technologically, such environments still require powerful machines to operate effectively, and so far, nearly all rely on separate downloadable software as opposed to running in simple ubiquitous clients such as web browsers. This state of affairs may not last long, however. In specifications for HTML 5, real-time, 3D, and immersive environments are being considered. Various real-time technologies are already fairly advanced—Google's Shuttle5 (code.google.com/p/shuttle5/) provides Jabber chat and uses HTML5 support for websockets, an emerging standard for enabling various protocols to work within web browsers.

Both Google and the Mozilla Foundation are working on ways to enable virtual immersive spaces within the browser, which may lead to standardization and distribution beyond the isolated server spaces of today. If and when this occurs, we may see the flowering of a 3D immersive web, perhaps developing into something not too far removed from William Gibson's original vision of cyberspace.

Group Toolsets in the Cloud

The ever-present closed email list has been and continues to be the workhorse of many effective groups. Email has reached a saturation point in many schools and workplaces such that one can count on learners having access to email and the ability to check their accounts regularly. This familiarity with the tools, in addition to the "push" to the attention of a group means that many groups in both formal and informal learning contexts rely on the group mailing list as the primary means of communication. Recently, large Net companies (Yahoo and Google Groups) and new Web 2.0 companies (MySpace, Facebook, etc.) have expanded and integrated new features into their group email tools to create rich group work and learning environments. These collections not only support email but also retain and organize email posts in web formats so that group members need no longer store individual copies of email in their increasingly full mailboxes. Rather, they can search and retrieve postings from the group archive. This is very useful for learners who join the group at a time after group communication has already begun. These systems also support a host of add-on features such as common calendaring, document sharing, picture archiving, group to-do lists, polls, surveys, and other tools designed to afford both synchronous and asynchronous communication among group members. A number of companies have recently stepped into the realm of educational service provision, offering richer and well-managed learning environments for group use in classes where existing tools are weak, such as Udutu and CourseLab, as well as many hosted versions of existing LMS products like Moodle and Blackboard.

EFFECT OF GROUPS ON ATTRITION

Distance learning has notoriously high attrition rates, though this is by no means true across the board (e.g., Guilar & Loring, 2008). Among the many things that help to reduce attrition rates, a central pillar is social support. While there are many factors that can lead to attrition and many mitigating factors that reduce it, sustained motivation is essential. It is very easy, without cues like the requirement to be in a particular place at a particular time, to allow other things to take precedence, so motivation plays a crucial role in success to a greater extent than it does in face-to-face learning. Ideally, that motivation will be intrinsic: rather than being coerced, cajoled, rewarded, or even working to achieve goals that align with self-image and self-worth, it is better by far to simply want to do something in the first place. However, intrinsic motivation is easily undermined; often by the very things we try to do to achieve it in the first place, such as reward systems or punishments (Ariely, 2009; Deci, Vallerand, Pelletier, & Ryan, 1991; Kohn, 1999).

According to Deci and Ryan (2008), there are three distinct components to intrinsic motivation. As a rule, if learning tasks give people control, are within their range of competence, and provide relatedness with others, they will enable intrinsic motivation to emerge. Without any of those features, intrinsic motivation is almost certain to be quashed. Although the relatedness portion of this triangle may emerge in, say, family settings, friends, social networks or public acclaim, a system for learning that embeds sociability is far more likely to succeed than one that does not. A social component is therefore an extremely important means of avoiding attrition. There are many examples of this recorded in the literature. Royal Roads University, an online Canadian institution, famously achieved completion rates approaching 100% by employing the relatively simple technique of fostering cohorts, groups of mutually supporting learners who helped one another when the going got tough, even averting disaster in classically dangerous times such as changes in job, bereavement, or illness (Guilar & Loring, 2008). A closed group is especially effective at providing such support because shared goals and values, combined with a culture of mutual support, can help to foster strong community ties.

EFFECT OF GROUPS ON SELF-EFFICACY

Self-efficacy—the belief that a learner can accomplish a goal—has long been associated with performance and persistence (Bandura, 1977) and resulted in a major theory and considerable study of self-efficacy in both classroom and distance education. In a major review of the sources of self-efficacy, Usher and Pajares (2008) isolate four sources of self-efficacy found in the considerable research literature. The largest source is mastery: having accomplished one goal leads to confidence that additional goals can be achieved. But after competency, the next two sources are decidedly related to social interactions that are common in group interactions. The first of these is labelled "social persuasion": inducements made by other group members and especially teachers increase a learner's sense that they can accomplish a challenging learning goal. Perhaps this is most clearly visualized in the sports group, where the coach and teammates' almost continuous communications that "you can do it" are vivid social persuasions leading to increases in self-efficacy. The second source of socially induced self-efficacy relates to vicarious experiences, where learners are able to observe the success of peers and come to believe that they too can achieve these goals. Obviously the intense interactions that define group activities give rise to many opportunities for such vicarious experience, with resulting increases in self-efficacy.

As we have already observed, groups differ from networks inasmuch as they tend to have:

- Structure and leadership
- Fixed periods of operation and identifiable stages of development
- Explicit membership

However, things are complicated by the latent possibility that groups may evolve into networks and back again. There are two distinct ways for designers to cope with this:

1. Ignore the problem and leave the network aspect to a different application or applications.
2. Build support for transitions to network modes into the software itself.

We favour the latter solution. We will start, however, by briefly examining the features needed to support group modes. We will not go into great depth on this topic: software to support group interactions has been available for several decades, and we do not intend to suggest new or revolutionary approaches to its design here, apart from in terms of the transition to network modes of interaction.

Structure and Leadership

Software designed for groups needs to embody roles that provide affordances, capabilities, and levels of control to different people.

It should be possible to see the mapping between the group structure and the individuals and resources composing it. In other words, we should be aware of the organizational structure of the group, with clear signals for different roles. This may be as simple as labels or icons to indicate that a person is a teacher or group leader, or it can be more sophisticated. For example, we could display the organizational structure as a tree, or indicate ownership of resources and discussions by images or text.

Fixed Periods of Operation and Identifiable Stages of Development

- Any group system should be capable of having a specified beginning and end date/time.
- Resources and discussions for groups should have the facility for expiring or archiving.

As groups pass through various phases, they need different kinds of electronic support, and these should not be mixed up. For instance, relics of experimental sharing and learning should not persist once groups have become self-sustaining and apply knowledge critically. Allowing or requiring resources and discussions to expire (or to be sidelined through archiving) is one approach to dealing with this issue. Another is to parcel the learning landscape in order to keep spaces associated with different development phases separate.

Explicit Membership

Groups imply membership, which also implies that those outside the group need to be excluded. Any application supporting groups needs explicit controls over not just authentication but also authorization. In addition, such a system needs support for subgroupings, including groups of individuals and the virtual spaces that they use. For example, this may be used to separate spaces for subgroup interaction (a common feature of LMSs), or at a higher level, to separate out instances of courses. This leads us to consider transitions from group to network modes.

Transition from Group to Network

It is not uncommon for groups to evolve into networks, especially in educational applications. Typically, people who have been in a class together may stay in contact, and even if they don't there is a great deal of potential value in using the alumni of a given course to provide support, encouragement, and other benefits to new cohorts.

Unfortunately, many systems primarily designed for closed groups (including most LMSs) do not make it easy to do that, and such networks tend to arise despite the system's design rather than because of it, through email or other more network-friendly social applications (Facebook groups, for example).

To support the transition from group to network modes, it would be better if designers developed group applications that fade into networks rather than those that abruptly end. The common approach to closed course management that is used in many institutional LMSs is to archive old courses when they have ended, thereby ending a given student's association with the course. Indeed, data models behind the applications enforce this by requiring separation for each instance a course runs. Because of the data models behind many LMSs, there is little alternative to this approach because were we to leave ex-students and their discussions active, it would be confusing to new cohorts. In unpaced/self-paced learning there are further problems as, without a specific cohort to be a member of, relics

of old discussions can quickly evolve into a chaotic tangle that is counterproductive in learning. In a paced (cohort-based) course it is very valuable to make use of
subgroupings for each instance of a course, but to maintain either a supertype or
superclass of the course that allows users to maintain membership in the broader
network.

For unpaced courses, the problem is more complex. Learners who progress
through a course at their own pace, typically with discontinuous overlapping
start and finish times, are in some senses a group with shared goals, a hierarchical
organizational structure, clear membership and so on, but in some senses they are
a set because individual ties are typically very weak, and while purposes are shared
at the large scale of the course, areas of interest at any given time will typically
differ.

CONCLUSION

In this chapter we have overviewed both the power and liabilities of group models
of teaching and learning. Groups can be used by educators to create the support,
solidarity, and community that encourage learners to continue the often-strenu-
ous work of effective learning. They are also important vehicles for transmitting
the cultural capital, often referred to as the hidden curriculum, which is associated
with the experience of formal education.

The benefits are balanced with the tendency for groups to suffer from groupthink and serve as cliques that bar access for some to group privileges. In formal
education, groups often suffer from teacher dependency than doesn't allow learners to practice the skills or develop the self-efficacy attitudes associated with self-
directed and lifelong learning. Nonetheless, we have seen the evolution of groups
from place-based entities to ones that can thrive and be effective in blended online
and place-based format, and on to groups that operate effectively with only online
interaction and collaborative work.

There are some notable downsides to the use of groups, one of the largest
being that such approaches typically impose heavy restrictions on time and pace,
and distribute control in ways that may not benefit all learners. Beyond these
problems, they scale badly and are very expensive to run (Annand, 1999). The
organizational complexity of managing large numbers of group-based learners and the effort involved in sustaining group technologies means that more
innovative ways need to be found to gain the benefits of groups at a lower cost
and without the concomitant loss of learner control that they necessarily entail.

Connectivist pedagogies appear to offer such an alternative, and with that in mind, in the next chapter we move beyond groups to the fluid and emergent structures we refer to as networks.

LEARNING IN
NETWORKS

Most learning is not the result of instruction. It is rather the result of unhampered participation in a meaningful setting. Most people learn best by being "with it," yet school makes them identify their personal, cognitive growth with elaborate planning and manipulation.

Ivan Illich, **Deschooling Society**

In this chapter we delve into a detailed discussion on the social form of networks, with a focus on the learning opportunities and challenges associated with this class of social interaction. Networks are a central social form in human societies. Sociology, anthropology, business, and other disciplines have studied their function and form for many decades, and there is ample literature on social networks in a wide variety of communities. However, networks have been used to a lesser extent in formal education, at least partly because their loose form often conflicts with and can be disruptive to institutional structures. They are not bound by processes, roles, or deliberate architectural sculpting. They can be formalized, but not formally constituted. And yet networks are among the primary knowledge conduits of the world; throughout our lives, we learn from people that we know. The spread of knowledge through a network closely resembles the spread of infection: learning is contagious (Kleinberg, 2007), for good or ill.

Recently, the development of low-cost and portable devices allowing for network development and engagement anywhere/anytime has accelerated interest in and the use of networks for distance learning. In the previous chapter, we saw that group norms and customs evolved largely in face-to-face contexts, in which presence, trust, and shared environment created the background context. Today's learning networks, however, operate and evolve primarily in a mediated context. There are new possibilities networked technologies enable that were difficult or impossible to reach prior to the advent of cyberspace. In this section we detail the underlying affordances of networks as a background to examining the learning activities and contexts that can be expected to thrive under these conditions.

A network, in the loosest sense, consists of nodes (the points on the network), and edges (the connections between them). Networks are not only visible in human interactions: in nature, ecosystems, chemical systems, geological systems, galaxies and solar systems can be viewed as networks. Similarly, designed physical systems such as the Internet, transit systems, power grids, and roads can also be viewed as networks. In systems that involve humans, networks can be seen in everything from the social connections between individuals (Wellman, Boase, & Chen, 2002) to the relationships of actors and actants within a dynamic system (Latour, 2005), from the epidemiologic patterns of disease diffusion (Watts, 2003) to the interactions that occur within a city (Alexander, 1988; Hillier, 1996). Human systems share much in common with their inanimate counterparts and obey similar dynamic laws (Watts, 2003). Our focus, however, is not so much on the abstract or even physical structure of the network, but on the social structures it enables for learning.

Networks are Concerned with Individuals

It is possible to see networks in any learning engagement that involves other people, including within, across, or beyond the perimeters of a group. Networks are constituted in connections not as formal or informal processes: they are of a different ontological type than a group. Membership of a group is by definition membership of a network, but this does not negate the value of understanding group processes as distinct from the network: they are different kinds of things. Although concerned with human interaction, the social network-centric view of the world is, perhaps ironically, heavily focused on the individual. Indeed, Rainie and Wellman (2012) explicitly describe this form of engagement as "networked individualism." It is possible for a researcher, informally or formally, to examine the topology of networks and explore their nodes and edges, and to perform analyses of the forms they take as though they were distinct entities. However, lacking a designed structure or concept of membership, from the perspective of any individual member of a network it is constituted egocentrically, as people with whom one has a connection of some sort. We do not do things for the good of the network as we do for the good of the group because this makes no sense— it is not an object as such. It is simply the description of our many connections with others, and with the visible limits of these connections.

Networks are Uneven

Diagrams and maps of social networks typically show multiple threads connecting network nodes or members in complex arrays. The hierarchical structures of groups give way to structures that are fluid, complex, and that evolve to create new linkages as old and unused ones atrophy. The network structure forces and affords individuals and sub-networks to engage in responsible decision-making for themselves rather than relying on others to make decisions or filter information flow. In aggregate, the people in a network make decisions and move in specific directions, but the direction and focus of this movement cannot usually be dictated by any individual member. Rather, in the interactions of networks, members' directions, strategies, and ideals are created and enacted. It is, however, an oversimplification to suggest that networks are topologically flat structures where all play an equal role. Small-world networks are an extremely common form in social systems, with parts of different networks joined by highly connected nodes and supernodes that are typically of greater relative importance than those with fewer connections, at least when we are looking at flows of information or feelings. However, this is a complex area of ongoing study: while highly connected nodes with many edges are important to the spread of knowledge through a network, they are not necessarily the most influential nodes in a human system, nor do they effectively close connections among other nodes. Rather, they are necessary conduits through which knowledge flows and may be filtered or transformed.

The unevenness of networks relates not just to their topology but to their temporal characteristics. Activity and clusters within networks occur in bursts and are often sporadic, with hard-to-predict ebbs and flows. This is unsurprising given that, unlike the group, there is no intentional coordination of behaviour in a network. Topics of interest emerge for a large number of reasons, and these spark conversation. Sometimes a particular blog post, article in the media, notable piece of news or TV segment may act as a catalyst for conversation. Sometimes, the internal dynamics of networks themselves spread ideas and dialogue. The spread of memes, replicating ideas, phrases, or, most often in modern cyberspace, images of cats, is easily facilitated through networks.

Networks are Uncertain

Network learning is qualitatively different from group-based interaction because it introduces elements of both uncertainty and opportunity. The audience for a networked communication is the heterogeneous members of that network who may share some values, interests, and qualities in common but, beyond the reason for the connection in the first place, are unlikely to share more. Groups share homogeneous goals and norms, whereas the differences between people and their interests in networks provide opportunities for the emergence of new friendships, development of social capital, emergence of conflict, and other unanticipated instances.

It is this openness to the possible that both attracts and repels potential network learners. For some distance learners, the lack of face-to-face interaction means trust can only be built after considerable exposure to group interaction, and they gain both personal and professional understanding of one another, combined with the trust engendered by context and norms that arise from membership in an institution or class. For others, the group's homogeneity creates sameness and boredom, with restrictive constraints entailed by the need to work at similar times and at a similar pace to others in the group; they seek out the network for its capacity to provide exposure to the learning opportunity of the unknown.

Networks are Diverse

We are typically connected to different people for different reasons. They may be friends, we may meet them at conferences, share groups with them, interests, locations, buy things from them, meet them at a party, know their aunt: the possibilities are endless. What defines a network is the sum of the people with whom we have a connection for whatever reason. The lack of homogeneity in networks means that problems that are shared with them are viewed from multiple perspectives, increasing the potential range of solutions and creative ideas to draw from (S. E. Page, 2008).

Networks are Clustered

The corollary of there being multiple reasons that we are connected with others is that it is possible to cluster people we know into different, typically overlapping sub-networks. Subnets are characterized by Google+ as "circles," which is a useful term that we commonly use to distinguish different parts of our network. We have different circles of friends, people who share professional interests, casual contacts, and so on. These subsets of networks make it easier to identify those who might help us in different learning contexts. If we have the technologically mediated means to distinguish them, we can focus questions or things we share on those who are most likely to have an interest or knowledge about them.

Networks Foster Cooperation

The network provides an ideal context for sharing information, ideas, and questions as opposed to collaborative working, where roles and rules are more appropriate. But sharing itself is not a unitary concept and has many culturally, contextually, and individually defined dimensions. Talja (2002) extracts from the literature on academic research communities four types of sharing activity:

1. Strategic sharing: information sharing as a conscious strategy of maximizing efficiency.
2. Paradigmatic sharing: information sharing as a means of establishing a novel and distinguishable approach or area.
3. Directive sharing: information sharing between teachers and students, or employees and employers or other networkers seeking to perform a specific task.
4. Social sharing: information sharing as a relationship- and community-building activity.

Networks in learning contexts are used for each of these four tasks, and the network gains in value when any of them bear fruit, as demonstrated by networkers' satisfaction and use.

Networks are Borderless

As Milgram (1967) famously showed and others have since confirmed, we are all connected to one another via a very small chain of people. In "Six degrees: The Science of a Connected Age," Watts (2003) reports on experiments that confirm the chain between one person and another is six or less, whoever they may be, wherever they may be in the world. In essence, viewed from above, the world can be seen as one huge network of people.

Networks are not Technologically Constituted

Networks are constituted in terms of connections with others and, while technologies can support and enhance them, there are no consistent or defining rules, processes, or methods in a network, whether implicit or codified. Networks are not, in and of themselves, technologies. Of course, individuals may overlay all sorts of processes on a case-by-case basis, and this is often the way networks coalesce into groups: some form of codification is created that distinguishes them from a loose assemblage, including the establishment of names, purposes, ground rules, schedules, and so on. Networks themselves are diffuse, bottom-up, and have undefined perimeters. Though often technologically enabled and benefiting from technologies that reveal them, no technology other than language (at least in most cases) is required for them to form.

The lack of technology or intentional architecture means that, if they are to be used in intentional learning, more effort is needed on the part of the learner. The roles, processes, and methods embodied in groups are designed to make things easier, and they are not available to the networked learner. While the group-based learner may be actively engaged in the social construction of knowledge, he or she is seldom involved in the construction of the process to achieve that. To learn deliberately is to assemble the means and methods of doing so. In groups, they are assembled for you. In networks, you must assemble them yourself. Networked learning, as Connectivism suggests, is as much about acquiring meta-skills in learning as it is about the learning itself. In the absence of a teacher role, this typically means that the networked learner must discover sources of inspiration from within the network through role models, or discover the learning design in some other way. Typically, the process of doing so will mean discovery of instructional resources in the loosest sense of the word, leaving the networked learner in a hybrid position: employing behaviourist/cognitivist tools yet at the same time engaging in authentic social practice.

MANY LEARNERS ARE LOOSELY TIED

Internet scholars have written about the distinction between "dense bounded groups" and "sparse unbounded networks" (Wellman et al., 2002). This work flowed from the study of informal organizations in wired communities, but similar forces are at work in the socializing modes found in networked-based groups. Wellman et al. (2002) found that group and network relationships are common in both work and community contexts. They note that groups are most often associated with locally bound communities where relationships evolve through proximity, even in the absence of choice. We are forced to interact with those we live, work, and attend class with, regardless of any affection or interest. Distributed networks, of course, eliminate this constraint and allow us to form both networks and groups with people who may be very widely physically distributed.

Beyond physical proximity, networks are supportive of the creation of weak ties (Granovetter, 1973) that serve as bridging connections to other groups and networks. Networks often have higher percentages of weak ties than strong ones, but each type has advantages and disadvantages. Strong ties are associated with closeness, multiplexity (multiple forms of interaction), and higher levels of intimacy, immediacy, and frequency of interaction. These are generally positive attributes, but strong links can also lead to "amplified reciprocity," where individual freedom is constrained due to obligations of mutual support, inertia, and lack of interest in building relationships outside of the group (Gargiulo & Benassi, 2000). Networks and other models of human organization associated with weak ties offer greater diversity, provide wider and less redundant sources of information and opinion, and increase individual and community forms of bridging capital (Ellison, Steinfield, & Lampe, 2007).

Gargiulo and Benassi found that the development of social capital is not directly related to the creation of stable and secure strong ties; rather, "managers with cohesive communication networks were less likely to adapt these networks to the change in coordination requirements prompted by their new assignments, which in turn jeopardized their role as facilitators" (2000, p. 183). In rapidly changing contexts, the creation of social capital remains important, but change requires flexibility and the diversity often associated with weak ties rather than stable, strong relationships. Moreover, Burt argues that these weak ties foster "structural holes" or disconnections that allow the nimble to exploit opportunities "to broker the flow of information between people and control the form of projects that bring together people from opposite sides of the hole" (1997, p. 340). Those with more extensive network relationships are thus "at higher risk of detecting and developing good ideas, because of which they enjoy higher compensation than peers, more positive evaluations and faster promotions" (Burt, 2009, p. 46), giving them more opportunities to create knowledge, social capital, and wealth.

Networks, with their bridging of structural holes, can in principle reduce the propensity for negative and inhibiting group behaviours and culture. However, the lack of structure also means that commitment may be lower, or at least of an ad hoc and unpredictable nature. Too much diversity can also be counterproductive, leading to chaos or randomness (S. E. Page, 2011). Without some redundancy, the dynamic and changing nature of networks can leave gaps when those filling a particular niche leave the network or move to the outer limits of its boundary.

COOPERATIVE FREEDOMS IN NETWORKS

The degree of freedom afforded in a network-based learning context is typically very high (see figure 5.1). This is both a blessing and a curse because choice is not equivalent to control (Dron, 2007a). Too many options, especially in a learning context where we may have little idea about appropriate tools, methods, content, or individuals from which to learn, can make it very difficult to choose between one path or another, and may leave the learner in a worse position for control than if he or she had no choice at all. The archetypal theory of networked learning, Connectivism, shows this in sharp relief. In many ways, connectivist methods are concerned with the meta-level of learning: learning how to learn in a white-water world of constant change and uncertainty.

Figure 5.1 Notional cooperative freedoms in a network.

Time

Compared to group-based ways of learning, freedom of time in networked learning is typically high, though there are often dependencies relating to the availability and activities of others in the network. If a learning path is instigated by a particular blog post, or involves interaction with others, the availability of other people determines when and how participants might learn. This is very dependent on context though: some kinds of learning conversation in a network can spread out over years while others, such as those about a recent news topic, can be over in hours or days. One of the most distinctive features of network-based learning, as the Connectivist model suggests, is that it is typically self-instigated rather than imposed by a designer, so not only can it begin with an inspiration from an interaction with others, it can also emerge from the individual. Learning often starts with a process of creation, be it a blog post, video, discussion post, question in a forum, or simply a comment on another post.

Place

As with all cyberspace learning, freedom of place is very high in network-based learning. There are a few exceptions where location may be important, for instance where a network develops through augmentation of a physical space by geotagging or virtual cairns left by others in a network (Platt & Willard, 1998), but these are relatively rare.

Content

Freedom to choose content is, by definition, high in a networked learning model. Net-based learning is often concerned with discovering and tracing paths to content through a network, for instance, following links posted in Twitter, LinkedIn, or Academia.edu, and freely choosing what and from whom we learn. There are some subtle constraints, however. An individual's view of the network is always limited and localized. Filter bubbles, where machines or individuals filter out all but confirming sources of data, can emerge where preferential attachment leads to certain resources, and particularly the content created by a limited range of popular network nodes that is far more likely to be selected. While the network may extend fuzzily outward to encompass almost anything available in cyberspace, the emergent organization of a network can strongly emphasize some while leaving others outside of it, only slightly connected and with little chance of being found. This is not necessarily a bad thing—most certainly, the range and diversity of content in networked learning will always be far greater than in a group-oriented learning context, and exponentially greater than in an instructivist setting. However, there is a concern that "popular" is not necessarily equal to "useful": what appeals to a diverse collection of people who have some shared learning goals but not others may emphasize the bland, the attractive, the powerfully stated, the easily digestible, and so on. This is particularly risky because connectivist models place a great deal of emphasis on members of a network being contributors and creators rather than consumers. Content is often curated, mashed-up, re-presented, and constructed or assembled by those in the network. This is a wonderful resource when seen as a co-constructed and emergent pattern of knowledge-building, but without the editorial control that a teacher or guide in a group provides, it can lead to network-think, a filter bubble in which social capital rather than pedagogy becomes the guiding principle. So, while freedom is high, there are still patterns shaping the selection of content, and unlike those in a more constrained group setting, these may not align well with learning needs. Furthermore, the wealth of content that is proactively flung at us in social networking systems may lead to an excess of choice, and hence diminished control (Schwartz, 2004).

Delegation

While grouped forms of learning include the reassuring role of a teacher to whom one can delegate control, with the concomitant risk that the teacher may take more control than one might wish, the strong emphasis on an individual's learning path in networked learning, especially given the read/write mode expected of networked learners, makes it much harder to delegate control to another. Networks have a social shape, not a cognitive shape, and the emergent guidance that is inherent in the form may not lead us to useful places. Because the path of connectivist learning is not carefully planned, it is not possible to fall back on a predetermined route, and the networked learner must therefore rely on the goodwill and availability of others if he or she needs to let go of the learning reins for a particularly complex or challenging sequence of learning activities. The problem is exacerbated by the fact that learners, by definition, do not know the subject they are trying to learn sufficiently well and therefore may not know how to ask the right questions, even if someone in their network may know the answers. Of course, should learners find the right person to help in their network, it may well be possible to delegate decisions about the learning trajectory to them; at this point, teaching becomes one-to-one, rather than a function of the network, with all the benefits that entails.

Relationship

Freedom of relationship in a networked context is maximized. Within a network we choose how, when, and whether to engage with others, without any constraints beyond that those we engage with must be, by definition, part of the network. Again, networks are about local interaction, not in the geographic sense, but in the sense that they are only ever perceived in relation to an individual node and its neighbours: networks can connect us with others only where connections between adjoining nodes are available to us. While a group may be viewed as a whole, a distinct entity apart from the people within it, a net is constituted only in the local connections between people.

Medium

The choice of medium in networked learning is typically very high. The networked learner is typically able to select from a vast variety of media to suit his or her needs and may deliberately cultivate networks that make one or another medium more significant. For example, networks of people on YouTube will make video a dominant form, while those in a social network for book lovers such as goodreads.com or even Amazon will tend to favour text or images.

Technology

The only constraints on the choice of technology in network-based learning are that the tools and processes we use must facilitate connection. They should directly or indirectly be connected with the network. We also acknowledge, however, that many of these tools are expensive, and thus there is an inherent constraint—especially on those with little or no disposable income.

Method

While there are no particular constraints on methods that may be used as a consequence of being in a networked-based learning context, the nature of the social form precludes the kind of controlled, paced, formalized pedagogies that may be the norm in a group-based learning context. Networks are very good for surfing ideas, following paths wherever they may lead, going on tangents, and connecting disparate ideas and skills, but to follow intentionally focused paths they are more limited. Having said that, there is nothing to prevent a learner from using the network to discover focused groups or behaviourist/cognitivist resources in order to take a structured path to learning, but the network form itself is by definition emergent and lacking in distinctive pedagogy. Connectivism, the most fully formed of networked learning theories, is more of a meta-pedagogy, specifying an approach to exploration and exploitation rather than designing a learning path.

Pace

Net-based learning typically offers a great deal of control of pace at a macro level, but the interdependence of learning with others can, like group-based ways of learning, lead to dependencies on the availability and interest of others. When a learning conversation opens up around, say, a blog post or a Twitter stream, it is important to engage in a timely fashion in order to be part of the learning dialogue. This dependence on the availability of others, is however, notably offset by the persistent nature of much networked communication. For instance, someone may respond to a blog post months or even years after it was posted, reviving interest and activity in it after a long period of dormancy. The pace of interactions and the expectation that it is a timely stream makes this less likely to occur in Twitter or similar micro-blog technologies.

Disclosure

Most computer-based systems with social networking facilities provide a significant amount of control over what is revealed and to whom, Facebook's constant battle to remove such control notwithstanding. Assuming the technology allows it, the networked learner is free to reveal as much or little as he or she wants. Having said that, there are limited benefits to a social network if everything is kept hidden. The inherent lack of structure and norms in a network means that, with the ease of digital replication that most social networking systems provide, information provided to a small range of individuals may spread through their networks to others.

TRANSACTIONAL DISTANCE AND CONTROL IN NETWORKS

Moore's theory of transactional distance (1993) assumed a formal learning context in which a single teacher or teaching presence was engaged in a learning transaction with a single learner. We have seen that, in group-based learning, the teacher role may be taken by other learners, which can lead to a reduction of transactional distance when measured as a communication or psychological gulf, but an increase in distance when measured in terms of control.

In a networked learning context, the teacher role is distributed among an indefinitely large number of teaching presences, from blogs to peers, from key network nodes to comments on discussion posts. An individual may be both teacher and learner simultaneously. Negotiation of control in networks is a constantly shifting, emergent phenomenon in which the learner is engaged in multiple relationships, each with their own dynamics of control and psychological distances but, in aggregate, transactional distance is low on control in both of these dimensions. From a learner perspective, control can increase and communication/psychological distance can diminish. However, that comes with a strong proviso: an increase in the number of choices may, without the means to choose between options, reduce the control of the learner. Having many choices is not the same as having control (Dron, 2007a; Schwartz, 2004).

Examining this more closely, if there are just two people in a network, then transactional distance may be lower or higher depending upon the strength of the network tie, bearing in mind that, as we have already observed, a dyad may be seen equally as a group, net, or set. If, say, we post a tweet and it is responded to by a follower of someone we follow, then the communication distance is low but the psychological distance may be quite high: we do not necessarily know them or their motivations, and understand little of the context in which they are writing. If the friend that links us then responds, this not only perforce reduces the overall aggregate psychological distance but also the psychological distance between us and the original poster, because their post has gained greater validation by the response of our friend, helping us to understand more of the context and value of their original contribution.

NETWORK TOOLSETS

In this section we describe some of the functionalities of the current generation of network technologies, relating them to the needs of learners who are making use of their networks for learning. Many of these functions are contained in suites of network tools such as those found in Facebook, Ning, Elgg, and others. However, whether through aggregation standards such as RSS and Atom, service-based architectures, widget-based systems, or even by embedding framesets, learners are also often able to "mashup" their own network tools to create personal learning environments. These mashups may be more or less integrated.

Many people maintain more than one network channel on their cellphones, tablets, and computers, with instant messaging applications, social network tools, and feed aggregators providing a constant flow of traffic from them. These are often bound together and linked through tools that integrate them in tablet apps, websites, and other devices: for example, a large number of iOS or Android apps allow content to be shared with other apps, such as Twitter, Facebook, or Google+ that may themselves be network-oriented applications. Given their diversity, it is thus challenging to describe in an exact sense the functions of network tools since they are constantly morphing in look, feel, and function, so our categorization is broad and flexible. In general terms, and in keeping with the individualist focus of networking, most network tools provide one or more means of representing the self, through profiles, presence tools, avatars, and so forth. Networks would be of no value without the means to communicate with others in them. As a result, network tools also provide a means of creating content and sharing it with others. These tools also normally offer facilities for building and sustaining networks of connections. We expand on these main features and some of their corollaries in the subsections that follow.

Profile Tools

The central component of most social networking systems is the profile, a means of displaying information about an individual used by others to find and add them to their networks. Profiles usually contain images (avatars) and a variable amount of other information about the person, which can range from just a name and perhaps location to a complete curriculum vitae, as well as shared content, records of interactions with others, contact details, and other information such as collectively generated reputation indicators and badges (we will explore these in depth later). Profiles serve as proxies for identity to help learners identify those with relevant interests or skills in their network, and assist them to discover more about people before connecting them to their own networks.

Content Creation and Sharing Tools

Networked learners, through participation in networks that reify their inter-actions, are almost always "prosumers"—people who both consume and produce network content (Bruns, 2008). Blogs, wall posts, instant messages, tweets, file sharing, video sharing, photo sharing, podcasts and many other tools for sharing content are an essential part of a modern social networking system, providing the medium and focus for further interaction to occur. The creation of content is one of the central requirements of connectivist learning pedagogies, and the means to create shared content is thus pivotal in providing tools for knowledge construction and tools for sharing and expanding on that knowledge.

Communication Tools

For network-oriented tools, there is a very blurred line between content sharing and creation tools and those whose main purpose is communication. The facility for commenting is ubiquitous, found on everything from photos and videos to shared blogs, curated items, and bookmarks, so in a sense, almost all modern social media facilitate communication. However, some network-oriented functions are concerned with direct dialogue: email, instant messaging, videoconferencing, IP telephony, SMS, direct messaging tools in social networking systems, discussion forums, and so on provide the means to contact one or more people in a network, typically managed through a list of contacts or address book. The means to carry out a sustained dialogue with one or more people in a network facilitates many social pedagogies in both the social constructivist and connectivist traditions of learning. The main difference between such tools and the embedded dialogue that surrounds blogs, for example, is the flexibility of purpose. While comments on blog posts can and frequently do diverge from the topic of the original post, the post acts as a basin of attraction, an object of dialogue that seats the conversation, and usually persists over time, while communication-oriented tools are concerned with the ephemeral process of conversation.

Presence and Status Tools

Networks allow learners to make their presence known or else conceal it, both asynchronously (typically through profile settings) and synchronously (e.g., status indicators in an instant messenger). Presence notification can support presence in physical space, as provided by the tools for mobile social networking, or for helping to identify those in social proximity who share a common interest in an educational- or discipline-related interest. Presence indicators are also being added to text, audio, and video communication and conferencing tools to allow us to see which of our friends or colleagues are available for instant answers, feedback, and interaction. Of course, this sense of presence must be under the control of the individual learner; there are times when we welcome the presence of "kindred souls," while there are other times when we need the freedom to protect and maintain our privacy and anonymity.

Often related to presence tools are status indicators that reveal current activities, interests, or moods. These may be as simple as "at a meeting" indicators or emoticons, or may be brief text messages. Author Dron, for example, travels a great deal and so typically indicates his location in his status message. Some tools integrate with others so that, for example, a status message indicates which piece of music a person is listening to. This rich information greatly increases a sense of social presence and connectedness that reinforces weak ties and sustains an awareness of another person's activities, making it simpler to catch up and more effectively lubricate the social wheels so that interaction is easier when people in a network more sporadically engage in richer conversation. Often, such status updates form a topic of conversation for a broad network, allowing further connections to be built and individual networks to be extended.

Notification Tools

The sporadic and bursty (occurring in bursts) nature of network interactions means that it is vital for all members to be proactively informed when people on the network are trying to connect. Contributing to a learning network and not receiving feedback or acknowledgement of that contribution quickly discourages further participation. Good networking software provides both push and pull forms of notification. Using push tools such as RSS, instant messaging, or even email provides notification to the learner when new content or communication is entered into a learning space. Quality networking tools also allow historical and persistent display and searching of these interventions, so that the learning space can be searchable and span across significant lengths of time.

Referral Tools

Some of the most successful commercial social networking software, such as LinkedIn, MeetUp, and Facebook, is based upon providing selective referrals to other persons for social or commercial motivations and effective encounters. Most of these referral systems assume that those people you regard as friends are more likely to become useful and interesting friends to one another than a random selection of individuals. Thus, mining both weak and strong connections allows us to become acquainted with, and possibly work or learn together with others, with a greater probability of developing profitable exchanges. A variety of network tools make the discovery of others easier, most notably the ubiquitous "friend of a friend" functionality that recommends people you may know. This is an example of a collective application used for networking. However, referral is often more direct and manual: many social networking systems provide the means to suggest people that others may know, and some allow one to suggest groups or sets that may be of interest. Referral may relate to other people, or communities of interest. One of the great strengths of networks lies in the ability to exploit weak and indirect network ties, a matter of great importance when the knowledge a learner seeks cannot be found within his or her circle of friends and acquaintances. As, seemingly, everyone is potentially connected to everyone else by a very small chain of network nodes and edges (Watts, 2003), it appears that someone not too distant from you in network terms may turn out to be the world's leading expert on what you wish to know.

Information Routing

One of the key roles of a teacher in a conventional classroom is to draw attention to information and resources that are of value to learners. The Internet is awash with information, some extremely relevant to us, but most of which is irrelevant and merely creates unwanted noise in our networked environment. By routing relevant information to colleagues in our various networks, we serve as filters for one another and become critical tools of networked information management.

Emotional Support

Networks were earlier conceived of as instrumental tools to afford the undertaking of tasks and support communities of practice. But as network tools have evolved and engaged larger and more diverse sets of users, their function as tools for the emotional support of others has grown. For example, most social networks can be set to alert you of the birthday of anyone in your list of friends. Unlike earlier tools to support this type of notification, Facebook provides a variety of tools the user can employ to express their wishes on a networked friend's "special day." They can, of course, compose a traditional email; send an electronic card; post to their Wall, making a semi-public contribution to the recipient's personal web space that is visible to them and their "friends"; "poke" the person to indicate that they are being thought of; post the information to a group or network to which the recipient belongs; engage in an audio, video, or text chat, or even compose an audio or video greeting. Thus, networks allow members to acknowledge and support one another in a variety of ways—most of which are totally free of charge and very easily composed.

VALUE OF NETWORKS IN FORMAL EDUCATION

As our brief overview of some of the main tools reveals, networks can be valuable to learners, especially in a lifelong learning context, but also within a more structured and guided context.

An oft-cited observation has it that citizens must be lifelong learners in order to maintain their currency, employment, and relevancy in the context of a rapidly changing knowledge-based society. Rather than immersion in full-time study for a few pre-professional years of postsecondary education, policy advisors and educators now argue that learners need to develop skills, attitudes, and connections that will afford their participation in many forms of learning throughout their lives. Most educational groups, especially those that are institutionally organized and led by professional teachers, end very abruptly at graduation. Networks, however, persist and can be used as the basis of lifelong professional education and learning, as long as the participants remain in the relationship. Further, networks made up of participants from the professional world and pre-professional students serve to connect the often theoretical study of the classroom with the everyday problems and challenges of real life. Networks provide opportunities for mentoring, recommendations, and posting queries and requests for help that are heard beyond the protected environs of group-based learning. The capacity to add value and gain recognition within a network also serves students when they complete their studies. They are not only established with membership in a set of existing networks, but more importantly they have experienced and practised the skills needed to effectively use networks throughout their professional careers.

Global Collaborations

Networks support connected learning on both local and global scales. Recent concerns over global warning illustrate the growing awareness of the connectedness of all who inhabit our globe. Many global problems will not be resolved in the absence of international dialogue and coordinated efforts. Networks afford opportunities for learners to associate, negotiate, plan, and execute projects on a global scale with others. For example, the Centre for Innovation in Engineering and Science Education (www.ciese.org/collabprojs.html) coordinates a range of projects that allow learners around the globe to share data collection and analysis in areas such as water and air quality, real-time weather, genetic variations in human body size, and other challenging and intrinsically interesting studies of life science. A similar and hugely successful project, Earthducation, has connected networks of schoolchildren across the globe to a team of researchers, and actively engages them in what Doering (2006) describes as "adventure learning," following him and his colleagues via the Internet on ecologically inspired expeditions around the world.

Workplace Networks

Although more commonly associated with informal and non-formal learning, networks offer flexibility, exposure, and the means to build social capital that warrant more serious consideration for their adoption in formal education. There are important lessons to be drawn from modern uses of networks in the workplace. These applications retain the purposive and task-oriented functionality needed for organizations to succeed, while representing a shift in thinking away from traditionally constituted hierarchical departments and centres. The most widely known research related to networks in workplace contexts is the work of Etienne Wenger on what he refers to as communities of practice (COP). COPs usually consist of co-workers located in a common workplace that develop and share their skills as needed, thereby creating solutions to common problems. In the process of completing these tasks, they develop mutually defining identities, shared jargon, and "shared discourse reflecting a certain perspective on the world" (Wenger, 1998, p. 125). Learning networks, however, are not defined as much by a shared location or description of work, but rather by an individual's need for task performance, learning, advice, or interpersonal support. The type of support or aid required causes the learning network to constantly morph its structure, rate of interaction among members, and communication tone in response to these tasks. A range of tools and environments support explicit group-oriented learning within a networked context, allowing groups to branch off from networks for specific learning purposes. For example, CoolSchool, presented primarily as a Facebook application, brings learners and teachers together through Facebook, providing a system for running real-time classes and requesting or offering a lesson, along with a scheduling subsystem.

There are numerous learning activities that can be imported from familiar group contexts as well as from instructivist methods based on cognitivist/behaviourist models of teaching. In many cases, discussions, debates, critiques, and presentations benefit when the audience is expanded beyond a specific group. We see this commonly in the networks that spread out from MOOCs, with Facebook groups, Twitter hashtags, and other foci providing the means for networks to develop beyond the formal group and connect with others. These less homogenous contributions add authenticity and divergence of opinion that is often the basis for enhanced motivation and learning. Even when the primary source of learning is the closed group, networks can be used effectively to expand learning beyond it. This expansion easily includes students enrolled in the program who have already completed a course of studies, and these alumni add experience and diversity to networked deliberation. Expansion to professional groups is perhaps most valuable in professional faculties, but even general studies can benefit from the experience of professionals who are in practice, have retired, or have even chosen to resign from professional life. As noted earlier, the Web's global connectivity and data collection capacity can be used to design new learning activities. Data collected, shared, and analyzed in global contexts creates an expanded context that is inherently more valuable, fascinating, and motivating then similar activities in only local ones.

Informal networked learning presents both a challenge and an opportunity for formal education institutions. As more open and freely available educational resources become available, the monopoly of formal institutions over learning content is weakened. Similarly, as learners are able to connect with one another without mediation by employees of a formal educational institution, they gain the capacity to collaborate, share, stimulate, and support individual cooperative and collaborative forms of informal learning. The interest by governments, professional bodies, and employers in measuring and tracking competencies as opposed to credentials fundamentally threatens this last remaining monopoly of formal educational institutions (see, for example, Richards, Hatala, & Donkers, 2006). Networked informal learning acts as profoundly disruptive technology to formal education institutions. Christensen described disruptive technologies as those that are "typically cheaper, simpler, smaller, and, frequently, more convenient to use" (1997, p. xv). Since most informal networked learning is completely free to the learner, it is obviously cheaper than institutionally provided learning opportunities. Informal learning is chunked, sequenced, and scheduled by the learners themselves, thus creating appropriate-sized opportunities to engage in learning. The fact that networks are centred on the learner, not on processes and methods of groups in institutions, means that they bypass the careful controls of the institution. Facebook, for example, is commonly used by networks of students to support their formal learning activities in study groups that, on occasion, turn into mechanisms for cheating: at least, this is how universities perceive it (and in some cases they are correct).

Course Hero, for example, a website that boasts it has solutions to over half a million textbook problems, has over 265,000 fans of its Facebook group (Young, 2010). The ability of networks to easily allow learners to share and collaborate is forcing institutions and teachers to radically rethink traditional attitudes toward assessment and accreditation. Given their pivotal role in educational systems, this in turn may mean a drastic restructuring of the purpose and methods of traditional education altogether, an issue we return to in our final chapter of this book.

We have already observed that networks can be scary places for teachers who are used to being in control. Effective network teaching involves some letting go, but also recognition of where a teacher can add value, whether as a subject expert, a reassuring guide, or a shaper of the study process. It is thus concerned with a balance between top-down and bottom-up control. In a group, rich communication and an identifiable hierarchy enables a teacher to engage in dialogue to enable learning even though it is likely that structure is, at best, tenuous. It is thus comfortably within Moore's notions of transactional distance. In a network, the fact that the teacher is just one of a myriad of signals in the environment means the potential dialogue that helps to guide the less autonomous student is diluted or lost in a cacophony of voices that struggle to be heard. It is all too easy for a student used to the comfortable certainties and cosseting of traditional group-oriented institutional instruction to feel out of his or her depth and forced to make too many decisions about what and who to pay attention to.

Some of these issues may be addressed through a more structured design of the networked environment. Many social networking systems, such as Elgg, make it possible to impose a structure and appearance on a site that supports a given network, allowing the owner of a community to control the experience of the learner to a greater extent than more freeform social networks. However, that controlled space is just one of many that the student may inhabit in his or her personal or networked learning space.

Given the varieties of networks that learners participate in, of crucial importance are tools to manage, filter, and control information so as to make learning in networks efficacious. Specific recommendations include:

- Using high-quality and, where possible, open tool sets for finding, joining, forming, and supporting new and existing networks and their archives;
- Developing and deploying tools to support individual control of network filters;
- Supporting network deployment in contexts that are as open as possible;
- Using tools to support identifying, evaluating, and annotating resources by individual and collaborative network members;
- Creating linked profiles and other sophisticated search tools so that network members can come to know one another and contributions to the network are recognizable and valued;
- Using means of identity management such as OpenID to enable persistence

of identity between systems;

- Allowing members to morph, parcellate, and combine networks as needs evolve;
- Using tools or processes, such as the soft security of wikis, which promote trust both of network artifacts and the people within them.

Connectivist models of learning are deliberately free from fixed learning outcomes. Because every learner's constructed network is different, and trajectories are based on currency and emergent needs, networked learning does not take easily to the formalization of learning outcomes that underpins traditional courses. This does not mean that such outcomes cannot be stated in advance; instead, they are decided at an individual level and are constantly subject to re-examination and modification as a learner progresses, especially over a longer trajectory. In an academic world that is defined by learning outcomes, comparable courses, and assessment based on such outcomes, this presents difficulties for those attempting to enable networked learning in a formal context. A two-pronged approach of learning contracts and portfolios can help to overcome such obstacles.

Learning Contracts

One simple and effective solution to the problem of variable outcomes is to employ a learning contract, in which the learner specifies in advance what outcomes are intended and plans a learning path in order to achieve measurable outcomes. If it is to have value, it is important that this contract is negotiated with an expert, direct or embodied in a toolset, who can ensure that at least the minimum competencies are covered. If a learner wished to, say, become a medical practitioner, then it would be important to ensure that the learning undertaken is sufficient to support such a role and thus limit risks to potential patients. The use of competence frameworks can be helpful here, especially when they are designed by a variety of experts in a field.

Portfolios

While learning contracts provide a suitable mechanism for accrediting networked learning in some cases, they have limitations. In the first place, much networked learning is likely to fall outside the parameters defined for the contract, and will thus go unaccredited. This is true of almost all learning, from the most formal instructivist model to the loosest problem-based methods, and it just means that there are inefficiencies in assessment: not all that is learned is assessed. A more troublesome difficulty is that a contract-based approach does not easily allow for direct comparison of individuals, nor does it easily fit with professional accreditation requirements. Competence frameworks and expert guidance can assist to some extent but, especially where learners are already competent in some aspects of a field, portfolios can play an important role in assembling evidence of competence for accreditation.

GROUPS EMERGE AS NETWORKS GROW

The fundamental role of facilitation, ownership, and other issues associated with leadership differentiate groups from networks. Educators, like other actors in hierarchical organizations, are used to creating learning environments in which students, as consumers, play their assigned role. Thus, many educators first approach network development as a task in which the learning activities are precisely outlined and students are commonly assessed by the teacher on their network participation. Many researchers, however, note the requirement for emergence in network learning models. See, for example, the special issue of IRRODL on emergence (www.irrodl.org/index.php/irrodl/issue/view/49). This implies that the members of the network have both the tools and authority to recreate the network's form and function in response to changes in the environment.

Author Dron (2007b) emphasizes the need to design for this change, through use of evolutionary change theories (survival of the fittest activities, modes of sharing and creation of knowledge), and the percolation of networks into new instances, or tighter groups. Dron also notes the need for network designers to delegate much of the control over the network to users; however, they must also allow the network enough central control and capacity for applying appropriate constraint to curtail abuse by spammers or other malevolent users.

The desirability of facilitation, promotion, and activism involved in leadership is a very contentious issue among network theorists. Community of practice theorists have argued (Wenger, 1998) that one cannot intentionally or artificially create a community of practice—rather they are by definition self-organizing. But at the same time, Wenger and others talk about individuals who play key "community development" functions that provide leadership to emerging networks. They go on to discuss strategies by which community developers exit from leadership roles in the community of practice when it reaches unspecified levels of size, participation, and sufficiency in governance. An individual's power in a network comes from influence, not design.

Our notion of learning networks has much in common with the work networks discussed by Nardi, Whittaker, and Schwarz (2002), referred to as *intensional networks*. They point out that, increasingly, networks and not groups are the defining features of much workplace activity, which we suggest relates to the work and study associated with formal learning as well. They argue that "intensional networks are the personal social networks workers draw from and collaborate with to get work done" (2002, p. 207). These networks are activated based on opportunities or requirements for production. This may be directly associated with a formal learning activity, but more often arise when an individual turns to their personal network in order to accomplish some learning activity alone. Like Nardi et al.'s intensional networks, learning networks consist of those directly enrolled with the learner in a formal course. They also consist of colleagues, family members, friends, former workmates, neighbours, and others who can be called upon to support the learning activity. Though learning networks may be stable and used by learners for a series of learning activities or courses, they can also be temporary and called into existence for one-off learning demands. Nardi et al. note that "intensional networks are not bundles of static properties. They dynamically pulsate as activity ebbs and flows, as different versions of the network come to life" (2002, p. 238).

Similar to Nardi et al.'s notion of intensional networks is the concept of ad hoc transient learning networks (Berlanga et al., 2008; Sloep et al., 2007), which are focused on lifelong learning that is intensely learner directed. Koper, Rusman, and Sloep (2005) define a learning network as "an ensemble of actors, institutions and learning resources which are mutually connected through and supported by information and communication technologies in such a way that the network self-organizes and thus gives rise to effective lifelong learning" (p. 18). An ad hoc transient learning network provides tools enabling learners to access, engage, and evaluate learning activities, often but not necessarily as individuals in ad hoc networks. They thus encourage developers to move beyond the class and course familiar in formal education to learning designs that allow and support learners to create their own learning activities, goals, and outcomes.

Unlike those of Nardi et al. (2002), Koper et al. (2005) are clear about the technological requirements for such coordination, and their team at the Open University of the Netherlands (OUNL) has developed a range of online tools that facilitate their formation. Somewhere between a traditional group and an informal network, ad hoc transient learning networks are loosely joined networks of people with shared interests who are brought together through the use of toolsets to assist their formation. The team at OUNL address design and implementation challenges to build systems that help networked learners find appropriate learning content and paths to knowledge acquisition, connect with learners embarked on similar or related learning activities, assess their own competencies, develop personalized learning goals, and assess and authenticate self-directed learning outcomes. The computer-based technologies that underpin ad hoc learning networks play some of the roles occupied by traditional teachers and the surrounding apparatus of formal learning: enrolling learners, managing contacts, enabling the co-creation and curation of content, and assisting in the management of the learning path, though unlike a traditional group-based approach, the focus (network-like) remains on the individual learner and his or her goals, rather than a shared group purpose. The use of such tools places the systems used by Koper, Sloep, and others in the holistic generation of distance learning, moving beyond the loose networks of connectivist learning to something more guided and structured, yet still benefiting from the emergent strengths of individuals in a crowd.

THE VALUE OF DIVERSITY

Learning and knowledge rests in diversity of opinions.
George Siemens, "Connectivism: A Learning Theory for the Digital Age"

For a learner in a network, there is typically greater value to be found in diverse networks than in those that are self-similar. If a network consists of many different people with various skills and interests, then there is a far greater chance that someone in the network will have the skills and interests needed to assist with a particular learning goal. Diversity encourages growth by making the likelihood far greater of different world views conflicting and being challenged. Such challenges require learners to examine their knowledge structures, reflect on their positions, and articulate their beliefs and opinions, thereby connecting and constructing a deeper and more meaningful knowledge system.

There are many different ways of measuring diversity in a system. S. E. Page (2011) identifies three main categories of diversity: variation, diversity across types, and diversity of community composition. Variation can occur between similar people of the same type: for instance, researchers in e-learning may have different notions of how best to evaluate a learning transaction. Diversity across types is concerned with a system containing multiple types of entities such as species, topics, or product lines, measurable in terms of entropy, network distance, or attributes. What defines a type is contextually situated: for example, gender may differentiate types for some kinds of network, such as those who breastfeed, but may be completely irrelevant in others, such as those who research e-learning. Diversity of community composition, measurable by population, is concerned with the ways that different combinations of the same things can lead to different entities, such as the many and varied combinations of carbon, hydrogen, oxygen, and nitrogen used to make proteins. Which form of diversity is of most value will depend to some extent on the context and learning task. As a rule, type diversity will offer the most opportunities to ensure that someone within the network will have relevant skills. For example, if we are learning about global warming, then it will be valuable to have philosophers, climate scientists, economists, and poets within the network. However, especially where the network is one that centres around an area of expertise, it may sometimes be more valuable to find variation: for example, a learner who is making use of a network of learning technology experts in order to learn more about such things may gain more from a range of relevant skills in that area than from the presence of particle physicists or poets. Conversely, the potential for border crossing, creative connections, and transformative learning may be better enabled by a more diverse crowd, including physicists and poets.

Too much diversity can be overwhelming: the benefits of diversity are applicable only if the range of options to choose from is manageable. One of the most notable benefits of many networks (especially those that are scale-free or sparsely connected) is that they are, from the perspective of any node, limited in scope. As well as acting as a natural brake on diversity, this feature also enables variation, speciation, and diversity to occur within a large network. If everyone can see what everyone else is doing, with maximal connectivity, then an evolutionary pattern sets in where only the fittest survive, however fitness may be measured. For example, imagine a nightmarishly distorted hypothetical network that works a little like Twitter, with the twist that everyone is following everyone else. In other words, every tweet from every one of its hundreds of millions of users would be sent to every other. Imagine then that, unlike the real Twitter, this network provides no means of filtering sets of posts by topic (hashtag), nor is there any concept of age or ageing of tweets, but this system retains the network-oriented feature of allowing retweets. The chances of a new tweet surviving an onslaught of existing retweets would be minimal. Almost all that anyone would ever see would be retweets, which would mean that almost the only posts retweeted would be ones that had already been retweeted. Unless further mechanisms to limit expansion were introduced or were extrinsic to the system (e.g. some news headlines might have a large enough effect to impinge), in a rampant example of the Matthew Effect (Merton, 1968) these would soon be reduced to a few that would entirely dominate the rest.

If everything is in direct competition for attention with everything else, without further temporal or spatial variegation, there will be only one or, at best, a very small number of winners within any given niche. This is true whether we are talking about memes, ideas, patterns of behaviour, or cultural expressions. Luckily, such hyperconnectivity is unlikely to be found in the wild, though larger network applications that fail to take such issues into account can and do suffer from problems caused by excessive connectivity between network members, as anyone with more than a few hundred Facebook friends is probably already aware. Attention is a limiting resource for which many posts compete. S.E. Page (2011) notes that, in a system like this that involves replication, variation and competition for survival, there are four main ways that this chaos of undifferentiated connectivity is avoided: "geographic heterogeneity (allopatry), isolation of a small subpopulation (peripatry), divergent neighboring niches (perapatry) and diverse niches in a common environment (sympatry)" (p. 95). These factors remain significant in a virtual environment as much as in a physical space. Limitation of scope (allopatry and peripatry), whether artificially induced through group formation or emerging along geographical lines, is a diversifying benefit of small communities, which inherently parcellate a set of individuals and, in many cases, impose or imply a set of shared values which develop differently from others around them. Perapatry (divergent neighboring niches) is a prime mechanism that saves networks from overconnection thanks to the innate limits of connectivity between individuals and the effects of groups that concentrate connections, which means that most networks are far from uniform. This differentiation is aided and abetted by limits to the speed with which ideas, patterns, memes and knowledge spread between nodes of networks and the clusters within them. Network diversity can also benefit from diverse niches (sympatry), such as those introduced through set-oriented mechanisms like Twitter hashtags or through individuals splitting a network into sets of individuals (circles) that relate to their different interests.

CONTEXT IN NETWORKS

Closely allied to diversity is network context. While Facebook founder Mark Zuckerberg famously proclaimed privacy to be dead (O'Brien, 2010), it is nonetheless true that people present different identities in different contexts, and are not participants in a single network but many (Dron, Anderson, & Siemens, 2011; Rainie & Wellman, 2012). This is particularly important in a learning context where the networks that relate to our academic or personal learning projects may be quite different from those that relate to, say, our hobbies or friends, and where there may be many sub-contexts that interest us, like different classes, courses, subject areas, and so on. If we are receiving a stream of information and updates via a social networking site, it is very convenient to split the stream into different areas of interest. In many cases, we may choose different social networking spaces for different networks that we belong to—Facebook for friends, LinkedIn for business contacts, academia.edu for academic contacts, and so on. Each will provide a slightly different, if often overlapping context. Alternatively, an increasing number of sites that utilize social networks provide tools for splitting networks into more manageable chunks: Facebook Lists, Google+ Circles, LinkedIn's variegated ways of specifying relationships, Twitter's Lists, Elgg's collections, and so on. These mechanisms go some way toward allowing manageable diversity, albeit at the cost of having to take time and effort to manage our circles, lists, or collections.

OWNERSHIP OF NETWORK ARTIFACTS

Debate over ownership of digital content has proved to be very disruptive issue on the Net and provides fuel for the emergence of many different forms of digital products. Publishers and media producers have seen their profits attacked, and in some cases obliterated, by the tools and techniques developed by both consumers and producers of media who often distribute their products at no cost to the user. In education we see equivalent disruption and opportunity brought about by Open Educational Resources (OERs).

The school or corporate entity that sponsored its creation has most often retained ownership of specifically designed educational content. This institutional ownership model, however, has been challenged in university contexts, where professors often lay claim to ownership of course content as a traditional right of academic freedom. This contention often leads to questions of ownership and disputes that have proven very difficult to resolve. In the worst cases these disagreements lead to "patent thickets" in which the threat of ownership and enclosure by one or more of the creators of the content makes it impossible for anyone to legally benefit from it (von Hippel, 2005).

When one moves beyond the familiar camaraderie of the group to the open network, effective management of one's identity becomes critically important. Before discussing the particular tools provided to both reveal and conceal the personal, it is useful to review the rationale and means by which users present themselves to the outer world.

Individuals are constantly walking on a balance beam where they attempt reveal enough of themselves to gain the benefits of social interaction, discourse, and commerce. At the same time, they try to protect themselves from the crowd, so that they have places and times when their actions and ideas are allowed to develop in privacy. The goal of all but the most reclusive hermits among us is not to maximize our privacy. Indeed, maximum privacy—as in solitary confinement—is used as a punishment in many criminal systems. Neither is the goal complete openness, where no actions, ideas, or words are held privately in the self or shared with only a small number of confidents.

The Internet has irreparably disrupted this balance, leading to instances of "identity theft" and both perceived and real invasions of privacy. For example, A. Smith and Lias note that "typically victims in the US may spend on average $1,500 in out-of-pocket expenses and an average of 175 hours in order to resolve the many problems caused by such identity thieves" (2005, p. 17). Further, the popular press and individual parents are aghast at the amount of personal disclosure engaged in by both young and more mature Net users. Conversely, cyberspace has been instrumental in the development of countless new personal friendships, collaborations, and even marriages. We often ask for a show of hands when delivering keynote speeches, querying the audience for those who know someone who has married another that they met in cyberspace. Invariably, the question reveals that many of us find camaraderie, love, and lust using the affordances of cyberspace, and specifically various social software tools.

We come to know one another through the presentation of ourselves in Net spaces. In his seminal 1959 work, Erving Goffman defined a new field of sociology that he called dramaturgical sociology (1959). He masterfully tied together metaphors of the stage and its actors to describe how people manage their "presentations" or plays for the benefit of self and others. Goffman's plays took place in real time and in face-to-face interaction. Nonetheless, the prompts, settings, front and back house etiquette, audience and actor interactions also are performed in cyberspace, and are often amplified.

Goffman describes two types of impressions we use during the course of our presentations of self. The first are those that are carefully crafted and presented or given to the audience. The second are those displays of self that are "given off" often inadvertently, through words, deeds, gestures, or expressions. These breakdowns or partings of the curtains arouse in the audience "an intense interest in these disruptions . . . that comes to play a significant role in the social life of the group" (Goffman, 1959, p. 14). In face-to-face interaction, given off displays include style of dress, accent, body language, choice of topic, and quality of discourse. They include the many ways we can stumble both physically and metaphorically, and how we respond to the unexpected. In cyberspace, these clues are somewhat constrained and often focus on written discourse. However, as Walther (1996) and others have pointed out, a host of compensatory tools and techniques are used, even in low-bandwidth Net contexts, to create forms of hyper-communication that compensate and in some ways create enriched contexts for developments of the self that exceed those available in face-to-face contexts. As cyberspace evolves to support immersive, videoconference, and other rich forms of interaction, we see continued means by which participants add novel channels of communication to present themselves.

Thus, cyberspace affords its actors a powerful set of tools which they can use to present themselves. But what exactly are they presenting? Higgins (1987) notes three quite distinct psychological entities that actors present to others. The first is the "actual self," the set of attributes that the individual actor possesses and displays, perceived by others. The second is the "ideal self," those attributes that the actor wishes to possess, and which defines his or her hopes and aspirations. Finally there is the "ought self," those attributes belonging to both the actor and those of importance to them that define what they perceive others expect of them. We shall see that cyberspace provides ample opportunity for presentation of each of these senses of self—the challenge for both actors and audience is to differentiate the context, time, and space in which each is presented.

A final attribute of the stage upon which we present ourselves is the role of others—both actors and audience. Goffman goes into some detail developing his stage metaphor to include interactions between audience and actors and the backstage discourse among teams of actors. Networks also support these interactions. As we have seen in group interaction, the discourse and collaborative activities team members engage in is critical to learning and the production of learning artifacts.

In networked interaction, exchanges between both active and potential network members are much more complicated. The complications arise most obviously in response to the size and fluid nature of network actors. But of even greater importance is the diminished certainty as to the nature of the audience. Network members share similar interests in the topic, ideas, or activities that motivate their membership and participation in the network. Yet they also have additional ideas, cultures, customs, and activities that are not shared, and some may be fraught with dissonance among other network members, especially when considering connections beyond those of the first-order—friends of friends and the like.

MEMBERSHIP IN NETWORKS

Unlike groups, for networks to operate effectively, participation needs to be as freely and widely accessible as possible. For this reason, the P2P Foundation uses the term "equipotency," which implies that each member of the network has the potential and power to participate in the network (p2pfoundation.net/Peer_to_Peer). Network participants have ample opportunity to witness the network's dependence on participation from large and diverse populations. The culture that evolves within the network therefore emphasizes openness and invites contributions from as wide a population as possible. Further, networks encourage members to join and participate in other networks, thereby providing conduits to cross-pollinate and invigorate existing ones.

Participation on the physical level is open to all who have access to cyberspace—a capacity nearly universally available in developed countries, but sadly unequally distributed in some developing countries at the present time. However, with the development of very low-cost hardware, the increase in portable and handheld devices, and the deployment of machines with mesh networking, we can expect physical access constraints to decrease rapidly in the near future. Nevertheless, network value may also be restricted to those who are able to adapt to the fluid culture, languages, and linguistic clues that are used to sustain networking cultures. Those whose technical skills are very limited, who harbour a deep distrust of network technologies, or who are comfortable only in highly visible and defined hierarchical organizations may find networking contexts both frustrating and suspicious.

Equipotency also speaks to the power of network members to define the extent of their participation in a particular network. Since networks offer a wide variety of participative roles, members must decide for themselves what roles they wish to play and be able to amend them as desired. They are free to define the extent of their participation, and to adopt roles of leadership, support, encouragement, or silence as required. Equipotency assumes a deep respect for democratic ideals, in that network members are free to define their own expectations and practice, while respecting the rights of others to do so as well. This freedom is not anarchical, though. Participation in the network requires a shared commitment to a common interest, goal, or activity of the network. Network members come to understand through observation that the realization of their object of cooperation will happen when they coordinate and distribute their activities, skills, and talents in effective ways. Thus, organization, leadership, planning, and coordination evolve within the network and are viewed as legitimate means of achieving network goals.

NETWORKS AND SOCIAL CAPITAL

Social capital has long been seen as an important facilitator and indicator of readiness for social activity. Through collaborative interaction, action, and discourse, groups and networks build social capital. Resnick notes that "use doesn't use it up; when a group draws on its social capital to act collectively, it will often generate even more social capital" (2001, p. 2). The social capital thus created empowers both individuals and their network(s), affording them increased opportunity, capacity, and a sense of efficacy that are used for subsequent individual and social actions.

Burt (2009) focuses on the value accrued to the individual by the exploitation and growth of their social capital. He discusses the role of a broker, someone who spans two groups or networks and serves as an introductory facilitator for more extensive social, and often, economic transactions. While Burt's work is especially relevant to business-oriented networks such as LinkedIn, it also points to the role of the teacher as one who brokers connections—not only to content, ideas, and facts, but to individual groups, networks, and collectives who can be called upon to expand and apply the ideas studied.

DESIGNING NETWORK APPLICATIONS

There are many books, websites, and papers that purport to provide formulae and techniques for designing successful social networking sites. While we will be highlighting some of the more obvious common features of these, our intention here is to focus on those that are significant in a learning context. Successful network-based learning is not just about building large numbers of connections (as in, for example, Facebook or LinkedIn), though numbers do matter (Rainie & Wellman, 2012). It is more about building systems that make it possible to gain the greatest value in a particular learning context. A small network of the right people is far more valuable than a large network of those who will not provide much help, although it is true that the chances of finding that small network are higher if we are more networked in general.

The looser aggregation of networks compared to groups leads to its own set of design problems. Networks do not, by definition, involve the same levels of commitment and purpose that define groups, do not have the same social hierarchies and structures that bring comfort and security in groups, and are less tightly controlled and defined. Indeed, most do not even have a name and, when they do, it is a label more than a definitional term.

Design to Encourage Participation

Unlike groups, there are seldom external structures and social clusterings that drive the membership in learning networks. While membership in a group may be the precursor for the formation of a computer system to support it, networks tend to arise through participation from the ground up. It is certainly possible to intentionally seed a network, but it is usually not so easy to define its membership in advance. It is therefore important for any software and surrounding systems designed to support networks to pay close attention to making participation (as well as ending participation) as easy and painless as possible.

Some aspects of encouraging people to join a network are mainly a marketing concern: if the intention is to seed its growth, the purpose of the network should be clearly stated, well-advertised in the right places and, more than anything, the *right* people should be encouraged to join, remembering both Reed's law and Metcalfe's law: individuals should be well-connected, well-known, or both. Some are a matter of design for applications to support the network:

- Make the process of joining clear: make the joining and login process simple and well-signposted;
- Make the process of joining simple: use of OpenID, Facebook Connect, simple forms, or progressive engagement. (Porter, 2008, p. 93)

Design to Encourage People to Stay

While much of the dynamics of a network application are determined by the interactions of people within it, there are many things that may be done to make it more likely that networks will persist and thrive. Techniques such as sending push reminders about new content via email, notifications when a user's content has been "liked" or commented upon, tools such as recommendation or referral systems to sustain network growth, and above all, making compelling content easy to find can help here.

Design for Change

Evolution occurs as much in groups as in networks but, commonly, the evolution of groups is an intentional process that at least passes through, if it is not derived from, the higher hierarchical levels of control within. In the network, the meaning of the word "evolution" begins to shift far closer to the specialized Darwinian notion of the term.

CONCLUSION

In this chapter we have seen that, though some of the tools may be shared in common with groups, networks are a very different social form, one that is fuzzy, bursty, emergent, and unbounded. Central to this difference is that fact that networks impose different and fewer structures and methods on their members, which means that they play a far more significant role in determining their own course of learning. Perhaps ironically, this most centrally social of forms is focused almost entirely on the individual and that individual's relations with others in the network.

6

LEARNING IN SETS

While the network has proved to be a useful structural principle and, in a minimal technical sense, underlies every social form enabled by the Internet and other networked technologies, and groups are well founded in practice and literature, they are not always the most useful way to look at the social structures that emerge in cyberspace. Sometimes we do not know people in any meaningful way, so "network" is too strong a word for our engagement, and sometimes we are not members of shared groups, yet people can make a big difference to our learning. In this chapter we will describe how the set, a simple aggregate of people and the artifacts they produce, can provide meaningful learning opportunities and how it differs from group and net social forms. Unlike previous chapters on nets and groups, there is not a copious bounty of literature to call upon that discusses sets because few, if any, researchers have explored their use in a learning context.

This is uncharted ground, and much of what we write here will be relatively new in academic literature, though the set has not gone unnoticed by the blogging community and popular press, nor by millions of users of social media. Eldon (2011), for example, observes that set-oriented social interest sites such as Twitter, Tumblr, and Pinterest have experienced massive growth. These are still often inaccurately referred to as "interest-based social networks" (Jamison, 2012): just as early network-oriented applications were called as "groupware," there is a tendency to see systems through the lenses of what we are familiar with, and we are currently familiar with social networks. Though under-researched as a social form, especially for learning, sets are important. It is not accidental that relational database technologies used to store and retrieve information about people and things in the world are based on sets, because categories matter, both to people and machines. To a significant extent, the ways that we categorize the world shape our experience of it, and represent what we know of it (Hofstadter, 2001; Lakoff, 1987; Wittgenstein, 1965). We do not just *know*. We know *things*, which fit into categories, and this is important. As Lakoff (1987) puts it, "Without the ability to categorize, we could not function at all, either in the physical world or in our social and intellectual lives" (p. 6). Categories according to Lakoff, were classically seen as things 'in the world' that we could simply identify through their common properties. Wittgenstein (1965) both problematized the issue and slightly side-stepped it by suggesting that, for at least some of the categories that we use, this is simply not true. Instead there are family resemblances in which things we identify through a single category may share some but never all of the same properties, and the boundaries that we put around particular categories are not fixed but socially constructed. More recently, thinkers such as Lakoff and Hofstadter (2001) have shown the deep psychological, social and linguistic complexity of the ways that we categorize things, showing how metaphorical meanings are not just a feature of language but fundamental to understanding, without which we would be unable to build cognitive models of the world around us. Categories allow us to symbolically represent collections of things in ways that are meaningful to our social, intellectual, and practical needs, while letting us extend our understanding across fuzzy boundaries, making connections and drawing analogies from which we construct our knowledge. In many ways, knowing the right names of things is a crucial step towards understanding them. This has an important pragmatic consequence in the context of the current enquiry: when seeking to learn, especially in academic disciplines, we typically begin by thinking of topics, areas, or categories into which our new knowledge can be classed and named.

DEFINING THE SET

Sets as a social form are made up of people with shared attributes. There are indefinitely many attributes that may be shared by individuals, which may be specific or relate to coming within a range of values: location, height, IQ, choice of automobile, and so on. Most of these attributes will be of little value to a learner, but some might. In learning, particularly useful set attributes might include a shared interest in a topic, a shared location, a qualification in a particular subject area, or a shared outlook.

In order to be useful, it should be possible to identify a set and to interact or share with people in it. In this sense, there is a minimal requirement for a mechanism for sharing and communicating with others in a set. Like groups and nets, sets rely on a substratum in which they are situated and observable.

Sets are About Topics and Themes

The notion of the set bridges both people and things. For instance, one may find resources that are part of the set of writings about networked learning, as well as people with an interest in networked learning. The social form of the set simply refers to any collection of people, and in a learning setting this is often related to artifacts that they produce or seek. In typical cases, what causes us to identify the set is the topic, artifact, place, or site around which they aggregate.

A concrete example of this is a page on Wikipedia. While groups and networks can and do develop around Wikipedia pages, the central thing that draws people to both edit and read a Wikipedia article is an interest in the topic it addresses. Beyond that, there need be no social engagement, no direct communication, no exchange of information, not even a shared purpose. The boundaries of this particular social set are the page, and beyond that boundary is everything else. While networks and groups may develop in support of topics and pages, and various inducements are provided by the site to reveal one's identity, such as greater editing rights, the ability to move articles or participate in elections, they are not a necessary feature of engagement with others on Wikipedia.

People may simply be identified by IP address which can be entirely anonymous (for instance, if an edit is made in an Internet café). This is not an uncommon occurrence. In one survey reported on Wikipedia itself of editors who made 500 or more edits (placing them among the most prolific), 5 out of 67 editors were identified only by IP address, not name (en.wikipedia.org/wiki/User:Statistics#Case_1:_Anon_Surprise.21). In 2005, Voss found that, across different language sites, anonymous edits accounted for between 10% (Italy) and 44% (Japan) of all edits made. It is notable, however, that it is increasingly difficult to find such statistics in recent research papers. The strong academic focus on networking in most research publications on social software means that anonymous edits are often deliberately excluded from results of studies (e.g. Nemoto, Gloor, & Laubacher, 2011; Wöhner, Köhler, & Peters, 2011) which tells us more about the biases of researchers than the nature of Wikipedia.

Similarly, when we create hashtags for public posts in Twitter, they are a signal that defines a set for anyone with an interest in the topic defined by that hashtag. When we search for such a hashtag, we rarely have any particular interest in or knowledge of the people that created it: they are just a set of people who have tweeted about that topic. Of course, Twitter supports a profound net form as well with the mechanism of following but, through the hashtag, it is equally powerful as a means to support sets.

Individual Identities are Seldom Important

Identities of people that are revealed in sets may be hidden, anonymous or, even where they are revealed, of relatively little consequence to others in the set. Those who engage in sets are typically more concerned with the subject than the identities of the people that constitute them. One of the characteristics that tends to be indicative of a set mode of interaction in cyberspace is that names of participants, if available at all, are often abbreviated to usernames, without the associated translations into real names or profiles found in networked and group modes of engagement. This does not mean that everyone in a set is unknown: sets overlap with networks and groups. We may participate in a set with people we recognize and people we do not know, and we may come to know people by their consistent pseudonyms. However, most of the time, the identity of the individual, even when known, is not the most important factor when engaging on a set-oriented social system.

Sets are seldom bound by temporal constraints, nor do they demand the use of particular tools or technologies, though both can be important in certain contexts: without the means to discover things, it would be hard to put them into sets. In the broadest sense, sets are found within networks and groups. Indeed, groups and nets can always be viewed as sets, and subsets of sets. A group is a set of people who are members of the group, and a network is a set of people who are in some way connected with one another through direct or indirect links. Similarly, one may find sets of groups, sets of nets and, of course, sets of sets.

Sets are not Technologies

At their simplest, sets are simply assemblages of people with shared attributes. They have borders that are defined by the categories that make them, but while the process of categorization might be considered vaguely technological, this stretches the definition of "technology" further than we would like. There are therefore no innate technologies that are required to engage as a set. Having said that, there are many ways that technologies can play a role in establishing, forming, and facilitating a set, beyond simply providing a real or virtual place where people with shared attributes may congregate. Tools like search engines, tagging systems, databases, and classification tools sometimes play a key role in making set modes of engagement possible in the first place. Such tools often take the place or augment the capacity of a human to organize and classify people and things.

Why Distinguish Sets from Nets?

The reason for distinguishing the set is twofold. In the first place, the ways in which we interact are different when the attribute(s) forming the set matters, rather than the people with whom we engage or the mission of the group. In the second place, the operations we can perform on sets are quite different from those that we perform on networks and groups, a factor of great significance when we come to talk of collectives. Many collectives are the result of set-based aggregations and transformations.

THE BENEFITS OF ANONYMITY

In some cases, the lack of an easy way to identify an individual who is learning in a set may be beneficial, especially when dealing with sensitive topics that require him or her to reveal things that may be uncomfortable or embarrassing. This may be due to the nature of the topic under discussion. For example, many medical sites, counselling sites, and sites relating to socially difficult things that people do not always want to reveal to their networks or groups take on the set social form. This is even true where the site appears to use the same tools and processes as a network or group site, simply because of the extensive use of more anonymous identities. In other cases, the value of anonymity in the set lies in selective disclosure. Self-determination theory suggests that there are three pre-conditions for intrinsic motivation in a learning task: feeling in control, feeling competent, and feeling relatedness with others (Deci & Ryan, 1985). If people are concerned about their level of competence, then fear of negative reactions from peers and teachers may reduce their inclination to share, leading to a vicious circle of doubt that undermines confidence, contribution, and motivation. In a group setting, one of the roles of a teacher is to reduce that sense of doubt, to offer encouragement and positive reinforcement to build confidence.

In a network, that safety net is often lost, because things released into the network may be seen beyond their original context. The products of learning are usually safe to reveal, but the process may be less so. Where anonymity is allowed, fear of disclosure will be lower. However, this is a double-edged sword, and there is a fine balance between the gains and losses that will vary according to context. Anonymity also reduces the significance of social capital (Nemoto et al., 2011) and the benefits of knowing one's peers, as well as feeling pride in a job well done that is recognized by a peer group, thereby reducing motivation on the axis of relatedness. If contributions are truly anonymous (as they are in, say, an anonymous Wikipedia page edit), rather than simply anonymized (as they are when pseudonyms are used on a question-and-answer site) then there are no opportunities to gain social capital by merging set-based interactions into net-based interactions.

IDENTITY AND THE SET: TRIBAL UNDERPINNINGS

While in many cases, membership in a set may have no significant impact on an individual and there are many ways to be a member of a set without even being aware of it, there are also many forms of set membership that are central to a person's identity. Race, gender, nationality, (dis)ability, sports team supported, fashion preference, profession, religion, and so on are crucial to a person's sense of being in the world and, much like a group (and unlike in a net), those who self-identify with a set may identify people outside it as "other." On some occasions, such identity is of little or no consequence: for instance, we may feel a distant kind of camaraderie that makes us wave or honk our horns when we see someone else driving the same kind of car or riding the same kind of bicycle. On other occasions, identification with a set means much more. The starting point for understanding this lies, obtusely, in the realm of groups and group dynamics.

E.O. Wilson (2012) suggested that group evolution has played a large role in our development as a species, and thus we depend on identifying with sets of others, or tribes we belong to. For Wilson, the dual driving forces that form us—individual survival and things done for the good of the group—determine our ethics and social being. The sociality of our species places emphasis on survival as a characteristic of the tribe, band, or larger group rather than the individual. In modern societies, this evolved aspect of our being has become more complex because we do not see ourselves as part of a single set but, typically, of many. Cross-cutting cleavages, diverse sets that intersect across many axes (S. E. Page, 2011), mean that we may feel a sense of identity with more than one set of people—a football team, a nation, a set of people with particular abilities or disabilities, and so on. A heavy metal fan who sees another person wearing a t-shirt advertising their favourite band may treat them as a member of the same "tribe," making assumptions about other shared attributes that relate to lifestyle, preferences, and behaviours, though those people may also be supporters of hockey teams, believers in a particular religion, or other sets that are also meaningful to their identity and create feelings of allegiance. Likewise, those wearing religious symbols such as crosses, turbans, veils, or beads may signify not just membership in a set of religious iconography-wearers but also a complete ethical, social, aesthetic, cultural, ontological, and epistemological outlook, as well as being parts of other sets. Of course, religious tribes do not simply relate to identity but often drift into group-modes of social organization, with hierarchies, prescribed behaviours, and rules of membership—the borders are blurred and variable.

Tribes are equally prominent in academia (Becher & Trowler, 2001): people are self-categorized by and identify with others sharing subject areas, uses of methodologies, schools of thought, interests in particular topics, past membership of institutions, classes of qualification, and many more attributes. Some sets are viewed by their members as mutually exclusive despite cross-cutting cleavages such as shared membership of institutions or professional bodies. What to an outsider may seem like remarkably similar things can be the cause of tribal divisions, to the extent that different languages evolve around them. For example, those who make use of activity theory are typically looking at the same things and using the same words with very similar purposes to those who employ actor network theory, yet seldom do the two tribes meet, and if they do, there are many ways they misunderstand one another. The mutually exclusive sets we belong to, though intersecting with other sets that cross those borders can lead to conflict, creative or otherwise. If they were completely isolated from one another then it would be of no consequence, but the cross-cutting cleavages bring them into juxtaposition.

Tribal sets, which involve many different attributes and a sense of membership, are potentially powerful social forms for organizing, motivating, and coordinating activities of members. Membership in a tribe can help create social confidence: knowing that others in a set share common beliefs or attributes can help to reduce the fear of the unknown that may beset those engaging with an unknown community. Conversely, they carry many associated risks when compared to sets that relate to a single attribute. That strong sense of identification can lead to heightened emotions when those who disagree are involved, especially thanks to the naturally anonymous or impersonal modes of engagement that tend to be found in sets. For instance, challenges to religious or political beliefs, criticisms of bands, sports teams or even tastes for certain cellphones can lead to harmful and bitter flame wars. This is one occasion where a transition from set to more interactive nets or group modes is not always helpful.

The social form of the set resembles that of the net in many ways, but without the social constraints where actions of others can strongly affect learning. Sets offer the greatest freedom of choice of any of the forms (Figure 6.1), though it is important to note that this does not necessarily equate to greater control, because too many choices without guidance or the means to make critical decisions is not control at all (Garrison & Baynton, 1987).

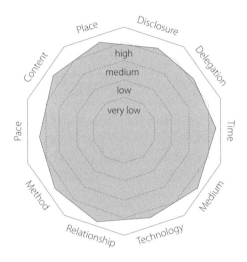

Figure 6.1 Notional cooperative freedoms in sets.

Place

Like all cyberspace learning, there are usually few limits on where a set-based learner can learn. However, there may be some constraints that depend on the attribute chosen to form the set itself, notably where geographical proximity is a significant factor.

Content

There are few limits on content in a set, and most revolve around content: people who are interested in x, people who know about y, people in a place. However, a major issue affecting all set-based learning is that it is not always easy to find the appropriate classification scheme to define the set in the first place. There are an indefinite number of ways to categorize anything, and it is an active, learned, social behaviour to do so (Lakoff, 1987; S. E. Page, 2008). The learner is often faced with a "chicken or egg" problem of not knowing which classifications relate to what he or she needs to learn, because he or she does not know what classifications are applied within a given domain.

Pace

There are virtually no constraints over pace in set-based learning, save for those that are intrinsic to the nature of a particular set. For example, those with an interest in sunsets may have limited opportunities or interest in gathering at other times of the day, and the set of those who attend a particular event will not exist long before or after the event.

Method

There are virtually no constraints over choice of method in set-based learning. However, it is very much up to the learner to choose the learning methods that are appropriate, and without much control over delegation, the difficulties for learners lie in finding appropriate methods.

Relationship

Sets are typically highly diffuse and impersonal, even though there is total freedom to choose with whom one may interact. Sets are often conduits into the more personal and social forms of engagement of nets and groups, however.

Technology

The main technology constraints in set-based learning are those of compatibility: the set exists in a particular technological environment or a constrained range of environments. There are therefore constraints imposed by the chosen instantiation of any given set: in order for the set to form, it needs a technological substrate to take hold in, and unlike a network, there cannot be alternative channels to a set that are not provided by its aggregator. That said, it is possible for individuals to amalgamate sets from multiple sources, in effect creating a set of sets or, maybe more accurately, a network of sets. Some kinds of set instantiation demand certain types of technology in order for the set to be visible: those that can aggregate, such as tagging or folksonomy systems, or those that can be aware of location, for example. In certain cases, technologies may determine or at least partially determine the set: owners of iPhones, for example, or those who use a particular app.

Medium

Medium form is irrelevant to set-based learning, unless the medium itself defines it, as in a set of writings, videos, songs, or media-constrained attributes such as colour or loudness. A set can, in principle, consist of any number of different media with shared attributes such as subject or theme.

Time

Because sets are about attributes of people and things, there are few if any time constraints affecting engagement in a set.

Delegation

While it may be possible to find people who are interested in something—a piece of software, a place, an idea, and so on—it is not always easy to sort out the valuable from the peripheral, misleading, or useless. Without even the social capital available in networks to guide people in a set, all content and dialogue is potentially suspect, and lacking other mechanisms, either net- or collective-based, there is no one to whom control can reliably be delegated. Sets provide a lot of choices, but the information required to exercise those choices may be limited.

Disclosure

The relative anonymity of sets means that people making use of them are able to retain some measure of anonymity and, on the whole, can be extremely selective about what they disclose and to whom. Having said that, sets only have value insofar as people *do* disclose knowledge and information, so while personal disclosure is highly controllable, it is necessary for people to reveal information in order for them to function at all.

TRANSACTIONAL DISTANCE AND CONTROL IN SETS

In a set, everyone is equally distant from everyone else in terms of communication, unless it is formed around a teaching presence: for instance, a Khan Academy tutorial creates a very high transactional distance between the tutorial creator and the learner who is using it, though this can be reduced if the creator of the tutorial engages in activities designed to feign a type of interaction by, for example, asking questions of oneself as if they originated from a live student or engaging in asynchronous discussions around the video tutorial. In such a case, that particular interaction drifts firmly into the networked social form with known individuals, albeit held together by weak and transitory ties in dialogue with one another. Within the set itself—that is, the people who are the discussants in the tutorial— transactional control, in the sense of the learner's ability to choose what to do next, is absolute: a set is defined by intentional engagement around a topic. While there may be some dependencies on whether or not a reaction is forthcoming when a problem or concern is posted to a set, sets are decided upon and identified by the learner, who is free to seek people with shared interests. There is neither the overt or implicit coercion of the group, nor the social coercion of the network.

Dialogue is, in most senses, freely possible and strongly encouraged, and therefore the *communication* aspect of transactional distance between learners in the set is very low, though it can vary considerably in intensity and volume and, like in the net, become a distributed aggregate value. For example, an online forum or bulletin board makes the process of exchanging messages very straightforward and largely unconstrained. However, the *psychological* gulf between one learner and another is typically very high, because those in the set may neither know nor care much about one another. While caring can be an important attribute in both group and net social forms, in a set the person as a distinct human individual seldom matters at a personal level. If they are visible at all, people often become ciphers, anonymous or near-anonymous agents with which to interact. Most importantly, the great number of choices available to set users does not always equate to control. Whether sufficient help is given with making choices or not depends on the nature of the others in the set, the topic, the degree of familiarity that the learner has with it, and many other factors. Transactional *control* may therefore not be as great as the number of choices suggest. Transactional distance in the set is a complex phenomenon that, as in the net, is difficult to pin down.

LEARNING IN SETS

Sets and Focused Problem-Solving

Sets are most useful to learners who are fairly sure of what they wish to know or at least the broad area of interest. Much set-based learning occurs "just in time," concerned with finding out something of value to the learner now, rather than a continuing path. For instance, we may visit Wikipedia, a Q&A site, or Twitter in order to discover an answer from the set of people who have posted on this topic to a question or perhaps establish a starting point for further investigation.

Sets and Focused Discovery

Another common use of sets is to maintain knowledge and currency in a topic or area of interest. For instance, we may subscribe to a feed on a site such as Reddit or Slashdot in order to get a sense of the buzz around a certain topic. The majority of people who use such sites are not actively engaged with the network, but visit or subscribe to them because of an interest in the areas that they discuss. Because such sites are socially enabled, we may contribute ideas, pose problems, seek clarification, and use the other contributors to construct our knowledge, thus helping us to become experts within a subject area, not just to find answers to particular questions or suit specific needs.

Sets and Serendipitous Discovery

Beyond that, just as we find overlapping networks, we also find overlapping sets. It is a rare set-based interaction that keeps within the precise limits of the topic of interest, because people have many and diverse interests, often revealed through exposure to cross-cutting cleavages. Thus, as we find with networks, sets sometimes provide opportunities for serendipitous discovery beyond the immediate area of interest. This is frequently enhanced through the use of collectives, especially by recommender systems that suggest other articles, posts, or discussions that may be of interest.

Another way that sets can aid serendipitous discovery is when we spot trends or patterns in behaviour. For example, if one were sitting indoors and noticed that everyone outside was using an umbrella, he or she can learn from the set that it is raining. Similar things happen online: an aggregated RSS feed, for instance, might contain multiple versions of a trending story, which might therefore pique one's interest. We may discover in a set-based conversation subtleties and areas of interest in a subject we were not formerly aware of. There are subtle blurs here, however, between sets, nets, and collectives. Such trends may be spread through social networks as memes, or be generated automatically by aggregators that combine set behaviours and that, consequently, drive the trend.

Sets and Multiple Perspectives

The vastness of cyberspace means it is rare to find only one site or page connected to a particular set. Topics are typically represented in different ways in various places and often present multiple perspectives, points of view, and ontologies, going far beyond the diversity found in nets (where we might see bias due to affiliation and similarity with others to whom we are connected). This has value in many ways. Every learner is different from every other, with different prior knowledge and experience and different preferences for learning, so the presence of multiple perspectives makes it more likely that one or more will fit with cognitive needs.

Perhaps more significantly, multiple perspectives require learners to make judgments, choose between alternative views, or reconcile them. This active process of sense-making is one of the cornerstones of connectivist approaches to learning: differences are embraced and nurtured because the result is a richer connection and more deeply embedded learning. Differences require us to establish our own points of view, and to better know why we hold them. Multiple perspectives also broaden our outlook, enabling us to see connections that a single point of view, such as one we gain from an intentional teacher, may obscure. For example, to one individual, the set of things connected with e-learning may be limited to what can be found on the World Wide Web, whereas to another it covers any computer-enabled learning activity, while for yet another it refers to pedagogies of cyberspace. By combining these perspectives, a learner may find a valuable intersection or broaden his or her outlook and discover other related issues and areas of interest. The flip side of this benefit is that, much as in a net, it is up to the learner to make sense of conflicting views that he or she discovers. This can be a powerful and creative learning opportunity or, if the area is new or complex, may increase confusion and reduce motivation.

Sets can Support Formal Learning

Sets are of value as part of an individual's self-paced learning journey, even in a formal setting. For example, at Athabasca University, undergraduate students start work on courses at any time and follow their own schedules within a six-month contract period. They seldom know other students in their course, and though the course itself is highly structured and led by tutors and teachers, the social form for student-student interaction is far more akin to a set than that of a group. There are few social interactions, no process-driven group engagement, few social norms, and few (if any) rules of engagement with other course members. They are not a cohort. They are just a collection of people bound together by the attribute of working over the same period on the same course. While students are not directly working with others or at the same time as others, they often benefit from the presence of others either directly (through contributions to question and answer sites), or through artifacts that others have shared. Course discussion forums provide both a repository of prior questions and answers, and a place to pose and answer such questions, though in our experience we find that set-based learners rarely engage in extended discussions. We should observe that, though very close to sets, these are tribal groups: there are still norms, expectations, and regulations as well as membership exclusions that make them set-like groups rather than pure sets.

BREADTH VERSUS DEPTH

Broad sets are useful when learning is exploratory and the questions themselves may be unknown. A set of students in an Athabasca University course or a subscriber to an RSS feed from a popular gadget review site will be open to a broad number of ideas and content that fall within a range determined by the shared attribute. At the other end of the spectrum, a person in search of an answer to a single question may turn to a social set-oriented site such as Wikipedia for answers that rely on the set's specificity, or a site that is so broad there is likely to be someone who knows the answer to any question. For a specific problem, the perfect set would be the global set of everyone. However, it is important that the two sets—people with specific problems and people willing and able to give specific answers—intersect, and that they can find each other. Where a site or service is specific and narrow, this is achieved by being in the same virtual location. For a more general purpose site, it is common for experts to classify themselves into sets, and/or for the site itself to be divided by classifications, often hierarchically organized or with a folksonomic, tag-based approach for identifying subsets. Once again, search engines play an important role in filtering out specific subsets of interest.

CATEGORIES OF THINGS

Sets are defined by shared characteristics. They are communities of homophily. Sometimes they are intentional, and sometimes they are latent in what is shared. For example, as I look out of my window now, I see a set of people who are currently sharing the same general space as me. Most are pedestrians walking by with whom I do not and will never share a connection beyond, at this moment, being in a shared space. However, if some event occurred (perhaps a whale poking its head out of the water) then that attribute of shared space may become significant because it would enable learning to occur. We would probably talk about what we were seeing and, in the process, learn. Someone might identify the whale, someone else might mention previous sightings, and another might say how unusual it is to see one in these waters. Others, seeing the set of people gathering and sharing the attribute of staring at the whale, might come and join us, perhaps contributing to the shared learning moment. For a transient few minutes, we would become a learning community, ad hoc and fleeting. When the whale leaves, the significance of the space recedes. Some may perhaps make connections and become networked as a result, but as a collection of people learning together, our shared context would no longer matter. In rare cases, the set may even coalesce into a group that continues to gather at other times and locations as whale watchers. Similar processes happen all the time across cyberspace.

We search for answers and solutions based on their attributes such as subject, keywords, and tags, or explore topics in Wikipedia, brushing against those with shared interests, knowledge, and learning, and then moving on. Indeed, a set-based way of learning has been the norm since the invention of writing. As soon as the volume of available material became impossible for one human to track, we relied on classification systems to discover books, papers, and reports, and latterly other forms of media. Writers, especially of non-fiction, have a set of attributes in mind when writing books: subject, expected level of ability, background, language and so on define the sets for whom something is written. The same is true for all media used for learning.

CATEGORIES AND TAXONOMIES

Categories are ways of putting things into sets and are one of our primary means of sense-making. To a large extent, how we think is determined by how we categorize the world (Lakoff, 1987). Our categories evolve as we learn. Expertise can be seen as an increased ability to both ignore attributes that are insignificant and to subdivide things that, to non-experts, appear to occupy the same categories (S. E. Page, 2008). Some of the work of a teacher is involved with helping learners to identify and focus on categories that are significant in a subject or skill being taught, to see both big patterns and small distinctions. Traditionally, categorizations of learning content tended to be performed by trained or otherwise knowledgeable individuals who would classify books, papers, journals, and media for easy discovery and organization. The builders of taxonomies created ordered sets of things, sorting them into easily identified clusters and groupings.

For the most part, taxonomies have a tendency to be hierarchical. It is no accident that ontologies used in the Semantic Web, though capable of taking any network form, are typically hierarchical in nature as they refer to sets, subsets, and further subsets of objects that are relatively easy for both humans and computers to navigate and understand. However, the world is not always so easily categorized. Many sets intersect, and connections are often more in a network structure than a hierarchy. For this reason, faceted approaches to classification, browsing, and navigation have gained much ground in recent years. Faceted classification allows objects, people, or data to be classified in any number of "facets" from which different combinations of set attributes can be selected for various classification purposes. Ranganathan's facets (2006) have found particular favour in the library community, offering a structured schema that takes full advantage of the intersection of multiple sets to find things we seek. Although it can cause difficulties when allocating objects in a physically ordered space such as library shelves, a faceted classification scheme lends itself well to computer-based organization. Perhaps more significantly from a learner perspective, facets provide ways of seeing the same things differently. By breaking out of a networked or hierarchical model of thinking, facets encourage a set-based view of the world where multiple orientations can be explored. If experts define such facets, then they offer a means of seeing the world from the perspective of different experts. However, when defined by a diverse crowd, facets may actually offer greater value.

S. E. Page (2008) argues, using fundamental logic and empirical data, that a random set of people will frequently provide better problem-solving in aggregate than a set of experts because of the greater diversity of perspectives, heuristics, interpretations, and predictive models they share. For Page, interpretations equate loosely to categorizations—they are ways of dividing up the world by lumping things together. Combined with predictive models, they provide a means of describing the world and, more significantly, taking effective actions. On the social web, interpretations are reified in the form of tags, metadata supplied by creators and users of content that help others to interpret and discover sets. In combination, the aggregate of such tagging is known as a folksonomy (Vander Wal, 2007).

FOLKSONOMIES

The growth of social media has concurrently seen the growth of a bottom-up method of faceted classification in the form of social tagging, whereby any resource (bookmarks, photos, videos, blogs, and so on) is tagged by one or more individuals. A machine to enable discovery of similarly tagged resources that others can find aggregates their classifications. These folksonomies define sets of things with shared attributes most commonly known as tags, and they can be used to guide a learning journey. Because of the diversity of interpretations of the world that such tags represent, they are a powerful way for learners to identify and explore both the vocabulary associated with a given subject area and the different ways that the area is conceptualized. Anticipating our discussion of the power of the collective in the next chapter, when combined in a weighted list such as a tag cloud where tags that are more frequently used are shown with greater weight through visual cues such as size, font, or colour, they can indicate not just the range of interpretations of the world that the crowd uses but also the relative importance of such interpretations in aggregate. Kevin Kelly has identified tags and the hyperlink as the two most important inventions of the last 50 years (2007, p. 75).

There are many set-oriented uses of tags in which learners help others to learn. Twitter hashtags help us to find discussions, snippets of knowledge, and hyperlinks to further resources from which we may learn. Flickr Commons (http://flickr.com/commons/) is an exercise in mass tagging, involving tens of thousands of people categorizing public domain photos for the benefit of themselves and others, allowing users to easily find relevant photos in huge collections. The cataloguing and discovery of images is a wickedly complex problem, because even the simplest of holiday snaps can be categorized in an indefinite number of ways (Enser, 2008). The social tagging in Flickr Commons is a great example of how a large, anonymous set of people can create value for others without any kind of social interaction. Some photos in the public domain collection have been tagged thousands of times, with tags identifying people, places, objects, themes, subjects, concepts, colours, and hundreds of other attributes that may be used to split objects into sets. Bookmark sharing sites such as Delicious, Furl, and Diigo are heavily dependent on tags that people provide to categorize websites of interest according to topic.

As well as enabling the set to help its members make sense of the world interpreted by others, the act of tagging itself is a metacognitive tool that encourages the tagger to think about the things that matter to him or her, helping the process of sense-making, embedding reflection in the process of creation, and thus enhancing learning (Argyris & Schön, 1974). This process may be aided by systems that suggest additional tags, previously applied by others, similar to tags first chosen, which helps to decrease a potential multiplicity of synonyms from becoming tags, but also limits variability with both positive and negative results. We will return to other downsides of tagging later in this chapter.

There are many tools available that offer and enhance set-like modes of learning. Typically, most set-oriented applications are not exclusively dedicated to the set, also providing tools to branch into networks and, in some cases, groups. We describe a few of the main examples of the genre below in order to provide a sense of the range of tools and systems that can be used in set-oriented learning.

Listservs, Usenet News, Open Forums, and Mailing Lists

For decades before the invention of the World Wide Web, people engaged in posting on bulletin boards, anonymous FTP servers, newsgroups, and other topic-oriented services with great enthusiasm. Though many of these developed into rich networked and group communities, with emergent or imposed hierarchies and complex economies driven by social capital, several others celebrated open engagement around subjects and themes without significant social ties. Such services are still very common today in the form of social interest sites—Pinterest, Wikia, and learn.ist being prime examples—sites dedicated to different kinds of software and hardware, and many more.

Socially-augmented Publications

It is rare to find any form of publication in the wild that does not allow some level of anonymous user interaction—newspapers, magazines, public blogs, and the like, all offer engagement at a public level, frequently anonymous or where the identity of the person making comments is irrelevant, concealed, or ambiguous. There is a fine dividing line between the anonymous set orientation of these and the networked mode of engagement, and many combine the two. Sometimes, networks are explicit in trackbacks, where one blog comment leads to a different blog site, or through engagement in a conversation by known individuals. Much of the time, the comments are from people that no one else in the dialogue knows, nor wishes to know.

Tags, Categories, and Tag Clouds

Folksonomic classification, where bottom-up processes are used to tag content, are archetypally set-oriented. When using tags to find content, our concern is not with the individuals who create them but with the topics that they refer to. Hashtags in Twitter, tags in Delicious, Flickr, and many other systems provide a set-oriented way of cooperative resource discovery. Sometimes, sites will use a combination of top-down categories and bottom-up folksonomies. For instance, Slashdot, Reddit, Digg, and StackOverload provide ranges of common topic areas around which posts occur.

Search Terms

When we enter a search term into a search engine, we are typically seeking a set of things that share the attributes of the keywords or phrases we enter. What we get back, if all has gone well, is a list of items where others have used those terms. Thus, the search engine mediates between creator and seeker, enabling a simple form of one-to-one dialogue between them. However, the intentions of the creator may be very far removed from the intentions of the seeker, even when he or she is skilled in the art of searching. Unfortunately, as we have already observed, expertise is in part a result of being able to use categories effectively and a learner will be unlikely to know which terms are most appropriate to his or her needs in a novel field of interest. The sets returned, in such cases, may be highly tangential and confusing. For example, if a learner enters a search for "evolution" with the intention of learning more about the theory, then the list of results are likely to include many ideologically driven creationist sites (often deliberately manipulated through search-engine optimization to appear on the list), sites using the word in the pre-Darwinian sense (like the evolution of a design or concept), a film by Charlie Kaufman, a number of beauty products, and plenty more results of little value. Like the tag, the search term is highly susceptible to various forms of ambiguity. Unlike most tagging systems, search terms may be refined. A search for "Darwin's theory of evolution" will result in a more focused set of results, but again, the anonymity of the set will mean that the learner is in conversation with not only evolutionary theorists and historians but also creationists. Bearing in mind that our hypothetical learner knows little or nothing about evolution, this places him or her in great danger. Without a theoretical framework to understand the manifold weaknesses and failings of the creationist point of view, he or she may learn inaccurate ideas that will make understanding the correct theory more difficult. Complexity theorists might view the potential range of useful and less useful results as a rugged landscape: there are many possible solutions or "peaks" that may be fit for the purpose, but climbing one (even a low one), will make it significantly harder to move from there to a higher, more useful peak (Kauffman, 1995).

While most search engines follow the logic of the set in an abstract sense, many make use of the set of people more explicitly in algorithms that mine similarities between searchers. Some, such as Google's use of PageRank, also use networks to help provide relevant results. We shall return to this powerful use of the set in our chapter on collectives.

Social Interest Sites and Content Curation

Sites such as Pinterest, Learni.st, Wikia, Scoop.it, etc., allow people to share collections of related content—in brief, sets. Curated content can be created by individuals, groups, and networks as well as sets of people, and can be directly authored and/or collected from elsewhere, but however it is created, it provides a set of resources that are clustered around a topic of interest. Many more general social sites provide tools for the aggregation of content around a topic or theme: YouTube Channels and Facebook Pages, for example, provide thematically organized content where the set is at least as important as the network or group that is associated with it. Though the genre has been common throughout the history of the social net, going back to (at least) Usenet News and bulletin boards, in recent years there has been a significant growth in social curation sites, not to mention sustained growth in older social bookmarking sites like Delicious, Diigo, and Furl, sharing options for personal curation tools like Evernote or Pocket (formerly ReadItLater), and ways of using more general-purpose tools like Facebook Pages or Google Sites to assemble and share information on a topic. Curated sites or areas of sites are concerned with niches—areas of interest that are often very narrow—for instance, food (e.g., Foodspotting.com) or fitness (e.g., Fitocracy. com). While most niche sites can be used by groups and often involve nets, publically available niche sites based around topics are deeply set-based in nature.

The vast majority of niche sites make extensive use of folksonomies for organization, often combined with a more top-down and hierarchical categorization system. From a learning perspective, curated sites combine many of the advantages of a traditional, teacher-created content-based behaviourist-cognitivist learning resource with the added value of sets, and optionally, nets and groups. Social curation sites, as the name implies, embed the ability to tag, rate, discuss, and comment. Not only that, most curated content can be re-curated, mashed up, and aggregated, extending the value by recontexualizing it for different communities and needs. Thus, different kinds of conversation can develop around the same content, new connections can be made between different topic areas, and the value of diverse perspectives and interpretations can be heavily exploited.

Shared Media

Many rich media sites share tutorials and exemplars, some user-generated, some more top-down but with associated discussion or comment options. YouTube, TeacherTube, The Khan Academy, Flickr, Instructables, and many other sites offer rich learning content around which set-oriented discussions and learning can evolve. Media act as anchors for learning a particular topic. Wikis are flagship set-based tools. Wikipedia, Mediawiki Commons, Wiki Educator, and a host of other reference and sharing sites are based around categorized content. While many wikis do support sets and networks, the primary engagement in a wiki is nearly always focused around content rather than social interaction.

Arguably the poster child for set-based learning, Wikipedia is without a doubt the most consulted encyclopedia ever written, and one of the top two tools for learning on the Internet today, the other being Google Search. If ever anyone expresses doubt that online learning has a future, we have only to ask him or her to what they turn to first when seeking to learn something new. In many cases, the answer is "Wikipedia" or "Google Search." Wikipedia organization is complex and highly social, yet it has few identifiable groups and very little in the way of networks. The vast majority of interaction is indirect, mediated through edits to pages by a largely anonymous or unknown crowd; most editing or visiting a page because they are interested in the topic it describes. In other words, they are part of a set with the shared attribute of interest in a topic.

With a similarly vast number of users, YouTube is another set-based system that is extremely popular for a wide range of uses, many educational in nature. Social networking in YouTube is not its main feature, and much of the interaction that occurs is centred on specific videos or clusters of videos (collections) rather than people known to one another. While the number of educational videos on YouTube greatly outnumbers those found on any other site, including Facebook, other similar sites like TeacherTube and SchoolTube provide services that are focused specifically on education. The benefit of such sites is their greater focus on formal learning, making it easier for learners to identify reliable and useful resources without the distractions of Lolcats and music videos. They are niche sites that contain further sub-niches or subsets categorized in ways designed to link learners with content and consequent interaction. Thus, the choice of the site itself acts as a means of classifying and organizing learning resources along set lines.

Locative Systems

Places are attributes shared by people who are in the same location. A wide range of social applications have been designed to take advantage of geographical co-location, from restaurant finders (e.g., Yell, Around-me, Google Latitude), to game playing as a means of discovering one's locale (Geotagging, FourSquare) to cooperative shopping and dining (Groupon). Many mobile apps make use of location information to both discover and post information relating to the locale: FourSquare, Google Latitude, Geotagging, and many more tools allow persistent interactions to occur around a place. Locations thus become augmented by the activities of people who inhabit them, with the location serving as the defining attribute of the set of people who visit geographical spaces.

Augmented Reality

2D bar codes such as Semacode, QR codes, and similar technologies enable physical objects to be tagged. These bar codes are used for advertising, allowing people to snap photos of codes using cellphones or similar devices and receive either small snippets of information, or more commonly, hyperlinks to websites providing further information. While these have some potentially valuable educational applications, they are not usually socially enabled. However, a particularly promising approach to learning as a set in a location is to provide virtual information via cellphone, tablet, or more sophisticated devices such as Google Glass, and to allow people to leave virtual cairns or tags that others may discover in the space if equipped with a suitable device.

Crowdsourcing

A particularly powerful use of sets in learning is found in question-and-answer sites and other approaches to crowdsourcing work, problem-solving, and creative construction. From simple Q&A sites such as Quora to more complex brokerages for skills and services, the crowdsourced solution to learning problems is popular and thriving. Again, many of these sites shift between network and set modes, sometimes intentionally, sometimes seamlessly. For example, Amazon's Mechanical Turk or Innocentive both provide a mediating role between those with problems and those able to provide solutions, typically using set-based characteristics to match the two, and facilitate the exchange of money between the parties. Other systems, such as Yahoo Answers and Quora, are less obviously incentive-driven: while social capital often plays a role, in which case interactions drift toward network-based models, many people contribute answers because they can. Altruism is a deep-seated human characteristic that has evolved in our species: one need look no further than the fact that people frequently risk their own lives to save those of strangers to see this fundamental urge in action (E. O. Wilson, 2012).

One of the most obvious ways to exploit the wisdom of crowds is to ask a question. Assuming the question is meaningful and has a correct answer, there is likely to be someone somewhere in cyberspace who knows it. Two giants of networking have tackled this opportunity in quite different ways.

Yahoo Answers is one of the older user-generated answer sites. Modelled after the wildly successful Korean site Naver Knowledge iN (www.naver.com), Yahoo Answers allows users to post and answer questions with no fees or concrete rewards. Questions and their responses are categorized and lightly filtered to remove obnoxious or nonsensical material. Users provide answers, and the questioner decides or allows the crowd to select the best one. Obviously, the site provides some value to users who can search or browse the archives for answers to relevant questions. Like all social sites, Answers gains value in proportion to the number of users. To support and encourage participation, Yahoo offers "points" for contribution. Five months after its launch in December 2005, Yahoo Answers was publishing nearly a half million questions per month, which generated nearly 4 million answers, an average of 8.25 answers per question (Gyongyi, Pedersen, Koutrika, & Garcia-Molina, 2008).

As in many publicly available sites, Yahoo Answers contains a great deal of "noise," or questions and responses that can charitably be classified as silly or inane. Interestingly, many of the questions seem to be posted to stimulate discussion as much as to obtain a definitive answer. A question posed by the user Gothic Girl illustrates both noise and a discussion stimulator: "What is your favorite food??? (it can be candy too, i say that's food)" received 41 answers! Alternatively, a question by Katie R. in the Math section, "If I calculate the variance of a collection of data to be .235214, does this tell me that there is large variance (that the data is spread out) or that there is relatively little variance?" received a comprehensive answer with examples from a top contributor whose profile explains "by education and profession, I am a statistician."

Rival answer sites such as Answerbag.com and Quora, a more network-oriented Q&A site, are developing rules and practices that attempt to better organize questions and answers and support the development of communities among their members. For example, they allow members to develop searchable profiles and engage in discussion via comments to either questions or comments. Google took a more traditional approach for Google Answers, a more commercially oriented service, allowing users to post bounties between $2 and $200 for solutions. Rafaeli, Raban, and Ravid (2007) analyzed all questions and answers submitted between 2002 and 2004, and found that over half of the 78,000 questions asked were successfully answered with an average payout of $20.10. After four years of operation, Google discontinued accepting questions and answers, and described the project as an interesting experiment. Its failure in the face of Yahoo's continuing success has raised an interesting debate in the blogosphere. It seems that many want to ask questions, a few want to answer, but few want to pay and even fewer want to handle the logistics of accounting, curtailing spam, and all the other issues that challenge Web ventures. This also speaks to the dangers of extrinsic motivation reducing the motivation to answer (Kohn, 1999). It is a very notable feature of most surviving Q&A sites that the rewards are intrinsic, and often provided for completely altruistic reasons, with no hope of even social capital being accrued. In recent years, StackOverload sites have become extremely popular because they offer not only set-based interaction but also a collective-based method of identifying useful answers, organized by those perceived as being the most accurate or beneficial.

The use of answer sites creates an additional option for teachers and learners that provides a more current social resource than more traditional web or print sources. This query of the crowd is however less definitive and reliable than more traditional reference resources including those such as Wikipedia, which garner much more critical and comprehensive review by peers for accuracy, connectiveness, relevance, and authority. Some learners use answer services merely as a means to lighten their workload, and as a consequence, likely diminish their learning by posting homework questions in search of "easy answers." Not surprisingly, this abuse of the crowd has given rise to the DYOH (Do Your Own Homework) movement.

Nonetheless, question and answer sites may prove useful for topical questions where discussion of especially socially constructed issues among answerers may be a forum to generate knowledge not available in more traditional resources. A review of the popular sites also reveals examples of explicit content that would be offensive and inappropriate for many learners.

TeachthePeople.com is another startup site that provides "experts" with server space to which they can upload teaching and learning materials in many formats, into "learning communities." The site shares ad revenues with "teachers" that are dependent upon the number of learners who access the site.

Crowdfunding

Increasingly, learners are funding their learning with the aid of the crowd. Crowdfunding sites for students such as Upstart (www.upstart.com) or Scolaris (www.scolaris.ca) match sets of people interested in funding learners with donors. While many still rely on group forms for this role (governments, families, companies, and so on), the set has proven to be surprisingly effective for connecting those in need with those who wish to give. Because such applications tend to be one-off requests, networks have little or nothing to add, save in helping to verify identity and, occasionally, allowing prospective funders to find out more about students seeking funds.

RISKS OF SET–BASED LEARNING

Reliability

The relative anonymity of sets makes it significantly harder to gain a strong sense of the reliability of content produced by the crowd than it does in groups and networks. The Internet is notoriously filled with distortions, lies, and falsehoods of many kinds, but even when data is accurate and meaningful, it does not mean that it will be of great value to a particular learner at a particular point in his or her learning trajectory. The problem is made worse by the fact that, sometimes, people deliberately mislead or distort the truth.

In the absence of cues such as the presence of advertising, an excess of exclamation marks, or a lack of references, there are three distinct ways that reliability of knowledge gained through sets can be ascertained inherent in the social form. The first is correlation: if more than one similar answer to a problem can be found in a set, then it increases the probability that the answer is reliable. The nature of sets, however, makes this a risky approach, because people in sets influence one another and it is very common for falsehoods to be propagated through and across them, each wrong solution reinforcing those that come before. The second is disagreement: where multiple perspectives and solutions are presented, this typically leads to argument, and by analyzing the strengths and weaknesses of the arguments, the learner can come to a more informed opinion about the correct solution. Disagreement is usually a good thing for learners in sets, because it encourages reflection on the issues and concepts involved, enabling learners to form a more cohesive view of a topic. Third, beyond the inherent capabilities of the social form, other social forms can play an important role in establishing veracity: we may, for instance, trust opinions voiced in our networks, turn to a group for discussion, or as we shall see, make use of the collective to establish reputation or reliability of information provided in the set.

Anonymity

On the whole, the relative anonymity of the set has notable benefits to the learner. There can be greater openness and keenness to participate, especially when topics involve sensitive personal disclosure. Where the crowd is contributing to, editing, and evolving a resource started by others (e.g., a Wikipedia article) the anonymity makes it far easier to make edits because editors are unlikely to feel as beholden to earlier authors as they would in a group or network. When using wikis in a group, we have found that the strong ties, roles, social capital, and the politeness that this leads to can significantly deter members from editing what others have laboured to produce. This may be a particularly strong tendency in the authors' two native countries, Canada and the UK, both known for cultures of politeness, but it seems likely that the more learners know one another, the less inclined they will be to modify one another's work in the peculiarly mediated world of the wiki, at least without extensive use of associated discussion pages or other dialogue options. However, the flip side of relative anonymity is that it makes it more likely for people to be treated impersonally, as ciphers, with feelings that can be ignored or, as we see in the case of Internet trolls, manipulated for fun. From the early days of Usenet News and bulletin boards, we have seen large anonymous communities brought down by flame wars and trolling.

Another drawback of anonymity is that the motivation to participate is significantly lower than in groups or networks. If individuals are not recognized and identifiable, there is sometimes less social capital to be gained, and there is no sense of being beholden to other individuals, either because they are known directly to us or because of the written or unwritten rules of a group. Size can play an important role in overcoming this limitation. Where many people are engaged, such as might be found on a large social site like Twitter or Wikipedia, there are more likely to be others willing to share and participate at any given time. The Long Tail (C. Anderson, 2004) means that someone, somewhere, is likely to share the same concerns, no matter how minor the interest.

THE TROUBLE WITH TAGS

Tags are a useful way to harness the collective wisdom of the crowd, and we will return to more advanced ways that they can be used in the next chapter on collectives. However, folksonomies suffer from a range of related issues and concerns.

Context and Ambiguity

Especially when learning, the meaning of tags may be closely connected with the context of use. The same word in a different context can mean something different, even though the dictionary definition is the same. For example, if an expert tags something as "simple," it means something quite different than if the same term was used by a beginner. Equally, "black" might designate a colour, a race, or a kind of humour, among many other things. "#YEG" is a hashtag commonly used by residents in Edmonton to refer in Twitter posts to the city, yet it also is the designation for the Edmonton International Airport. The word "chemistry" used about an image might refer to the subject of chemistry, or equally to the bond between two lovers in a different context. In some cases, the same word may have multiple distinct meanings in a dictionary. Context is also important when dealing with lexical and syntactic ambiguities where longer descriptions are applied. For example, "Outside of a dog, a book is a man's best friend; inside, it's too hard to read" (attributed to Groucho Marx (van Gelderen, 2010, p. 42)) or "they passed the port at midnight."

Bruza and Song (2000) describe a diverse set of categories that might become tags: S-about (subjective-about, broadly scalar qualities), O-about (objective-about, broad binary classifications), and R-about (contextualized to a group of users). R-about is particularly interesting, as it suggests that different communities may use the same terms differently. This is confirmed by Michlmayr, Graf, Siberski, and Nejdl (2005), who looked at the properties of tags describing bookmarked sites on the Web obtained from Delicious. They postulated that those who bookmarked similar sites and described them with similar tags would share other tags, interests, and perhaps, already belong to, or be interested in developing, existing networks or groups. They found, however, that users who tagged similar sites did not have large intersections of other resources that they tagged. An average of 84% of sites bookmarked by users who share a common site were not bookmarked by other users sharing a common bookmark. Furthermore, they found surprisingly little correlation between folksonomic tags and those developed as a component of the more formal tagging systems developed by the Open Directory Project (www.dmoz.org). This suggests that folksonomic classification may serve personal and perhaps group needs, but beyond showing popularity and tag cloud images, the extent to which inferences can be drawn based on folksonomic tags or the taggers is limited without further examination of context.

Homonymy

Sometimes, especially in English, the same word means more than one thing. These are subcategorized as homographs, heteronyms, and homophones. Homographs are spelled the same but with different meanings: for instance, bat (an animal) and bat (a stick for hitting balls). When the pronunciation is different, they are usually referred to as heteronyms: for instance, "bow" (a ribbon tied in your hair) and "bow" (to lower your head). Equally, homonyms may be homophones (sounding the same but spelled differently), for instance "through" and "threw."

Synonymy

Even where terms are distinct, more than one term may be used to tag the same thing. Some are obvious: for instance, "people," "persons," and "person" refer to very similar resources. Stemming dictionaries and tools like WordNet can deal effectively with such simple cases. In other cases, the words have quite distinct and precise meanings that are not synonymous, but will typically be used to describe the same object: for example, e-learning, online learning, and networked learning, at least for some, refer to the same set of objects. This can be a particular problem when using metonyms—for instance, "Hollywood" to refer to the US film industry and the place where it is most concentrated—where the term is not only a synonym but also is ambiguous.

Binary versus Scalar Tags

Nearly all tag-based systems treat tags as simple binary classifications which, in some instances, are what is needed. However, many tags are fuzzy and constitute fuzzy sets (Kosko, 1994): something may be fun or less fun, red or more red, cute or less cute (Dron, 2008). Golder and Huberman (2006) list seven distinct varieties of tag: identifying what (or who) a resource refers to, identifying what it is, identifying who owns it, refining categories, identifying qualities or characteristics, self-reference, and task organizing. Very few systems, notably those created by author Dron, make use of fuzzy tags that allow degrees of membership in a set (Dron, 2008; Dron, Mitchell, Boyne, & Siviter, 2000). We hope to see more such systems appearing in future, but they are beset by the inevitable complications of entering and using fuzzy tags. Binary tags take little effort to create, and are typically a comma-separated list of words. Fuzzy tags require not only the tag but also its perceived value to be entered, and raise further issues as to how they are presented and aggregated—for instance, should the values be simply averaged, or should there be some form of weighting based on number of uses too? Such problems also beset simple rating systems on, things like review sites, and the solutions are similarly imperfect: showing numbers of ratings separately, for example.

Lack of Correlation

These and other related concerns matter considerably when learning in sets, because a learner may find it harder than an expert to distinguish context and ambiguity, not be aware of relevant synonyms, or fail to observe closely related but distinct homonyms. While it can be argued that the process of discovering such uncertainties is an effective way to become adept in a given subject area, this may equally reduce motivation and increase the time needed to learn something new.

SETS IN THE ONLINE CLASSROOM

Within a formal, group-based educational setting where cohorts of students work in lock-step with one another on shared activities, set-based tools and communities can provide great augmentative value.

While traditionalists throw up their hands in horror at the problems that emerge from students using Wikipedia in traditional courses, citing concerns about reliability, superficiality, and plagiarism, the online encyclopedia has a place in almost any learning transaction. It is a wonderful way to enter into a topic, providing not only a fairly reliable overview (especially in academic topics) but also links, references, and further reading that can greatly assist the exploration of a subject area.

Moreover, many teachers have reported success in encouraging students to make active contributions to the site: they create pages, correct errors, and engage in the often rich discussions that emerge around a particular page. However, volunteer Wikipedia experts have also complained about the mess of forked (or unrelated) articles, and poorly written or incomplete edits that some students have left. In true wiki spirit, there is an editable page on Wikipedia (en.wikipedia. org/wiki/Wikipedia:Assignments_for_student_editors) discussing how to make the most effective use of a Wikipedia article as a writing assignment for students.

Similarly, tutorials available through sites such as the Khan Academy, eHow, WikiHow, HowStuffWorks, provide not only useful supplements to classroom learning but also a chance to engage with others, to see how they conceptualize and mis-conceptualize subjects and topics, and gain a sense of their own knowledge in relation to others. Within a formal setting, the widespread availability of varying quality resources that can take the place of some of the traditional roles of a teacher makes it possible to "flip" the classroom (Strayer, 2007), a term that describes what many teachers have always done: leave content for self-guided homework and concentrate on richer learning activities in the classroom. Content discovery and activities that in more traditional settings form the material of the learning process, whether online or not, can be offloaded to the set, allowing the teacher to concentrate on social knowledge construction processes that are more appropriate to a grouped mode of learning.

Teaching Set Use

We have noted that one of the major problems with set modes of interaction, as well as one of the greatest opportunities, is anonymity. This means that it is vital for users of sets to develop well-honed skills in identifying quality, relevance, and reliability of both people and resources. Teachers in conventional courses can play an important role here, modelling good practice, providing feedback, recommending strategies, and offering opportunities for safe practice.

Self-referentially, the set itself can provide resources and clues about the reliability of information found within it, particularly if it incorporates collective tools that emphasize reputation, provide ratings, or show other visualizations that give hints about the value of a contribution or individual. Even where that is not the case, it is often possible to follow conversations and identify which participants hold the upper hand in controversies or disagreements.

One important role for the teacher wishing to make use of sets is to define or identify relevant vocabularies and narrow down the attributes by which sets are classified. This may simply be a question of sharing vocabularies, identifying relevant search terms, and providing exercises that use the appropriate wording. However, the diversity of views and vocabularies that may be discovered also open up many opportunities to explore the ontological assumptions of a subject area, and much can be gained from comparing and contrasting different ways of seeing the world as a result.

The choice of appropriate sets is an important one, and relates to the purpose and context of the learner. A diverse crowd may be useful in solving some problems and less effective in others. Generally, when learning, a set of experts is better than a random set, or one made up of beginners, or things they come up with will be entirely random. But too narrow a focus may mean they will not meet the needs of the learner. Sometimes, proximal development is an issue. A set of subject experts is probably not useful to help learn the basics of a subject because the vocabulary and assumed knowledge of the set may not just render the subject incomprehensible but actually demotivate the learner. For beginners, it is better to find a set of expert teachers, explainers, demonstrators, and co-learners, each of whom has a certain amount of knowledge. The set will represent a range of perspectives and views of the subject, which together will offer diverse opportunities to connect existing knowledge to new discoveries.

Designing and Selecting Set-oriented Applications

There are two main issues that a set-oriented system needs to deal with: publication (or sharing), and discovery (or finding). On the one hand, there needs to be sufficient data organized effectively so that sets can be discovered and formed in the first place. On the other, it should be possible to use tools to find, organize, and make use of them.

Unless a networked application or site is highly focused on a finely differentiated subset, it is almost a defining characteristic for a set-oriented application to have the means of classifying content. The most popular approaches to this are to offer top-down categories or topics, bottom-up tags, or both; some go further in providing RDF-based ontologies or faceted classification schema. Search tools are also vital, in some cases circumventing the need for explicit categorization, though use of metatags, keywords in titles, and other cues still play a strong role in helping the search system to find what you are looking for. A richer search system is often valuable: at its most extreme, this might take the form of a visual query tool that generates SQL or similar commands to extract data from a relational database.

Curation tools are of particular value in set-oriented applications. Users should be provided with the means to collect and assemble content, and to create it. This may be as simple as a wiki—the popular Wikia site, for example, which is making great efforts to be a social networking site and build group-like communities, is a predominantly set-oriented application almost entirely wiki-based. It allows people to create tagged wikis and provide anonymous edits, much like Wikipedia. Other tools, such as learni.st and Pinterest, provide tools for aggregation that allow people to assemble content around particular topics, with a focus on presentation and classification. RSS feeds and other push technologies that provide channels, such as listservs or mobile apps making use of social site APIs, can be very valuable in certain kinds of set-oriented, curated content application, allowing a learner to identify a particular set or subset, which can feed him or her with a stream of information. This is especially relevant to broad sets that provide rich content around a subject area. Such aggregation may be less important on question and answer sites or similarly narrow-focus social systems, where engagement is unlikely to persist beyond dialogue relating to the presenting problem. Curation tools gain value if they are able to use common standards such as HTTP and RSS to retrieve content and metadata. Where access to otherwise restricted content is needed, such as from a closed network system, it is also valuable to provide the means to access them through their APIs. For our own Elgg-based site, Athabasca Landing, we created tools to use and provide authenticated RSS feeds, tools for importing feeds into different site media (such as wikis, blogs, and shared bookmarks), and tools to embed Google Gadgets.

Beyond the set, site analytics that monitor usage and hits on various pages or artifacts can also be useful in providing feedback, indices of value, and even fodder for advertising services to a set curator.

Relational databases are ideally suited to set modes of interaction because of their formal basis in set theory. However, looser kinds of database management systems may have greater value for some kinds of set data, especially where either very high performance trumps the need for accurate classification, or classifications are fuzzy, unspecified, or shifting.

Like all other social applications, communication and sharing tools are a prerequisite in set-based systems, with a greater emphasis on sharing than that found in network or group social systems. Because of the sporadic and bursty nature of set interactions, tools to notify people via other systems such as email or SMS are useful.

Verifiable identification of an individual in a set-oriented application is seldom as important as it is in networked and group applications, though profiles that reveal interests, skills, and purposes are very helpful in filtering for useful topics of interest. That said, one of the biggest difficulties when dealing with sets is determining the, accuracy, truthfulness, and trustworthiness of others in the set, so it is helpful to provide a means for allowing people to reveal some kind of persistent identity, even if it is pseudonymous and shifts between one set and another.

Another range of potentially valuable tools for set-oriented applications are those that provide controllable filtering. Given that there may be diverse viewpoints, and that some content may be boring or disagreeable to some members of the set, it is important to allow features such as the blocking of individuals, filtering based on keywords, and tools that enable learners to focus on specific things—again, curation tools are useful, as are personal "dashboards" that enable a learner to assemble collections of content and dialogue. It should be noted that filtering is a potentially double-edged sword. Though well-suited to anonymous engagement in a set, in network or group applications it can impose implicit censorship on members and thus play a powerful role in shaping the community and reinforcing its values, creating an echo chamber or filter bubble (Pariser, 2011) that may have harmful and unforeseen effects. Because sets, by definition, do not involve any distinct community, filter bubbles are less problematic, assuming that other sets addressing similar concerns are available for those that find their interests or beliefs are excluded.

Associated with the relative anonymity of their members and perhaps more than in any other social form, sets are frequently intertwined with collectives. It is rare to find a set-oriented application without at least some collective features and/or a large amount of editorial control. Rather than dwell on this in detail here, we will return to it in the next chapter.

CONCLUSION

Sets are a ubiquitous social form we all engage in both on and off the Internet. The characteristic forms of social engagement that emerge in sets in a learning context typically have to do with cooperation rather than collaboration. Set-based learning is about sharing ideas, resources, tools, media, and knowledge, and engaging with others on an ad hoc, transient basis. On many occasions, others will make use of what we have shared without our knowledge or consent: the value of the set therefore grows over time. Once persistent dialogues start to occur, set-based systems blur into net-based systems: one of the most notable uses of sets is as a means for forming networks and, occasionally, groups.

Arguably the greatest value from sets comes when they are the social form behind collectives, and the most effective sets make extensive use of collectives by creating structure and dynamic processes to drive them and capitalize on their features. We turn to collectives in the next chapter.

7

LEARNING WITH COLLECTIVES

But here is the finger of God, a flash of the will that can,
Existent behind all laws, that made them and, lo, they are!
And I know not if, save in this, such gift be allowed to man,
That out of three sounds he frame, not a fourth sound, but a star.

Robert Browning, "Abt Vogler"

So far we have looked at collections of people. Networks, sets, and groups are aggregations of individuals that define the relationships, norms, behaviours, and activities they perform, together and alone. We have seen that, though nets and sets offer many benefits to the learner, the loss of the technological structures of groups combined with the lack of teacher input can place a large onus on the learner to make decisions he or she may not be suitably equipped for, potentially leading to sub-optimal paths and, occasionally, fear and confusion that stands in the way of effective learning. In this chapter we turn to a different kind of entity, composed not of people but an amalgamation of their actions and products. We describe this entity as the *collective*. The collective can, under the right circumstances, replicate or even improve upon the organizational value of groups, networks, and sets without the overhead of group processes, and take on many of the roles of a teacher. Collectives are thus crucial to realizing the potential of the crowd; they are perhaps more than anything else, what gives modern social software the potential to be a truly radical departure from traditional educational approaches. We are only beginning to realize the benefits of collectives for learning, and there are many pitfalls and obstacles to overcome before they can fulfill their promise, some of which we address in this chapter. Collectives may be teacher-like, but without great care, they can be very bad teachers.

This chapter is organized much like those on groups, nets, and sets, but the emphasis in each section will be somewhat different for two main reasons:

- A collective plays the role of a teacher, not of a collection of learners. We are interested therefore not so much in how to learn in a collective as we are in how a collective can teach, or how we can learn from collectives.

- In cyberspace, a collective is usually a cybernetic technology, composed of both people and software. We will thus pay more attention to technological design principles for collectives in learning.

In terms of learning, the relationship is not between many and one or many and many in the same sense as we find in a group, set, or net, but is instead a one-to-one relationship between an individual and a single entity composed of many parts. Thus, in many ways, a collective plays the role of a teacher in a one-to-one dyad. The potential benefit of collectives as educational tools is great. Done right, they offer the benefit of human judgment as a driver of artificial intelligence. Traditional AI approaches attempt to mimic the thinking behaviour of humans or other creatures, whether as a direct analogue (e.g., neural nets) or as an identifiably alien means of giving the appearance of thought. Collectives do neither: done right, they are simply a means of mining and using crowd activities to create wisdom. If we are able to harness such tools to help the learning process, then the wisdom of the crowd could guide us on our learning journeys. Mishandled, they can magnify and enable mob stupidity, and will only guide us in unhelpful directions.

DIFFERENT MEANINGS OF COLLECTIVE

The word "collective" may stir up many associations of loss of personal identity. There is something threatening about the loss of individuality associated with the hive mind or fictional Borg collective, of course amplified when human choice to participate is eliminated, as exemplified in the Borg's assertion, "Resistance is Futile." Sandberg (2003) explores this concept, drawing unfavourable analogies between hive minds and those of humans, where the benefits of the super-organism are available only to those who have given up their individualism. Turchin and Joslyn in their Cybernetic Manifesto similarly describe metasystems that are created "when a number of systems become integrated so that a new level of control emerges" (1989, para. 5). They show that these higher control systems have developed from the control of movement, through control of individual thinking to the emergence of human culture. Again, we don't like the coercive connotation of the word control, but we acknowledge that as life has evolved into more complex entities, metasystems are necessary for survival. However, there is no reason that a human collective should subsume its participants. It grows as a result of their activities, in principle taking nothing away from the individuals who form it. We see collective activity in a more tool-like fashion where one exerts individual agency to exploit an affordance provided by collective tools. We realize activities in cyberspace are constantly being extracted and shared at high speeds, and that there is a great risk to becoming enmeshed in a single world view, or caught in an echo chamber as the victim of a filter bubble (Pariser, 2011). But we don't think this entails more loss of control than what we give to a traffic engineer or a radio station traffic reporter counting the number of vehicles using an intersection at any given moment. Indeed, it is less controlling because the whole Internet is only one URL away, and we do not need to use that intersection to get there. As the Internet ingeniously routes itself around damaged nodes, knowledge of the collective activity and possibility helps us make individual decisions. A collective is an addition, not a subtraction.

Of course, the collective can and often does make mistakes, and we see evidence of groupthink, erroneous or slanderous meme proliferation, filter bubbles that strain out uncomfortable ideas, echo chambers that amplify mundane or even evil ideas, path dependencies, preferential attachment, confirmation biases and more, not to mention illegal or immoral extraction of individual and identifiable activity from collective activities. There are potential dangers in collective creation that need to be dealt with through careful design, and we will discuss these at greater length, but such weaknesses are not strictly features of collectives: misuse and inefficiencies accompany all forms of human organization. One must judge the value of the tool's use as compared to these costs, and the collectives of which we speak are tools, not mindsets. Even though, as a quotation attributed to Marshall McLuhan (1994) reminds us, "we shape our tools, and thereafter our tools shape us" (p. xi), we need practice and time to develop tool use in ways that allow us to optimize our individual and social selves in a complex universe. Resistance may not be futile, for in the resistance we recreate the technologies to meet our individual and social needs.

Many authors have attempted to grapple with what defines collective intelligence, but in ways that significantly depart from our usage. Malone, Laubacher, and Dellarocas (2009) describe a set of design patterns for different forms of collective intelligence of which the *Collective* itself, as we define it, is only one. For many, collective intelligence is the result of the combination of coordinated behaviours that represent the ability of a group to solve bigger, more complex problems, or to solve simpler problems more effectively than an individual alone could. Howard Bloom, for example (2000, pp. 42–44), lists five essentials for this kind of successful group intelligence:

- Conformity enforcers—mechanisms to ensure similarity among members
- Diversity generators—mechanisms to ensure some differences
- Inner judges—mechanisms to enable individuals to make their own decisions
- Resource shifters—mechanisms to reward success and punish failure
- Intergroup tournaments—competitions between subgroups.

Howard Bloom's notion of the collective is both broader than ours, and narrower. Broader, because he sees collective intelligence as a combinatorial effect of many intentionally coordinated individuals, in which technology may play only a supporting role. Narrower, because his concern is with leveraging conventional group processes to achieve a good outcome. A slightly different way of viewing collective intelligence is provided in the field of distributed cognition. This is similarly concerned with a form of collective intelligence that is spread among many, including the artifacts they create: cognition necessarily occurs with others as a result of the shared objects and tools we use, and in the different skills and abilities of people who work and learn together. These definitions are compelling, but differ from our more bounded use of the term as they are concerned with ways we consider collective intelligence to spread among individuals and their artifacts, not as a distinctive agent in itself. We are not just concerned with collective intelligence as a form of distributed cognition, but with distinctive individual entities. This is why we call them "collectives" rather than "collective intelligence." We are treating the combined behaviours of crowds as identifiable objects that in their own right embody a kind of collective intelligence.

DEFINING THE COLLECTIVE

Collectives are composite entities made up of the aggregated effects of people's activities in groups, sets, and networks. In the natural and human world, collectives are commonplace. They are emergent, distinct actors formed from multiple local interactions between individual parts, either directly or mediated through signs, without top-down control. For example, ants leave a trail of pheromones when returning to the nest with food, and they act as a guide to the food for other ants, who leave their own pheromone trails in turn, thus reinforcing the trail and attracting other ants until the food runs out, when the trail evaporates (Bonabeau, Dorigo, & Theraulaz, 1999). The collective is the combination of ants' interpretations of the signals they leave and those signals, which lead to the self-organizing behaviour of the whole that is distinct from the behaviour of any single individual. Similarly, a crowd gathered in a street acts as a magnet to individuals to join the crowd, which in turn increases the attraction of the crowd. Trading in currency, stocks, or shares reciprocally influences the market for those items, encouraging buying or selling by others, which in turn affects the behaviours of those who initiated the action and those who follow. It is not solely the actions of individuals that affect other individuals, but the emergent patterns left by the multiple interactions of many that engender changes in the behaviour of single individuals. Each individual interacts with a single collective of which he or she is a part.

Collectives can be intentionally created and mediated: for instance, when a teacher asks for a show of hands, or voters vote in an election, individual decisions are aggregated by some central authority and in turn influence the later decisions of those who make up the crowd. This can, for instance, help to swing undecided voters one way or another in an election. In cyberspace, a collective is often this kind of intentionally designed cyber-organism, with a computer or computers collecting and processing the behaviours of many people. Such collectives are formed from the intentional actions of people linked algorithmically by software and made visible through a human-computer interface. It is partially composed of software and machines, partially of the individual behaviours and cognitions of human beings. It is important to distinguish the role of the mediator in such a collective from an independent artificial intelligence. For example, a search engine that returns results solely based on words or groupings of words is not mediating the actions of a crowd: it is simply processing information. However, if that search engine uses explicit or implicit signals from its users or preferences that are implied by links in web pages—such as Google's PageRank—then it is making use of the aggregated actions of many people to influence those who follow: it is a collective. It can be seen as a substrate for interaction more than a processing machine. While natural phenomena like ant trails and termite mounds are utilizing the physical properties of the world, computers allow us to manipulate the physics of interaction and create new ways of aggregating and processing what people have done, greatly extending the adjacent possibilities.

Groups, sets, and networks are defined by membership, commonalities, and relationships between people who usually share a common interest. Collectives involve no social relationship with other identifiable persons at all, unless social relationships happen to play a part in what is being combined. A collective behaves as a distinct individual agent: we do not interact with its parts but with the whole, to which our own actions may contribute. A collective thus becomes a distinct and active entity within a system, with its own dynamics and behaviours that are not necessarily the same as those actions of the individuals who caused it.

Collectives as Technologies

Most human collectives can be thought of as cyborgs, composed of human parts and a set of processes and methods for combining them that are, whether enacted in people's heads or mediated via a computer, deeply technological in nature. As much as groups, collectives are defined by the technologies that assemble them. Just as a group is inconceivable without the processes and methods that constitute it, a collective is inconceivable without an algorithm (a set of procedures) enacted to make it emerge. While an algorithm is essential, this does not necessarily imply a technological basis for all collectives: there are plenty of natural collectives, such as flocks of birds, herds of cattle, swarms of bees, and nests of termites that are not assisted by any technology, at least not without stretching the definition of "technology" beyond bounds that we normally recognize. However, when an algorithm is enacted as a piece of software, as is the case in most cyberspace collectives, the collective is part machine, part crowd.

Some Corollaries of the Collective

From our definition of a collective, it follows that

- Someone or something has to perform the grouping of actions that make up the collective. This may be distributed among the collection of individuals, or centralized by an individual or machine.

- The subset of specific actions to observe must be chosen by someone (or some collection of people, or by a machine) from the range of all possible actions.

- What is done with the aggregated or parcellated behaviours has to follow one or more rules and/or principles: an algorithm is used to combine and process them.

- The result has to be presented in a form that influences actions by individuals (who may or may not have contributed to the original actions). Were this not the case, then the collective would have no agency within the system, and there would be little point to creating it in the first place.

We illustrate the collective graphically in figure 7.1. Note that individual components of the collective can be people, machines, or both, at each stage of the process.

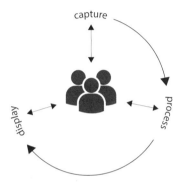

Figure 7.1 A model of how a collective forms.

A collective often involves a feedback loop of mediated and transformed interactions. Behaviours of individuals are

- Captured (by observation or by technological mediators such as computers or vote collectors)

- Processed and transformed by algorithms (which may be applied by those individuals or by some other agent, human or machine) and

- Fed back or displayed more or less directly to those and potentially other individuals who, in turn, affect their behaviours.

A computer may or may not be involved with any part of that continuum. Significantly, it is possible for all the necessary processing and presentation that drives the system to be facets of individuals' cognition and behaviour, as we see in the formation of crowds on a street. Each individual makes a decision, the aggregate forming a crowd, which itself then acts as a recommendation to join the crowd, thus driving its own growth. The crowd is both a sign and the result of that sign. Equally, even when a collective is mediated, the computation and presentation may be performed by a human agent: a teacher collecting and summing a show of hands in a classroom to allow students to choose between one of two options, for example, is using collective intelligence to affect his or her behaviour. The decision that a teacher makes is not based on dialogue with an individual but with the complete set he or she aggregates, so that the whole class becomes a decision-making agent. Sometimes both human and computer are combined.

People and/or machines may perform the shaping and filtering. This may occur at several points in a continuum:

1. During the selection of relevant actions filtering is likely to occur, where the machine (controlled by a programmer) decides which actions to record from which people.

2. During processing, where the machine allocates priority or relevance in order to produce rankings and/or reduce the number of results returned.

3. During presentation, where the machine filters the items displayed or shapes the form of the display so that some are more prominent than others (e.g., through visual emphasis, list order, or placing at different points in a navigational network or hierarchy).

Because a collective may be seen as an individual agent, then recursively, it is possible to treat one as a part of other collectives. For example, when a collective such as Delicious, CoFIND (Dron, Mitchell, Boyne, et al., 2000) or Knowledge Sea (Farzan & Brusilovsky, 2005) is used to aggregate links pointing to other sites on a single page, that page is treated by Google Search (a collective) very much the same as one that has been created by an individual person. This recursion can reach considerable depth.

STIGMERGIC COLLECTIVES

The term "stigmergy," from the Greek words for sign and action, was coined by the biologist Pierre-Paul Grassé to describe the nest-building behaviour of termites and other natural systems where indirect or direct signs left in the environment influence the behaviour of those who follow, leading to self-organized behaviour.

Many collective systems are stigmergic, and in nature they afford many advantages. Stigmergy fosters actions and ideas that collectively allow the performance of "problem-solving activity that exceeds the knowledge and the computational scope of each individual member" (Clark, 1997, p. 234). Stigmergy can be seen in many systems, from money markets (where money is the signal), to nest-tidying in ants (where untidiness is the signal). It is rife in cyberspace, influencing search results returned by Google, for example (Gregorio, 2003), and is the foundation of educational systems that employ social navigation (e.g. Dron, 2003; Dron, Boyne, & Mitchell, 2001; Farzan & Brusilovsky, 2005; Kurhila, Miettinen, Nokelainen, & Tirri, 2002; Riedl & Amant, 2003), allowing users to become aware of the actions, interests, categorizations, and ratings of others.

Many systems that collect and display user-generated content have some stigmergic characteristics whereby individuals are influenced by the collected behaviours of the whole. For instance, users are influenced by the ratings or number and depth of postings to a forum, or by the number of viewings of changes on a social site's front page. In each case, the system provides an interface that shows some aspect of crowd behaviour, which in turn affects the future behaviour of individuals making up the crowd.

NON-STIGMERGIC COLLECTIVES

While very common in collective applications, stigmergy is not a defining characteristic of a collective, or at least, not in a direct and straightforward manner. There is a variation on the theme that is as useful and in some ways superior to the self-organizing, dynamic form in which the choices and decisions of a crowd are mined, applying similar principles to other collectives to identify some decision, trend, or calculation. Such systems are almost all based around the use of sets, because those in groups and nets are usually far more aware of one another's actions and are influenced by them. Classic examples of the genre are recommender systems and collaborative filters that make use of independently mined actions or preferences to identify future interests or needs. This is positive because as Surowiecki (2004) pointed out, crowds are only wise when they are unaware of what the rest of the crowd is doing. By definition, stigmergic systems break this rule, at least on the face of it. There is compelling evidence that Surowiecki's assertion is true. The disastrous out-of-control stigmergic effects that fuel bank runs, where the people withdrawing money serves as a sign for others to follow suit, shows all too clearly the potential downside of people being aware of others' actions. Similarly, Salganik, Dobbs, and Watts, (2006) show that when people can see the choices others have made for rating songs in a chart, it profoundly alters the overall charts: social influence in their study made for unrecognizably dissimilar chart results when compared to independent choices, and when compared to individual choices, the rankings are less satisfying for all concerned. This is not an entirely simple equation, however.

Author Dron performed a study to explore the influence of others' choices on behaviour that showed a mix of behaviours from copying to rational decision-making, and on to deliberate obtuseness in selecting items that were as different from the items selected by others as possible (2005a). At the time, such effects seemed surprising: the expected behaviour was that people would generally make worse choices by copying those who came before, not deliberately avoid such behaviour. These results are, however, borne out by other research. Ariely (2009), for example, discovered that the beer-ordering behaviours of individuals in a group, as opposed to independent individuals, was significantly different. In this experiment, participants showed a tendency to deliberately order differently from their peers, even though their preference without such influence might have been for a beer that had already been ordered. While the influence of earlier people can skew results of collective decisions so that they are, at best, only as good as the first contributor, aggregated independent choices are far more successful at eliciting crowd wisdom.

We have a tendency to be influenced by decisions that came before, whether positively (we follow them) or negatively (we deliberately do not follow them). This is clearly evidenced on social sites such as Twitter, where what is "trending" or most popular is promoted, leading to sometimes vast waves of viral interest. However, as we have already observed, this can be problematic. There are some simple solutions, however, which do not limit crowd wisdom but still bring the benefits of adaptation and dynamic change that a feedback loop engenders. The most effective of these is the simplest: to introduce delay to the feedback loop (Bateson, 1972). If a crowd does not know what the rest of the crowd is thinking, then it is far easier for it to be wise. This is evident when poll results are displayed as an incentive to vote, but only after one's preferences are entered. Flickr uses this to good advantage when supplying tag clouds for the previous day, the previous week, and overall: recent tag clouds are seldom valuable, though they can occasionally show the zeitgeist of the crowd. But as delay creeps in, they provide more relevant and potentially useful classifications.

While many collectives are not directly stigmergic, stigmergy may nonetheless re-enter the picture when results are returned to individuals. Google, for example, mines independent implicit evaluations of websites, but because it plays such a prominent role in helping people find pages of interest, it is more likely that pages appearing at the top of search results will be linked to, therefore reinforcing the position of those that are already successful in a stigmergic manner.

While the collective is not in itself a social form, and so is not directly comparable to individual, group, net, and set modes of learning (it relies upon those social forms in order to exist at all), there are some distinct benefits that emerge from its effective use. Most notably, although it will often inherit the limitations of its parent social form(s), it can be a gap-filler, adding freedoms that might have been unavailable in the other social forms. We do not present our customary diagram of cooperative freedoms for the collective, because it depends entirely upon the kind involved, but we describe some of the ways that collectives contribute to, or in rare cases, detract from cooperative freedoms.

Time

Collectives tend to inherit the limitations of the social forms they arise in. For instance, those that emerge in immersive and other synchronous contexts tend to appear in real-time, though timeline-based tools can add extra richness to such experiences and, if they are recorded, can add layers to the original interactions, for instance by showing patterns that may have occurred within the original interactions of earlier participants. Donath, Karahalios, and Viegas (1999), for example, used this to good effect in the stigmergic ChatCircles system, which was otherwise constrained to real-time dynamics. Similarly, when they emerge out of discussion tools, they can distil or mine patterns from them. For example, one of the earliest collaborative filters used for learning, PHOAKS (People Helping One Another Know Stuff), provided its recommendations by mining discussion forums for links to resources, and used those as implicit recommendations to others (Terveen, Hill, Amento, McDonald, & Creter, 1997), thus allowing freedom of time to engage with the system separately from the actual discussion that generated them.

Place

As with all networked tools, collectives provide few limitations on the location learning can occur in, except where they emerge in real time from collocated crowds.

Content

Freedom of content depends a great deal on the form that the collective takes. Many are used as recommenders of people or content, suggesting an assortment of alternatives that narrow down the choices that can be made. The effect of this can be very large and is always significant: the chances of a user clicking one of the first two items presented by Google Search, for example, are many times higher than they are for him or her clicking the last item on the page, even when results are deliberately manipulated to show the "worst" options first (Joachims, Granka, Pan, Hembrooke, & Gay, 2005). Interestingly, however, the chances of the user clicking on middle-ranked resources are even lower than they are for clicking the last item on a page. When we trust the collective, belief in its accuracy frequently overrides even our own judgments of quality (Pan et al., 2007). In some cases, such as when a user clicks "I'm feeling lucky" in a Google search, there may be no choice presented at all. Of course, we must remember that the user is always free to search somewhere else or for something different. We are aware of no collectives as yet that are used coercively; their role is always one of persuasion.

Delegation

The ability to delegate control to a collective is dependent on context. In many ways, accepting a recommendation or allowing a collective to shape an information environment is to intentionally delegate control to someone or something else. However, the typical context of collective use in current systems is that of the self-guided learner who has made an active decision to use the collective. Thus far, there have been few attempts made to use collectives to shape an entire learning journey, and those who have tried have not succeeded.

Relationship

Apart from the use of collectives to recommend people or shape dialogue use, collectives have very little effect on freedom of relationship. However, because a collective is an active agent akin to a human in terms of its behaviour, it is often possible to engage more or less fully with the collective itself. Typically, one gives information to the collective in order for it to provide better information or advice. For example, the more information it has about you, the more Google will give you personalized and accurate results if you are logged in as a Google user, (i.e., it is more likely to give the results you are looking for). Similarly, many collaborative filters use explicit ratings and/or preferences (e.g., MovieLens or Netflix for movies, Amazon for books) to improve the accuracy of their predictions of what you may like.

Medium

As a rule, collectives are neutral to medium: they may or may not place constraints on the media used and, as we have already observed, they are usually used in a context where the learner has control over whether and which collectives are used for learning.

Technology

Many collective systems work equally well across various technology platforms. Again, however, the details depend on the precise context of use: a system that uses one's location, for instance, is constrained to uses where the technology can provide that information.

Method

Once again, the context determines whether collectives provide a choice of method. Because they are mainly used by independent learners, the choice of method is more dependent on the learner than on the tool. Collectives on the whole act like controllable teachers, allowing the learner to choose what method suits him or her best. Very few existing collectives apply any intentional pedagogy, and this is an area that demands greater research.

Pace

There are few occasions where pace makes a difference when using a collective for learning, though there are sometimes constraints due to the time it may take for a collective to gain a sufficiently rich knowledge of both individuals and crowds to provide useful help. The vast majority of collective systems suffer from a cold-start problem: they only offer value when sufficient numbers of actions have been captured, so until then, there is no reason to use them, which creates difficulties for them to gain sufficient numbers to begin with. Most systems deal with this by making use of previously shared information (e.g., Google mines links from websites, PHOAKS mines posts in Usenet News, Facebook uses EdgeRank, and Delicious uses browser bookmarks), information from other domains (e.g., Amazon book "likes" may be used to identify similar people in order to recommend movies), or by using automated guesses based on content similarity or approximations from statistical data to provide reasonable recommendations earlier in the system's development when there is insufficient crowd data.

Disclosure

For any collective to work at all, some disclosure of actions is required. However, in most mediated collectives, this is essentially anonymous. Though we may fear the motives of companies that provide collectives, this is a fear of disclosure to an organization, not to the collective itself. Where software is performing aggregation, it knows who you are but other people in the collective rarely, if ever, do. There are some exceptions, especially when collectives are concerned with establishing reputation. In such cases, there is a double concern: first, that one must disclose information about oneself to the software and, in principle, its owners in order to participate; and second, that it involves the delegation of one's reputation to the crowd. In such cases, fear of exposure may be justified.

TRANSACTIONAL DISTANCE IN COLLECTIVES

The collective, as an emergent entity composed of a collection of people in sets, nets, and occasionally groups, plays the role of a teacher in a learning transaction, guiding, suggesting, collecting, clustering, and re-presenting the knowledge of the crowd. A learner interacting with a collective is engaged with something dynamic and responsive in a way that is quite different from engagement with a static book, website, or video, yet without the social engagement he or she experiences when interacting with an individual human being. At least for the foreseeable future, there will be little or no psychological connection between a human and a collective, or if there is, it will be one-way: collectives do not care about individual people. From the point of view of the individual, interacting with the collective is seldom more psychologically engaging than interacting with any artificial intelligence. This is not to suggest that the interaction is not powerful for the individual concerned, and one can claim that two-way communication has meaningfully occurred, just as with Furbies, Tamagotchis, or more recent AIBOS and Paros (robot baby seals intended to provide companionship for the elderly—www.parorobots.com; Turkle, 2011).

The two-way dialogue with a collective can occur in many ways. One of the motivations behind Kay & Kummerfeld's (2006) scrutable user models is to allow people to talk back to the collective, which otherwise can make decisions on the behalf of users that are not helpful. Many people have deliberately watched content that they would not otherwise choose on collaborative filter-based TiVo devices, for example, to stop the machine from making wrong or embarrassing predictions about what they would like to see (Zaslow, 2002). A very distinctive feature of collectives is that the individuals who interact with them are also typically a part of them, active contributors to the collective intelligence. This is distinct from our engagement with people in social forms: we may be part of a net, set, or group, but the individuals within them are still distinct, and at least in principle, identifiable. The collective is an active individual agent of which we are a part. All of these complexities make transactional distance between learner and collective a very unusual but quite distinctive phenomenon. The collective creates high structure, shaping the information space that the learner inhabits, but the learner is part of the collective, and in many cases can control the results, whether through direct intervention (e.g., in Netflix, specifying the kinds of movie he or she would like to see), behaviour modification intended to affect results, or simply by choosing from one of multiple options.

EXAMPLES OF COLLECTIVES

Rating Systems
The majority of systems that provide a means to implicitly or explicitly rate someone or something make use of collectives. These vary in sophistication from simple aggregators to full-blown collaborative filters, where ratings are used to compare an individual with the crowd, and on to rich metadata that provide ratings across a range of dimensions.

A few examples include Slashdot Karma Points and categories, Facebook Likes, Google+ Plus-ones, and countless systems that provide Lickert scale-style ratings such as Amazon and YouTube.

Collaborative Filters
Collaborative filters are recommenders that make use of similarities between people (e.g., people who share a similar pattern of interest for things like books or movies) or similarities between crowds of people implicitly or explicitly liking

particular items (e.g., people who bought this also bought that). Some examples are Amazon Recommends, Netflix, and MovieLens.

Data Mining and Analytics Tools

A number of collective applications mine existing content in order to identify patterns, preferences, and structures that might otherwise be invisible. For instance, Cite-U-Like and Google Scholar provide recommendations based on citations to scholarly papers, Google Search ranks results according to the number of links mined from web pages, and PHOAKS looks at links in newsgroup postings to identify implicitly recommended articles.

Swarm-based Systems

Swarm-based systems mimic the behaviours of groups of ants, birds, fish, and other naturally occurring crowds in order to bring about self-organization in a crowd-based system. These are most often used to control work of very simple robots to collectively complete a complex job. Tattershall and his colleagues have used this process to provide sequencing recommendations for learners (2004; van den Berg et al., 2005). Though it can work reasonably well with a closed corpus such as a conventional course where there are limited potential paths and defined goals, this kind of approach falls flat in the large open corpuses of set and net interactions. Particle swarm optimization systems take a slightly different approach, and are typically used in goal-oriented systems to optimize multiple behaviours towards a single solution. They are sometimes used with Genetic algorithms (GAs) to rule out inappropriate resources to filter results (Huang, Huang, & Cheng, 2008).

Ant Colony Optimization Systems

Systems using ant colony optimization techniques make use of virtual pheromones to capture paths and actions taken by the crowd in order to adapt content, presentation, process, sequence, and other elements of a user's experience. Some examples are AACS (Yang & Wu, 2009) and Paraschool (Semet, Lutton, & Collet, 2003).

Social Navigation Systems

Systems that employ social navigation capture browsing behaviours and actions such as tagging or commenting in order to modify an interface to emphasize or (sometimes) determine certain paths at the expense of others. For example, CoFIND used rank order, font style, and font size to indicate resources that are viewed as useful by the crowd (Dron et al., 2001). Educo used representations of individuals as clustered dots surrounding resources that were more widely used (Kurhila et al., 2002), Knowledge Sea 2 used colour depth to indicate more visited resources (Farzan & Brusilovsky, 2005), and CoRead used different highlight colours to indicate passages of texts that have been more or less highlighted (Chiarella, 2009).

Social Network Discovery Engines

The vast majority of social networking sites use some means of discovering others with whom to connect. The algorithms may be quite simple, such as link analysis to discover friends of friends. Indeed, the commonly used FOAF protocol was explicitly built to exploit this. Others may simply identify other people in groups an individual belongs to, but some can be more complex, taking into consideration profile fields, browsing behaviours, and the content of posts. A sophisticated example is Facebook's EdgeRank, which takes a range of factors (a trade secret) including not just connections but numbers and frequency of interactions into account when presenting content, as well as numerous set-oriented factors (Pariser, 2011). In a learning context, we have provided an Elgg plugin that assists discovery of both friends of friends and people in shared groups (community.elgg. org/plugins/869921/1.2/suggested-friends-18x).

Crowdsourcing Tools

Crowdsourcing systems typically rely on user-generated content in response to a particular problem, question, or project request. While some rely on the person posing the problem to sort through potential solutions, such set-oriented applications are very often enhanced with collective tools that solicit implicit or explicit ratings from the crowd in order to rank the effectiveness of the solution: these include Yahoo Answers, Quora, Amazon Mechanical Turk, and Innocentive.

Tools to Assess Reputation

A number of systems mine data such as citations and references in order to discover experts rather than content; for example, Cite-U-Like and Connotea. There is abundant literature on refinements to these approaches (Ru, Guo, & Xu, 2008; Smirnova & Balog, 2011). Social networking systems such as LinkedIn make use of networked endorsements to provide a collective indication of reputation within a field while others, such as academia.edu, make use of citations and papers to help emphasize reputation within a field.

In many network-oriented systems, the connections explicitly made between one individual and another by "friending," providing links in a blogroll, commenting or linking within blog posts and so on, provide the necessary recommendations for us to trust others. If someone I admire admires someone else, that acts as an effective indicator of reputation. It is an old technique that can be quantified and turned into a collective with relative ease: weighted citation indexes use the same kind of approach to indicate the significance of an academic paper.

Going beyond those we know in a large network, reputation (apart from for a few of the most well-known people within the network) can be harder to identify, and collectives rapidly become the most important tool for identifying value. Systems such as Slashdot, Spongefish, or Graspr can be remarkably effective self-organizing learning resources because of the methods they use to identify reliable/useful contributors and resources. Slashdot and Graspr (now defunct) both make use of a karma-based system, whereby "good karma" is gained through a variety of crowd-driven mechanisms.

Spongefish (a how-to site that folded in 2008) took a simpler but more comprehensible approach where coins denoted social capital for a teacher. In each system, there is an economy: those who already have points/coins are able to distribute them to others, thus ensuring that reputation is decided by those who already have a reputation, an approach that ensures at least some assurance of quality. However, the failure of so many systems points to the difficulty of getting algorithms right and designing interfaces that do not overwhelm their users with complexity. Slashdot (with its tagline, "News for Nerds"), one of the earliest, and still the best of collectives, survives largely due to its target user base that not only tolerates but also revels in its complexity.

Within an educational setting, such systems can offer several affordances. For example:

- Learners can be encouraged to gain reputation and submit that as part of a formal assessment. Used with care, and bearing in mind the risks of subverting such a system, this can offer motivation in the right places.

- Learners can use such systems to identify resources and people of value, thus filtering out those who may be distracting or misleading.

- Learners can be encouraged to rate/rank/pass on points or coins to others, encouraging critical and reflective thinking and encouraging them to engage more deeply with the community.

In previous chapters about groups, nets, and sets, we have labelled this section "Learning in x." In this chapter we deliberately describe this as learning *with* collectives, as the collective is an active and influential participant in a learning process, far more akin to a teacher or content than it is to a collection of people. At once human and mechanical, the collective is an alien kind of teacher engaged in a dialogue with its parts.

There are many roles teachers must play in a traditional educational system. Here is a short list of some of the main ones:

- Model thinking and practice
- Provide feedback
- Design and assemble learning paths
- Schedule learning
- Convey information
- Clarify and explain complex topics
- Assess learning
- Select and filter resources and tools for learning
- Care for students and student learning
- Provide a safe environment for learning

The majority of these roles, if not all, can be played by a collective to some extent. It should be noted, however, that enthusiasm, caring, passion, and many of the most valuable personal attributes of a teacher will not be present, though they can be mimicked by a collective. The collective plays the functional roles a teacher might perform.

Modelling Thinking and Practice

Little will substitute for observing a real teacher modelling good practice and demonstrating how he or she thinks about an issue, but of course collectives occur within social communities where such things are already possible. However, some kinds of collective can be used to promote and aggregate such behaviours. Karma Points and ratings, for example, can combine to show the informed user not just relevant content, but also the cream of the crop—not just a single teacher, but the "best" of those who contribute to a discussion or a debate. The collective is, by the judgment of the crowd contextualized to the needs of the viewer, an "ideal" composite teacher.

Providing Feedback

Even a simple rating system of "thumbs-up" or page view counters can tell a learner his or her work is valued. However, this is not particularly rich feedback, serving a motivational purpose more than offering guidance. Moreover, in some cases this can be demotivating, if it is viewed by the learner as an extrinsic reward (Kohn, 1999). Such guidance is still more a function of the social modes of engagement, group, set, or net, than of the collective. Having said that, a range of collective systems have been developed that provide somewhat richer feedback, including the nuanced rating system of Slashdot, and the more freeform "qualities" used in CoFIND (Dron, Mitchell, Siviter, & Boyne, 2000). These systems allow ratings across multiple dimensions that, at least in the case of CoFIND, can be pedagogically useful. People may, for instance, choose to rate something as "complex," "complete," or "well-written," thus giving valuable feedback that in some ways betters that of an individual teacher, if sufficient ratings are received. Such systems also show rater variability, which itself can be more instructive than the stated preference of a single teacher (even a wise one).

Designing and Assembling Learning Paths

A number of social navigation-based systems provide weighted lists of recommendations of what to do next (Brusilovsky, 2004; Dron, Mitchell, Siviter, & Boyne, 2000; Kurhila et al., 2002; Wexelblat & Maes, 1999). Others have used techniques such as ant-trail optimization, swarming, and other nature-inspired techniques to offer recommendations (Wong & Looi, 2010; Semet et al., 2003). Many recommender systems that use various forms of collaborative filtering similarly present alternatives of what to look at next, based on previous behaviours of other learners (Drachsler, Hummel, & Koper, 2007; Freyne & Smyth, 2006; Hummel et al., 2007). However, it has proved difficult to do more than present suggestions for the next step in the path. Generating a plan of activities for a learner to follow poses significantly greater challenges, though many have tried (Pushpa, 2012; van den Berg et al., 2005; Yang & Wu, 2009). There are several reasons why they have not yet been wholly successful: learning is a process of change in which it is hard to predict in advance how a learner will develop as a result of each step.

When teachers design courses well, they do so based on their experience and conceptions of the topic as well as pedagogical considerations and knowledge of learners, resulting in an assembly that is intricately connected and cohesive, involving deep content knowledge, and importantly, an understanding of how to tell a story about it. Many adaptive systems have attempted to do the same and can work fairly well for individuals or group-based learners, but few (if any) have succeeded when dealing with an open corpus of knowledge, which is commonplace in net-based and set-based learning situations.

Some have used ontologies for connecting sequences of resources that are collectively generated (Karampiperis & Sampson, 2004). Though computationally elegant, this has been a profound failure from a learning perspective. The main reason is because pedagogically appropriate paths are not the same as expert opinions of the relationship between one topic and another. Even assuming a sufficient body of material can be effectively marked up and put in relation to others, subject discipline relationships seldom translate into good learning paths.

A promising approach is to combine recommendation methods with expert-generated curricula (Herder & Kärger, 2008) and these are relatively easy to generate in a constrained set of well-annotated resources within a group-oriented institution (Kilfoil, Xing, & Ghorbani, 2005; van den Berg et al., 2005).

Scheduling Learning

Closely related to the design of curriculum and learning paths is the means to synchronize activities and pacing. This has long been an important role for a teacher, often played by an institution in group-based learning, and is a common characteristic of group-based approaches, but it is usually difficult to achieve in network and set learning. However, collectives can take on some of that role. The simplest tools for this task allow an individual to specify a list of possible dates and others to indicate their availability. The tool aggregates potential times, and automatically or semi-automatically, suggests the most appropriate time when as many learners as possible are available. Plentiful free tools of this nature such as MeetingWizard, Doodle, Congregar, Setster, and Tungle are available on the Web and, in some cases, for cellphones.

Conveying Information

On the whole, collectives are not used to convey information from the ground up, but to collect, filter, refine, order, and display information that already exists. They provide ways to organize information rather than generating it in the first place. This organizational process can be quite powerful, however. Slashdot, for instance, is able to tailor content to specific needs, and allows relevant and reliable posts to provide nuanced insight into the topic under discussion that greatly surpasses what any individual teacher might be able to say on the subject, simply due to diversity and breadth of coverage. Other systems can help to visualize a complex subject area or social connections that might otherwise remain hidden (Buckingham-Shum, Motta, & Domingue, 1999; Donath et al., 1999; Vassileva, 2008).

Perhaps one of the most important sources of learning content today and a notable exception to the norm is Wikipedia. Wikipedia arguably uses stigmergic and similar collective processes, largely enacted in the minds of its contributors, underpinning and affecting ways that pages grow (Elliot, 2006; Heylighen, 2007; Yu, 2009). Basically, people are affected by signs left by other people in the environment but, for the most part, this is simply an anonymous mediated dialogue, a set-based interaction where each edit builds on the last, but without the distinctive self-organizing character of a true stigmergic system. However, there are a few genuinely stigmergic elements. Changes made by others affect not just content but also style, in ways that are analogous to stigmergic processes in nest-building ants or termites. Similarly, the use of wiki tags—metadata that relate to the content of pages—leads to predictable patterns of editing: the tags act like pheromones that guide others in their editing (den Besten, Gaio, Rossi, & Dalle, 2010).

Wikipedia also provides some embedded intentionally designed collective tools, such as pages showing trending articles that are truly stigmergic: frequency of use and editing affects the behaviour of others that follow. While it does include some collective elements, it is important to observe that Wikipedia is more of a farm than a self-organized jungle, and its power lies in its organizational and automated tools for assuring quality, not in collective processes. The collective aspects of the system simply help to shape its development rather than playing a major role in content production.

While difficult to generalize beyond specific contexts, there have been some interesting collective approaches to the creation of artwork, many of which have persisted and grown for ten years or more: www.absurd.org, www.potatoland. org, or snarg.net, for example. More recent systems like PicBreeder (PicBreeder. org), Darwinian Poetry (www.codeasart.com/poetry/darwin.html), and a wide variety of music evolution systems (Romero & Machado, 2008) use the crowd to choose between mutated forms of artworks, thus acting as an evolutionary selection mechanism. As a means of reflection on what creates value, this may be useful in an educational context. The potential for actually providing educational resources beyond such specific domains, however, seems limited.

Clarifying and Explaining Complex Topics

Collectives can be used to extract meaning and sense from a complex set of materials. For example, CoRead is a tool that allows collective highlighting of texts, in a manner similar to that employed on Amazon Kindle devices (Chiarella, 2009). Learners can see other learners' highlights, and a simple colour scheme is used to indicate which words and phrases have been highlighted the most. This allows those who come to a text to identify the words and phrases that others have found important or interesting. Similarly, tag clouds within a particular site or topic area can help learners to get a sense of the overall area and keywords associated with it. This can be particularly useful where the tag cloud is combined with a collaborative filter showing recommended tags that appear with selected tags more often, as can be found in Delicious. By viewing associated keywords, the learner is able to make connections and see generalizations that situate a topic within a network of ideas and concepts.

Assessing Learning

Several social systems provide rating tools. In many cases, these are simply variations on good versus bad: simple "thumbs-up" links such as Facebook "Likes" or Google +1s, for example. Unfortunately, this is seldom valuable to a learner seeking feedback on the success of his or her learning, unless the context is highly constrained, because there is not sufficient information to identify the reasons for the "like." It can, however, work reasonably well within a group, especially in a large group such as one found in a MOOC, if the meaning of "good" and "bad" has been explicitly identified within that context. In sets or nets, there are few opportunities to provide such constraints.

Moving beyond simple ratings, some systems contextualize ratings within specific sets of qualities or interest areas. This can provide far more useful feedback on learning, though typically at the cost of far greater complexity for the people contributing ratings. CoFIND (Dron, Mitchell, Boyne, et al., 2000), for example, allows learners to not just rate a resource as good or bad, but to use fuzzy tags known as "qualities." Qualities are tags with scalar values attached, allowing their users to both categorize a resource and say that it is more or less good for beginners, complex, detailed, accurate, reliable, authoritative, well-explained, or nicely structured. This kind of rich feedback can be very helpful. However, it is harder to use qualities to tag items than to use more conventional discrete tags, because their users must not only provide a category but also a rating for it. Other systems such as Slashdot provide a more constrained list: its basic comment filter allows users to identify whether comments are insightful, informative, interesting, or funny, which assists in filtering content and also helps the poster to know how others feel about the post. Though not intended for assessment, LinkedIn endorsements provide an intriguing and effective way to use collectives generated from networks to judge an individual's skills. Skills that have been tagged in a user's profile may be endorsed by those who are in that user's network, thus providing a collective view of a person's accomplishments that is both bottom-up, and in aggregate, trustworthy. LinkedIn makes good use of reciprocity, social capital, and individual vanity: when someone has endorsed you, it is hard to resist viewing your growing list of endorsements, and the site then prompts you to endorse others based on the skills identified in their profiles.

Selecting and Filtering Resources and Tools for Learning

The selection and filtering of resources and tools for learning is an important role for most teachers and is, in principle, what collectives do best. This is the role that Google plays when providing us with search results, using many collective processes to help assure quality and relevance of the results that it provides. Likewise, when Amazon provides recommendations of books we may want to read, it employs item- and user-based collaborative filtering techniques to make it likely that we will find something of value. Both are powerful learning tools, and this point has not been lost on the academic community. Over the past two decades, there have been many systems explicitly designed to use the crowd to recommend resources in a learning context (M. Anderson et al., 2003; Bateman, Brooks, & McCalla, 2006; Chiarella, 2009; Drachsler, 2009; Dron, Mitchell, Boyne, et al., 2000; Farzan & Brusilovsky, 2005; Freyne & Smyth, 2006; Goldberg, Nichols, Oki, & Terry, 1992; Grieco, Malandrino, Palmieri, & Scarano, 2007; Huberman & Kaminsky, 1996; Hummel et al., 2007; Jian, 2008; Kurhila et al., 2002; Tattersall et al., 2004; Terveen et al., 1997; van den Berg et al., 2005; Vassileva, 2008).

These systems include approaches such as social navigation, swarm-based methods, collaborative filtering, rating, and many more. When done well, crowd-based approaches to recommending resources, parts of resources, people, and tools have many benefits. Many hands make light work, and a crowd (especially a diverse set) can trawl through far more resources than an individual teacher. Depending on the way the collective is constructed, crowds can also be wiser than individuals (Surowiecki, 2004), succeeding in identifying facts or quality where individuals may fail.

Resource discovery is of great value in a formal setting. Because of the focused nature of closed groups in educational institutions, resource databases can become an extremely valuable facility, allowing the group to engage in developing a read/write course with relatively little effort. This offers a wide assortment of learning and practical benefits:

- It reduces the cost of course production
- It keeps the course current and topical
- It gives students a strong sense of ownership, which in turn increases motivation
- It provides a simple means of learning by teaching: selection of resources, combined with some ranking and annotation, encourages reflection on both the resource and the learning process (i.e., how and in what ways it is helpful to the learner in his or her own learning process)
- It multiplies the possibilities of finding good and useful resources, leading to a far greater diversity and range than a single teaching team could hope to assemble alone.

It is best if such systems include at least some form of collective ranking, so that students can vote resources up or down, or provide implicit recommendations by clicking on links that can be fed back to the crowd through social navigation features. If such a system is not available, the next best thing is the capability to annotate or comment on links other learners have provided: the presence of comments can act as a simple stigmergic indicator of interest, positive or negative—both have value. If the system itself does not allow anything of this nature, then it is better to either use a more free-form system such as a wiki, or to go beyond the managed environment and make use of systems such as Delicious or Furl to create closed lists of bookmarks where commentary and tagging is allowed.

Tag clouds are a potentially powerful means of making resource discovery easier in a group, once resources have been added to the system. Within groups they are often different from and can sometimes offer greater value than those in large networks, because they adapt more quickly to the changing foci of the group. In a teacher-dominated environment, they can provide a more constrained and closed folksonomy than one allowed to develop without such control, a sort of hybrid of top-down control and bottom-up categorization. In some circumstances this can be useful: a shared vocabulary, if understood by all, helps to make sense of a subject area as well as making it easier to locate relevant resources. By categorizing the world, the teacher is enabling students to understand it better.

Caring for Students and Student Learning

There are some vital things teachers do that are far beyond the grasp of collectives. As our analysis of transactional distance in collectives suggests, the psychological gap between collective and learner is about as big as it can get. We know that other people have helped the collective to provide us with information, structure, process, or design, but that does not help us to feel closer to them and there are virtually no ways they can care for us or what we do. Collectives are only part of a solution to providing a rich and rewarding learning experience, and some things are, at least for now, best left to humans. Having said that, collectives can provide a gauge to let us know that unspecified others care about us: the "plus ones" or "likes" from popular social sites can improve a sense of social well-being and worth, albeit seldom with explicit pedagogical intent. They can also provide support for establishing connections with those humans. There are even aspects of the caring role a collective can play. For instance, they can be used to help nurture and guide learners to become more engaged and motivated (Glahn, Specht, & Koper, 2007).

The field of learning analytics has been experiencing rapid growth in recent years. It draws from a variety of fields: web analytics, educational data mining, adaptive hypermedia and social adaptation, and AI. Its purpose is to uncover indicators of learning, obstacles to learning, and information about learning pathways to help guide learners' journeys. For teachers, it improves teaching methods and discovers weaknesses and risks before they become too dangerous. Some have extended this purpose to include analytics that interest administrators, institutions, and employers of teachers but, though such uses can and do have an impact on learning, we are of the opinion that it is no longer about learning when the process is applied this way: it is more a question of teaching analytics or institutional data mining.

The value of learning analytics to a teacher's ability to provide care is that it allows him or her to become a part of a collective, in much the same way that asking for a show of hands to check if students have understood a problem in a classroom uses the crowd to change behaviour. Processed results that inform a teacher of the progress of students leads to changes in his or her behaviour, and thus can help the teacher to provide more assistance when needed. For example, if analytics show that, in aggregate, many students are having difficulty with particular lessons or concepts, the teacher can be more supportive in those areas. Analytics can also help to identify particular learners or groups of learners who are at risk. It can help to uncover patterns in behaviour for disparate students or identify commonalities that lead to difficulties. For example, if it appears that most of those who submit work after a certain date or who lack particular qualifications have difficulties, then the teacher can intervene to advise them of the dangers. In effect, the teacher becomes part of a crowd-based recommender system.

While collectives can play several teacher roles in a system, they do not always make good teachers. There are many ways in which a wise crowd can become a stupid mob.

The Matthew Effect

The Matthew Effect, coined by Merton (1968) from the biblical aphorism attributed to Jesus "Whoever has will be given more, and he will have an abundance. Whoever does not have, even what he has will be taken from him" (Matthew 13:12). In the specific learning contexts examined here, this saying can be interpreted as a result of path dependencies and preferential attachments that set in early in a collective system's development. If the system affects behaviour (e.g., it encourages clicking of one resource or tag, or suggests people with whom to connect), then those who gain an early advantage are far more likely to retain it and be more influential than those who come later. The rich get richer while the poor get poorer. A classic example of this is presented by Knight and Schiff (2007), who discovered that early voters in US primary elections have around twenty times the influence of late voters on the results. This is because media reports the relative swings of voters, which in turn influence those who are undecided as to how to vote. Voters want to make a difference, usually by being on a winning side or, occasionally, to defend a candidate in danger of losing. Similarly, Salganik et al.'s (2006) study of artificial pop charts, mentioned in Chapter 6 shows strong Matthew Effects on music preference.

Many collective systems suffer from this problem. Google's search results are a particularly prominent sufferer from the Matthew Effect. Because Google mines for links that are treated as implicit recommendations (L. Page, Brin, Motwani, & Winograd, 1999), and because people are far more likely to click on the first few links in the search results (Pan et al., 2007), this means that they receive greater exposure to pages that are already popular. Of course, it is only possible to provide links to sites that one already knows about (Gregorio, 2003) so such links are more likely to appear in the future. Because Google commands such a large share of search traffic, the overall effect is quite large. Many systems provide checks and balances to prevent rampant Matthew Effects from overwhelming new or equally valuable resources. Some use deliberate decay mechanisms (Dron, Mitchell, Boyne, et al., 2000; Wong & Looi, 2010), some introduce deliberate random serendipity, while others, including Google and Facebook, use a wide range of algorithms, collective and otherwise, to massage results so that there are no single persistent winners.

Unfortunately, many collectives occur without deliberate planning or forethought. For example, the presence of many or few messages in a discussion forum can act as an incentive or disincentive to others to contribute to a discussion, or a rating system can be used, as in Salganik et al.'s (2006) study that does not prevent runaway preferential attachment. The spread of viral memes in a population is another example of the Matthew Effect in action, where repeated exposure from multiple channels spreads through a network with increasing repetition (Blackmore, 1999).

Filter Bubbles and Echo Chambers

As Pariser (2011) observes, collectives play a very large role in the creation of filter bubbles. A recommender system, be it Google, Amazon, Slashdot, or any other system that filters and weights resources according to implicit or explicit preferences, runs the risk of preventing us from seeing alternative views to those we already hold or accept. This can function recursively and iteratively, especially where implicit preferences are mined on our behalves, creating a "bubble" over us that allows only similar ideas to those we already hold to penetrate. If what we see is limited to a subset of possibilities, then there are great risks that we will increasingly be channelled down an ever more refined path until we only see people we agree with and things we already know. For learners who, by definition, wish to move beyond their present boundaries, this can be a particular issue. As long as there are many alternative channels of knowledge this is not a major problem, but with increasing aggregation of data through things like tracking cookies, especially when we are using more personal devices like smartphones and tablets, the number of channels is quickly diminishing.

In a single browsing session, Felix (2012) reported that Facebook alone sets well over 308 tracking cookies without the user granting any explicit permissions, and these can be used by any subscribing sites to customize content and presentation. The lesson this teaches is that it is not always wise to join Facebook, but if one does, blocking tracking cookies using browser add-ons like TrackerBlock for Firefox, or AVG's (currently free) do-not-track browser add-on may help to prevent many recommendations based on past activity. A simpler but less reliable approach is to ensure that one is not permanently logged in to a particular commercial social system. The penalty to be paid for such methods is, however, a loss of functionality: things such as Facebook "like" buttons will no longer work, for example. While one of the worst offenders, Facebook is far from alone in performing wide-ranging tracking. Google's many services, for example, make extensive use of knowledge about who you are to shape the kind of results you receive from their search engine.

Sub-Optimal Algorithms

To err is human, but a collective can really make a mess of things. While the results of a Google search or a recommendation from Amazon or Netflix can be remarkably useful and accurate, they can equally be off the mark, unsuitable to our learning needs and, even if valuable, there may be better alternatives. The recommendations of collectives may be better than those that come from the reflective and critical skills of a human curator, but it depends on many things, notably the selection pool, the algorithm employed, the means of presentation, and the kind of problem being addressed. Despite the best efforts of many researchers and developers, we are some distance away from a perfect set of solutions for all learners and contexts.

Deliberate Manipulation

Another problem with collective systems is that it is hard to build them in a manner that prevents abuse by those who understand the algorithms and presentation techniques they employ. For example, author Dron had a student who added his own work to a self-organizing link-sharing collective system, and who then made use of the naïve social navigation methods the system employed to emphasize and de-emphasize tags, (which was little more sophisticated than a click-through counting system at the time), to promote his own website. Although the system did stabilize in the end as people realized where they were being sent and found it wanting, for a while his site became quite popular. More problematically, the experience left other students feeling less trust in the system. It would be nice to think that this problem had gone away with the increasing sophistication of social systems but, at the time of writing and for at least the past year, Flickr's recent tags are dominated by advertisements and other more dubious content that fails to represent the wisdom of the crowd and results from intentional abuse. This particular collective within Flickr is to all intents and purposes useless but, sensibly, Flickr employs a wide range of other collectives at different time scales capturing different actions so that they may still be usefully employed to find things of good quality and interest to many.

Loss of Teacher and Learner Control

Like networks and sets, collectives pose issues of control that take away some of the traditional power of the teacher in an educational environment. Author Dron has been writing and using collective applications since 1998 and has experienced both more and less delightful results. For example, when he placed his own lecture notes in a collectively driven link-sharing system, (which used advanced tagging and annotation along with self-organizing algorithms to raise or lower resources in ranking according to perceived usefulness), he found that they did not always stay at the top of the list, and once vanished into the second page of results. While it is possible that his notes were terrible, previous evaluations of them had been good and they had been used internationally by other teachers. Instead, this seems to be a positive sign that the collective was better and made more useful recommendations, a supposition borne out through interviews and observations (Dron, 2002) but still potentially bruising to a teacher's ego.

Lack of Pedagogical Intent

Most cybersystem users have "wasted" time following links suggested by systems. Learning is hard work, and more often than not requires focused effort. Collectives are not great at reinforcing such solitudes. The wisdom of the crowd requires the crowd to share a purpose of learning. For example, when using a system with a combination of wiki- and MOOC-like elements which are self-organized according to a combination of stigmergic principles and a design inspired by Jane Jacobs's principles of city design (Dron, 2005b), postgraduate students studying the effects of using communication technologies actually wound up creating a set of resources about chocolate, which interested them more than the subject at hand. Apart from the students' interest in chocolate, there were two main causes of this: on the one hand, this was group work and a poorly defined context and lack of direction made it unclear what was expected. On the other, the process was self-reinforcing and ran out of control, a common problem in stigmergic systems, whereby the rich get richer and the poor get poorer (the Matthew Effect). The combination was good for learning about chocolate, but less effective as a means to think about how we are affected by communication technologies. This was an experimental system, and the episode helped to establish and refine principles for limiting such divergence that we discuss in this chapter.

Shifting Contexts

A collective that has evolved for one purpose may be counter-productive when used for another. For example, collaborative filters that identify preferences based on past preferences may be of little or no value to learners because, having learned what they need to, they no longer require similar things (Drachsler et al., 2007; Dron, Mitchell, Boyne, et al., 2000). In a different context, we need a different collective.

DESIGN PRINCIPLES FOR COLLECTIVE APPLICATIONS

Collectives are predicated on the existence of collections of people, whether in groups or networks. A collective application, perhaps to a greater extent than network, set, or group applications, is potentially far more influenced by the designer, so it is no coincidence that this section of this chapter is larger than those on designing for social forms.

As a cyborg, a collective consists not only of the actions and decisions of individuals but also of the algorithms and interfaces designed by its creator. People are the engine that drives the vehicle, and on occasion perform most of the work in giving it form and function (for instance, in deciding whether the level of threading in a discussion forum is too great or too little to be of interest), but the vehicle itself usually plays a far more significant role in the application than in those designed for networks and groups.

It is important to identify those elements that relate to each of the stages of a collective application: selection, capture, aggregation, processing, and presentation. This must include the things that our programs will do, what we expect people to contribute, and which actions to monitor. Without such a guiding heuristic model, we are likely to be surprised by the results.

In the following subsection we provide a range of issues and heuristics to be considered when designing collective applications for learning. It is not difficult to create a collective application, but it is more complex to create one that helps people to learn. This is very much an overview of large design patterns rather than a guide to building collective applications for learning. Knowledge of collective intelligence mechanisms such as Pearson Correlation, Euclidean Distance, neural networks, and Bayesian probability is very useful, even essential if one is to seriously engage in building such systems, but we will not be covering these technical issues here. Instead, we refer programmers who are interested in the mechanics of collective applications to Segaran's *Programming Collective Intelligence* (2007), which is an excellent primer on the topic and relates almost exclusively to the kind of collective we speak of here. The socially constructed wiki, "The Handbook of Collective Intelligence," (scripts.mit.edu/~cci/HCI/index.php?title=Main_page) is a more formal but less practically oriented treatment of the topic that also covers related ways of thinking about collective intelligence.

Parcellation

As Darwin (1872, chapter XII–XIII) was the first to observe, parcellation is an important feature of an evolving system. This is especially significant when considering large sets, nets, or groups of a tribal form. Without some means of separating out smaller populations, path dependencies mean that the Matthew Effect keeps the successful at the top of the evolutionary tree and makes a system highly resilient to small perturbations, such as new or different ideas. To enable diversity, the evolutionary landscape must be parcellated in some way. This is why many of Darwin's greatest insights came from his visit to the Galapagos Islands, where different species had evolved in isolation. In a learning context, a massive site like YouTube would be of little value if it were not possible to separate out subsections: videos of cats would likely overwhelm those of broader educational value. Similarly, it is possible to parcellate according to temporal scale, paying more attention to, for example, recent and topical items than to an entire body of posts spread over many years. To illustrate the issue, tagging systems in large networks have a tendency to display very uniform and bland sets of tags. For example, over the past six years, over 80% of the most popular Flickr tags have stayed the same, despite a massively growing and presumably changing collection of people that use the system.

The reinforcement caused by existing tags combined with a stable set of generic interests in photography—the tag list includes many obvious ones such as "portrait," "landscape," and "black & white." This means that the list remains very stable over time. Of the less than 20% of tags that changed in that period, most were related to large-scale shifts in interest caused by external factors, such as the season of the year and the popularity of movies. In 2005, for example, New Zealand was a much more popular tourist destination as a result of the Lord of the Rings films than it is today. Smaller groups, conversely, will create tag clouds of popular tags that change as the needs of the group evolve, reflecting change as it occurs. Small populations are more dynamic, and follow the same pattern of parcellation that we see in populations rapidly evolving in natural environments. This situation points again to the importance of parcellation: the smaller the subset, the more likely it is that relevant content will be discovered because the collective will be operating within a more precise context. Evolution happens fastest in small, isolated populations (Darwin, 1872; Calvin, 1997). Natural ecosystems exist in a highly variegated landscape that is frequently divided by borders which species find hard or impossible to traverse.

Relationship of Collectives with Groups, Sets, and Networks

Collectives may form in any size group or network. However, while a number of collectives have equal applicability whether they arise in groups, sets, or networks, some kinds are more relevant to one than the other. For example, in closed groups it is rarely a significant issue to identify the trustworthiness, reliability, and roles of members: it is part of the definition of a group that there will be leaders, that people will know or could come to know other members, and that shared norms and supportive behaviour will arise. In sets, this is far from the case, and there are many collective applications concerned with discovering and establishing reputation, from eBay to Slashdot. Conversely, the fact that we do know more about the goals and needs of people within a group makes some kinds of collective application more effective in groups than in sets. For instance, simple rating systems, especially in large networks, are seldom effective in sets because the needs of people across the set vary widely. However, in a closed group, simple ratings can give an accurate and useful reflection of a group's opinions and beliefs that is valuable within that closed context. In networks, the greatest value of collectives is in mining connections between people to identify relevance. Often, such recommendations are hybrids that also consider set attributes. Facebook's EdgeRank, for example, takes into account professed interests and keywords extracted from content users post or read.

Evolution

Because the content of social sites largely comes from users, they are shifting spaces and, in many set and net forms, there can be a great deal of content of extremely variable quality. Especially once we start to employ collective processes to organize this information, a social site may be seen as a bottom-up organization, an ecology of multiple postings, discussions, videos, podcasts, and more, all competing with one another. As in natural evolution, there is replication with variation. Good ideas spread and become refined, changing to fit the perceived needs and interests of their viewers and participants. When designing a collective system it is therefore important to mindfully introduce selection pressure, prevent out-of-control Matthew Effects, and allow the crowd to sculpt the collective as efficiently as possible. This can be achieved in many ways, through active culling of poorly rated resources, the use of weighted lists through tag clouds or ordered search results, capturing successful paths, and selective or weighted display, among other things.

Diversity

For evolution to occur there must be sufficient diversity so that novel solutions have a chance to compete. The Matthew Effect may stifle diversity but, especially in groups, there is also the risk of groupthink setting in. Parcellation is one way to assist diversity, but it is equally important to create isthmuses between populations, to allow ideas and problems to seep beyond isolated islands. A little randomness can go a long way: it is worthwhile to introduce random results here and there that allow novel and seldom-used resources to be shown.

Constraint

Like natural systems, the evolution in a social site exists within a landscape. Some aspects of this landscape are comfortably familiar—spatial layouts, structural hierarchies, colours, and pages. Others have more to do with process—the algorithms, formal or informal rules, and temporal constraints imposed by the software. How we build the landscapes in which collectives form can have a massive impact on their effectiveness. Whenever we make a design decision regarding the structure or behaviour of our software, we are shaping the landscape in which the ecosystem will develop: if we create oceans, we will get fish. If we build mountains, we will get mountain goats. Constraints can be very useful, allowing the designer to consider not just a broad and unspecific crowd but also one that is using the system with the intent to learn. For example, it may be a valid and helpful constraint to deliberately filter out certain forms of content from the results based on the target audience, or to create top-down categories that relate to anticipated interests. Active shaping can also be used to specify the kinds of activity the user is expected to engage in and make learning more purposeful. For example, using wording like "provide tags that describe the value of this resource to you as a learner" can help maintain a focus on pedagogical rather than less valuable tags.

Very few attempts to use collectives thus far have embedded more than a passing attempt at pedagogy. Collectives have been used as tools within a broader pedagogically driven context, applied within a constrained traditional group context, or relied on as simplistic models of human learning. There is a desperate need for programmers to design systems that use collectives with pedagogic purpose and an architecture built for learning, and to do so in the open world of sets and nets rather than the closed academic groups that most adaptive systems have been created for, if they are to reach their full potential. Google is a wonderful learning technology, but it is not designed explicitly for learning and often recommends resources that are not ideal for a learner's needs.

Context

Particularly in educational settings, the broader context in which we use our social software can play a crucial role in determining the shape it takes. For a collective to have value, it should be derived from and used in a context that relates to current learning needs. As we demonstrated with the group of communication studies students who taught one another about chocolate, it is very easy for a collective to bend to a different set of needs and interests than those that are of most value. In some cases, context can be flexible. Collaborative filters, for example, typically base their recommendations on past interests, which may be poor predictors of value when context changes; but with small adaptations that allow a learner to deliberately specify interests at the time of searching, these filters can still be useful as long as others in the crowd have also specified similar contexts. Unless a system is extremely tightly focused, tags and/or pre-specified categories or topics can help to make a context clear. Tags are most useful when there are alternative means of ensuring that ambiguities will be minimal, for instance by limiting results to those of a specified sub-community through categorizations or special-purpose sites, or by making use of collaborative filtering mechanisms to identify people with similar needs and interests. Another way to make context more relevant is to consider recent items preferentially to overall items rated, increasing the chance that the results are relevant to the current context. This helps to deal with the problem that, once we have learned something, we rarely need to see other resources to help us learn it some more. In some systems, such as CoFIND (Dron, Mitchell, Boyne, et al., 2000), a decay weighting, proportional to relative activity and use of the system, is applied to older resources so that they disappear from the list of recommendations.

Scrutability

Many of the algorithms that generate collectives in cyberspace are trade secrets, jealously guarded by their owners. Outside of Google, Amazon, Facebook, and similar commercial organizations, and beyond the relatively small amount of published work they produce, we can only guess at the means they use to aggregate the wisdom of the crowd to shape our experiences. Where possible, the behaviour of algorithms and the decisions that they make should be explicit, or at least be discoverable. If possible, users should be able to adjust the workings of algorithms and what they display to suit their changing needs. For an end user, however, it is not necessarily a bad thing that some of the details are kept secret. As Kay and Kummerfeld (2006) and Dron (2002) have discovered, while scrutability of algorithms and the ability to adjust weightings is much to be wished for, it increases the complexity for the end user, often with little or no benefit. One way to reduce that complexity is to provide templates, wizards, or a fixed range of settings that fit most needs. However, for those willing to make the effort to fine-tune the collective to their needs, it should be possible to access a wider range of settings as well. Amazon provides a good example in making use of broad-brush algorithms by default, but allowing individuals to provide explicit ratings to improve their recommendations, and to specify items to exclude from the pool used for recommendations. In principle, it is better to allow people to make adjustments at the time when they are needed, rather than as a general setting, but this again increases cognitive complexity.

CONCLUSION

This has been a long chapter that, though it has covered much ground, has barely scratched the surface of the teaching and learning benefits of using collectives. We think it is worthwhile to spend time on it because collectives are central to opening up cost-effective, responsive, socially enabled lifelong learning. We have seen that nets and sets afford rich and varied opportunities for learning but, unlike groups, they are not technological forms and thus do not provide the supporting processes that have evolved over hundreds of years of educational group use. Collectives have the potential to be organizers of learning, teaching presences that can guide and assist learners according to their needs, while allowing them to retain control of the learning process and engage in rich, social learning. Although we have had collectives since the dawn of human civilization, the scale of cyberspace and the potential of social software to generate new and more complex forms of collective makes it perhaps the most significant distinguishing feature between the new generation of online learning and what came before it.

The capacity to examine large-scale networks, and especially sets, allows us to catch glimpses of the group mind that were invisible before, and exploit crowd wisdom in new and pedagogically valuable ways. The dangers of mob stupidity should not be underestimated, however. In entrusting our learning to the crowd we are also entrusting it to the algorithms, both within the minds of the people in the crowd and in the software that aggregates and transforms their use. Careful design of collective applications for learning and mindful awareness of their strengths and weaknesses can go a long way to increasing their reliability, but it is also important for learners and teachers to develop collective literacy: to know what collectives are doing, how their learning experience is being shaped by them, and to know where the dangers lie. In chapter 9 we explore these and other dangers of social software in greater depth.

8

STORIES FROM THE FIELD

In this chapter we discuss a range of examples of social systems used for learning that employ the different social forms we have been speaking of. These are not case studies. Rather, as the chapter title suggests, they are stories, exemplars that illustrate how our model can be used to illuminate different ways of teaching and learning. Beyond that, the stories provide concrete examples of some of the issues and concerns that emerge when attempting to implement a social system for learning, and some of the benefits of doing so.

Our focus will be on a small subset of the systems that we have actively played a part in developing or have created ourselves, each based on the Elgg social framework; a toolset for creating social software environments. This is partly because we know more about these systems than any others, but mainly because they have been informed by, and have informed, our evolving model of crowd-based and social learning. While we have worked with and developed a wide range of other social software systems, these have been either small-scale or constrained by the limits of the tools.

Elgg has provided us with a full palette of possibilities to create a social software environment, and the relatively large-scale institutional uses of these systems have made it possible to examine a broad range of issues that arise. We will begin by briefly describing the context and some of our early attempts to both use existing tools and create our own, and the lessons learned from them. The bulk of this chapter will be concerned with the development and uses of Athabasca Landing, an Elgg-based system that we have been working on for the past three years. It is introduced with a discussion of two Elgg-based systems that we worked with prior to that, which taught us some valuable lessons in social software design and management. We will describe uses in both self-paced and paced distance education online courses, and ways that learning has happened outside formal courses, concluding with some observations on the knowledge bridges that have formed between different learning contexts, courses, and experiences.

LEARNING MANAGEMENT SYSTEMS

Like all pioneer online teachers, we have been exposed to and created courses using a variety of computer conferencing discussion boards, initially with static web pages and associated newsgroups, next with learning conferencing systems, and then using early and later versions of multi-functional learning management systems (LMS) or, as they are referred to in the UK, managed or virtual learning environments (MLEs, or VLEs). Indeed, in the late 1990s and early 2000s, author Dron was co-leader of a team that created such a system. It is thus from first-hand experience that we can assert the organizing metaphor of the LMS has always been the classroom. The vast majority of LMSs have been designed to automate and virtualize processes, pedagogies, methods, and procedures that already exist in institutions and business, and are thus quintessential group environments. Learners are typically assigned to groups by the institutional register, and are presented with a host of management, interaction, and content display tools. Notably, these groups are nearly always paced by the instructor and they march along in sync, typically for a semester of study.

LMS systems almost always feature strict role definitions wherein teachers, or in some cases only course designers, add various interaction modules and the content. An LMS is a very different technology to a teacher than it is to a student. Some kind of assignment drop box and resulting gradebook display serves to automate the reception, marking, and return of assignments, along with the transmission of records of student achievement and class participation to the registrar. With rare exceptions, anonymous participation is prohibited and students are forced to be personally responsible for their contributions and comments. The closed nature of the LMS course serves the group well, as it both defines who is a member of the group, and provides a degree of privacy and opportunity for growth of trust. We have often heard teachers decree that "what happens on the LMS stays on the LMS," and despite the technical capacity for cutting, pasting, and reposting in the public domain, students generally accept the benefits of the closed online context.

The mirror of functionality between the campus classroom and the LMS context is both the system's greatest strength and weakness. Teachers are presented with online equivalents of classroom activities—discussions, presentations, grade books, quizzes, and so on—that have long been institutionalized and become familiar social architectures of formal education. Thus, there is a relatively familiar learning path along which comfortable patterns can be transformed from face-to-face to online contexts—albeit with the added novelty of mediation and time- and place-shifting. However, this tight transposition from classroom to online also militates against the exploitation of new affordances, notably networks and sets that can be harnessed for social learning online. The closed group environment typically prohibits networks of learners, notably those from other sections of a program, alumni, and those with similar interests and learning needs, from contributing to the learning context. The strict privacy control prohibits sharing and commenting, and thus limits opportunities for social capital growth beyond the immediate group. Commonly, the pervasive enrolment control means that contributions from previous cohorts or knowledge resources built through time scales that extend beyond the course completion date are lost—in effect, every cohort starts the learning journey afresh, with no opportunity to benefit from the insights or learning of students who came before. It does not have to be that way, but given the surrounding organizational requirements and habits learned from centuries of face-to-face teaching processes, it is this path of least resistance that is usually taken.

We are not alone in thinking about, building, and testing systems that "go beyond the LMS," and in the next sections we discuss our efforts to do so.

ELGG

In 2005, Dave Tosh and Ben Werdemuller von Elgg released a social software system based on their research into personal learning environments they called Elgg. The system acquired its name because Ben, whose family name is Elgg, ran a website with that name and that is where the first system first resided. Like many developed at that time, Elgg sought to provide a fairly complete social software solution, including blogs, social networking, groups, wikis, file sharing, social bookmarking, and content curation.

While the early 2000s saw many social software systems emerge, from its inception Elgg had some distinguishing features that separated it from the crowd, at least partly due to its evolution within the context of research into online learning. Chief among these was an extremely fine-grained, bottom-up set of access controls. There is no single privacy setting that meets the needs of all potential users. What for one user is an inherent right to free expression and an important way to build social capital through creation of an online identity is for others an invasion of privacy. Moreover, these settings must be dynamic, as one blog message may be thoughtfully restricted to a circle of tight friends, or for a teacher, while the next might be addressed to a network, and a fourth meant for reading across the Internet. Thus, each user (and notably not just the teacher) should be afforded the capacity to set the permissions level on everything they create (Figure 8.1).

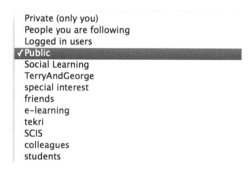

Figure 8.1 Screenshot of Elgg's fine-grained access controls.

COMMUNITY@BRIGHTON

Author Dron was previously employed at the University of Brighton, UK. It is a traditional campus-based university, centred in the city of Brighton & Hove but spread across many campuses in different communities around the south coast of England. After sporadic and independent efforts throughout the 1990s to provide a range of virtual learning environments, including one designed by the author, in the early 2000s a Blackboard-based learning management system was established that integrated with student record systems and other tools, known collectively as "studentcentral." The course orientation of studentcentral and the hierarchies of control that it embodied made it hard to adapt to learner-controlled methods of teaching, and made us painfully aware of the shortcomings of LMS systems. In response, Community@brighton was created by the university's Learning Technologies Group in 2006. Based on the Elgg framework, it was an attempt to provide a richer online social space to bind this distributed community, embed learning beyond coursework and the university, build richer social networks, and perhaps most significantly, enable methods of teaching and learning that were difficult or impossible in the existing studentcentral system. In particular, it was meant to increase opportunities for learner participation and control (Stanier, 2010).

The system was set up so that everyone at the university was automatically given an account, making it possible to claim that it was, at the time, the world's largest Higher Education-based social network, with some 36,000 registered users, growing over the years to nearly 100,000 members at the time of writing. A total of 79% of all those who might log in did so at some point, though few persisted and fewer contributed, with only 4.5% active after two years of operation (T. Franklin & Van Harmelen, 2007).

At first, growth was impressive and the system was used in a wide variety of situations, including academic, social, and support settings. A particularly powerful illustration of its value was its key role in the prevention of a student suicide (T. Franklin & Van Harmelen, 2007). Many innovative uses were made of the system, including some popular alternate reality games to introduce prospective students to the university community (Piatt, 2009), and some innovative pedagogical uses (Dron & Anderson, 2009).

Author Dron was an avid promoter of the system. He was one of the most active contributors to the site, providing presentations and exemplars to colleagues and brought in invited luminaries from the world of online learning to promote the ways it might be used to enhance learning. This, combined with the facts that most viewed the system in a frame within the studentcentral system and students were forced to subscribe to course groups, led to an increasing perception of the site as simply an extension of the existing, institutionally controlled learning management system. Its use polarized, and as alternatives like MySpace, and later, Facebook became more popular, the social and support uses diminished.

A further blow was dealt when, in 2008, the system was upgraded to a new and very different version of the Elgg software which, though more modern and functional in design than the original and far more architecturally elegant, stripped away some of its most important friendly, useful, and usable features, and worse, resulted in the loss of some of the content and presentation work that many had invested in, as well as rendering all existing hard-coded links to parts of the site unusable. Among elements that were lost were the ability to import RSS feeds from other sites, and the means to receive comments from users who weren't logged in. This removed much of the beyond-the-university value of the site in one fell swoop. Other things that were lost included the Presentation Tool, a portfolio system created for the University of Brighton, which further reduced its value as a pedagogic device. Other small but important losses included the means to identify the access settings of particular posts, reducing faith and trust in the system, and a far less effective search tool, reducing the ability to find things across the site. Unwittingly, the new design also more clearly emphasized the institutional role of the system, with a large banner showing announcements and a feed widget displaying institutional announcements. It also began to lose its champions.

Though author Dron remained employed in a part-time capacity at the University of Brighton, he left its full-time employment in 2007 and his involvement, including his strong promotion of the system, diminished from then on. By the end of the first decade of 2010, a financial crisis was beginning to hit UK academia and resources that were at the best of times thin on the ground were increasingly channelled into other projects at the expense of the community@ brighton site. An enthusiastic and skilled learning technologies group still managed to continue with a small amount of development but, on the whole, the site entered maintenance mode.

Community@brighton persists today, but its future is in jeopardy, and currently it is in visible decline. For the past couple of years its main roles have been to provide an advertising bulletin board for students sharing or seeking accommodation, institutional announcements, and a diminishing amount of course-related use, typically involving student blogging—usually only engaged in under duress for course grading. As we write this, of 98,766 users, only three are logged in and a widget displaying "hot topics" is completely devoid of content. The Wire, its microblog (the equivalent of Twitter on an Elgg system) has not been used for 27 days and most posts to it are classified advertisements or requests to meet similar people in the area. We sincerely hope that the system may yet be saved, but the signs are ominous. [1]

PROBLEMS WITH COMMUNITY@BRIGHTON

There are many complex factors behind the slow demise of community@ brighton. We will identify some of the more salient issues.

---

1   As this book goes to the press, we are sad to relate that community@brighton has just been decommissioned.

Interaction Design

Elgg has never been noted for its innate usability. The modularity that gives it great flexibility can, without very complex theming, also lead to a fragmented and often confusing user experience. This is, to some extent, inevitable in a rich toolset without a clear centre or focus, but it is also not helped by unintuitive metaphors, too much click-distance between related items, and inconsistent navigation and action tools. Use of terminology and tools like dashboards, profiles, and widgets confused people, even those familiar with the earlier version of the site, and without a compelling need to stay, drove them away.

Change Management Concerns

We have already noted some of the problems that occurred when moving from one version of Elgg (0.9) to another (1.0). The enormous discontinuity between the two versions came at a time when the site was still finding its feet, and for many, the loss of data and formatting reduced trust and commitment to the site. Had the new version been a compelling improvement things might have settled down quickly, but the loss of functionality that its users had come to depend on, including lecturers who had incorporated it into their courses and those who had simply provided a little content, as well as large changes in terminology and implementation, made the move painful and abrupt. The then-developers of Elgg were widely criticized for the lack of support for existing users, and there was much ill-feeling in the community, despite recognition of the underpinning design's excellence and acknowledgement of the value of the new direction the software had taken.

The old version of Elgg was poorly engineered but very well evolved, while the new version was very well engineered but untried, untested, and lacking in features. None of the many plugins that had been developed for the old version worked in the new one, disenfranchising many in the buoyant and distributed open source developer community so much that some who had invested large amounts of time and effort in developing for the platform felt betrayed. It was like the shift between piston engines and jet engines in the aircraft industry: for nearly twenty years, piston engines outperformed jet engines in nearly every measurable way, until jet engines became sophisticated enough to surpass their predecessors (Arthur, 2009). The new Elgg had immense promise, but in its first iterations, failed to deliver and moreover failed to facilitate a smooth transition from old to new.

Mismatched Social Forms

Elgg supports groups and nets well, and offers a few set-oriented tools like the Wire (its Twitter-like microblog) and tagging. However, this flexibility is a double-edged sword. At any given moment, all of these social forms might be visible and only a click away. One might be in a group context and click a blog link, only to find oneself in a network context. Similarly, one might click a tag to find oneself in the context of a set. This fluidity is a strength in many ways, but also means that it is very hard to get a sense of place on an Elgg site. Furthermore, support for sets is not strong: many of the groups that were created on community@ brighton were actually more set-like than group-like. For example, author Dron's particular favourite, "Grumpy Old Gits"—a group for people to complain about modern life—required users to become members in order to post a complaint, even though what drew them together was only a shared interest in whining about life. For such a set-oriented interest, there is no need for the trappings of group membership—the hierarchies, rules, and norms simply got in the way, and when the group owner lost interest, it became unsustainable.

Another mismatch in forms arose from the fact that academia is a highly discontinuous and hierarchical group form. Students are members of course groups they are periodically engaged with, but the groups have sharply delineated start dates, end dates, and demarcation lines between one course and the next. Furthermore, students and staff are members of faculties and schools that are largely separate from one another, with loose networks connecting them. There are strong boundaries between year groups, with little overlap among networks within them. These and other discontinuities mean that the fluid engagement found in a public social network like LinkedIn, Facebook, or MySpace takes on a more clustered form in academia. Students and staff frequently move between different networks, groups, and sets, often in predictable ways. While Elgg's fine-grained access controls are very useful for keeping these separate, it remains a single space viewed through different filters, and what is suitable for one context may not be suitable for all (Dron et al., 2011).

Lack of Ownership

Partially to compensate for its lack of centre, community@brighton's role as an institutional organ was made too prominent: announcements, banners, and embedding with the institutional LMS fill the main real estate of the site, and conspire to detract from a sense of individual ownership. Because a major point of the site is to provide personal control, anything detracting from that reduces the chances it will be enthusiastically used. A user-owned community site must embody a much different look and feel, and contain different content than the "official" website of an institution. Many users lost trust in the site after content, formatting, and functionality were taken away when Elgg was upgraded, further reducing their sense of control. When changes were made, it seemed that they were being inflicted from above, rather than emerging from the needs and interests of the site's users.

Competition and Overlap on Many Sides

On the one hand, the institutional Blackboard LMS system has added tools such as wikis and blogs that, in limited group contexts, compete favourably with Elgg's tools. If the purpose of an educational innovation is solely to share user-generated content within a closed group context, there are no great benefits from using a system that supports network- and set-oriented modes of engagement. On the other hand, the fact that the vast majority of students have Facebook or other social network accounts makes the need for social networking within the institution less compelling. This reality was compounded by the increased insularity introduced in the newer version of Elgg installed on the site. Another competitor in the form of Microsoft SharePoint, a staff-oriented tool that performs some similar social functions, has reduced the need for a tool that enhances sharing and social cohesion among staff.

Lack of Champions

Less than 5% of the site's population contributed significant content and, among those, many were forced to do so because of course demands. This was a site with a very long tail. Over half of the 30,000 or so blog posts were created by author Dron, or more accurately, by a very buggy RSS tool provided with the earlier version of the site that imported the same posts repeatedly. Even so, Dron contributed some hundreds of unique posts over a period of several years. The loss of a single prolific poster, especially one with a strong evangelical mission to promote the site, was therefore a significant loss. While there were still a few champions after he left, there remained insufficient numbers of people with critical passion to sustain a sense of liveliness and topicality on the site.

Lack of Diversity

The flip side of the very long tail was that a small number of people appeared far more visible than the rest, thus establishing a culture and themes that would not interest everyone. We encounter this issue again later in this chapter when we discuss a site developed to deliberately address the problems raised here. Author Dron over-promoted the site as an educational tool for use in courses, which led to a stronger focus on educational issues and a consequent lack of emphasis on social and support uses. A number of students realized that the site could be a useful bulletin board to advertise rooms wanted and for lease, as it provided a free channel that would be seen by sufficient others to make it successful. The Matthew Effect took hold, driving greater and greater concentration of such uses, eventually leading the development team to design a plugin to support this main use.

Meanwhile, site administrators spotted value to be gained from being able to quickly and easily disseminate information, deliberately promoting such news to the most visible top corner of the site's front page. Although many groups were created for a wide range of interests, clubs, societies, religions, and hobbies, they were overwhelmed by the dominant uses. In order for a generalized social system catering to a set of people to thrive, there must be sufficient reasons for users to be there, otherwise they are like the areas in cities that Jane Jacobs (1961) identifies as dangerously monocultural, such as city centres where people go to work and then leave when the day is done, making them dead and dangerous at night or on weekends.

Periodicity

Students come and go with predictable regularity, typically for three or four years at a time. Champions who created groups and sustained and nurtured them while they were students of the university left, and with their departure the groups they created faded away. Even though many group members and new students might still have had an interest in their topics, the fact that their owners were no longer present meant that newcomers were faced with the choice of joining a moribund group, or trying to start a new, competing one with a similar purpose. This was particularly problematic when the "groups" were really sets—collections of people with shared interests. The mismatch between the group form imposed by Elgg and the social form of the set it was trying to cater to led to fragmentation and dissolution.

Critical Mass

A social networking system only has value if it has many users. This circumstance creates a "cold start" problem, where users do not participate in a new networking system until a significant number of people are present. While enforced enrolment on the site provided a large population at the start, this served to highlight the limited amount of participation relative to the number of users. As user interest waned, it became self-reinforcing. It is not only important for there to be a lot of content, but on a social site, there must be visible and recent activity: the network effects of Metcalfe's Law (1995) also works in reverse, with value decreasing proportionally to the square of the number of nodes in the network when nodes are removed, as MySpace found to its misfortune as its users left for Facebook in droves. The punctuated and time-limited nature of academic life, with ephemeral courses and fixed terms of engagement, meant that groups and networks experienced massive and catastrophic drops in membership every year, every semester, and sometimes in between, reinitializing the cold start problem once again. Only sets and groups, often devoid of active members and sometimes lacking owners, persisted. With ever-reduced resources being put in place to sustain and build these afresh, the site waned.

ME2U

At roughly the same time as community@brighton was being rolled out, author Anderson instigated another Elgg site at Athabasca University (AU) in Canada, named me2u. The reasons for installing the system were broadly similar to those informing community@brighton, though me2u's ambitions were focused on a smaller community. While it did gain members from across AU over time, the site was mainly intended to encourage in-course, beyond-the-course, and open learning within a single academic centre, the Centre for Distance Education. At its peak, it had around 600 users. This smaller and more focused community developed into both a group-based support space and a means to support personal learning through portfolios and social networking within the community, including with its alumni. Its relatively small size meant that it was a mix of groups and tightly knit networks, and activity on the site remained fairly high because its use was required for a significant portion of its users at any one time as a coursework element. With a shared and cohesive vocabulary and purposes, the site appeared to be thriving, but it gained little from the benefits of network- and set-oriented modes of learning, and mostly kept a distinct disciplinary focus.

With far fewer resources than those available at the University of Brighton and without institutional backing, me2u remained a backwater research project but gained some avid users and supporters, driven particularly by Anderson's enthusiastic endorsement of the system, bolstered by Dron on his arrival at AU in 2007. This was shortly before the new and ultimately improved version of Elgg that had caused so much disruption at the University of Brighton was released. Together, the authors of this book combined to build on me2u to achieve broader, more sweeping goals. The changes we planned were to encompass the whole university and beyond, to become a social learning space for formal and informal learning.

ATHABASCA LANDING

The authors' home institution, Athabasca University (AU), is unusual in many ways. It is an open university that accepts anyone regardless of qualifications, though a few senior and many graduate courses do require prerequisite know-ledge or skills. It is almost entirely a distance institution, apart from a handful of courses, mainly at graduate level, with a small residential requirement, and another handful of courses that may be taken at partnered face-to-face colleges. One of its most distinctive features is that almost all of its undergraduate courses are self-paced: students can start a course in any month of the year and have six months to complete it, or up to twelve months with paid-for extensions. They can study and submit assignments and write exams at any time they wish. This provides great freedom of time, place, and pace, but traditionally does so at the cost of limited social interaction and virtually no opportunities for collaboration. Because the chances are very slim of two students with coincident timetables being at exactly the same point in the course at the same time, most interactions that occur in courses are limited to dialogue with tutors, or sporadic questions and answers on shared forums. This means that, though much high-quality learning goes on, the student experience can be lonely, disjointed, and lacking in some of the benefits of learning with others on a shared campus, where serendipitous encounters and the rich interactions of a community of scholars offers benefits beyond those of the formally taught classes. More than that, the focused nature of the dialogues that do occur ensures that it is very easy for gaps to emerge where one hard system does not perfectly interlock with another. Some students fill those gaps by asking questions of others and their tutors, but others see them as gulfs that are disincentives to continue. Dropout rates once a student has leapt the biggest gap of starting to submit work are quite low and compare very favourably with those of conventional universities, but before they ever submit a piece of work or start their course of study, these rates are very high.

The distance nature of the institution is not only limited to students. AU has traditionally followed a production model for most of its courses that evolved in the print and correspondence age of distance learning, with production teams including editors, learning designers, multimedia specialists, subject-matter experts, and a host of supporting roles developing well-engineered courses that are designed to be delivered more than taught. When courses are running, they are supported by teams of mostly part-time tutors and managed by a course coordinator who is often a member of permanent faculty. Faculty themselves are widely distributed geographically, most working from home and living in places spread across Canada, with concentrations in Edmonton and Calgary, and a very few at AU's central headquarters, in the town of Athabasca, which is two hours' drive from the nearest city. Not quite the middle of nowhere, but you can definitely see nowhere from there.

This means that the majority of interaction within the university is at a distance, and despite a plethora of communication technologies used to connect its staff, this makes it a victim of Moore's theory of transactional distance (1993). There are many forms, processes, and procedures required to offset the relatively limited opportunities for dialogue when compared to a traditional institution. Manifold computer-based systems are used to disseminate information, and communicate to and between staff, but in the process, things fall between the gaps. However, communication tools can fill many of the gaps when used effectively. Email, Skype, telephone/teleconference, Adobe Connect, Moodle discussions, Zimbra groupware, and video conferencing facilities help to some extent, but each has limitations. Email is a powerful and effective technology than can be bent to almost any communication and information sharing task with sufficient effort, especially in conjunction with listserv technologies, but it takes a great deal of individual effort to manage effectively. It can be a scheduling system, a content sharing tool, an archive facility, a coursework submission tool, a voting tool, a personal networking tool, and a million other things, including its primary purpose as a communication tool, but each of these uses requires effort as well as organizational and interpretive skill on the part of sender and recipient. Email is also prone to error, inefficiency, and lack of reliability.

Moreover, email is a technology with the individual at its centre, a tool that almost completely blurs boundaries between multiple groups, networks, and sets. Moodle has facilities for discussion and sharing, but its hierarchical, role-based approach and the fact that it mirrors the organizational structures of traditional courses and classrooms makes it inappropriate for more diverse uses. Furthermore, it provides limited personal control over disclosure and connection, especially in set and net social forms. Various forms of synchronous interaction are provided through Adobe Connect webmeeting software, Skype, and dedicated videoconference facilities between AU sites, with consequent limited cooperative freedoms of time, pace and, in some cases, place. Zimbra provides a wide range of tools such as scheduling, chat, file sharing, and collaboration, but it is highly oriented toward group forms of interaction, and because of AU's unusually transient and self-directed student population, is not available for students.

None of the tools that were available provided the kind of variegated, connected social space where many people could co-reside, selectively share, and experience a sense of what others were interested in and doing outside the restricted social roles in which they encountered them. In short, there was very limited support for networks and sets. This was especially problematic for interactions with students, who were at the bottom of the control chain in almost every kind of engagement.

Development of the Landing

In late 2009, with institutional, provincial, and federal funds, the authors helped to create a social site, a kind of virtual campus or learning commons for Athabasca University that was christened Athabasca Landing. Athabasca Landing was named after the original name of the town (a nineteenth-century landing on the Athabasca river) in which Athabasca University is based, but the site has, from the start, been commonly referred to as "The Landing," which is not only shorter but also reflects both its role as a place to land and gather, and a space between other spaces.

The Landing was designed from the start as a place to connect, share, and communicate, to reflect and inform the ideas that we have expounded in this book and in our earlier work, building upon our earlier experiences and benefiting from what we had learned about advantages and pitfalls in Me2U and community@brighton. We intended the Landing to be a place that filled the gaps, both in social engagement and in process, left between our well-engineered, hard, and purpose-driven tools. There were several principles that we formulated early on and that continue to inform its development:

- Ownership and control: the site should be by and for the people that use it, who should have complete control of what they create, who they engage with, and who they share with, without significant hierarchies or top-down control. This made Elgg one of a small range of possible candidates as a platform for the site, as the vast majority of other systems embedded roles, access hierarchies, and top-down control in their design.

- Diversity: the site should be designed to cater to every need, avoiding an excessive emphasis on teaching activities.

- Sociability: social engagement and the ability to connect should be embedded everywhere throughout the site. Related to this was the notion that it should be a trustworthy and safe site, free from commercial motives, hidden agendas, advertising, or manipulation. Once again, Elgg presented itself as one of only a few alternatives that embedded social engagement everywhere, not just in confined spaces.

We discuss more fully some of the concerns, rationales, and discussion we had on these features in the following subsections.

Ownership and Control

We believe one of the reasons that community@brighton failed to reach its potential was that it was perceived as an extension of the institutional system. This perception was significantly reinforced by its most prominent use as a teaching tool: in effect, it became an extension of the classroom for many students, or was viewed as a communications tool for university administration despite its many social networking features and tools to create personal learning environments and bottom-up engagements. This perception was further reinforced by its tight integration with the university's learning management system, a design that emphasized announcements rather than community-created content on its front page, and students' forced membership in course-related groups. Furthermore, all students were automatically enrolled in the system when they registered with the university; they were not given a choice as to whether they were members or not. This immediately took away some of the benefits of deliberate group joining noted by Kittur, Pendleton, and Kraut (2009), and may have reduced motivation to participate as a result.

All of our design decisions about the Landing were based on the principle that its users are its owners. Before even starting to design the site, we enlisted a diverse group of over 50 AU staff and students to choose the tools and technologies to use, and to define its purpose. When the site was opened, we invited these people to join a set of individuals to guide the development of the site: they formed a group we christened "Friends of the Landing." This group has thrived—at the time of writing, it had 97 members: we will report on some of the learning that has occurred within it later in this chapter.

Elgg was not the only possible choice of infrastructure for this new site. When choosing a technology from 50 possible systems that provided the kind of tools we needed such as blogs, bookmarks, wikis, and file sharing, once we had weeded out commercial systems (we needed the flexibility of open source), and those that were hosted elsewhere (there was a need for privacy, in addition to flexibility and long-term ownership), the choice was narrowed down to two: Elgg and Mahara. We were very impressed with a number of content management and blogging systems, such as Drupal, Plone, Wordpress, Joomla, and LifeRay, and many involved in the project argued for extending the existing Moodle learning management system to meet our needs. However, all of these candidates embedded role-based or access hierarchies that meant end users would not be in complete control of their content, or if they were, ensuring they could exercise the rights we wished to give them without impinging on those of others would be an unsustainable management burden.

Mahara is a tool explicitly based on Elgg that specializes in the production of e-portfolios. While it is very good in this role, incorporating social networking and several tools such as blogs, file sharing, and wikis, and it was a highly polished product, its other features were decidedly lacking when compared to Elgg, and the effort required to add new features would be considerably greater. Both were extendible, but Elgg was vastly superior at that time: Mahara had a small handful of plugins compared to many hundreds available for Elgg. Elgg's architecture had been completely reworked shortly before we were choosing systems in order to make it more of a social software construction kit than an extendible system, and so, as it was our intention to mould the system as closely as possible to the social forms we had identified and principles of design we had established, the final choice of the Elgg system was almost unanimous. We note, though, that the psychological lock-in to a system we were familiar with through development of Me2u may have influenced our decision. There were practical benefits to leveraging existing knowledge and skill sets, even though Elgg itself had undergone major revision.

Context Switching

Academic life for both students and faculty is a disjointed affair, with frequent and abrupt shifts between different social contexts: classes, courses, research areas, departments, terms, and so on, demarcate borders between areas of interest and sets, networks, and groups of people. Access permissions and the functionality of groups, networks, and collections allow users to both selectively reveal different things to different people and filter what they see according to various needs. We have built a number of tools that make switching between contexts more explicit and intentional by allowing people to place highly configurable widgets on different tabbed spaces for different purposes:

- Super-widgets: Widgets are small objects that can be placed on the screen to display (but usually not add to) different kinds of content—for instance, to view blog posts, files, recent activity, groups we belong to, and so on. Users of widgets can also access different social sites and services such as Twitter, newsfeeds from other sites, et cetera. Widgets can be placed in groups, on personal profiles, and on the user dashboard (a learning space used to organize and personalize an individual's view of the site), and serve to alert users about fresh content, upcoming events, or important addresses. We have made extensive modifications to the widget functionality provided by Elgg so that users have far greater control over what they show, allowing filtering according to group, network, or set (through tags), date range, individually selected posts, and more. We added sorting and display options that make it easy to configure a group, profile, or dashboard according to individual needs and contexts.

- Tabbed profiles and dashboards: to support the super-widgets, we have extended the single-page views of individual and group profiles as well as dashboards to allow multiple panels for different contexts (see Figure 8.2 below). People can create tabs for particular courses, interests, and intentions, each filled with different widgets showing different content. This allows individuals to both switch between contexts—for example, to separate social from academic interests—and present different facets of themselves or their groups to others. Because each tab has the same sets of permissions applied to it as all other objects on the site, people can display one aspect of themselves to their friends, another to their teachers, and a third to the world at large. Similarly, research groups can have a tab that supports internal working processes and another to display their outputs to the world.

Figure 8.2 Profile page on the AU Landing, showing widgets, tabs, and the "Explore the Landing" menu.

A Soft Space Made of Hard Pieces

The Landing is highly componentized, both in architectural terms (Elgg has a very small core and gains almost all of its functionality from plugins) and in interaction design. For an end user, Elgg provides a set of tools that can be assembled, aggregated, reassembled, and integrated in an infinite number of ways. Creating a different use for the Landing is simply a question of assembling and configuring components to suit specific needs. The intention is to escape the prescriptiveness of a role-based hierarchical system such as an LMS, but to reduce the difficulties of building a system from the ground up. Widgets, tools such as blogs, wikis, bookmarks, and files, groups, tabbed groups, and individual profiles can be combined in many ways to meet diverse needs. The balance between ease of use and flexibility is difficult to achieve, and we are still some way from getting the balance right for everyone; indeed, this may be a quixotic search. One of the most frequently voiced complaints about the Landing is that it is complex, confusing, and hard to navigate. To deal with this, we are currently adapting a range of strategies, including story-sharing, social menu organization, and community-led design.

Sharing of Stories and Ideas

The help system of the Landing is constructed using the wiki tools available on the site, and we have attempted to encourage users to share their stories and suggestions within this context. However, few have done so, perhaps because the wiki is available in a Help group context, whereas it is more clearly and obviously a set-oriented activity: it would be unusual to feel a sense of membership for a help system unless one was explicitly recruited to it. Unwittingly, we have made use of the wrong social form to provide help within the system. However, a few Landing members have independently begun to share their stories and insights. A student, for instance, started "the Unofficial Landing Podcast" and interviewed other students, Landing founders, and even the AU president on topics of interest to AU members. A member of staff created a podcasting group in which he and a few others present ideas, links, and tutorials on podcasting though, once again, the group form acts as a barrier to entry, and means it remains primarily the domain of a single enthusiastic user. Another student started a videocast series that explored similar themes to the Unofficial Landing Podcast, but has since left the university. As we saw with the University of Brighton, individuals' sporadic and time-limited involvement in the community causes problems of continuity and acts as a barrier to ongoing engagement.

Social Organization of Menus

Instead of the default tools-oriented menus natively provided by Elgg, we have reorganized the structure of the site in accordance with our model of sets, nets, and groups. The menus we provide are:

- You: profiles, dashboard, settings, options to view one's own activity and content, and to post new content.
- Your network: options to see what people one is following are doing, as well as to discover and connect with new people.
- Groups: options to see one's groups, the activity within them, and to join new groups.
- Explore the Landing: options to focus on specific tags and keywords relating to topics of interest (sets).

These explicit perspectives help to control the kind of interactions people have with others on the site. Those who wish only to engage in group contexts should be less distracted by network interactions, those who are interested in their connections with others should find them more easily, and those with specific interests should find it simple to discover and explore subjects and topics that matter to them. However, once users follow a link, they may soon find themselves in different contexts from those where they began, and this reality limits the extent to which the social organization of menus achieve the desired goals.

For example, when exploring the site-wide categories, as soon as an individual clicks on a specific post, they are immediately flung into whatever social context it was created in, often a group or a network, which requires a subtle transformation of perspective to understand the relationships between what they are viewing and what else it relates to. This remains an ongoing design problem.

Community-led Design

We are also engaged in a constant cycle of refinement that incorporates feedback and suggestions from the Friends of the Landing and others on the site. We have added an instant feedback link on every page using AJAX, so individuals can make comments without leaving the context in which their issue arose, or instigated discussions to which many have contributed. The ideas we have gathered as a result are beyond our technical capacity to deal with in a timely manner, but we are making progress all the same.

We also realize that even within closed communities, users may purposively or inadvertently post content that others find objectionable or unlawful. Thus, we have a link on the footer of each page where users can report content that they feel violates norms or laws. Fortunately as administrators we have yet to see use of this link, but there has been controversy and discussion about a number of posts (we will discuss this later in the chapter).

The Friends of the Landing have monthly or bi-monthly meetings via web-meeting tools, and we have evolved a process of round-robin discussion where people share their experiences, concerns, and interests. This is not only a useful source of feedback for design purposes but also a means of sharing stories and ideas that spread through the community.

Diversity

Both Me2U and community@brighton became, for different reasons, monocultures. Me2U's limited user base, largely drawn from a single, highly focused academic centre and just a few courses, was never evolved into a general purpose environment. The combination of academic focus, lack of ownership, and the exigencies of being a face-to-face university where, though campuses were distributed, most people who needed to meet in person did so, led to community@brighton eventually serving only three main purposes: teaching, announcements, and advertisements attempting to fill shared rooms in houses. While many other communities were created and some flourished for a little while, there were few reasons to visit the site outside of those specific needs, and so visits tended to be brief and task-focused.

As a starting point, we expended a fair amount of effort on migrating as much of the content and users from the older Me2U site as possible because it was being actively used in teaching and we could not sustain two social sites at once. This had a number of repercussions, not the least of which was an extremely strong emphasis on distance learning interests right from the start. As we observed in the last chapter, the impact of path dependencies and the Matthew Effect meant that we were starting in a weak position from which to encourage diversity. We adopted a number of mitigating strategies in an attempt to swing the balance away from this focus, actively recruiting our assorted group of Landing Friends to contribute from their diverse fields of interest, running events and giving talks to encourage people from across the university to engage, and deliberately shaping the environment—for example, we removed a tag cloud at the start that showed virtually nothing but education-related tags. Despite this positive discrimination and much work to encourage diversity over the past three years, the effects of this early bias continue to be felt. On the bright side, because AU is a distance university, many people who are not actually studying distance education do take an interest in and benefit from the rather large amount of content and interaction on this subject.

Sociability

One of the reasons for choosing Elgg over alternatives such as the institutional Moodle site was that sociability was built into every part of the system. Unless people choose otherwise, the default behaviour for every object created—be it a file, a photo, a blog post, a wiki, a bookmark or a calendar event—is to enable comments and discussion to evolve around it. Whenever such commentary does occur, the individual who made it is shown in avatar form, with a hyperlink that allows people to follow them.

We deliberately changed the default Elgg vocabulary of "friends" to "followers," partly because that is a more accurate description of the one-way relationships enabled by Elgg. I do not necessarily "follow you" if you follow me, unlike the reciprocal relationship of Facebook friends. We mainly did this because we did not wish to suggest a specific kind of relationship when one person connected with another. In many cases, we knew that people would be following the activity of teachers, for example, and using the relationship as a means of sharing work with them. We also recognized that many people would be sharing work with and following the work of colleagues, co-researchers, and others who may not accurately be described as "friends." Elgg supports a feature known internally as "collections" that allows one to group those one is following into sets. One can create collections labelled with anything, such as "friends," "co-workers," "COMP602," and so on. We improved this functionality to make it easy to create such sets at the time of following, in a manner almost identical to that which was later used by Google+ when it introduced Circles. Because of the subsequent popularity of Google+, we renamed "collections" as "circles" in order to make them easier to recognize.

We built a tool to enable comments on public posts from people who were not logged in, to support beyond-the-campus interactions, and extend the site beyond a closed, group-like community to broader sets and nets around the world. To make it easier to find people, we provided a tool that identifies followers of people one follows and fellow group members.

The Social Shape of the Landing

The Landing supports social networking functionality, but is not exclusively a social network like Facebook, LinkedIn, or Bebo. As Chris Anderson puts it, social networking is a feature, not a destination (2007). Many of the uses of the Landing are group-oriented, but the fact that the technical form of a group has been employed does not always mean that the social form is appropriate: many groups are simply used to collect a set of resources around a single topic. For example, several students have created groups to amalgamate individual portfolios or research findings, while other groups have been created as a focus for areas of interest, such as the "Zombie Research Group" or "First World Problems"; a staff member has created a site to share photos of convocation events. Because of this, we have built a plugin explicitly intended to support sets that we call the Pinboard. Pinboards are technically similar to groups in the functions they provide but do not have any notion of explicit membership: essentially, they are containers for objects akin to boards on Pinterest or Learni.st. Unfortunately, though our Pinboard is a powerful plugin that has been taken up by many other Elgg-based sites around the world, it is far from easy to use and has not been as widely adopted within our own community as we had hoped.

Default Access

The capability of Elgg to provide fine-grained access control has worked well. However, thanks to the power of the default (Shah & Sandvig, 2005) permission setting has proven to be a powerful determinant of user choice. In the very early days, we hoped to attract outside readers and thus left the default permission to "public." However, we soon found that many users had left this as their default, and a few were not pleased with the exposure on Google search engines that resulted. We thus changed to default to "logged in users" for general posts and to the members of a group, for content posted within groups, leaving it open for the user to set more or less restrictive permissions if desired.

A second useful feature of Elgg is the capacity to open or close membership to the site. We have chosen to allow login by any member of the university community (teachers, students, staff, and alumni) and have integrated the single sign-on used for other university systems. Although we have manually added a few guests working on research projects and so on, this has meant that potential contributors from outside the Athabasca network and set have been denied the opportunity to participate. We did, however, build in a moderated comment tool for outsiders to add comments to posts that are explicitly made public after appropriate moderation by the poster, to prevent spam comments. Thus we have described our Elgg installation as a "walled garden with windows." Membership in the site is restricted, but any member can open a window through which their contributions can be viewed and commented on from outside.

At the time of writing, the Landing has more than 5,000 users who have, between them, created over 20,000 resources, including around 8,000 blog posts, over 6,000 file uploads, and thousands of other objects like bookmarks, wikis, photos, polls and events, along with countless comments and annotations of other posts. There are nearly 400 groups. It is hard to analyze the precise purpose of all of these without interviewing the individuals who create and use them, and groups have a tendency to evade neat categorization: for example, groups that are purportedly related to a course may turn out to support a specific research student or project or, in a couple of cases, students may have set up their own versions of official course groups. Such is the bottom-up nature of the Landing. Bearing this in mind, we have attempted to classify the kinds of uses, using an iterative coding process. Relying on the descriptions provided and some informed guesswork, for instance, by identifying course names and numbers or recognizing specific organizational groups, we see the following breakdown:

> Research-related: 16%
> Personal: 5%
> AU business (e.g., committees and working groups): 15%
> Academic centre or faculty: 5%
> Non-formal learning (e.g., support groups for computing or hobbies): 9%
> Course-related (e.g., study groups, project groups): 21%
> Course administration (e.g., development or tutor groups): 2%
> Course (formal): 18%
> Social (e.g., local meetups): 2%
> Subject area: 2%
> Landing-related (groups supporting research, operations, etc. in the Landing): 4%
> Experimental (set up and forgotten): 1%

While there is still plenty of room for increased diversity and an understandably large emphasis on things that are related to teaching and learning, we have achieved some success in making the site sufficiently diverse so that there is more than one reason for someone to visit the site. Among the biggest of these is in formal course use. In the following section, we provide a few examples of the way that the Landing is used to support and enhance formal courses.

Information Technology (COMP 607)

Ethical, Legal, and Social Issues in Information Technology (COMP 607) is a gradu-ate- level course provided to students in a distance-taught MSc in Information Systems at AU. The previous iteration of the course was based around a book, with weekly discussion forums centred on different chapters. It was a classic group-based course, with tutor-guided discussions enabled on Moodle, shared study of a single text, a set of short essays, marks given for participation, and a final examination, taken at home. Because study was paced, the group form was an appropriate approach but, as all students were working in the IT industry and had rich experiences to share, there were opportunities to draw more broadly from their own knowledge and gain from "teachback" (Pask, 1976) in a more networked manner. Furthermore, each iteration of the course had started with a blank slate, a newly replicated version of the original Moodle course, so none of the learning and knowledge building of previous iterations carried forward to new cohorts.

For the new revision of the course, a Moodle course was created with a broad and flexible course outline and a few selected readings, and the Landing was used as the platform where all course activities occurred. A group (defined in Elgg as a container for content and interaction with members) for the course was created. This automatically opened up the opportunity for a persistent record of student activity that would remain for the next cohorts to draw upon. The group would therefore naturally draw in more of the set, and open up opportunities for a net-work to develop, if previous group members remained in the group (membership after the course being voluntary).

The course was structured around a variety of social processes, a mix of debate formats such as fishbowls, team debates, Oxford-style debates, and small group discussions, and combinatorial cooperative strategies such as sharing bookmarks and contributing to an "encyclopedia." Each week revolved around a topic that, after some introductory exercises in ethical and moral debate, explicitly focused on topics in the news. This emphasis on events within a few weeks of the course beginning ensures that students learn from previous cohorts but do not copy them. Basic arguments and viewpoints can and do repeat from one cohort to the next, but the content is always different and draws from a broader network.

Having run through two iterations, the course has been successful from the point of view of the experience and outcomes. Comments from students were positive: "I was impressed by the level of intellectually stimulating debate. It certainly twisted my brain in a new direction and I am among a great group of folks!" and "I've enjoyed the discussions and the debates, and have learned a lot from people with different viewpoints," and "it's nice to see how many people have contributed to the discussions, almost everybody answering a different question." However, the positive benefits were largely the result of pedagogical design that could have been achieved within a Moodle course using conventional group tools. The set and net benefits were thin on the ground, but some were seen. The second iteration of the course benefited notably from access to the work done by the previous cohort, especially when it came to the ongoing development of the "encyclopedia," and there were two interjections from previous course members, which suggests value in ongoing networked connection with a course. Some benefits were seen from references to other posts by people from other faculties on the site, and one staff member from a different department contributed a couple of comments on open posts. However, the fact that the group was closed militated against deep involvement from across the set/net of the rest of the site, despite many of the students posting their work for all logged-in users and, in a couple of cases, public viewing.

All of this is, in retrospect, an inevitable consequence of following a traditional, closed-group process and the highly task-oriented instrumental approach used by most students accustomed to this mode of teaching. A major benefit of using the Landing, however, is that it is within the power of the teacher to implement change. In the next iteration of the course, it will no longer be a closed group. While assessment will, as ever, be limited to the paid-up members of the course, the group on the Landing will be open to anyone wishing to join. We hope that this will bring about a more interesting dynamic and encourage engagement from others beyond the course.

Planning and Management in Distance Education and Training (MDE605)
This semester-length course operates in paced mode and is compulsory for students in a distance Masters of Education program. The course has run for a number of years in Moodle, and the major assignments revolve around iterative development of extensive business and evaluation plans. The Moodle environment was used to store content and for the assignment dropbox, but all interaction took place in a closed Landing group limited to registered students in the course, though additional students were added each year. Students could choose to remain in the group and receive notifications of activities in subsequent years

and add comments, or resign from the group upon completion. Thus, unlike typical LMS systems, students were able to review contributions, blogs, comments, wiki pages, and most importantly postings of assignments—draft iterations of business plans from former students. In addition, students were encouraged to post links to useful resources they found on the Net, and were required to post a summary blog in which they reflected on their contributions and experience in the Landing context. The course ran for three years, and thus a considerable "archive" accumulated. Students could choose to share their assignments with or without the marks and audio marking annotations inserted by the instructor (Terry Anderson). Interestingly, some chose to address deficiencies identified before posting assignments, while others chose to leave them.

Almost all the students expressed enthusiastic appreciation for the archive, especially the submitted and marked assignments. In a follow-up research study, students made comments, such as, "I had no idea how to approach this assignment until I saw what other students had done—it was great!" However, a minority were uncomfortable with this exposure to others' work, and stated, "I came to learn this material myself, looking at the work of others would be cheating." It strikes us that the latter attitude inhibits the great affordance of the Net: to search for and build upon the contributions of others, a process which has defined scientific publication and knowledge growth for centuries.

Also of interest was the decision made by the next teacher of MDE605, after Anderson moved to other teaching assignments, to discontinue using the Landing and revert to the standard Moodle presentation. This may illustrate the challenges of implementing change and the conservative nature of many academic institutions. Or perhaps it only illustrates the need for enthusiastic early adopters to propel exploratory use of new technologies.

THE LANDING IN A SELF-PACED COURSE

Athabasca University's undergraduate courses are all based on individual study. Students enrol any month of the year, are assigned tutors, and then have six months to complete the course as it suits them. While catering well to many of the cooperative freedoms, it has historically been almost impossible to gain the benefits of group processes (collaborative or cooperative learning) in this self-paced context. Most people take courses in isolation, with occasional contact with tutors via email or telephone, and formal points of contact established for feedback on regular assignments.

Over the past decade or so, course designers and instructors have increasingly used learning management systems, particularly the centrally supported Moodle system, and many courses have incorporated group forums as an attempt to increase a sense of social presence and reduce the loneliness of the long distance learner. To some extent this has worked, inasmuch as forums have become places where students can ask questions about the course, and on the whole, get answers, sometimes from tutors and sometimes from other students. However, the group discussion forums are, as the name implies, designed for groups, whereas these independent learners are, in most respects a set, only bound together by the characteristic of taking the same course at the same time. Typically the forums are little used and often not effectively moderated by tutors, who are not paid for this "extra" work. Unlike a group, there is no shared collaborative purpose: everyone is doing his or her own thing at his or her own time, without dependencies on other people. Most of the time, beyond a name or occasional shared profile (optional, of course), the rest of the group remains anonymous, part of an undifferentiated crowd.

COMP 266

Introduction to Web Programming (COMP 266) is a course in HTML, JavaScript, and related technologies that had been running for a number of years as a textbook wraparound course. A study guide, available on a Moodle site, provided guidance on readings and exercises in the textbook. Moodle was used to provide a set of self-assessment multiple choice questions, a means of submitting the four assessment exercises for the course, and a threaded forum. The forum was almost exclusively used to get answers to specific questions and, as a result, over a period of years became a poorly organized but well-used repository of knowledge for students seeking information. Most students contributed nothing to the forum however, and for many, their only human interaction was with the tutor in the form of feedback on assignments. At the end of the course, students sat an exam at one of many exam centres around the world either run by AU or franchised out to other institutions. The course appealed to a few, but there were many complaints and many who registered but failed to complete the course.

In the course's revision, author Dron applied many of the ideas and principles expounded in this book. While there were clearly few, if any, opportunities to make use of group-based learning, the natural set orientation of the self-paced course mode of delivery suggested a range of possible approaches. There were also opportunities to foster the formation of networks and, at least in principle, to use collectives to help harness the wisdom of the crowd.

Figure 8.3 COMP 266 group profile page on the Landing.

The course makes use of Moodle to provide fixed content, a place for students to submit work, and self-assessment exercises. Students are required to follow a guided and scaffolded process to build a single website that gains in sophistication as the course progresses, starting with a design unit the rest of the work is based upon, then working through HTML, CSS, JavaScript, library re-use, and AJAX integration. Students choose what the site is about, what functions it will have, and everything else about it. There are stop-points throughout where tutors give feedback but no grades, to ensure that students stay engaged and do not take on too much or too little to succeed. The only assessment for the course is a single portfolio: students are given a grade for each intended learning outcome rather than on work performed for particular units. Throughout, students are required to submit all the work they do via a closed group on the Landing (see Figure 8.3 below) in a learning diary that contains reflections, design artifacts, code, and so on, as well as links to their publicly visible sites. Students are permitted to set any permissions that they like for this work, as long as the tutor can access it as well. Many limit access to the group (the default), almost as many allow access to all logged-in users (members of the larger Athabasca community), and a few provide access to the whole world. A very limited number restrict access to only their tutor. Because grades are given for learning outcomes rather than specific pieces of work, students may submit any evidence they like of having met them, including annotations of links shared with others, help given to others, and general commentary in their learning diaries. This helps to align marks with incentives to participate in the set, without enforcing sociability on those who do not wish it. Those who do not want to engage or who wish to remain peripheral participants can be successful simply by creating a good website and set of reflections, but there are still dividends to be had from sharing.

From the point of view of the students, the course has been a huge success by allowing a full range of cooperative freedoms. However, this is again the result of pedagogical design, although unlike our previous examples, such a pedagogy would have been difficult or impossible without the ability to selectively share anything with anyone. Many students comment on the value of being able to see what others are doing and thinking, and benefit from the amplification effects of tutor and student feedback on work posted. Notably, students explicitly mention that they are inspired by what others have done, and are motivated to excel by the fact that others are not just looking at their work but displaying an active interest in it. There is a great deal of camaraderie in the course, with some students referring to their fellow students as a "cohort," despite the fact that it is nothing like one from an organizational perspective—by and large, this is a set, with cooperative sharing and mostly unsustained dialogue forming the bulk of social interaction.

Nevertheless, the overwhelming amount of communication has caused problems for many—we do not yet have powerful collective tools to provide the necessary filtering for this, though a collaborative filter is in testing as we write this book. This is exacerbated by a poor design choice to require students to share a single course blog. Although this does have benefits in making everything visible, which was the intention, there is simply too much to pay attention to. In other courses author Dron has created on the Landing, students either share their own personal blogs or make use of hierarchically structured wikis so that their work is still visible but separate from the rest. The wiki approach is more successful in a group context and still provides the benefits of visibility, but the personal blog approach has value in extending the course into the broader network. Beyond these issues, the interface is often seen as unintuitive, at least partly because of the ongoing confusion, despite our best efforts, of group, net, and set social forms, as we described in an earlier paper on a similar course run at the University of Brighton (Dron & Anderson, 2009).

INFORMAL LEARNING ON THE LANDING

While course-based uses of the Landing have shown the potential for social tools to expand the number of pedagogies we use and improve the motivation and engagement of learners, even beyond the course period itself, one of our biggest hopes for the site was that it would support learning outside of courses, to help build a richer learning community and foster forms of engagement that navigated the formal boundaries.

The Friends of the Landing

In the formal constitution of the Landing, we deliberately avoided the usual nomenclature of "steering committee" to describe the people who would help guide its development; opting instead for a "steering network" we christened it "Friends of the Landing." We wanted it to be an informal and inclusive collection of people who engaged as based on interest and propinquity rather than as a result of the formal group edicts and processes that guide a typical closed-group committee. Anyone who uses the Landing can be a Friend of the Landing, and like most friends, the commitment does not require them to follow schedules, meet quorum requirements, or adhere to established rules of conduct. Though we described it as a network and implemented it in an Elgg group, this is in fact more akin to a set, bound together by a shared interest in how the Landing develops. The Elgg group is simply a container where social objects of interest like discussions, links, minutes, wiki pages, and blog posts are shared. Almost all activity that goes on within the group is provided by people who set access rights to all logged-in users rather than to the group alone, demonstrating and reflecting its set-like nature. Similarly, though the vast majority of set members have chipped in from time to time, the fact that engagement is driven by current interest rather than commitment to a group, its members, and norms, strongly suggests that the set mode of engagement dominates this collection of people.

However, there are more complex patterns of social engagement overlaid on the group that make it a far from equal set. While some are unknown to others, many are networked with one another in different contexts, sharing the same groups or working together as staff members, friends, and fellow students. As in any formal education institution, there are power relationships in which AU staff are recognized as a different set from AU students, as well as more complex divisions within the staff that contribute both on academic and organizational lines: faculty, learning designers, administrators, and others exist in formal and informal juxtapositions within an institutional context. Notably, the core development team has a particularly strong role in an informal hierarchy, as the majority of decisions and suggestions made within the set are channelled through them, interpreted, and filtered, before being implemented on the site. Adding to those inequalities, people have to actually join the group to fully engage with all the tools: while most allow anyone with the rights to see them to comment, wikis and discussion forums are, at the time of writing, a peculiar subset of Elgg technologies that can be seen but not engaged with by people outside a group. We will be changing this in our new "set" developments, but unwanted mismatches between the set and various group and network social forms occur, since people deliberately have to become members because of the group's technological form, and a group has owners.

There are synchronous meetings held monthly via an Adobe Connect web-meeting system to which all Friends of the Landing and, emphasizing the set-based nature of the engagement, anyone using the Landing are invited, but a lot of involvement takes place via the Elgg group itself. In addition to members of the core development team, the group contains faculty, support staff, administrators, graduate and undergraduate students, interested bystanders, alumni, and executives of the university. The proportions are not determined by any formal constitution—those who are members are those who have self-selected to join. Sometimes, people contribute from beyond the group of members, as virtually all communications within the group are shared with all logged-in users of the site and a few are available to the whole world.

The other collection of people intimately involved with Landing development is the Landing Operations Group. Unlike the Friends, this is a true group in most senses of the word. It has a distinct mission and purpose, is closed to non-members, involves strong social ties, and is hierarchically organized: there are three co-leaders, the authors of this book and George Siemens. Most of its online activities take place in its closed Elgg group but it has regular weekly meetings in person/via teleconference, and also uses other tools such as the Bugzilla software management tool to manage interactions.

BRIDGES AND ISTHMUSES

As well as the relatively formal uses of the Landing that we have reported on so far, threads of knowledge weave back and forth across the site, breaking out of course boundaries, sets, and formal groups and spreading across the network. To help foster this diversity, we have designed the site with a number of tools that make it likely for one to encounter the posts of others, with related content displayed in several places, a configurable activity river that shows posts from across the site and for specified groups and circles of people one follows, a random content widget that displays posts from across the site, and more. The Landing is a thriving community where comments are very common, including those that come from beyond the walled garden, and there is diverse activity and a strong sense of awareness of what others are doing. Although we have (yet) to implement real-time chat capabilities, several people have commented on the sense of reassurance and value gained from seeing that others are online, displayed via a counter on the site's front page. There are typically 20–30 people logged in and identified as active (i.e., having loaded a page within the past two minutes) at any one time during the day. As I write this at 2 a.m. on a Sunday morning, even allowing for time zones (from 1 to 4 a.m. across most of Canada), I see that there are seven other people logged into the system. I have no idea who they are, but the collective thus plays a role in giving me a sense of relatedness with others.

The Landing is a work in progress, and there is a long way to go before we can trumpet its success. We outline some of the remaining issues in the following subsections.

Punctuated and Time-limited Engagement

Some of the problems that beset community@brighton remain on the Landing, and in some cases are magnified in the Athabasca University context. In particular, the fact that many students are visitors taking a single course who are not even enrolled in a program means that the punctuated nature of engagement that played a strong role in community@brighton's dynamics is an even greater problem at AU. It is very hard for a student who is taking a single course for less than six months, with little social engagement in most cases, to feel any sense of ownership or belonging in a transient community. While we make it clear that, unlike access to most other university services, Landing accounts persist for the foreseeable future even when students have left, for transient students there are few compelling reasons to join or remain in the community at AU. Given the rarity of in-course communication between students apart from those created on and for the Landing, there are seldom networks of people to make it worthwhile to remain on the site; even when they form, close personal friendships or professional relationships are more likely to be maintained on a purpose-built and heavily populated site like Facebook or LinkedIn.

Lack of Diversity

For all our efforts to foster diversity, the strong Matthew Effect caused by an early influx of distance education students, combined with the fact that the most persistent users of the site are staff who have an inevitable interest in distance education, means that distance and online learning is by far the most prominent area of interest on the site. Because we have a strong policy of technological non-interference, all we can do to ameliorate this problem is evangelize about alternative uses, nurture these when they occur, and make explicit our celebration of diversity. But, though we are among the most prolific posters to the site, and we do run workshops and presentations, particularly to encourage staff members to participate, our views are just two among many.

Sets, not Groups

As we have already mentioned, the Friends of the Landing should be a set but is embedded in a group tool and is comprised of multiple overlapping groups and networks, all playing a significant role in its formation. We illustrate this with an example of a discussion that occurred around a problem users had commented on both in the group and across the site: that people sometimes post things others find distasteful, offensive, or boring. On the whole, the access control facilities on the site prevent such things from occurring, as people usually recognize there is a limited audience and deliberately post sensitive materials so that only those with an interest will see them. However, that is not always the case, and on some occasions, there are very good reasons to make controversial or sensitive posts public. Yet because of the diverse sets of people on the site, some of whom are engaging due to coursework requirements, and all of who have diverse tastes and ethical or religious stances, this caused problems for some users. A couple users commented that they usually accessed the site from the workplace, where some content is forbidden or disapproved of. The discussion was started with a message outlining the problem and providing three solutions that Friends of the Landing had suggested, none ideal:

1. To provide the means to filter out/ignore specific individuals
2. To (optionally) censor specific words
3. To encourage people posting potentially sensitive content as "not safe for work"

For the purposes of this story and in the interests of preserving the right to privacy of the participants, we do not examine the discussion in detail, but will observe some of the outcomes that occurred to illustrate how the discussion was a valuable learning experience, how it failed to achieve the initial goals of its initiator, and how it resulted in further conversations that highlighted the complex interplay of group, set, and net modes of interaction on the Landing.

The discussion was a rich learning dialogue, in which many diverse points of view were brought to the table, with distinct camps in computing, social sciences, education, and support/administration staff. The discussion often revolved around the complex issue that the participants were not all equal, some being students of the staff involved, others being recognized researchers in their different fields, bringing expertise and vocabularies that required a great deal of unpacking and explanation. These explanations and clarifications provided benefits for many participants, several of whom commented on the enormous value they were getting from it as a transformative learning experience. Many difficulties were caused because some treated the Friends of the Landing group as a community, while others saw the whole Landing (the tribal set) as the community under discussion, and some were interacting with people they knew from other contexts. The fact that this was not, technically speaking, a typical hierarchical group, but more of a set, made it very difficult to come to conclusions.

Suggestions that problems should be resolved by establishing a cooperatively designed social contract, for instance, were difficult to bring to fruition because the discussants recognized that the Landing is not a single community but many, with different social forms including groups and sets and networks. Each of these cross-cutting cleavages has different, sometimes overlapping but often divergent needs and interests. By the time the discussion fizzled out, after branching into two further sub-discussions, over 180 messages had been exchanged, many of them lengthy and filled with references and links to further readings, and the discussion continued for some time in ensuing reflective blog posts. As we write this, no solution has been found that satisfies everyone, and it remains an ongoing wicked problem.

Ownership

We have noted the central importance of ownership and commitment, but it takes a huge leap of faith for an individual to commit posts and effort to build a network when the future of the site itself is unknown. One the many things that was done right at the University of Brighton was to make a commitment for the long haul (Stanier, 2010). It was recognized from the start that a large-scale social system needs time to grow, and growth cannot occur unless the people occupying the space feel it is more than an experimental campsite that may disappear at a moment's notice.

To date, the Landing has been funded and supported as a research project, championed by this text's two authors. However, the site's creators have always intended for it to be an integral and (we hope) essential component of our distributed university's infrastructure. Thus, we wish to migrate it to a place of permanence and continuity and to normalization within the university's administration and budgeting cycle. As financial background, the project was initially funded by $150,000 (CAD) of research development funding and has since received about $80,000 a year from a variety of internal and external research funds. Almost all of this funding is used to support a full time PHP programmer with part-time support provided for systems administration from the university research centre.

We have had a number of discussions with our computer services (cs) department, and find that much of our development process parallels the ones used by the university to support its open source and proprietary administrative systems—including Moodle. However, we have evolved the Landing at much faster speed than a typical cs project, and do much of our development and testing following the Web 2.0 mantra: "release early and release often." This results in a culture clash and occasional misunderstandings as we negotiate a future long-term home for the Landing. We are currently negotiating with the Library, which is attempting to reinvent itself, and we hope that the Landing will become an appropriate feature of this "library of the future."

The Perils of "Release Early, Release Often"

Our preferred development process has been successful, inasmuch as the site has not failed, had its security breached, or been brought down (apart from once due to hardware issues we resolved using mirrored recovery systems), since it was first installed. However, some people have complained that the site changes too much. For those who are trying to use it as part of formal courses, instructions provided elsewhere go out of date very quickly: the Landing is not friendly to top-down group processes. For others, however, the Landing represents a constant learning challenge as new features and improvements provide new challenges. We do not have an easy solution to this problem. Our goal is to provide an ever richer, more valuable toolset, not a fixed single-purpose tool, but the price to be paid for increased functionality is increased complexity.

Achieving the right balance is difficult, especially as we are in the thrall of path dependencies whereby, if someone is using a tool, we cannot remove or change it so that data are lost. The Friends of the Landing have only approved the removal of one tool in the course of three years, a marketplace plugin that was hardly used, thanks to the distributed nature of the university.

CONCLUSION

In this chapter we have attempted to illustrate how the model and methods presented in earlier chapters play out in a complex, institutional setting. An overarching theme that emerges from this is the complex interplay between different components of the institutional machine and the social software embedded in it. Technologies, including institutional methods, procedures and techniques, pedagogies, tools, and information systems are assemblies, constituted in relation to one another, together creating a complex adaptive system where each plays a part in the whole. However, the role different parts play is not equally influential. Like most complex systems, the large and slow moving affect the small and fast moving more than vice versa (Brand, 1997). The pre-existing structures of institutional life, including the course form, punctuated engagement, formal requirements, existing software tools, as well as the external environment of competing systems and differing contexts of distance learners have played a major role in constraining the activities and methods used on the social systems we have described. We return to these and other concerns in the next chapter, where we discuss the darker side of social media for learning and some of the problems, solved and as yet unsolved, that emerge.

9

ISSUES AND CHALLENGES IN EDUCATIONAL USES OF SOCIAL SOFTWARE

Turning and turning in the widening gyre
The falcon cannot hear the falconer;
Things fall apart; the centre cannot hold;
Mere anarchy is loosed upon the world
                W. B. Yeats, "The Second Coming"

In this chapter we explore some of the risks and dangers of using social software. We have touched on some of these already in our discussion of each of the social forms, and in our stories—out-of-control feedback loops, privacy, identity, safety, reliability, access, usability, and a host of other issues have emerged in the context of the tools, methods, and systems we use in social learning. In this chapter we focus on issues that arise within an institutional education context, rather than in purely informal and non-formal learning, because many problems are a result of the clash between novel adjacent possibles and the baked-in norms, methods, and behaviours that have evolved in a different evolutionary landscape. The fact that you are probably reading this as a book rather than a more socially mediated form demonstrates that we are in a period of transition, where old ways of thinking and learning are overlaid on and co-exist with the new.

DISRUPTION AND CHANGE

Institutions seldom accept with relish major changes to practice, especially those that impact long-held norms and beliefs, and resistance is common. C. Christensen observes that disruptive innovation, of the sort we are observing here, is almost never successfully developed and adopted within existing systems (1997; Christensen et al., 2008). This is not surprising, because disruptive innovations are nearly always initially worse than the existing systems with which they compete. Most technologies evolve primarily by assembly, slowly gaining in complexity and sophistication. Only rarely do novel innovations come along, and when they do, they are nearly always less compelling, functional, or useful than what they replace at first. As Arthur (2010) explained, it was around twenty years before jet engines were able to compete with their piston-driven propeller forebears, and at first, they did so in separate, non-competing niches. Educational systems may be viewed as complex adaptive systems, and like ecologies, novelty rarely survives unless the evolutionary landscape changes or they are introduced from a different ecosystem.

Disruptive innovations can therefore only take root where they are allowed to incubate without direct competition with existing technologies. Christensen cites the growth of microcomputers which, he claims, initially targeted children and gaming systems in order to establish a market where they could evolve without clashing head-on with the monolithic mini- and mainframe computers that already had the adult market well sewn up. Net, set, and collective technologies used in learning have evolved outside the educational system in social networks, Q&A sites, blogs, and wikis, filling niches not already taken. Some, at first, crept into the educational system unbidden and are hardly noticed as they sow seeds for change: Wikipedia, the Khan Academy, and other social systems present faces sufficiently similar to existing models that are the thin end of a wedge to prise open educational systems to new technologies.

Net, set, and collective-oriented social technologies for learning, as we have seen, demand a different way of thinking about the learning process than those built for groups. The whole apparatus of institutional learning, including the processes and methods used in schools, universities, and colleges, is a highly evolved set of technologies that does what it aims to do very well. Social technologies designed to support net and set modes of interaction, when placed in direct competition with other tools such as purpose-built learning management systems built to fit with the other technologies of education, will likely fare poorly. In particular, there is a mismatch between the technologies of institutions and those of network, set, and collective-centred social systems. Technologies such as classes, timetables, hierarchical management, assessments, lesson plans, and teacher-oriented pedagogies are unlikely to be well catered for by tools that centre on individuals and networks. This puts a brake on change and progress. It is exacerbated because existing systems such as Moodle, Blackboard, and Desire2Learn are highly evolved monoliths that perform a wide variety of functions and are purposely incorporating a growing number of tools that, superficially, look like network tools: wikis, blogs and similar features are increasingly included in such systems. However, though the tools may look and act in a similar manner to their counterparts in the wild, the group-based teaching that they are intended to support changes them. They use the same tools, but they are different technologies with different purposes, utilizing different phenomena with subtly different functionalities. Moreover, they are combined with different assemblies, and it is the assemblies that matter more than the parts of which they are comprised. Wheels appear in many different technologies, but it is the cars, watches, boats, cookers, and doors that matter to us, not the fact that they all contain wheels of some sort. It is the same for blogs and wikis: simply providing a tool as part of an assembly does not necessarily make that assembly into a different kind of social technology.

If we are to make effective use of networks, sets, and collectives within an institutional setting, then the greatest impact will be achieved by supporting needs and interests not already catered to by a well-evolved and entrenched set of tools. Potential niches within a formal setting include:

- Inter-/cross-disciplinary learning (e.g., support for using common research tools, cross-course projects, etc.)
- Learner-driven (as opposed to syllabus-driven) pedagogies
- Beyond-the-campus learning (incorporating others beyond the institution, whether formally or informally)
- Beyond-the-course learning, supporting disciplinary activity and interest across cohorts
- Self-guided research
- Self-organizing groups (e.g., study groups)
- Just-in-time learning
- Enduring committees, clubs, and student organizations
- Peer support (e.g., for learning to use research tools, computers, etc.)

INSTITUTIONAL CROSS-CUTTING CLEAVAGES

One of the first issues typically raised when a social software system is proposed that empowers students to share with others relates to dealing with posts that are critical, abusive, illegal, or objectionable—especially if the system allows public viewing beyond institutional boundaries. However, we have rarely experienced anything like this, either at Athabasca University or the University of Brighton.

Tens of thousands of posts have been created, almost none of which caused problems for others or threatened the institution, and none, so far as we know, included intentionally malicious or harmful material. Far from it: for the most part, public posts have served as an advertisement and invitation, something to be proud of, not hidden. We do, however, acknowledge the harm caused by bullying, especially in school systems.

Perfectly legitimate posts, taken out of context, can be offensive or disturbing for others using the system. Most university courses in the arts and humanities actively encourage students to explore complex adult issues and, in many cases, be provocative. In the comfort and safety of a role-controlled, group-based LMS, such posts are read by others with an understanding of the context, course requirements, expectations and norms. When this moves into a network, or worse, a set mode of engagement, posts that are made visible beyond the group might be seen out of context and may not be understood or may be deemed offensive by others. Discipline boundaries may make this more difficult to address. For instance, a religious student who is using a social media system as part of her course and treats it as an extension of the classroom—a safe space, a functional tool—especially if she objects to, say, swearing, may not appreciate a work of art posted by a student of fine arts deliberately constructed with profanities and blasphemies to challenge sensibilities. Some respond to this kind of problem with a knee-jerk reaction of censorship, asking for tools to hide such things, while others suggest self-censorship or tutor regulation of activities, but that denies the point of the provocative piece in the first place. Such anomalies are rare but important, affecting the beliefs, opinions, feelings, and relationships of individuals within a social system. This relates closely to the problem of contextual ambiguity.

CONTEXTUAL AMBIGUITY

Within an institutional setting, learners are constantly switching between different groups, networks, and sets, in a far more diverse and discontinuous manner than, say, when engaging with a social network of friends or people in similar businesses. A single tool that supports group, network, and set modes of interaction can soon become an unwieldy and confusing space unless it has been carefully designed to take these discontinuities into consideration. Traditional learning management systems, being group-oriented, carefully divide spaces into well-defined, course-oriented segments. Social networks base their design models on the assumption that a single individual has a single network, a single persona, a single facet that is displayed, with more or less filtering, to others. Some systems, such as Elgg, Google+ or, in an inelegant way, Facebook lists, explicitly recognize the discontinuous nature of networks and offer support for filtering different content to and from different people, but these are simply filters: the underlying presentation of content does not vary, it's just that some people see more than others, and some content is preferentially displayed depending on its originator. One very common way to get around this problem is to use different tools for different groups, nets, and sets. However, this raises important issues: it becomes significantly harder to maintain and for users to master, especially given the fact that groups, nets, and sets often overlap with one another in multiple dimensions, so similar lists of the same people may often recur in different systems. It also raises the spectre of duplicate functionality.

We have created a range of solutions in Elgg for the problem of contextual ambiguity clustered under the umbrella term of "context switching" (Dron et al., 2011). The tools allow anyone to switch between different social and personal learning contexts, and to show different things to different people in different ways. Tools include tabbed profiles, dashboards, and group profiles, which allow an individual or a group to organize their learning life into separate spaces, each built with highly configurable widgets. These spaces may have different appearances and display quite different content and, crucially, may be visible to different people. The circle-like collections that allow people to create sets of networks make this highly configurable: people can reveal what they want to reveal, how they want to reveal it, and to whom they want to reveal it too easily and fluidly. Different dashboards can also be configured to make navigation and retrieval easier as a user switches from task to task. We have added many different widgets that make it possible to show fine-grained results not just from personal content but also from networks, groups, and sets that are of interest. We have also created a "set" tool that enables people to group collections of related content together so that they can more easily represent different interests and identities to different people.

"DUPLICATE" FUNCTIONALITY

One of the largest problems that we have faced in encouraging uptake of the Landing at Athabasca University is that it is perceived to offer little that is different from other systems in use at the institution. This is a valid concern. It is, for example, possible to use email to replicate almost anything that can be done with social software, from a discussion forum to an LMS or social networking system. However, the complexities of doing so for anything that departs from one-to-one or one-to-many messaging are immense, requiring a great deal of effort, interpretation, and coordination by people involved in the dialogue, and slowing the pace to the extent that, for many uses, would be highly impractical. For email to be a shared repository, for example, every recipient would have to keep a copy and organize it in a way that would make it easily discoverable when others refer to it; in contrast to the simplicity of sharing a web page or link to an online repository, this is clearly a poor approach. The same is true of many tools, especially when they provide rich toolsets. For example, an LMS may offer messaging (like email), chat (like an instant messenger), wikis, blogs, discussion forums, bookmark sharing, file sharing, and many other tools duplicated in social systems. Conversely, Facebook may provide many tools that are similar to or improve on tools provided by an institutional LMS. The toolsets that we use for different networks such as LinkedIn, Google+, Facebook, Bebo, Hi5, or MySpace may offer very similar functions to one another, or subsume others. Most systems have Twitter-like microblog variants, for instance. However, quite apart from the different networks and sets that inhabit these spaces, there are very few cases where systems are drop-in replacements for other systems. All have some differentiating value in terms of access control, role systems, aesthetics, usability, price, manageability, tools, long-term prospects, support communities, capabilities for integration, and so on.

Faced with a potential infinitude of alternatives, it makes no sense to choose them all. This is especially true of social systems, where the fact that someone is using one system may act as a disincentive to use another, and make it pointless to do so: if everyone in the world were using a different, non-interoperable social system, then they would not be social at all. In an ideal world, tools would be interoperable so that one could be integrated with any other, and any community could extend its tool use in any way appropriate to the social form. Where possible, such interoperable, mashable, and connectable tools should be used. However, real-world decisions seldom provide this luxury. Apart from the ability to use tools together, there are few general rules for making decisions about which to choose. We have found our framework of social forms very useful in establishing criteria and heuristics for selecting appropriate technologies. For example, our selection of an Elgg system was due to the lack of support within Moodle for set and net modes of engagement. However, this left us with many further choices to make. We list a number of weighted criteria here that may be useful to others faced with similar decisions, but it should be borne in mind that the context of every decision of this nature will strongly determine important factors, and this is far from an exhaustive list:

- Cost
- Support (internal and community/company)
- Potential longevity
- Control (personal, and at group level)
- Usability
- Accessibility
- Import capacity
- Export capacity
- Interoperability with other systems
- Device support
- Learnability
- Diversity of tools
- Scalability
- Hosting (local, cloud)
- Access control and role models
- Network/set/group features

We encourage those who are trying to decide whether to implement social tools in their learning, and which to choose, to extend and amend this list to fit their own constraints, interests, and contextual concerns. When selecting the technologies for the Landing, we gathered stakeholders together and asked them to contribute the things they wished to see and what they wished to avoid in the new system: our list was many times longer than the one presented here. Every sociotechnical context will be different and should be dealt with on its own terms.

PRIVACY AND SOCIAL SOFTWARE

Many a parent has been shocked by the personal disclosure exhibited by their children on networked social software sites. Do they really want the whole world to see the pictures or read about their antics at last weekend's beach party? Will they want those images retrieved in ten years, when the not-so-young person applies for a new position or runs for public office? The affordance of cyberspace to provide and in some senses *become* a personal newspaper, radio, and television station broadcasting 24 hours a day to a global audience raises very profound questions about privacy, openness, and identity. The persistence of digital data on a network, and the fact that it may be seen in a very different context from its original posting, makes this a pressing concern. For many of us, the Net forces a profound rethinking of privacy and public identity. Privacy issues have likely been of interest since prehistoric times, when we shared our caves with others. The advent of both mass and personal communications has served only to speed up and magnify these concerns.

In his ground-breaking work, Altman (1976) noted the interest in privacy from many discipline perspectives shown by citizens, social institutions, and governments. He lists three ways in which privacy is defined and understood. To some, privacy revolves around exclusion, the avoidance of others, and keeping certain types of knowledge away from others. A second definition focuses on control, individuals' abilities to open and close themselves to others, and the freedom to decide what aspects of themselves are made accessible to others. Paradoxically, privacy is not defined merely by the presence or absence of others, as is implied in the sense of being anonymous or "lost in the crowd." Likewise, privacy is not valued in and of itself: it is relative to changing needs. An ultimately private life might look like a sentence of solitary confinement in jail, or being shipwrecked on a desert island. Finally, privacy is not static: each of us has moments when we desire both more and less of the presence of others, and similarly, there are times when we want to share more or less of ourselves and our ideas. Thus, Altman's second definition, with its focus on privacy as choice and control, suggests we need mechanisms that allow us to control the boundaries in time, space, perception, and communication so we may selectively open and close ourselves to both general and particular sets of "others."

Altman also describes the systems, tools, and behaviours we use to create, defend, and appropriately modify our sense of privacy to align with our ever-changing needs. He notes three types of boundary tools. The first use verbal and non-verbal behaviours: we invite others to enter or to leave our individual spaces. The second is built upon on environmental constraints we build and inhabit such as doors, fences, and speaking platforms. Finally, Altman notes cultural constraints, such as the type of questions that are appropriate to ask, the loudness of voice, and the amount of physical touch we use to build and reinforce interpersonal boundaries that culturally define privacy spaces and practices. Each of these boundary behaviours has evolved over millennia and been finely honed by evolutionary selection. The Internet, however, has evolved with breakneck speed, and has created privacy concerns with which we have had little experience, nor enough time for us to evolve appropriate boundary tools and systems.

Palen and Dourish (2003) invite us to unpack our concepts of privacy for a networked context . They note that "with information technology, our ability to rely on these same physical, psychological and social mechanisms for regulating privacy is changed and often reduced" (p. 130). If we return to Altman's three sets of boundary tools, we see that each is fundamentally altered by network affordances. Verbal and nonverbal behaviours certainly change in networked contexts, and their diversity, from text messages to immersive interaction with avatars, makes generalizations challenging. Most notably, networked behaviours span boundaries of time. A Google search reveals not only the comments I made this week or last, but reveals my comments from years past. Given that the boundaries I use to protect and define my privacy comfort zone are ever-changing and context-dependent, it is important that I know who threatens these barriers, so that I can raise the appropriate level of boundary protection. Unfortunately, such awareness of others is often not possible on the Net. The searcher of my name can easily be a trusted colleague, a potential new friend, an aggressive salesman, or an identity thief. Furthermore, the audience changes over time. Trusted colleagues one year may become aggressive competitors the next, and information that I may be proud to share this year may prove highly embarrassing in the years to come. Worse still, the place where I left private information may change its privacy rules and technologies without me being aware of this. Many users of Facebook, in particular, have suffered because of the network's ever-shifting privacy controls that have often revealed more than they originally intended to different people.

Environmental boundaries also are morphed in cyberspace. All but the most tightly encrypted activity in cyberspace leaves traces. Many Net users use multiple email addresses and maintain multiple identities in immersive environments and open social software sites so that they can contain these traces. Passwords, access to members and friends, and other security tools replace locks and keys from the physical world but fill similar functions. And just like in the real world, locks, doors, and barriers require active maintenance and attention to adequately serve as boundary defenders.

The cultural boundaries are perhaps most profoundly altered in networked contexts. There are as yet only emerging standards and social norms that are acknowledge and adhered to by Net citizens. For example, many of us have different standards with regard to email functions such as use of blind copies, forwarding messages with or without approval, and the release of our own email addresses or those of others. In even newer contexts such as SecondLife, World of Warcraft, and other immersive environments, social and cultural practices are constantly evolving and altering, and currently these customs change while millions of new users are exploring these environments.

We see that the maintenance of privacy and the boundary tools that we use in the networked world are in many ways markedly dissimilar to those we encounter in real-life contexts. Thus, it should come as no surprise that privacy issues are a major concern for all who use the Net, and perhaps especially so for those using social software tools for both formal and informal learning.

Many social software suites allow users to set privacy controls on personal information, permitting them to effectively select the amount of disclosure they allow and to what audience this information is revealed. However, studies are showing that the majority of users do not alter these privacy settings, leaving the default settings of the system (Govani & Pashley, 2005). In a 2005 study at Carnegie Mellon University of over 4,000 students registered on Facebook, Gross and Acquisti (2005) found "only a small number of members change the default privacy preferences, which are set to maximize the visibility of users profiles" (p. 79). Govani and Pashley (2005) found that over 30% of university students in the US had given permission for people they had never met to be their "friends" on the popular social networking site, allowing these strangers access to their entire profile, containing contact information, photos, and other personal details. As awareness of the dangers increases, however, users are becoming more careful. A US-based Pew Internet Study in 2011 revealed that 58% of adult users of social networking sites limited access to only friends, 26% of them adding further access controls, and another 19% making them partially private (Rainie & Wellman, 2012). Even so, this still means that 23% of users make no effort at all to control their privacy.

It is interesting to speculate on the reasons why users are not more actively constraining the visibility of private content. This is likely not because of a lack of awareness about the problem, given the coverage in the popular press on issues related to identity theft and cyber-stalking. In a 2007 qualitative study of Facebook users, Strater and Richter found that "while users do not underestimate the privacy threats of online disclosures, they do misjudge the extent, activity, and accessibility of their social networks." (2007, p. 158). The participants in this study did realize that posting personal information could have negative repercussions, but they assumed (often incorrectly) that such data was only accessible to a selected group of trusted friends. One might also wonder about the user-friendliness and design of social software tools. It may not be clear to users exactly who has access, and perceived as difficult to restrict access further. But what is more likely is that those users realize the value of social software increases in proportion to their support for connections with new and current friends and acquaintances. The balance is always a trade-off: many social software systems provide their services in return for information about individuals.

Taken to its logical conclusion, those most concerned with privacy would not participate in social networks at all, and indeed, this does happen—we have relatives who avoid all but personal communication online. Thus, we can assume users need very flexible systems that allow them to hide and reveal information at a low level of granularity, both in regard to the nature of the information and the membership of the various audiences who are allowed access to it. These decisions are very personal, and defy generalizations based on socio-demographic details. For example, the authors release their cellphone numbers only to a small group of very close friends and family. Yet for others, their mobile number is very public knowledge and is listed in many places on the Web just as many home phone numbers appear in paper-based telephone directories even today. We also provide information to select and changeable audiences. For example, we might share our calendars with associates at our workplace, but would withdraw this if either we or our colleagues left our current place of work.

PRIVACY AND TEACHERS

The mismatch between the social forms of classroom groups, with their formalized hierarchies and social networks and sets, has led to many difficulties for teachers, especially in schools. The formal relationship between teacher and student causes difficulties for some when teachers disclose information about their personal lives, reveal preferences and interests outside the professional context of the classroom, and engage in social chat with students. Indeed, recognizing this mismatch, the makers of Facebook provide explicit advice on separating the formal context of the teacher from the networks of their students (Dwyer, 2009). We understand that the formality of teacher–student relationships can lead to difficulties in a network context that, in extreme cases, lead to teachers losing their jobs, or at least their credibility in the classroom. Many teachers deliberately refuse to accept "friend" requests from students and former students for this reason. On Athabasca Landing, we deliberately renamed "friend" as "follower" in order to address the fact that there are complex ethical and practical issues for some teachers and students treating one another as friends. However, the corollary to this issue is that a blurring between student and teacher networks can allow richer, longer-lasting, valuable relationships. By enabling students to see their teachers as human beings, warts and all, they can gain a clearer idea of what it means to be a lifelong learner, to see that education is not divorced from life but is an integral part of it.

The notion that teachers should be role models is deeply embedded in the way the profession is viewed in society, but we question the value of a role model who demonstrates secrecy, and by implication, hypocrisy. We believe that teachers should present themselves as they are, not as they should be. Institutional values need to be seen in a human context, not as aspirational rules but as lived behaviours. This is not to suggest that teachers should reveal every aspect of their private lives. Context matters, and some things are rightfully kept private from some people. But the notion that the solution to the problem is to keep everything secret to the extent that we reject personal connection with those we teach is taking secrecy too far, and represents a failure to embrace an adjacent possible that can greatly enrich the learner experience.

WHY DO PEOPLE DISCLOSE?

"Several objects motivated blogging in our sample. Bloggers blogged in order to:

1. Update others on activities and whereabouts.
2. Express opinions to influence others.
3. Seek others' opinions and feedback.
4. 'Think by writing.'
5. Release emotional tension." (Nardi, Schiano, & Gumbrecht, 2004, p. 225)

The previous sections reveal that the control of privacy is a challenging and ongoing task. Effective management must work at a number of levels and entails a partnership of software designers, ethical and attentive systems managers, and knowledgeable and empowered users.

The design constraints of this context focus on three challenging propositions:

1. There is no single control setting that meets both the privacy and dissemination needs of all users.

2. There is no single control setting that effectively both secures and exposes all of the components of my personal profile and contributions or postings I wish to share.

3. There is no single setting or control that effectively both secures and exposes information over an extended period of time, since users' needs are subject to change.

The first constraint leads naturally to the solution that each individual should be able to easily set the privacy controls over personal information. While such a solution works for informed adults, it presents further challenges when educational social software systems are used by children who require either institutional or parental guidance.

Linked with concerns about privacy, and in some sense predicating them is the notion of online identity. Increasingly, we establish a range of online identities across social networks, on the websites that we visit, in our email systems, and in the online group tools we use. Despite efforts to consolidate identities through systems such as OpenID, Facebook Connect, Twitter, or Google+, those who choose to engage with cyberspace have to deal with multiple ways of revealing identity across different contexts. Our own context-switching approaches are one way to deal with this (Dron et al., 2011), but the bulk of solutions involve using different social systems and tools for different purposes.

TRUST

Beyond issues of privacy and identity, networks and sets (in particular) raise issues of trust and security. We have already observed that one of the most significant issues driving the use of collectives in networks is to establish faith in the credentials of those with whom, and from whom, we learn online. The popular press is full of examples of ways that trust can be broken online, notably in the behaviour of some pedophiles and other stalkers in cyberspace, who take advantage of the many-to-many strengths of the Internet combined with the potential for anonymity to achieve nefarious ends. While we hope such problems are rarely present in learning communities, it is vital to their success that learners feel safe and secure when learning. Learning outcomes are far more easily achieved if, in particular:

• One trusts the skills and capabilities of a teacher, both in subject matter and in pedagogical abilities
• One feels safe from attack or lesser antagonism by one's peers

Learning is, by definition, a leap into the unknown, and the unknown is scary. While we may justifiably be scared by what we know is harmful, what we don't know is often scarier. It is a sensible evolutionary adaptation that makes us fearful or wary of dark places and novel situations: until we gain awareness of the potential risks, it is safer to assume that danger may be lurking than that there is no danger at all. This is only true up to a point, of course—risk avoidance also means opportunity avoidance, so it is more an issue of being wary than of not doing anything that might be dangerous. It is also true that many of us positively relish the tingle of fear that comes when starting a new learning trajectory, the thrill of uncertainty that comes with learning something new, but again, only up to a point. This is perhaps itself a learned behaviour, something we have come to recognize as a result of previous successful experiences, probably with the kind of assistance and safety that a teacher provided, even if we have now learned to teach ourselves.

One of the many roles played by teachers and teaching institutions is to provide reassurance and a measure of safety. This is an essential process: if the only way we had to learn how to swim, perform surgery, ride a bicycle, or hunt a wild animal were to actually do so in real life, then far fewer would survive the process. Any child who has learnt to swim by being thrown in at the deep end is unlikely to have a very comfortable memory of the process, even though it might have been tempered by an underlying trust in the one doing the throwing. While learning about medieval history, how to be a teacher, literary criticism, or how to play the piano may lack the risks and dangers of the previous examples, there can still be fear involved, if only of failure to achieve our learning goals.

Whatever the risk factor of our learning is, nevertheless, it is helpful to be led by one who we believe knows the paths. We need teachers not just because we can achieve more with the aid of an expert—remember Alan Kay's warnings about the danger of a "chopsticks culture," when learners are provided with technologies but no examples from which to learn (1996)—but because the expert reduces uncertainty and/or reassures us about what we do not know, and offers us the security of knowing someone will be there to catch us when we fall. Similarly, if there are fellow travellers, we usually want them to, at the very least, not wish us harm in achieving our goals. We need supportive fellow learners not just because they help us to explore perspectives, including our own, but because they reduce the danger. We generally feel more comfortable when entering an unknown place or situation if there is someone else we know and trust with us.

All of this leads to some interesting problems in networked learning. We have seen that collective approaches can help in establishing trust, but when learning and engaging with others, it is the purely human and social processes of communication that we fall back on. Different cues in what people say can help: it is usually obvious, for example, when someone is being provocative, flaming, or trolling. Equally, it is generally clear when someone is using dialogue to be supportive and helpful. Unfortunately, when the former has occurred, it may poison us against a particular community or network, reducing our willingness to participate. We, the authors, have experienced some responses to our thoughts and discussions on the subject of this book in a networked environment that were discouraging, infuriating, or just plain useless or irrelevant. Partly we are supported by each other, partly by a belief that the medium is worth persisting in, and partly we have been inured to such things over many years of participation, but it is easy to see how such experiences might dispirit someone feeling uncertain and insecure. Indeed, if it happens often enough, it may prevent them from wanting to participate at all in any network.

This is a larger problem than it might be in a closed group context because our networks are typically joined and borderless, so withdrawal from one network may mean withdrawal from others. To make matters worse, there are subtler problems than simple antagonism. People may use a network as a platform to discuss things that do not interest us, get sidetracked by things we consider irrelevant, or simply talk at a level that is either beneath or above us, leaving us feeling alienated or bored. The very diversity that gives networks much of their strength also, potentially, contains the seeds of their demise. Much of the work that we have performed in the area of context-switching and context awareness has been an attempt to reduce such dangers by allowing people greater control of how and what is disclosed, and with whom it is shared.

ACCESS ISSUES AND THE DIGITAL DIVIDE

Although access to cyberspace is fast becoming the norm in both highly and less-well developed countries, the majority of people in the world still do not have access to an Internet-connected computer. This proportion becomes significantly smaller when we take into account those with mobile phones but, despite over 2 billion broadband-connected mobile devices, most cellphones used at the time of writing have limited access to the totality of cyberspace, and that still leaves billions with limited means to access even a small part of it, let alone the Internet whether for economic or political reasons. This remains the case despite the growth of services like U2opia (www.u2opiamobile.com) that bridge the gap by allowing Facebook or other service access through traditional "dumbphones." The topic of mobile telephones raises a further concern that there is much inequality in access speeds and the capabilities of machines used to gain access to cyberspace.

What can be reached and how fast it can be accessed with a basic cellphone is far less than what can be achieved with a top-of-the-line laptop or tablet with a high-speed connection. The massive growth in such technologies seems set to continue for some time to come, but inequalities will still remain even when, by 2017, it is projected that a broadband connection will be available for almost everyone on the planet (Broadband Commission, 2013, p. 14). In the authors' own country (Canada), the majority of the population is at least able, if they wish, to gain high-speed access to the Internet, but even in this highly developed country, there are huge areas where dial-up or, surprisingly often, satellite access is still the only option available. This immediately discounts a wide range of the technologies we have written about, including VoIP telephony, videoconferencing, live web meetings, immersive 3D environments, and more, as well as making even common websites, especially those using rich media, Flash, or AJAX technologies, unbearably slow to access. Having said that, access to more basic technologies like books, desks, and even pencils remains an issue in many parts of the world, so the problem is not new. Moreover, while the costs of initial access remain relatively high and still beyond the reach of some poorer families, once a connection is made into cyberspace, the cost of networked information is typically much lower than that of traditional books (Renner, 2009).

At Athabasca University we are making the transition from paper to electronic books and have calculated that, even given publishers' often exorbitant textbook prices (whether electronic or on paper), the cost of a good e-reading device, whether a tablet or dedicated reader, will be offset after the purchase of two or three textbooks for an average course, while the cheapest tablets now cost significantly less than a typical textbook, and come with access to tens of thousands of free books from sites such as Project Gutenberg. Such devices offer more than just an alternative means of reading: they also provide access to the Web, email, and many other facilities of cyberspace. While many issues remain, such as the cost of network access, the availability of infrastructure, and the complexity of calculating environmental impact relative to the cost of paper, storage, and transport needed for books, the accelerating move to ever greater cyberspace access for an ever-increasing diversity of people seems inevitable for economic reasons alone. There are large economic and gender inequalities that must be overcome but we are already at the point where access to the Internet is more widespread than to a decent traditional education, especially at higher levels, and so we are optimistic about the future. We hope that the ideas we promote in this book, particularly as they apply to networks, sets and collectives, may suggest ways that learning can happen without a formal educational process, enabled by the massive growth in socially-enabled technologies that is bound to occur.

MOBILE LEARNING

Mobile technologies offer many affordances. A modern smartphone is far richer than the average personal computer in its input capabilities (e.g., voice, video, velocity, direction, text, geo-location, Bluetooth, Wi-Fi, cellular networks, and more); even the simplest cellphones offer text and speech capabilities. Cellphones are typically with us all the time and smartphones allow us constant, uninterrupted access to cyberspace. At the same time, they have at least as many limitations as affordances, such as small screens, deeply incompatible standards, limited processing power, limited battery lives, expensive tariffs and overly diverse interfaces. With some exceptions, content developed for the Web needs to be re-presented for use on cellphones. Indeed, content and applications developed for one make and model of cellphone may fail to work on another, even from the same manufacturer. Despite the growth of popular platforms like iPhone, Blackberry, Windows Mobile, and Android, most applications will fail to work across even two of them, let alone all.

There are pedagogical challenges too. It would be wrong to suggest that the migration from traditional media to the Web was unproblematic, but it was a far simpler transition process than it now is from the Web to mobile platforms. Partly this was due to the fact that most uses of digital technology in education, as in other industries, do not show an imaginative leap when presented through a new medium: the typical LMS is a classic example of the "horseless carriage phenomenon," a mirror of existing face-to-face processes in an online environment, with little heed for the affordances of the medium. The small-screened, incompatible devices with awkward systems at best for text input do not succumb so neatly to mimicry, apart from some limited contexts such as language learning. As technologies such as Twitter Bootstrap (twitter.github.com/bootstrap/) that allow multiple representations of content for different devices become more prevalent, awareness of these issues is increasing and the tools to address them are more widely available.

The global nature of networked environments poses a range of challenges to many of our legal systems in different countries, states, and provinces. We have seen in recent years a sharp reaction from governments to the increase in network freedom new technologies allow. From the extreme black hole of North Korea and the censorship activities of China, to the subtler scrutiny and control of the US (as evidenced by the provisions of the Patriot Act), governments are becoming more active in controlling the use of the Internet by their populations. Even in relatively libertarian countries such as Canada and the UK, service providers are required to keep records of activities that may be scrutinized with, some would argue, insufficient concern for the rights of citizens.

Copyright (Cross Country/State/Province Concerns)

The increasing economic value of videos, blockbuster novels, and sound recordings has provoked governments to respond to pressures from their media and cultural industries to increase the length and enforcement of copyright protection for intellectual property. This has resulted in extensions of the exclusive but temporary monopoly granted to creators to market their intellectual products in many parts of the world. As a result, educators have had to wage extensive battles with copyright owners, who are often major for-profit publishers, rather than content creators, to assert their right to Fair Use of content for education and research purposes. Recently in Canada and elsewhere, the tide seems to be turning, and courts and legislatures are realizing that allowing dissemination, review, and critique in the education system actually enhances and stimulates the development of cultural and intellectual content, which was the original aim of copyright legislation.

Also of increasing importance is the capacity to lawfully share intellectual products while retaining some or all copyright, typically through various Creative Commons licensing schemes. It is a tragedy that so much potentially valuable educational content lies unused and unusable, not because educators or other creators want the product to be restricted from educational use, but because, prior to the Net and Creative Commons licenses, there was no cost-effective way to share it while retaining rights such as attribution, restriction from others commercially exploiting the product, or changing parts and then redistributing product.

Openness, Interoperability, and Integration

We should disclose a personal bias at this point: the authors of this book are strong advocates of open sharing of knowledge, and chose AU Press at least partly because it is committed to making its books available freely for education and non-commercial download. In a social learning context, a lack of openness can cause difficulties. For example, if a wiki has been worked upon by multiple authors, then ownership is hard to ascertain and the solution in a non-open context is often to default to that of the service provider—a university, publisher, or closed company. This situation both reduces motivation to contribute, because contributors do not have control of distribution, and prevents the free flow of knowledge. The issue becomes more complex when data are aggregated and re-presented, as may often occur when, for example, pulling in and redisplaying an RSS feed. There is a tension between personal ownership, the social capital that accrues as a result, and the sharing of knowledge that is essential for learning to occur.

The issue goes beyond simple questions of ownership, however. It is not quite enough that we own and share the data we produce: we also have to be able to re-use it, integrate it, and re-present it. For this, protocols and standards such as TinCan, OpenDD, Europass, RSS, and Atom are required to enable the easy movement of data from one system to another. Unfortunately, many proprietary systems are deliberately designed to make such transfers difficult. As is often the case, the dominant social software provider at the time of writing, Facebook, is one of the worst offenders: although user pressure has forced the company to allow people to export their own data, it is in a form that cannot easily be re-used in a different and potentially competitive social system. Facebook, Twitter, and other commercial systems often assert some degree of ownership over the content produced by their millions of users, and their business models are based on analysis and sale of "their" content. This is one of the reasons that boutique systems such as the Landing are valuable, because they make it possible to return ownership to users. However, efforts to do this on a larger scale, such as Diaspora, have failed to gain momentum so far.

CULTURAL CONSIDERATIONS

Despite a widespread feeling that we inhabit McLuhan's global village, cultural identities remain strong. As with personal identity, we are typically not just part of a single culture, but engage in many cultures in many contexts. One of the most popular means of distinguishing differences in cultures comes from Hofstede

(2001), whose study of a multinational corporation across 40 different countries revealed five distinct dimensions of culture. Of these, the dimension that showed most variation and has been frequently verified and observed in other studies (Church, 2000; Triandis, 2004) is the collectivist/individualist dimension. In individualist cultures, people see themselves as separate individuals and prioritize their personal goals over those of others, motivated by personal needs, goals, and rights—culture in the US, though diverse, provides a classic example of this set of behaviours, but it may be found in most Western cultures. In collectivist cultures, on the other hand, people see themselves as parts of "collectives" (note that this is not in the technical sense that we have used the term, but rather used in a more general social sense) such as families, organizations, tribes, and nations. Their motivations are more closely aligned with those of their social aggregations, and are driven by norms, duties, and expectations of these groups, nets, sets, and collectives.

Indian culture, though arguably even more diverse than the US, provides a good example of a more socially oriented set of attitudes. Given the great differences between cultures in this dimension, one would expect significant differences in uses of social networks, and this is indeed what we find (Kim, Sohn, & Choi, 2011; Vasalou, Joinson, & Courvoisier, 2010). Even more significant, from a learning perspective, is what happens when people with divergent cultural attitudes inhabit the same virtual spaces. Many of these differences are masked because social groupings need to share a common language. But, increasingly, as English competencies are developed by citizens of all nations in the world, we expect to see more confrontations and misunderstandings resulting from differences in this collectivist/individualist dimension. This is particularly significant inasmuch as, to a greater extent than when meeting face to face, obvious signals that a person belongs to a particular culture may be less prominent or not be observable at all.

Social software is only part of a learning system: content, behaviours, norms, existing social forms, and many other factors play strong roles in determining the shape it will take. Because of the way that structure can determine or influence behaviour, there is a risk that a social software system designed with one set of cultural expectations in mind may work against the dominant (or conversely, dominated) culture that uses it. Conversely, where a strong culture exists, it may undermine the effectiveness of software built to support different needs. Where, for example, as in India it is the cultural norm for teachers to be treated with a particular kind of respect (Jadhav, 1999), a system that deliberately equalizes participants in a learning transaction may cause discomfort to some or all participants.

Author Dron experienced this firsthand when working in a cross-cultural collaboration between English and Indian computing students in the early 2000s, where different norms posed a major threat to effective collaboration (Singh & Dron, 2002).

After trying and failing to encourage discussion through closed forums, at least partly because such exchanges were not the norm in India, a large part of the solution to this problem was to use a set-based, topic-oriented collective bookmarking application, CoFIND, that largely anonymized interaction and required little direct contact beyond cooperative sharing. By focusing on a shared topic of interest to both groups of students, many of the social differences and imbalances could be safely ignored, while both groups benefited from the process. This topic-oriented sharing was a common denominator that reflected common practice among students in India, where sharing of notes was common but challenging the wisdom of elders, including those within the student body, was frowned upon or caused discomfort. This was in almost total opposition to the more constructivist, guide-on-the-side approaches taken with the UK group, where argument and conflict were seen as part of the process. As a result, what little dialogue there was when these cultures were blended was stilted and strange. On a smaller scale, we have observed that cultural expectations of teachers by learners trained to stand up and bow to their professors can make for a similarly strange and stilted dialogue in an open learning environment like the Landing. The fact that some students, especially those from collectivist cultures, feel uncomfortable addressing us as anything other than "Dr. Dron" or "Professor Anderson" overlays a different kind of ethos to that of the casual, first-name culture we typically encourage and that students from more individualist cultures more often find easier to adopt. This tendency is exacerbated by the formal context of institutional learning that reinforces and sustains roles and hierarchies, regardless of the equality we deliberately encourage on the Landing. Like all cultural differences, there is huge variety to be found among individuals and a great deal of blurring between cultures, but the propensity of groups to converge on norms and develop groupthink behaviours means that such behaviours can spread in both directions. Whether this is a good or a bad thing depends on one's perspective and the context of the group. On a good day, it can help to provide a sense of membership and commonality. On a bad day, it can clash with the pedagogies and processes intended to bring about learning, either by preventing easy sharing or by causing discomfort to those for whom such sharing may feel unnatural.

Sherry Turkle's book, *Alone Together* (2011), is a tightly argued warning against the alienation and increasing separation between people that cyberspace technologies can create. As we increasingly cease to engage in physical spaces, often preferring the convenience and controllability of sms, email, messaging, social networks, and other forms of electronically mediated interaction, the breadth of our social inter-action increases while becoming shallower, less engaged, less human. Our know-ledge of others becomes what they choose to represent with avatars and profiles, abbreviated and edited, essentially a narcissistic performance where friendship is measured in quantity rather than quality. This is indeed a worrying trend, though Turkle's arguments are diminished somewhat by studies that show those who engage more online and through mobile devices also spend more time in face-to-face interaction (Rainie & Wellman, 2012). There are also notable benefits for those who have found communities and engagement with others who would otherwise have found it difficult to do so (Wei & Lo, 2006) and huge benefits that Turkle acknowledges in sustaining relationships at a distance (T. H. Christensen, 2009). However, even when active users of social media have extensive contact with others in person, that face-to-face time may not be full engagement. We have all sat in public spaces surrounded by others who are at once with us but also texting, messaging, and talking to people at a distance on cellphones and tablets. Whether or not we find this disturbing, for distance learners something is usually better than nothing. Without such technologies, many distance learners would be far more isolated than they are.

INFORMATION OVERLOAD

The ease with which information can be shared is both a blessing and a curse. In a formal course setting, students with who tutors might have had sporadic and formal contact in the past may now require or at least expect far more attention. One of author Dron's students, studying the "benefits" of social media in online learning, proudly proclaimed the effectiveness of her intervention by point-ing to increased satisfaction levels, greatly improved grades, and deeper learn-ing outcomes. On further investigation, the interview responses quickly revealed the reason for this. For instance, instant messaging was seen as especially useful because, according to one responder, "It was wonderful to be able to contact your teacher any time, even after midnight."

One of the greatest benefits of social media lies in their potential to create richer channels that let great teachers do what they do best. However, dedicated online teachers are rapidly drowning in a torrent of interaction where there are no longer quiet times of the day, no longer holidays or conference times when they cannot be contacted. Some have taken email sabbaticals, or specified online hours during which they will attempt to reply, but the torrent continues for most of us regardless of good intentions to constrain our availability to others. This is an unfortunate result of the combination of network and group forms.

The group form typically includes, as part of the implicit or explicit rules that govern it, the requirement for a teacher to be responsive and demonstrably caring. That expectation has, however, arisen in a controllable environment in which caring need only be evidenced during class and office hours. More network-oriented social media such as social networking tools, blog comments, and email increase both the volume of traffic and the expectations of a response: the many-to-one nature of the engagement can quickly overwhelm a teacher. It is essential for the network-engaged teacher to make response time expectations clear at the outset and, in designing learning experiences that incorporate the crowd, to ensure that there are opportunities (and expectations) for others to answer questions and discuss issues.

A similar problem afflicts the online learner. A popular connectivist MOOC can generate hundreds of posts a day, and sorting the wheat from the chaff can be a major problem. Collectives can help a great deal in this case, however, providing assistance in filtering and searching for dialogue.

FILTER BUBBLES AND ECHO CHAMBERS

We have already written of some of the ways that the Matthew Effect and preferential attachment can lead to mob stupidity rather than wise crowds. The perils of groupthink, echo chambers in which we only hear what we choose to, and the blind leading the blind are particularly problematic in a learning context (Pariser, 2011). Network and set forms of engagement remove the comfortable assurance of accredited sages telling us what to learn and how, replacing it not only with the difficulties of deciding who and what to trust but also a set of dynamics that may actually make things worse by their very nature. In a formal learning context, it is therefore of vital importance that teachers challenge and refocus students who are led to low fitness peaks and into filter bubbles.

CONCLUSION

We have solutions to some of the risks of a networked learning environment, but many risks and uncertainties still remain. The greatest risks all come back to difficulties in understanding the nature of social engagement in social media. Excessive content is often a direct consequence of superimposing a network or set form on that of the group, without adjusting the processes and methods used by the group. Privacy concerns often occur as a result of misplaced assumptions in a closed group, when in fact the social environment is net-like, or worse, set-like. Alienation and separation occur when people mistake Net-enabled interaction for relationships in meat-space (i.e., the non-cyberspace "real world"). Shifting contexts become hidden in simplistic, one-dimensional models of identity provided by many networked social environments. Collectives, used uncritically, are as likely to lead to stupid mobs as they are to wise crowds, perhaps more so, and the dangers of filter bubbles creating echo chambers where vision becomes narrow are great. We hope that the clearer understanding of social forms we have provided in this book will help networked learners and teachers to at least be aware of the risks and be more mindful of the ways that they engage. These issues will continue to emerge as technologies develop in years to come. With that in mind, in our final chapter we move on to discuss current and projected innovations that are currently emerging, providing new challenges as well as exciting opportunities.

10

THE SHAPE OF THINGS
AND OF THINGS TO COME

It is little short of a miracle that modern methods of instruction have not already completely strangled the holy curiosity of inquiry. . . . I believe that one could even deprive a healthy beast of prey of its voraciousness if one could force it with a whip to eat continuously whether it were hungry or not.

Albert Einstein, Autobiographical Notes

In this chapter, we identify current trends in learning, make some tentative predictions about what will happen next, and proffer some wild speculations about what might happen if the world were a less complex place and there were fewer constraints on the effects and affordances of social systems on education.

We head toward the end of this book with some observations and speculations that probably reveal as much about us and our philosophical stances as they do about the future. It is fair to say that many generations have felt their educational systems were failing them. Near the beginning of the twenty-first century, this is as true as ever. However, not to be deterred, we would like to suggest that there are some significant differences between the current era and earlier times, and that a significant number of them relate to the growth of cyberspace, both in terms of opportunities and threats.

THE PROBLEM WITH INSTITUTIONAL LEARNING

We are in the midst of an ongoing revolution. Whether it is a continuation of the industrial revolution, the start of the knowledge revolution, the green revolution, some blend of these, or something else entirely, what we can say with assurance is that in these first decades of the twenty-first century, the rate of technological change is greater than ever before (S. Johnson, 2010; Kelly, 2010). This is an inevitable result of the increase in the adjacent possible that our technologies bring, which engender more technologies that change how we connect, perceive, and value people and things in the world.

As a direct result of technological change, the world is getting better, and it is getting better faster than ever before (S. Johnson, 2012; Ridley, 2010). By almost any measurement—wealth, health, life expectancy, pollution, crime, violence, education, accessibility, discrimination, population growth, exploitation, inequality—many societies in the world shows significant, and in several cases, exponential improvement when viewed over a period of decades. However, this improvement is not evenly spread. There are huge local fluctuations, and it would be misleading to suggest that everyone in the world has experienced every benefit. But, on average, the world is getting better and better at a faster and faster rate.

The learning revolution is a part of this improvement, both benefiting from and driving change. Increasingly, learning is being separated from the formal institutions that we have created to facilitate it, not just through visible and hyped technologies such as MOOCs. Knowledge (or at least information), once centrally held in libraries and universities, corporations, and isolated individual groups, is more available than ever before. As it has always been—but at a far greater scale thanks to cyberspace—knowledge is held within the network of people and the artifacts that they create. More importantly, that knowledge is accessible on demand. We can offload the need to know facts and details to the networked totality of cyberspace because we know we can access it when we need to. Rather than being the result of lengthy study, we can learn things we need to know in a short period, often only seconds from identifying that need. Whether we need to know who has written what about networked learning (and, through collectives, whose thoughts are most valued by the crowd), how to fix a leaking tap, or how to produce overtones on a saxophone, we can turn to the crowd and its reified knowledge for answers. This does not mean that the need for lengthy study has gone away, and we need to hone our skills in both discovering and evaluating the knowledge that we find in cyberspace, but it does mean that knowledge is more easily attained that it has ever been, and it is getting easier by the second. And yet, for all this massive increase in learning and the ability and opportunity to learn, we continue to run institutions as though it had never happened.

This is not just a problem about learning. It is also a problem about the purpose and structure of learning. We are less likely than ever to stay in the same place, highly unlikely to stay in the same career, and many of the "careers" that we embark on would be unrecognizable to our parents, let alone our grandparents. Children born today will have career paths we can barely imagine at the moment. What marks this trend is an increasing need for creativity, flexibility, analysis, and synthesis skills in the use of information. Yet our educational systems have been phenomenally slow to change their approach in response to these issues. Indeed, many changes are extremely regressive, as governments try to prove they are doing something to deal with the gaping holes in education visible to all by measuring the measurable (e.g., SAT scores, or the number of hours spent on centrally speci-fied tasks) and controlling what should not be controlled (e.g., setting standard-ized lessons and outcomes for curricula). There is, and has always been, a tension between the role of education as a means of reproducing cultural norms for stabil-ity and as an instrument of change.

There is a pervasive, if sometimes fuzzily formulated, recognition of the value of education to society. This leads to top-down and bottom-up demands for an increase in the numbers of people entering higher education that makes their traditional processes and infrastructures creak at the seams. It is not surprising, therefore, that institutions turn increasingly to mass-production methods in an attempt to cope with the demand. However, we are seeing a neo-liberal reluc-tance to fund formal education systems from public revenues. Thus, as universi-ties become more expensive for students to attend, and these institutions fail to meet their bloating needs, they adopt a particularly retrograde form of instructiv-ist learning: industrial-sized lectures, mass media use, and MOOC (massive open online course) formats, with regulated outcomes and fixed modes of delivery. But this approach is, if more than a century of research in constructivist learning has taught us anything, fundamentally wrong. An industrialized methodology is exactly the opposite of what is needed if we want to nurture the skills of new gen-erations, infusing them with a love of learning. They must have the ability to be self-directed and self-motivated learners in order to cope with ever-more rapidly changing (and perhaps more dangerous) times.

SAVING INSTITUTIONS FROM IRRELEVANCE

Before the twelfth century, people used to visit scholars in order to learn (Norton, 1909). They sat around while the great masters (who were always men), shared their wisdom, wherever they happened to be located. These students were, of course, quite rich—going to spend a few years at the feet of scholars was not something the average peasant ever dreamt of, and grants were few and far between. At around the same time, city burghers in Bologna and Paris saw the benefit of having many rich students populating their streets for years at a time, and helped to establish Europe's first universities. At first, there were two distinct models of university: the university of masters, with Paris as the prototype, which set teachers up as arbiters of all things; and the university of students, stemming from the processes used in Bologna, where students determined what was taught and who taught it. Over the centuries, the Parisian model came to dominate. A concentration of self-moderating scholars soon led to things like

- The housing and collection of books into libraries;
- Buildings to house and teach students and faculty;
- Administrative procedures to manage ever more complex processes;
- Formal awards and testing methods to validate both institutions and their learners,
- "Efficient" methods of teaching like lectures (and the infrastructure to match);
- Restrictive subject ranges born of economic and physical necessity (communities of scholars needed critical mass);
- Large, complex bureaucratic infrastructures to maintain and organize the educational machine to handle timetabling, student registration, award-giving, hiring, and firing;
- Overseeing bodies (often governmental) to ensure quality, consistency, and so on;
- Restrictions on entry to ensure students' capability, class, and finances to succeed.

A few centuries later, in the late eighteenth century, the written exam was born in the form of the Cambridge mathematical Tripos, which came to supplement or replace the traditional *vive voce* oral presentation and defence of a thesis. This innovation spread fairly slowly over the next century, driven largely by economic and standardization benefits: written exams were cheaper than oral tests to mark and administer. Beyond that, there were few major innovations. Except for minor technological innovations such as slates and quills, and later ballpoint pens and whiteboards, the occasional restructuring (e.g., Humboldtian universities) and the incorporation of subjects other than the original three of theology, law, and philosophy (including, after some hundreds of years of being treated as a manual trade, medicine), there was little change. The teaching methods and organizational structures used in most institutions today would be instantly recognizable to Abelard, one of the early medieval education pioneers. Nearly every techno-logical innovation in education since medieval times has been an attempt to overcome some of the unwanted consequences of the basic technologies that remain unchanged.

Even modern open and distance universities that should not have to conform to patterns that emerged out of their physical and historical context, replicate structures designed to fit scholastic life in medieval Europe. And so we continue to see the dominance of a group-mode model, including the evolved trappings such as courses, semesters, libraries, deans, faculties, convocation ceremonies, medieval gowns, classes, grades, exams, scholarly covens, doctors and master's degrees, and an incipient hidden curriculum of class and gender (Margolis & Romero, 1998).

Higher Education has spawned a wealth of industries: copy houses, essay mills, textbook publishers, gown makers, schools that "prepare" students for university, companies that filter based on qualifications, government departments dedicated to grant awards, professional societies to defend their disciplines, tourist industries to employ the mass of students every summer, student unions, faculty associations, institutional furniture suppliers, whiteboard and computer manufacturers, and so on. It is very well integrated into our social and economic lives. More than that, the central credentialing role continues to serve as a filter for many jobs in aca-demia, government and industry.

But sometimes, technologies can do more than repair the damage done by others. Sometimes they open up new adjacent possibles that allow us to replace the whole system, because the paths they clear ahead of them lead somewhere better. C. Christensen has called such innovations "disruptive" (2008; C. Christensen et al., 2008). The Internet is one of those technologies. Right now, we in academia are mostly using it to shore up the old technologies and entrench them deeper with tools that automate medieval ways, like LMSs and web analytics to drive per-formance according to limited criteria.

Sets, nets, and collectives do not fit comfortably in this medieval model of teaching. If we are to reap their benefits on a large scale, then institutions must adapt, and in many cases, radically change. We propose a number of changes to help break this cycle.

VARIABLE-LENGTH COURSES

This book has shown how courses are far from the be-all and end-all of inten-tional learning. They are, however, so central to the design of educational systems that it is easy to forget the enormous effects they have on the shape of institutions. Courses are the main temporal unit that determine the ebb and flow of activity within a university. They are units of work allocation to teachers, administrative units for payment of fees, assessment determinants, constituents of a final award, and dictate class sizes and structures, among other things.

Courses are, for the most part, fixed denomination currencies that, for reasons of organizational efficiency, are divided into a very limited range of unit sizes. In Europe, especially after Bologna Accord (Sanders & Dunn, 2010), and much of the rest of the world, there are credit transfer points that make it relatively easy to compare one course with another by considering the expected study time involved, including teaching activities, personal study, and assessment activities. Typically, such credit points relate to a notional 10 hours of study, so a typical 10-credit course would, with some notable regional variations, normally equate to around 100 hours of study for an average student expecting an average grade. This is, in principle, a flexible approach that might allow a course to be created of any size. However, in most cases, this does not happen. Courses are normally divided into chunks that fit traditional term lengths: a single-term course usually accounts for 10 or 15 credits, a double-length course accounts for 20 or 25, and so on. It is extremely rare for courses to provide less than 5 credits and unusual to find courses worth more than 30 or 40. Smaller chunks are much harder to administer for a group-oriented model: it leads to complexities of timetabling, credit transfer, and difficulties identifying appropriate prerequisites. In short, smaller chunks make the bureaucratic technology of educational institutions creak at the seams, massively increasing costs. At the other end of the spectrum, courses that are too large make things more difficult for students because failure is far more devastating and transferability is more difficult because of the increased risk of parts of a course overlapping with others. Much of the reasoning behind the sizes that are chosen relate to traditional academic term lengths, which are determined on the one hand by religious holidays (in historically Christian cultures, Christmas and Easter) and on the other by the expectation that students need to return to their homes to help with the harvest during summer months. This has little to do with pedagogic, disciplinary, social, or psychological needs in modern societies. Educational systems contribute in a large way to the continuation of such seasonal breaks, accounting for rhythms of work and vacation that reverberate through entire societies.

In North America, for historical reasons, things are much worse. North American institutions use credit points relating broadly to the amount of *teaching* rather than the amount of *learning*: this very bizarre inversion means that two apparently very similar 3-credit courses, the norm for a single-term course, may equate to anywhere between 100 and 200 hours of study, depending on subject. A single credit in an American institution thus equates to anything from around 30 to 60 hours of study. This equates to a more standardized 39 hours of teacher instruction which, of course, is irrelevant in an asynchronous online environment, and gives no clue as to the amount of time spent learning. The combination of fuzzy and inconsistent expectations and coarser granularity makes the system even more bureaucratically dense and less flexible.

Whichever system is used, its value is not for the student but for the bureaucratic machinery of higher education, with lengths determined not by any pedagogical or organizational rationale, but by a pattern of holidays relevant to medieval times. Among the biggest problems that arise from this kind of chunking is that, from the perspective of acquiring any given competence, there are no fixed limits on how long it might take. For most people, a skill such as learning to tie a shoelace can probably be acquired in minutes, but for some it remains a challenge for years. For some people, becoming a proficient programmer may take years, while others may become productive in days. Literacy in many arts or sciences may take a lifetime to acquire, but different levels of literacy can be reached in minutes or hours.

COMPETENCE–BASED ASSESSMENT

For over a century, the most popular approach to assessing competence in university courses has been the previously unseen written examination. The popularity of this form of assessment has much to do with the fact that they are perceived to reliably ensure the person who claims to have learned something has actually done so, and they are relatively cheap and easy to mark in small numbers, or at scale. Unfortunately, they achieve neither goal. Exams are expensive because they do not contribute to the central goal of learning. In fact, it is considerably worse than that: they actively reduce motivation to learn because they impose extrinsic rewards and punishments, thus massively reducing intrinsic motivation (Deci & Ryan, 2002; Kohn, 1999).

Given their strong extrinsic role of punishment and reward, it is unsurprising that over 70% of high school students admit to cheating in exams (McCabe & Trevino, 1996). Measures to reduce this level of cheating are extremely expensive, and it is a never-ending arms race that cannot be won by educators. If exams were accurate discriminators of skills then this would be less of a problem but, except in some very limited contexts, they are not. With the exception of a few trades such as journalism, the competence of writing or problem-solving using a pen or pencil, with no access to the Internet or to other people, without a computer, in silence, with extreme time constraints and under extreme stress to perform, is seldom if ever again required. Exams reward those who work well under such pressures and punish those who do not, even though these pressures are almost never going to exist in any real-world application of skills and competence. At best, they lead to the development of gaming skills that students use strategically to pass examinations, not to gain scholarly competence.

What is required is accreditation that shows what you can actually do, not whether you can pass a test on fixed-length courses; accreditation that is transferable to wherever you need to go next, that is precise, that does not bind you to one institution, and that allows you to receive recognition for what you are provably able to do, whether the context is academic, professional, or personal (Berlanga et al., 2008; Koper & Specht, 2006). Partly due to the unreliability of university assessments in identifying the skills and qualities of candidates, and partly because it is easy, an increasing number of employers are either ignoring or reducing the weighting of formal qualifications when hiring new employees. Hiring managers consult sites such as LinkedIn and even Facebook, especially where skilled professional work is needed, leveraging networks and associated collective tools (such as reputation tagging) to identify those with appropriate and appropriately verified skills.

BADGES

To partly formalize learning achieved in sets and nets as well as groups, increasing attention is being paid to the use of badges. Badges are symbols or indicators received for demonstrating some competence, skill, quality, or interest. The Scouting movement and other organizations of its ilk have used the physical variant of the idea for many years. The modern update of badges involves the use of images that indicate one's accomplishments: these are as simple as participation in a forum or as complex as receiving a doctorate. Each is certified by an issuer (the "badger"), so they cannot be easily faked, and tied to a person's identity so that they cannot be reissued to someone else. Badges may be set to expire after a certain time for volatile skills. While anyone can issue them, some issuers will have higher reputations than others. They have many benefits beyond simply signalling achievement. The Open Badge project (openbadges.org) identifies a range of uses, observing that badges can:

- Signal achievement
- Recognize informal learning
- Transfer learning across spaces and contexts
- Capture more specific skills than traditional degrees
- Support greater specialization and innovation
- Allow greater diversity
- Motivate participation and learning outcomes
- Allow multiple pathways to learning
- Open doors
- Unlock privileges
- Enhance your identity and reputation
- Build community and social capital
- Capture the learning path and history
- Recognize new skills and literacies
- Provide a more complete picture of the learner
- Provide branding opportunities for institutions, organizations, and learning communities

  (Adapted from the Open Badges FAQ (n.d.) at https://wiki.mozilla.org/Badges/FAQs#What_are_the_benefits_of_badges.3F)

There are many ways that badges provide a way out of the institutional course stranglehold without necessitating a massive change to traditional ways of doing things in one fell swoop: a badge can represent accomplishment of a course as easily as it can any other competence. It is notable that many of the benefits are of great potential value in groups (e.g., allowing faster establishment of norms, expectations, and trust based on past accomplishments and known skill levels), nets (e.g., providing social capital, enriching projections of identity, and easing entry into different networks), sets (e.g., providing attributes to identify sets and subsets, and assisting in trust management), and collectives (e.g., discovering trends, identifying patterns of reputation and clusters of related skills). Badges are thus not just signals of accomplishment but act as mediating objects for social engagement outside group contexts. They offer a potential means of enabling networked and group learning to move beyond formal educational boundaries and enter into mainstream and lifelong learning.

However, on a cautionary note, there is a risk that badges may be seen, like traditional assessments, as extrinsic rewards. The wealth of evidence that such rewards are almost always deeply demotivating, especially when related to complex skills or creativity (Kohn, 1999), means that it should always be made clear that badges are simply credentials, evidence of achievement, not things to be striven for in and of themselves. We have some concern, especially when they are used as motivating objects, that there are big risks they could lead to unintended and unfortunate systemic consequences, much as the use of grades, gold stars, and awards in classrooms and the workplace have demotivated and hobbled generations of learners. We hope that they will eventually be seen as nothing more than evidence of ability, not as a substitute for success. Unfortunately, their prominent use in large-scale teaching systems like the Khan Academy and large MOOCs suggests otherwise.

At the time of writing, the specifications for badges are still in flux and, though used in a number of formal institutions and organizations, it remains to be seen whether they will become ubiquitous. However, they or something like them represent the technological means to enable the revolution in assessment and accreditation that is necessary if education as a formal process is to survive by moving beyond the rigid course format. Badges provide the means to transition between top-down accreditation and bottom-up recommendation. In principle, they can be aggregated and reassembled to fit different needs and purposes, signal specific competences rather than broad disciplinary knowledge, and equally used to describe still-broader facets of individual accomplishments. It is possible to envisage uses beyond the purely academic that may be of great value to potential employers, such as, for example, recognition of creativity, stickability, stoicism, or sociability. We can already see instances of such broad recognition having value in, for example, LinkedIn endorsements, which do not only show subject skills but also personal qualities. It is easy to imagine a PageRank-like collective process that uses networks to judge the reliability of such assessments and, just as Google currently provides greater weight to academic pages than to commercial pages, so we might see greater weight given to certain badgers relative to others. This may, over time, lead to a self-organizing system of accreditation in which universities carry no innately greater weight than individual academics, employers, social networks, or sets of people with relevant skills.

Libraries provided a strong rationale for establishing an institution before the advent of the Internet, and were often central to the institution and its functioning. Books, journals, and other resources were too expensive for individuals to buy for themselves, and it made sense to centralize them. The word "lecturer" derives from the fact that a single individual would read texts to classes of scholars in the Middle Ages because books were too rare to share. This is no longer such a strong imperative. In the course of writing this book, we have barely touched a piece of paper. While some books (particularly those published more than a decade ago), are still only available in paper form, the vast majority of the papers and books we have referred to existed on our computers as electrons and patterns on a screen. Libraries are still valuable, largely as a means to negotiate terms with closed publishers to gain access to electronic versions of papers and e-books, and we have used our own institutional libraries extensively in researching this book. However, the papers and books themselves are, for the most part, held by the publishers or freely available on websites. The library has become a junction in a network, not a repository of knowledge.

Beyond the library, in several cases we have been able to make use of our networks to contact original authors to receive not only their work but also engage in dialogue about it. This is the thin end of a large wedge. In many cases, work is published in blog form, and we can engage in and benefit from discussions with many others about it. We see this as an increasing trend that may eventually transform or even oust the traditional processes of peer review. Literature, especially *academic* literature, is enlivened by the dialogues that develop around it. Like medieval glosses, scholarly works are explained, illuminated, criticized, and extended by the conversations around them and these may provide equal or greater value to that of the original work that is being annotated.

Blog posts are typically seen as a less worthy form of academic publication because they lack peer review. However, the truth is sometimes almost exactly the opposite. The problem with this point of view is that it assumes that a blog post is simply a new way of presenting information that is like a newspaper or journal article. It is not. A "publication" is not just the blog post, but also the diverse dialogue that is associated with it: a blog post is the work of a crowd, not an individual. A post from a popular blogger in academia is not a standalone work like a traditional academic paper but an extended process, in which the comments are often as important as the post itself, where errors are examined, implications observed, and contrary views expounded. Often, through trackbacks, the blog becomes part of a network of shared knowledge that explores an issue in depth. The article that spawned such reified dialogue may itself be part of a larger network of connected posts. For writers of books such as this one, targeted at a largely academic audience, this presents a problem. How can one cite such a connected jumble, whose character is constantly changing and whose essence is discursive, where good and bad is mixed with sublime and awful? This is not the same kind of publication as an academic paper to which references have been made in other papers, despite apparent morphological and topological similarities.

There are two main reasons for this. Firstly, the pace is different: the slow rate of reply through academic publication of the traditional kind, where it is not uncommon for an article to take two years or more to reach publication, means that the dialogue is cumbersome and the original author may well have moved on to another topic by the time he or she might have replied to a response that appears in a follow-up peer-reviewed journal paper. Moreover, on many occasions the nature of academic rewards suggests that there is little motivation to respond: academics may not wish to tread old ground, and will have moved on to other considerations. Secondly, the conversation through academic journals is spatially discontinuous. A blog forms a centrepiece around which discussion and critique evolves in situ, whereas academic papers engender responses in different journals, conferences, workshops and presentations across the world, with few easy ways to link them together as a coherent dialogue. There are few places where the chasm between traditional modes of communication and the new forms that social software enables are so starkly highlighted.

Beyond simple blogs, collectives can provide powerful means of filtering and shaping these kinds of dialogue to provide a meta-review of the reviewers. On sites such as Slashdot, the use of the collective, through technologies such as rich metadata and karma points, can shape a large dialogue to reveal posts that are highly valued by the community for different needs, creating more reliable, richer, and more diverse co-authored resources than the best traditionally authored texts. An early system for computer-supported collaborative argumentation, D3E, formed the basis of JIME (Journal of Interactive Media in Education) in which conversation and disputes around papers provided rich peer review that was often as valuable as the articles under review.

While the existing author model persists, such systems are unlikely to see persistent use. It is notable that the JIME experiment was eventually abandoned, though recently revived in a different and less adventurous form, and efforts to make an educational equivalent of Slashdot have foundered, largely due to its geek-friendly design that appears arcane and complex to people of a less technical orientation. Less geek-oriented approaches such as that used by the StackOverflow family of sites have been far more successful, but have yet to see much transfer to academic environments. However, even more formal processes, such as those that sustain PLoS One, are increasingly open and inclusive: PLoS One has a panel of over 3,000 expert reviewers, and the reviews generated are aids to understanding for not only the writer but the reader of the article as well.

FLATTENING ORGANIZATIONAL HIERARCHIES

Institutional hierarchies and associated bureaucracies were once thought to be a necessary evil that had to be tolerated so large groups could work together efficiently. On the whole, they still work moderately well when the world does not change too fast. They are highly evolved social species, usually formalized group forms that have solved many of the problems of coordination on a scale necessary to support large populations. Without such technologies, we would be limited to the hunter-gatherer demes humans are so well adapted to live in (Caporael, 1997). However, they come at a cost in time, effort, and space. One big reason for this is transactional distance. Each level of a hierarchy separates one sub-community from another. This limits the capacity for dialogue between those in different organizational units and requires dialogue to be replaced with structure—formal reports, memos, announcements, and the like—that condense and impose structure upon what may have been less formal dialogues, with the truly informal being lost or diluted in committee meetings and other formal channels of information exchange. This channelling and condensation up and down the hierarchical structure is a necessary feature that makes such hierarchies possible. Those at the trunk ends of the tree would not be able to cope with the mass of detail from the branches without such methods, and those at the branches would be overwhelmed if they had to pay attention to everyone else in the organization.

However, it does not have to be that way. The capacity of cyberspace to support larger set-like tribes as well as groups and nets, especially with the aid of collectives that can provide the filtering and channelling formerly delivered by formal condensations of reports and top-down edicts, creates opportunities to rethink how and whether such hierarchical technologies are needed. Just as individual learners can learn effectively in nets and sets, so can a whole organization. In a tumultuous world, there is a need for structures that are flat, distributed, and agile, adaptable to changing needs, interests, and groups, yet still capable of effective and efficient coordination. Large, hierarchical organizations inevitably introduce rigid and slow-moving structural elements that preclude rapid change.

BREAKING DISCIPLINARY BOUNDARIES

Part of the hierarchical structure of educational systems is based on subject and disciplinary divisions. These academic tribes and territories are deeply embedded (Becher & Trowler, 2001). They start in earliest schooling, with lessons, classes, and teachers becoming more and more specialized as academic careers progress. To an extent, this is inevitable. There are natural path dependencies that mean when we take one path we cannot take another, and so we become more and more focused in the direction of our interests. As we take such paths, we develop cognitive tool-sets that are appropriate to different ways of seeing the world: the toolsets that we need for the appreciation of literature are quite different than those we need for physics (S. E..Page, 2008).

It is not a surprise, therefore, that communities of interest form around more and more refined disciplinary areas, where cognitive toolsets are similar enough to enable richer communication about a subject. These disciplinary divisions are reinforced by hierarchical group structuring: the schools, divisions, faculties, and similar expressions of difference with which we are all familiar. Because these are constructed as groups, and because groups thrive on exclusion and difference, it is equally unsurprising that the systemic effects of disciplinary clustering reinforce that clustering. It is embedded at such a deep level in everything from research funding to teaching practice that it is hard to imagine it could ever be otherwise. It is hard to be a renaissance person in a system that is fundamentally divided at its most basic architectural roots. Unfortunately, the world of real problems does not respect disciplinary boundaries.

A world of constant change demands ever-increasing creativity. Creativity thrives at the boundaries and borders (Wenger, 1998) and is driven by diversity (Florida, 2005; S. Johnson, 2010; S. E. Page, 2008; Vaill, 1996). If we create bound-aries that are hard to cross, the potential for timely evolution, at least of the indi-vidual, is thwarted. This is a more complex issue than individual growth, however. It can be argued that the parcellation caused by such divisions allows for greater system-level diversity and so, if there are opportunities for those from different disciplinary foci to work together, they will bring richer cognitive toolboxes to the problem. As S. E. Page (2008) demonstrates, a diverse group will usually outperform a less diverse one, even when the less diverse group is composed of experts, for most problem-solving and creative activities. So, while disciplinary areas reduce individual cognitive flexibility, they can increase it for society as a whole. The problem is one of balance: it makes no sense to completely demolish subject boundaries, because that flattening would reduce overall capacity and creativity, and anyway, would be impossible: people do have diverse and incommensurate interests in areas of study, and that is as it should be. Nevertheless, it makes no sense to sustain subject boundaries to the extent that crossing borders is too difficult for individuals. The solution lies in recognizing that these are not groups, but sets of people with shared interests. People will always focus on what interests them, and path dependencies mean they will always cluster in particular sets. If we are to make greater progress toward creative and agile educational institutions, then deliberate flattening is required, which means getting rid of inappropriate group forms.

If people wish to form groups for particular purposes, for instance to perform some substantial research or to further the study of teaching in their set(s) of interest, then that should be possible. Those groups may be composed of people with similar cognitive toolboxes, but they may not. However, groups should not be created out of sets simply through tradition or for bureaucratic convenience. Is there a case for groups of mathematicians who work together on problems or as teachers? Yes, absolutely. Is there a case for departments of mathematics? There may be far less compelling reasons for this, almost all of which revolve around a circular assumption that they exist within a hierarchical bureaucratic structure where such a department is needed (for administration, funding, research recognition, and so on). But, as we have already suggested, such structures no longer make the sense that they used to make. As a result of this disaggregation of boundaries, new organizational models that recognize and facilitate knowledge production within cross- and multidisciplinary sets of interest and focus (e.g., environmental issues, urban construction, education) may be created as needed, when needed.

CHANGING THE PATTERNS OF TEACHER REWARDS

Legend has it that the open sleeves of gowns worn by professors are pocket-like because students would drop money into them if they were satisfied with a lecture. Had universities developed along the lines of the student-led Bologna model, a variation on this approach might persist today. However, for most of those in academia, payment comes in the form of a predictable pay packet. In

North American systems, though not commonly elsewhere in the world, those wishing to become full-time permanent professors must endure a curious trial by fire known as attaining tenure. This requires them to jump through a series of hoops to show that they are well-rounded (and conventional) academics who can teach, research, and participate in the university and broader community. Once they've achieved tenure, all can and some do rest on their laurels. As a process, it leaves much to be desired. However, the world over, it is the norm for a Humboldtian model of research, teaching, and community service to be fossilized into the structure and organization of an institution. This has some unfortunate consequences, such as the fact that students are often taught by researchers who cannot teach, and that research is often performed by teachers who are not great researchers.

The notion that every academic should be an all-rounder accounts for much of the dissatisfaction expressed by those in the profession—high workloads, low teaching standards, and mundane or pointless research. It is one of the structural forces that propel academia along its well-trodden furrows and away from potential change. It is particularly strange in an institution like Athabasca University, the authors' academy, which distributes the teaching role among many such as learning designers, editors, graphic designers, and technologists, and employs people in roles such as coordinator and tutor that are primarily concerned with teaching and its coordination. Individual academics still need to support the three pillars: teaching, research, and community engagement, despite the fact that they are no longer individual academics in the traditional academic sense. As we move more fully into the sets and networks where learning happens, these restrictive roles will seem stranger for everyone.

For some, and we are among them, the three pillars of academic life are fulfilling: all of the roles are interesting, valuable, and enjoyable. For others, this is not the case, and as a result, many who would play one or two of the roles well are deterred from engaging in the profession, or leave it early. In the US, the mean length of an academic career is less than 11 years (Kaminski & Geisler, 2012). Some institutions have dedicated themselves to research or teaching at the exclusion of the other, but this too has dangers. Research informs and motivates learners, and teaching at a high level is difficult without a passionate and ongoing interest in the subject being taught, stimulated by active research. Some forms of research can appear pointless if they are not disseminated and explored through teaching.

No research has value without a community context, where work is grounded in, driven by, or meets the needs and wants of society. Once again, the way out of this dilemma lies in sets and nets. Problems arise because of the group-oriented view of a university, with fixed roles and rigid organizational demarcation. Academics are nearly always involved in cross-cutting cleavages, their sets intersecting with others across the world, their networks extending far beyond a single institution, and these connections are not only encouraged, but facilitated through institutional formalisms like conferences, journals, and workshops. However, within institutions themselves, the lines are often more distinctly drawn. Author Dron, for example, only found out that a colleague in the next office shared a research interest because he was a member of the same globally distributed set, a subject-oriented mailing list.

With greater organizational flattening, those with different interests and skills, whether in research, teaching, or community engagement can connect more easily. Our own Athabasca Landing demonstrates the value of this, connecting people in sets and nets who would otherwise have no knowledge or interest in what others are doing, and allowing good practice in research and teaching to spread organically throughout what is otherwise a hierarchy. Once this step is taken, it becomes easier to balance strengths and weaknesses. If some of one's learning is mediated by those who teach well, some is inspired by those who research interesting things, and some is embedded in the social and business life of the community, then classes and subject divisions are simply obstacles that prevent the best use of resources.

This brings us back to how academics are paid and rewarded. While we do not have a quick and easy solution to the problem, it seems worthwhile to consider not the breadth of skill in an academic, but the diversity of skills across a networked institution, including the people, the technologies, and the structures that enable that knowledge to be spread and organized. As long as we retain isolated groups connected hierarchically, then well-rounded individuals are a necessity. However, if we assume a network and sets, supported by collectives, then it is the collective intelligence of the system that matters, not the skills of a single individual. To some extent, of course, this is already the case. Anyone who hires a team will make a point of choosing a diverse range of people knowing that they will contribute differently. Yet, a team is a group, and an institution, though inevitably carrying some of the trappings of a group, veers more toward the set or net in its social form.

ADAPTING TO LEARNERS

In an ideal world, we would provide methods of learning that are fitted to the subject and people learning them, not the needs and capabilities of institutions teaching them. This is what learning in sets and nets, with the aid of collectives, allows. It opens possibilities for people to learn differently. The role of the institution becomes more like that of the modern networked library, a hub to connect people with other people and resources that will help them to learn.

THE MONKEY'S PAW

"The Monkey's Paw" is a story by W. W. Jacobs about a talisman that grants wishes which always come true with horrific consequences. This resonates deeply as a metaphor for technological change. While we have observed many systemic and path dependencies in the current system of education, there is no doubt that widespread changes would lead to equally unforeseen and potentially negative consequences. If we made these changes across the board, then the monkey's paw would no doubt work its usual mischief. For example, breakdowns in disciplinary boundaries might lead to increasingly shallow insights, albeit with greater breadth. The loss of examinations would impact a range of businesses and social structures that depend on them, and make it easier for some types of incompetence to be enabled that were previously restrained. But this particular set of wishes has held sway for too long, and it is no longer fit for its purpose.

BEYOND THE INSTITUTION

For some years now we have been asking academic audiences at education and online learning conferences and venues where they turn first when seeking to learn something new. With almost no exceptions, the answer is a search engine (nearly always Google) and/or Wikipedia. Such audiences are, perhaps atypical, and at this time these remain starting points, not for most, the end-point in their search for knowledge, but it does help to demonstrate the massive penetration of social software, especially that which supports sets, networks, and collectives, in the service of learning. We are not speculating about the future when we talk about educational uses of social software in this book, but describing the present. In the past, such an audience would have turned first to libraries, books, reference works, and so on, and perhaps to courses and programs for more ambitious learning activities. Such things still have a place, but even here cyberspace is making massive inroads. In the course of writing this book, we have barely contributed to the destruction of a single tree, let alone the small forests that we both consumed when writing our Ph.D. theses. These exemplars of set, net, and collective applications show the enormous existing impact of learning with others beyond the traditional groups of formal education.

MOOCS AND SELF-STUDY RESOURCES

MOOC (massive open online course) is an acronym coined by Dave Cormier to describe an open-to-enrol free course with many participants. Current popular examples of platforms for MOOCs include Udemy, Udacity, edX, and Coursera, but the market is shifting rapidly, and we are seeing a proliferation of competitors as this book goes to press, such as Open2Study, WorldWideLearning, and FutureLearn. How many of these will stand the test of time remains to be seen, but there is clearly a growing demand for MOOCs. Coursera alone has grown faster than Facebook or Instagram, garnering more than 1.8 million students in just over a year (Cadwalladr, 2012). These represent only the visible edge of a massive movement to self-directed and institution-free learning.

There are two distinctive forms of MOOC emerging. One, the original bearer of the name that is championed by people such as George Siemens and Stephen Downes, is based in a connectivist model of learning, and the other takes a more industrial and instructivist approach, using behaviourist/cognitivist models of teaching. These have been referred to, respectively, as CMOOCs and XMOOCs (Siemens, 2012). Both XMOOCs and CMOOCs typically, though not universally, follow a paced model of learning: courses have start and end dates.

In XMOOCs, it is normal for those wishing to take a course to sign up and engage in many individual learning activities and some group discussions (usually with an instructor) that are closed to non-members. The CMOOCs typically also ask for enrolment, but this is mainly for coordinating a looser network. They seldom have formal groups of any kind: clusters of learners connect, form their own networks, and link up to the broader network, typically through a hub that aggregates networked content explicitly linked or tagged. This does not mean that there are no groups involved, as they may be used with or in formal classes. When creating the first MOOC to bear the name, for instance, George Siemens and Stephen Downes used a closed course run within an institution so that others could participate, offering accreditation to paid-for students and open participation to anyone and everyone else (Downes, 2008b). David Wiley had done this a year or so previously, but on a smaller scale.

A further subdivision of the genre that sometimes gets lumped with the others is the more flexible, bite-sized tutorial approach exemplified most prominently by the Khan Academy, that may also be found in many places such as Instructables (www.instructables.com), eHow (www.ehow.com), HowStuffWorks (www.howstuffworks.com), LifeHacker (www.lifehacker.com), Ted Talks, and countless others. We christen these kMOOCs (Khan-style MOOCs). They are almost entirely instructivist in approach, but their small size makes them more easily assembled by different learners and, unlike most xMOOCs and cMOOCs, they do not follow a paced model that requires learners to move in lock-step with one another. The Khan Academy alone has helped over 10 million students (Cadwalladr, 2012). There are similarities between kMOOCs and the goals of proponents of re-usable learning objects (RLOs), but unlike the RLO, these "courselets" are inherently social, with commentary, remashability, and engagement built in from the ground up. Interestingly, these courselets are aggregable, appearing in set-oriented categories and including both top-down and collective-generated recommendations of what to learn next. The combination of fine granularity, social engagement, and collective guidance suggests that such methods may have a great future.

While much discussion is currently taking place about appropriate models and the different virtues or vices of these approaches, we observe that the reality for many learners differs surprisingly little between the three models. Large and small networks, sets, and both face-to-face and online groups have emerged around all of these courses, supplementing and enriching the learning experience provided by the course itself, whether or not this was intended in their original design. This is a benefit of scale: with enough people learning at the same time, the traditional group form of course-based approaches becomes at best tribal in nature, filled with multiple networks, smaller groups, sets, and clusters. In the case of cMOOCs, a rich network is an essential element of the experience, but in the rest, it has happened as networks coalesce and form into study groups, online and face-to-face, or sets that form around topics, posts, or themes in the larger MOOC. Given the scale, even in a paced MOOC such as those developed for Coursera there are always people (often strangers) who form tribal sets to help one another. As Koller, co-founder of Coursera, puts it,

> We built in the opportunity for students to interact with each other in
> meaningful ways and have one student help another through the hard bits so

they could work together to achieve a better outcome for everyone. There was a real community built up where students felt incredibly motivated to help each other and answer each other's questions to the point that in the Fall quarter of 2011, the median response time for a question posted on the forum was 22 minutes. Because there was such a broad worldwide community of students all working together, even if someone was working at 3:00 a.m., chances are that somewhere around the world, there would be somebody else who was awake and thinking about the same problem. (Severance, 2012, p. 9)

For the unpaced, small-chunk kMOOCs, the set that gathers around an individual tutorial, often instantiated in asynchronous comments, can be rich and pedagogically valuable, exploring and explaining the skills or concepts of the static tutorial, much like a blog post. In some cases, MOOCs have formed a structural backbone and content for traditionally taught classroom-based or online courses. The reason this can happen is that, despite intent in the case of some xMOOCs, without the binding group form of the institution, a single social form no longer formally binds learners.

Much has been made in the popular press of the relatively high attrition rates in MOOCs of all descriptions, but we think this is a not much of a problem. Relatively low completion rates are only a failing from the point of view of the purveyors of MOOCs, not from that of their participants, who often sign up on a whim, and may have little interest, time, or commitment to sustain their ongoing participation, at least when compared to the large commitment made in a traditional paid-for course. Freed from the coercion in conventional institutional courses, it is no surprise that MOOCs may be treated much like any other free resource on the Web. People get what they need, if the timing is right, and leave if they do not get what they want or if their curiosity is satisfied in the first week or two. There is one major benefit of this attrition rate, however. In part as a result of what are perceived to be high non-completion rates, the average length of xMOOCs appears to be getting shorter. This increasing focus and consequent diminution of group-like character means that they are becoming more and more aggregable, enabling learners to take ever more control over the learning process and integrate them into other social forms for learning. As course lengths become shorter, it would not be surprising to see xMOOCs becoming part of the "content" of network-oriented cMOOCs as well as formal closed-group classes, just another resource for learning specific skills or competences on a broader learning journey. This further emphasizes their set-like nature.

Central to CMOOCs and widely used in many other situations is the concept of a personal learning environment, or PLE (Attwell, 2007). The PLE can take any technical form, from a collection of documents and links in Evernote to a purpose-built space in an environment like Elgg, which provides a dashboard designed for this role. Echoing Rainie and Wellman's concept of networked individualism (2012), this personal space acts as a hub to a world of connected people and objects that are of value in a learning context. We have built our own extension of the concept, the context-switcher used on the Landing (Dron et al., 2011), in order to allow for the variegated, discontinuous, and multifaceted nature of learning. Within any tab of an Elgg dashboard people can store files, link to blog posts, show RSS feeds, posts from particular groups, Twitter searches, and items tagged with metadata that may be of interest, supporting sets, nets, and groups in equal measure. However, the same functionality can be achieved in many alternative ways, even using something as simple as a paper notebook, though such tools make it considerably harder to aggregate and organize the dynamic flow of information from the network.

Related to the personal learning environment and often combined in the same toolset is the e-portfolio. Like PLEs, e-portfolios can be used to aggregate learning resources, and though the typical use case is to present these aggregations to others, they may equally be used in the learning process as tools for organizing and sense-making, as well as social networking. Elgg and Mahara are good examples of the genre, both straddling the PLE/e-portfolio border due to their capacity to selectively reveal things to different people in different ways, including entirely privately. As we move creakily toward an open and interoperable future, standards such as TinCan (scorm.com/tincan/) will enable us to assemble evidence of learning from diverse sources, probably augmented by badges of proficiency, which we may use to make sense of our own diverse learning and assemble it in different ways for different needs. In the language of TinCan, learning management systems become learning record stores (scorm.com/tincanoverview/), repositories of evidence and tools to manage learning journeys rather than tools for teaching.

WHAT WILL THE FUTURE OF FORMAL LEARNING LOOK LIKE?

The time has come to move on from the present and into the near or not-so-near future. It is difficult to predict if, let alone *when* the kinds of things we talk about in the next section may happen. This is not just because we do not have enough facts (and we don't) nor because we cannot anticipate disruptive new technologies that have not yet been imagined (we can't), but because this is an increasingly networked world, a complex adaptive system encompassing much of the planet in which cascades of change can happen very suddenly and with little warning (like the appearance of a black swan; Taleb, 2007), at least until viewed in retrospect.

We think that a tipping point is on the near horizon, but it may be decades away. Like all good prophets, we hedge our bets and tread with caution. What happens may bear no resemblance at all to what we predict, and we will definitely be wrong in places. Most notably, the momentum of medieval values in universities is huge and heavy: though the format may change here or there, there are massive organized forces that have, for centuries, proudly sustained equilibrium. A fundamental change to how we learn and accredit learning will certainly be resisted by the varied interconnections between educational institutions and the rest of society: from governments to tourist industries, banks to small businesses, schools to old-boy's-club networks, our institutional forms are attached throughout the system. Academia will defend its position for the best possible reasons, and the worst. It is interesting that, whenever such issues are discussed within institutions, the default position is always "how will we deal with this threat?" or "how will we survive in this new environment?" without ever considering whether "we" the group *should* survive. Groups *want* to survive. The group forms that have sustained academia this far will not give up easily. With those provisos, we present our projections for what may be coming next.

Just-in-Time

As we already see for the small things of life, learning will happen more and more when it is needed, enabled by mobile technologies and beyond these on to forms of social learning that will increase as we become more trusting of and dependent upon the crowd and its productions. The focus will increasingly be on connecting the dots, sense-making, and taming the torrential stream of knowledge that is available to us.

Situated

Learning will occur in context—place, organization, project, and so on. Places to gather for specialist and large tools will still be necessary, though increasing use will be made of simulacra, immersive environments, and remotely controlled devices and experiments, and the tools of many trades are becoming smaller, cheaper, and more affordable. Genetic sequencing, for example, that a mere ten years ago took weeks or months and required massive and expensive equipment, can now be done with a chip and carried in a briefcase, with a turnaround measurable in hours. For many things that do require physical presence, learning will be carried out in situ, at the place where it has value.

Personalized

We already engage in personalized learning every time we do a Google search (your results will likely not be the same as mine) or look something up on Wikipedia, or find a lesson in the Khan Academy. In the future, collectives and curated sites will allow us to learn more easily what we want to learn, and to gain appropriate accreditation for it. Learners will be in control of how, what, and when they learn.

Disaggregated and Re-aggregated

The course, for which we will perhaps retain the term if not its denotation, may be anything from five minutes to five years in length. Accreditation will be through badges or similar certification systems. It is likely that the badgers themselves will be badged, perhaps using a collective that filters reputation rankings from multiple sources in order to identify the value of the provider, or that uses a PageRank-like algorithm to provide a weighted rating of value derived from the crowd's opinions and actions. Interestingly, some of those achieving high rank will be individuals, some companies, some institutions, and perhaps, some collectives: karma ranking in Slashdot or endorsements from LinkedIn may well become a more important currency than certification by institutions or learned bodies.

Some providers will be individuals, some will be companies, and some may be universities. The collective may rank some individuals more highly than all the universities combined. Universities will compete to gain attention from such superstar accreditors, who may be employed part time or on a contractual basis by them. Institutions whose credibility rests on a path dependency stretching back to medieval times will no longer dominate the formal learning space. There will be diversity of provision. Publishers and libraries, pushing into markets to replace those lost as a result of the non-rival nature of their wares, will become providers and accreditors that compete directly with universities and colleges. This is already happening—Pearson University, for example, follows just such a model. Indeed, even individuals will begin offering credentials certified only by their individual reputations as David Wiley, one of the main instigators behind open badges, has already done. All will be swamped by the wealth of freely available, paid-for by advertising or sale of associated products, and app-based learning tools.

Teachers may or may not be employed by single institutions. For many, their particular skills may allow them to work in many places, paid according to the work they do. Others may prefer the security and benefits of a single institution: there will be scope for diversity. Physical location will seldom play a strong role, though some researchers and teachers may still be drawn to physical facilities and toolsets offered by institutions.

Distributed

No longer will institutions be virtual monopolies that lock individuals in to a limited set of fixed-length courses for the duration of a program. If institutions like universities do exist, they will be both hubs for other services and service providers for individuals and other hubs. Learners may choose institutions much as they choose cable network providers, for the range of channels they provide, though unlike these, there may be other more social and academic benefits, especially the presence of an academic community, the opportunity to engage in organized groups around topics and, at least in some cases, to provide expensive, dangerous, or complex facilities like laboratories, meeting areas, or large-scale computing devices. Face-to-face institutions will ubiquitously provide something similar to flipped classrooms, where learners engaged in learning from the distributed web of cyberspace may gather and explore what they have learned, perhaps using approaches like action learning sets (Revans, 1982) to provide motivation, depth, and diversity to their learning.

Disciplinarily Agnostic

Universities and colleges have, in the past, deliberately prepared students for particular occupations. While it is true that many subjects are non-vocational and have broad application, this is often because of their coarse chunking, which is a good thing if you are seeking generality. With the disaggregation of courses, people will acquire far more diverse skillsets, and continually build on them as needs emerge. The use of badges that relate to specific competences will allow a much more nuanced and realistic perspective on the skills that have been attained, and will make it simpler to cross disciplinary boundaries, as accreditation will no longer be bound to a single school or college.

Old School Tie-less

Because most individuals will no longer be directly affiliated with institutions, there will be little opportunity for groupthink and the lack of diversity often entailed by, for example, a Harvard or an Oxford education. While there are benefits for alumni of institutions, especially in terms of social networks and elite status, it is precisely the shared culture of thinking that gives academic value. The lack of diversity may, however, reduce the potential for acquiring rich cognitive toolboxes. Because formal learning will be occurring in a patchwork of sets, nets, and groups, learners will be exposed to a greater range and diversity of perspectives, heuristics, and ways of understanding the world. This will be beneficial to adopting a creative and multi-layered understanding of the world.

Open Research

When we, as researchers, publish a paper, a blog post, a research finding, or a comment on a blog, our readers will be able to award us badges. We will be awarded social capital for what we do, not by citations (that may frequently be critiques of our points of view) but by actual commendations. A PageRank-like algorithm will drive a collective that gives weightings to our commenders and thus calculates the value of our commendation. We see the potential beginnings of this operating already in the much wider base of citations used to calculate impact in Google Scholar, as opposed to more traditional World of Science citation rankings, albeit without the use of explicit commendation (Harzing, 2010). There are already crowdfunded research projects and education initiatives. This will become more common, allowing for a greater diversity of projects, including those that fail to attract funding at present because of their lack of obvious application—the long tail of the crowd (C. Anderson, 2004) has many interests. It will also benefit those that fall between research councils and cross broad disciplinary boundaries.

WILDER SPECULATIONS

There are many technologies on the horizon whose growth is influenced by increased communication and connectivity and whose repercussions are difficult to imagine. Genetic engineering, medicines, and increasing knowledge of health and safety may make us smarter and able to live longer. This is a trend that has continued unabated for over 100 years and shows no sign of stopping. A job for life when that active life may continue for 100 years is not a likely outcome. We will work longer, in more rewarding and varied ways, and we will take longer to grow up, have children later, and be exposed to ever richer and more challenging stimuli that make us smarter still (S. Johnson, 2006). Lifelong learning, formal, augmented, and informal, will be a way of life for all.

The primitive augmented reality tools like Google Glass or location-aware apps on our cellphones will become lighter, smarter, more responsive to our context and eventually disappear, becoming contact lenses, implants, or less invasive augmentations to our own bodies (Waterfield, 2012). More than ever, we will know about the world without having to keep that knowledge in our heads. These technologies will be networked. We will have instant access to the crowd, bringing new and powerful challenges to our sense of identity, our privacy, and how we deal with massive cognitive overload, but also remarkable opportunities to know one another better than ever before, to tap into the knowledge of the crowd, to learn from and with one another. Collectives will play a large role in helping us to cope with this, along with smarter AI that will understand context, language, and perhaps what we think. Man–machine interfaces already allow us to control machines, exchange thoughts and ideas, and even to know what others are thinking and dreaming, though not, at least for a while, as spookily as the popular media would have us believe. It is already an anachronism to learn by rote things that we can know in seconds by looking them up. As our tools for searching become integrated with everything we do and see, the ability to remember passages from Shakespeare or to know how to service the engine of our vehicle will seem quaint: they won't go away, because we love to learn and love to explore, but they will become unnecessary, as much as the ability to operate a horse-drawn plough is unnecessary but, for some, rewarding still. What we will need to know is how to use this immensity of knowledge, how it fits together, what is useful and what is harmful, what is valuable and what is dross.

We think it highly unlikely that the pointless arms race with exam cheating in large-scale written examinations will continue under these conditions, and we confidently predict the end of this steam-age barbaric anomaly. It is not that the cheaters will win, but simply that everyone will realize, as they should already, that there is less than no point. The means of demonstrating competence will be authentic, targeted, and embedded in the social networks and traces that we leave as we learn. The skill of assembling such traces to demonstrate our competence to others will be crucial, and no doubt augmented by the crowd. Reflection and the skills of analysis and synthesis will be pre-eminent capacities in this not-so-distant future. Similarly, if there are still teachers of children, which we think may in some capacity exist, then they will not be the primary sources of information:

children will have access to that as easily as they do. Instead, teachers will become not so much guides as co-travellers on the learning journey, helping children to accommodate their vastly enriched and interconnected worlds. If they run into difficulties, help will be just a thought away.

Most universities will not, ultimately, survive in their current form, though some will almost certainly be kept alive as we keep alive old farming traditions and hand-weaving. We will probably look at them wistfully and think that life was so much easier, so much finer, so much more refined in those days. And we will be wrong. The arguments between advocates of online and face-to-face learning will be largely forgotten, much as we have mostly forgotten the arguments between proponents of scrolls and supporters of bound books. All learning will be both online and situated in an ever-shifting context.

Though we have great hopes for technologies that enhance and augment our cognitive abilities, we do not hold out the hopes of Kurzweil (1990) and others that the singularity, the point at which machines become smarter than us in every way and start to create still-smarter machines, will allow us to transfer ourselves into machines, nor vice versa, at least not using any conceivable technology at the moment. However, the potential for change at that point, however it may play out, is unknowable and vast. We recommend the reader to the vast body of speculative fiction on that topic for better ideas than we can come up with, almost all of which are wrong—if only we knew which ones! With that, we have reached the end of what we can reasonably extrapolate from current trends and inventions.

CONCLUSION

We have traced social learning from the dim past, dwelt long in the present, and ended in the future. It has been a long story, but it is one that will continue at an exhilarating rate, branching in diverse ways that will continue to challenge and ennoble us, while humbling us. As crusty old academics writing skeuomorphically within the system we suggest is fading, in a format designed for a technology whose sun is setting, we will enjoy what we can of the ride, but will view it perhaps as outsiders, like the dinosaurs watching the asteroid streak across complacent skies.

REFERENCES

Alexander, C. (1988). A city is not a tree. In J. Thackara (Ed.), *Design after modernism: Beyond the object* (pp. 67–84). London: Thames and Hudson.

Allen, C. (2004). Tracing the evolution of social software [Web log post]. Retrieved from http://www.lifewithalacrity.com/2004/10/tracing_the_evo.html

Altman, I. (1976). Privacy: A conceptual analysis. *Environment and Behavior, 8*(1), 7–29.

Anderson, C. (2004). *The long tail.* London: Random House Business Books.

Anderson, C. (2007). Social networking is a feature, not a destination [Web log post]. Retrieved from http://thelongtail.com/the_long_tail/2007/09/social-networki.html

Anderson, J. (1979). Teacher immediacy as a predictor of teaching effectiveness In D. Niimo (Ed.), *Communication yearbook three* (pp. 543–59). New Brunswick, NJ: Transaction Books.

Anderson, M., Ball, M., Boley, H., Greene, S., Howse, N., Lemire, D., & McGrath, S. (2003). *RACOFI: A rule-applying collaborative filtering system.* Paper presented at the COLA'03, Halifax, Canada.

Anderson, T. (2001). The hidden curriculum of distance education. *Change Magazine, 33*(6), 29–35.

Anderson, T. (2002). Revealing the hidden curriculum of e-learning In C. Vrasidas & G. Glass (Eds.), *Distance education and distributed learning* (pp. 100–15). Greenwich, CO: Information Age Publishing.

Anderson, T. (2003). Getting the mix right again: An updated and theoretical rationale for interaction. *International Review of Research in Open and Distance Learning, 4*(2). Retrieved from http://www.irrodl.org/index.php/irrodl/article/view/149/230

Anderson, T. (2005). *Distance learning: Social software's killer app?* Paper presented at the ODLAA, Adelaide, Australia. Retrieved from http://auspace.athabascau.ca/bitstream/2149/2328/1/distance_learning.pdf

Anderson, T. (2009, June). *The dance of technology and pedagogy in self-paced distance education.* Paper presented at the M-2009 conference, Maastricht, Netherlands.

Anderson, T., & Dron, J. (2011). Three generations of distance education pedagogy. *International Review of Research in Open and Distance Learning, 12*(3). Retrieved from http://www.irrodl.org/index.php/irrodl/article/view/890

Anderson, T., Rourke, L., Garrison, D.R., & Archer, W. (2001). Assessing teaching presence in a computer conferencing context. *Journal of Asynchronous Learning Networks, 5* (2), 1–17.

Annand, D. (1999). The problem of computer conferencing for distance-based universities. *Open Learning, 14*(3), 47–52.

Arbaugh, B. (2007). An empirical verification of the community of inquiry framework. *Journal of Asynchronous Learning Networks, 11*(1), 73–85.

Argyris, C., & Schön, D. (1974). *Theory in practice: Increasing professional awareness.* Oxford, UK: Jossey-Bass.

Ariely, D. (2009). *Predictably irrational* (Revised and Expanded ed.). New York: Harper Collins.

Aristotle. (1997). *Aristotle's poetics.* (George Whalley, Trans.). Montreal: McGill-Queen's University Press.

Arthur, W. B. (2009). *The nature of technology: What it is and how it evolves* (Kindle ed.). New York: Free Press.

Attwell, G. (2007). Personal learning environments–The future of eLearning? *eLearning Papers, 2*(1), 1–7.

Austin, J.L. (1979). A plea for excuses. In J.O. Urmson and G.J. Warnock (Eds.), *Philosophical papers* (pp. 175–204). Oxford: Oxford University Press.

Badges. (n.d.). In *Wikipedia.* Retrieved from https://wiki.mozilla.org/Badges/FAQs

Bandura, A. (1977). *Social learning theory.* Englewood Cliffs, NJ: Prentice-Hall.

Baron, R. S. (2005). So right it's wrong: Groupthink and the ubiquitous nature of polarized group decision-making. In M. Zanna (Ed.), *Advances in experimental social psychology* (Vol. 37, pp. 29–253). San Diego: Elsevier Academic Press.

Bateman, S., Brooks, C., & McCalla, G. (2006). *Collaborative tagging approaches for ontological metadata in adaptive e-learning systems.* Paper presented at the Fourth International Workshop on Applications of Semantic Web Technologies for E-Learning, in conjunction with the 4th International Conference on Adaptive Hypermedia and Adaptive Web-Based Systems, Dublin, Ireland.

Bates, A. W. (2005). *Technology, e-learning and distance education* (Kindle ed.). New York: Routledge.

Bateson, G. (1972). *Steps to an ecology of mind.* London: University of Chicago Press.

Becher, T., & Trowler, P. R. (2001). *Academic tribes and territories* (2nd ed.). Buckingham: SRHE & Oxford University Press.

Bell, B., & Kozlowski, S. (2002). A typology of virtual teams: Implications for effective leadership. *Group and Organization Management, 27*(1), 14–49.

Benkler, Y. (2006). *The wealth of networks: How social production transforms markets and freedom.* New Haven, CT: Yale University Press.

Berlanga, A. J., Sloep, P. B., Kester, L., Brouns, F., Rosmalen, P., & Koper, R. (2008). Ad hoc transient communities: towards fostering knowledge sharing in learning networks. *International Journal of Learning Technology, 3*(4), 443–58.

den Besten, M., Gaio, L., Rossi, A., & Dalle, J. M. (2010). *Using metadata signals to support stigmergy.* Paper presented at the Self-Adaptive and Self-Organizing Systems Workshop (SASOW), 2010 Fourth IEEE International Conference, Boston, USA.

Blackmore, S. (1999). *The meme machine.* Oxford: Oxford University Press.

Bloom, B. S. (1984). The 2 sigma problem: The search for methods of group instruction as effective as one-to-one tutoring. *Educational Researcher, 13*(6), 4–16.

Bloom, H. (2000). *Global brain: The evolution of mass mind.* Toronto, ON: Wiley.

Bonabeau, E., Dorigo, M., & Theraulaz, G. (1999). *Swarm intelligence: From natural to artificial systems.* New York: Oxford University Press.

Brand, S. (1997). *How buildings learn.* London: Phoenix Illustrated.

Broadband Commission. (2012, September). *The state of broadband 2012: Achieving digital inclusion for all.* Retrieved from http://www.broadbandcommission.org/Documents/bb-annualreport2012.pdf

Broadband Commission. (2013, September). *The state of broadband 2013: Universalizing broadband.* Retrieved from http://www.broadbandcommission.org/Documents/bb-annualreport2013.pdf

Brown, J. S., Collins, A., & Duguid, P. (1989). Situated cognition and the culture of learning. *Educational Researcher, 18*(1), 32–42.

Brown, J. S., & Duguid, P. (2000). *The social life of information.* Boston, MA: Harvard Business School Press.

Browning, R. (n.d.). Abt Vogler. In *Selected poems.* Retrieved from http://www.munseys.com/diskone/brwnsel.pdf

Bruner, J. S. (1966). *Toward a theory of instruction.* Cambridge, MA: The Belknap Press.

Bruns, A. (2008). *Blogs, Wikipedia, Second Life, and beyond: From production to produsage.* New York: Peter Lang Publishing.

Brusilovsky, P. (2004, May). *Knowledge tree: A distributed architecture for adaptive e-learning.* Paper presented at the WWW 2004, New York.

Bruza, P. D., & Song, D. W. (2000). Aboutness from a commonsense perspective. *Journal of the American Society for Information Science, 51*(12), 1090–105.

Buchanan, R. (1985). Declaration by design: Rhetoric, argument, and demonstration in design practice. *Design Issues, 2*(1), 4–22.

Buckingham-Shum, S., Motta, E., & Domingue, J. (1999). *Modelling and visualizing perspectives in internet digital libraries.* Paper presented at the Third Annual Conference on Research and Advanced Technology for Digital Libraries, Paris, France.

Bullas, Jeff. (2012, April 23). 48 significant social media facts, figures and statistics plus 7 infographics [Web log post]. Retrieved from http://www.jeffbullas.com/2012/04/23/48-significant-social-media-facts-figures-and-statistics-plus-7-infographics/#JiYeSCtjGkBtjS62.99

Burt, R. (1997). The contingent value of social capital. *Administrative Science Quarterly, 42*(2), 339–66.

Burt, R. (2009). Network duality of social capital. In V. Barkus & J. Davis (Eds.), *Social capital: Reaching out and reaching in* (pp. 39–65). Cheltenham, UK: Edgar Elger.

Buus, L., Georgsen, M., Ryberg, T., Glud, L. N., & Davidsen, J. (2010). Developing a design methodology for Web 2.0-mediated learning. *Proceedings of the 7th International Conference on Networked Learning 2010, Aalborg, Denmark.*

Cadwalladr, C. (2012, November 11). Do online courses spell the end for the traditional university? *The Observer.* Retrieved from http://www.guardian.co.uk/education/2012/nov/11/online-free-learning-end-of-university

Calvin, W. H. (1997). The six essentials? Minimal requirements for the Darwinian bootstrapping of quality. *Journal of Memetics, 1*. Retrieved from http://cogprints.org/3217/1/1997JMemetics.htm

Candy, P. C. (1991). *Self-direction for lifelong learning: A comprehensive guide to theory and practice.* San Francisco: Jossey-Bass.

Candy, P. C. (2000). Reaffirming a proud tradition. *Active Learning in Higher Education, 1*(2), 101–25.

Caporael, L. R. (1997). The evolution of truly social cognition: The core configurations model. *Personality and Social Psychology Review, 1*(4), 276–98. doi: 10.1207/s15327957pspr0104_1

Chang, K., Sung, Y., & Lee, C. (2003). Web-based collaborative inquiry learning. *Journal of Computer Assisted Learning, 19*(1), 56–69. doi: 10.1.1.94.8754

Chen, Y.-J., & Willits, F. K. (1998). A path analysis of the concepts in Moore's theory of transactional distance in a videoconferencing learning environment. *Journal of Distance Education, 13*(2). Retrieved from http://cade.athabascau.ca/vol13.2/chen.html

Chiarella, A. F. (2009). *Enabling the collective to assist the individual: A self-organising systems approach to social software and the creation of collaborative text signals* (Doctoral dissertation). McGill University, Montreal, Canada. Retrieved from http://www3.telus.net/andrewchiarella/pubfiles/AndrewChiarellaPhDThesis.pdf

Chickering, A., & Gamson, Z. (1987). Seven principles for good practice in undergraduate education. *American Association of Higher Education, 39*(7), 3–7.

Christensen, C. (1997). *The innovator's dilemma—When new technologies cause great firms to fail.* Cambridge, MA: Harvard University Press.

Christensen, C. (2008). Disruptive innovation and catalytic change in higher education. In *Forum Futures 2008*, (pp. 43–46). Educause.

Christensen, C., Horn, M., & Johnson, C. (2008). *Disrupting class: How disruptive innovation will change the way the world learns.* New York: McGraw-Hill.

Christensen, T. H. (2009). "Connected presence" in distributed family life. *New Media & Society, 11*(3), 433–51. doi: 10.1177/1461444808101620

Church, A. T. (2000). Culture and personality: Toward an integrated cultural trait psychology. *Journal of Personality, 68*(4), 651–703.

Churchill, W. (1943). HC Deb 28 October 1943, Vol . 393, c403.

Clark, A. (1997). *Being there: Putting brain, body, and the world together again.* Cambridge, MA: MIT Press.

Coates, T. (2002). On the augmentation of human social networking abilities [Web log post]. Retrieved from http://www.plasticbag.org/archives/2002/12/on_the_augmentation_of_human_social_networking_abilities.shtml

comScore, Inc. (2011, March 8). *The 2010 Canada digital year in review* (white paper). Retrieved from http://www.comscore.com/Press_Events/Presentations_Whitepapers/2011/2010_Canada_Digital_Year_in_Review

Conole, G. (2010). Facilitating new forms of discourse for learning and teaching: harnessing the power of Web 2.0 practices. *Open Learning, 25*(2), 141–51.

Dalsgaard, C., & Paulsen, M. F. (2009). Transparency in cooperative online education. *The International Review of Research in Open and Distance Learning*, *10*(3). Retrieved from http://www.irrodl.org/index.php/irrodl/article/view/671/1267

Daniel, B., Schwier, R., & McCalla, G. (2003). Social capital in virtual learning communities and distributed communities of practice. *Canadian Journal of Learning and Technology*, *29*(3). Retrieved from cjlt.csj.ualberta.ca/index.php/cjlt/article/view/85/7

Daniel, J. S. (1996). *Mega-universities and knowledge media: Technology strategies for higher education.* London: Kogan Page.

Darwin, C. (1872). *The origin of species* (6th ed.). London: Murray.

Dawson, C. (2012). Blackboard buys Moodlerooms...And no, this isn't an early April Fools. *ZdNet Education*. Retrieved from www.zdnet.com/blog/education/blackboard-buys-moodlerooms-and-no-this-isnt-an-early-april-fools/4866

Deci, E. L., & Ryan, R. M. (1985). *Intrinsic motivation and self-determination in human behavior.* New York: Plenum Press.

Deci, E. L., & Ryan, R. M. (2002). The paradox of achievement: The harder you push, the worse it gets. In J. Aronson (Ed.), *Improving academic achievement* (pp. 61–87). New York: Academic Press.

Deci, E. L., & Ryan, R. M. (2008). Self-determination theory: A macrotheory of human motivation, development and health. *Canadian Psychology*, *49*(3), 182–85.

Deci, E. L., Vallerand, R. J., Pelletier, L. G., & Ryan, R. M. (1991). Motivation and education: The self-determination perspective. *Educational Psychologist*, *26*(3/4), 325–46.

Demiray, U., & Sharma, R. (Eds.). (2009). *Ethical practice and implications in distance learning.* Hershey, NY: Information Science Reference.

Dewey, J. (1897). My pedagogic creed. *The School Journal*, *56*(3), 77–80.

Dewey, J. (1916). *Democracy and education.* Retrieved from http://www.ilt.columbia.edu/academic/texts/dewey/d_e/

Dewey, J. (1933). *How we think.* Boston: D. C. Heath.

DiPrete, T. A., Gelman, A., McCormick, T., Teitler, J., & Zheng, T. (2011). Segregation in social networks based on acquaintanceship and trust. *American Journal of Sociology*, *116*(4), 1234–83.

Doering, A. (2006). Adventure learning: Transformative hybrid online education. *Distance Education*, *27*(2), 197–215.

Donath, J. (2007). *Signals in social supernets. Journal of Computer-Mediated Communication*, *13*(1), 231–251.

Donath, J., Karahalios, K., & Viegas, F. (1999). Visualizing conversation. *Journal of Computer Mediated Communication*, *4*(4). Retrieved from http://onlinelibrary.wiley.com/doi/10.1111/j.1083-6101.1999.tb00107.x/full

Downes, S. (2007). Learning networks in practice. In D. Ley (Ed.), *Emerging technologies for learning* (Vol. 2, pp. 19–27). London: BECTA.

Downes, S. (2008a). An introduction to connective knowledge. *Media, Knowledge & Education: Exploring new Spaces, Relations and Dynamics in Digital Media Ecologies. Proceedings of the International Conference held on June 25–26, 2007.* Retrieved from http://www.downes.ca/post/33034

Downes, S. (2008b). Places to go: Connectivism and connective knowledge. *Innovate*, 5(1). http://bsili.3csn.org/files/2010/06/Places_to_Go-__Connectivism__Connective_Knowledge.pdf

Drachsler, H. (2009). *Navigation support for learners in informal learning networks* (Doctoral dissertation). Open Universiteit Nederland, Heerlen.

Drachsler, H., Hummel, H., & Koper, R. (2007). *Recommendations for learners are different: applying memory-based recommender system techniques to lifelong learning.* Paper presented at the SIRTEL workshop of the EC-TEL 2007 Conference, Crete, Greece.

Dron, J. (2002). *Achieving self-organisation in network-based learning environments* (Doctoral dissertation). University of Brighton, UK. Retrieved from http://www.cmis.brighton.ac.uk/staff/jd29/thesisorrectedfinaldraft.pdf

Dron, J. (2003). *Sidewalks on the information superhighway.* Paper presented at the AACE E-Learn 2003 Conference, Phoenix, AZ.

Dron, J. (2005a). *Discovering the complex effects of navigation cues in an e-learning environment. E-Learn 2005*, 2026–2033.

Dron, J. (2005b). Epimethean Information Systems: Harnessing the power of the collective in e-learning. *International Journal of Information Technology and Management*, 4(4), 392–404.

Dron, J. (2007a). *Control and constraint in e-learning: Choosing when to choose.* Hershey, PA: Idea Group International.

Dron, J. (2007b). Designing the undesignable: Social software and control. *Educational Technology and Society*, 10(3), 60–71.

Dron, J. (2008). *The trouble with tags: An approach to richer tagging for online learning.* Paper presented at the AACE E-Learn Conference, Las Vegas, NV.

Dron, J. (2012). The pedagogical-technological divide and the elephant in the room. *International Journal on E-Learning*, 11(1), 23–28. Retrieved from http://www.editlib.org/p/33288/paper_33288.pdf

Dron, J., & Anderson, T. (2007). *Collectives, networks and groups in social software for e-learning.* Paper presented at the AACE E-Learn Conference 2007, Québec City, Canada.

Dron, J., & Anderson, T. (2009). Lost in social space: Information retrieval issues in Web 1.5. *Journal of Digital Information*, 10(2). Retrieved from http://journals.tdl.org/jodi/index.php/jodi/article/view/443/280%C3%82

Dron, J., Anderson, T., & Siemens, G. (2011). *Putting things in context: Designing social media for education.* Paper presented at the European Conference on E-Learning 2011, Brighton, UK.

Dron, J., Boyne, C., & Mitchell, R. (2001). *Footpaths in the stuff swamp.* Paper presented at WebNet 2001, Orlando, FL.

Dron, J., Mitchell, R., Boyne, C., & Siviter, P. (2000). *CoFIND: Steps towards a self-organising learning environment.* Paper presented at WebNet 2000, San Antonio, TX.

Dron, J., Mitchell, R., Siviter, P., & Boyne, C. (2000). CoFIND—An experiment in n-dimensional collaborative filtering. *Journal of Network and Computer Applications*, 23, 131–42.

Dron, J., Seidel, C., & Litten, G. (2004). Transactional distance in a blended learning environment. *ALT-J*, 12(2), 163–74.

Dunbar, R. I. M. (1993). Coevolution of neocortical size, group size and language in humans. *Behavioral and Brain Sciences, 16*(4), 681–93.

Dunbar, R.I.M. (1996). *Grooming, Gossip, and the Evolution of Language.* London: Harvard University Press.

Dwyer, J. (2009). Back to school: Tips for teachers on Facebook. Accessed 2014, March 10. Retrieved from http://www.facebook.com/notes/facebook/back-to-school-tips-for-teachers-on-facebook/137948147130

Eldon, E. (2011, December 30). A new era for social interest sites: Twitter, Tumblr and Pinterest go big in 2011 [Web log post]. Retrieved from http://techcrunch.com/2011/12/30/twittertumblrpinterest/

Elliot, M. (2006). Stigmergic collaboration: The evolution of group work. *M/C Journal, 9*(2).

Ellison, N. B., Steinfield, C., & Lampe, C. (2007). The benefits of Facebook "friends": Social capital and college students' use of online social network sites. *Journal of Computer-Mediated Communication, 12*(4), 1143–68. doi: 10.1111/j.1083-6101.2007.00367.x

Engeström, Y. (1987). *Learning by expanding. An activity-theoretical approach to developmental research.* Helsinki, Finland: Orienta-Konsultit.

Enser, P. (2008). The evolution of visual information retrieval. *Journal of Information Science, 34*(4), 531–46. doi: 10.1177/0165551508091013

Erickson, T., & Kellogg, W. A. (2000). Social translucence: an approach to designing systems that support social processes. *ACM transactions on computer-human interaction (TOCHI), 7*(1), 59–83.

Fabro, K., & Garrison, D. R. (1998). Computer conferencing and higher-order learning. *Indian Journal of Open Learning, 7*(1), 41–54.

Farnham, S., Chesley, H. R., McGhee, D. E., Kawal, R., & Landau, J. (2000). Structured online interactions: Improving the decision-making of small discussion groups. *Proceedings of the 2000 ACM Conference on Computer Supported Cooperative Work.*

Farzan, R., & Brusilovsky, P. (2005). *Social navigation support through annotation-based group modeling.* Paper presented at the 10th International Conference on User Modelling, Edinburgh, Scotland.

Feeley, R., & Brooks, S. (2007). Updated Facebook network numbers. Retrieved Jan. 2008 from https://spreadsheets.google.com/pub?key=pGKddWq3qzxlMCQrBPRQbNw

Felix, S. (2012, September 9). This is how Facebook is tracking your Internet activity. *Business Insider.* Retrieved from http://www.businessinsider.com/this-is-how-facebook-is-tracking-your-internet-activity-2012-9

Finkelstein, J. (2006). *Learning in real time: Synchronous teaching and learning.* San Francisco: Jossey-Bass.

Fletcher, J. D. (2009). Education and training technology in the military. *Science, 323*(5910), 72–75.

Florida, R. (2005). *Cities and the creative class.* New York: Routledge.

Fox, S., & MacKeough, K. (2003). Can eLearning promote higher-order learning without tutor overload?. *Open Learning, 18*(2), 121–34.

Franklin, T., & Van Harmelen, M. (2007). Web 2.0 for content for learning and teaching in higher education. *JISC*. Retrieved from www.jisc.ac.uk/media/documents/programmes/digitalrepositories/web2-contentlearningand-teaching. pdf.

Franklin, U. M. (1999). *The real world of technology* (Kindle ed.). Concord, ON: House of Anansi Press.

Freyne, J., & Smyth, B. (2006). Cooperating search communities. In V. Wade, H. Ashman, & B. Smyth (Eds.), *Adaptive hypermedia and adaptive Web-based systems* (Vol. 4018, pp. 101–10). Berlin / Heidelberg: Springer.

Frymier, A. (1993). The impact of teacher immediacy on students' motivation: Is it the same for all students? *Communication Quarterly, 41*(4), 454–64.

Gagne, R. (1985). *The conditions of learning* (4th ed.). New York: Holt, Rinehart & Winston.

Gardner, H. (1993). *Frames of mind: The theory of multiple intelligences* (10th anniversary ed.). New York: Basic Books.

Gargiulo, M., & Benassi, M. (2000). Trapped in your own net? Network cohesion, structural holes, and the adaptation of social capital. *Organization Science, 11*(2), 183–96.

Garrison, D. R. (1991). Critical thinking in adult education: A conceptual model for developing critical thinking in adult learners. *International Journal of Lifelong Education, 10*(4), 287–303.

Garrison, D. R. (2000). Theoretical challenges for distance education in the 21st century: A shift from structural to transactional issues. *International Review of Research in Open and Distance Learning, 1*(1).

Garrison, D. R. (2006). Online collaboration principles. *Journal of Asynchronous Learning Networks, 10*(1). 25–34.

Garrison, D. R., & Anderson, T. (2003). *E-learning in the 21st century: A framework for research and practice.* London: RoutledgeFalmer.

Garrison, D. R., Anderson, T., & Archer, W. (2000). Critical inquiry in a text-based environment: Computer conferencing in higher education. *The Internet and Higher Education, 2*(2), 87–105.

Garrison, D. R., Anderson, T., & Archer, W. (2001). Critical thinking, cognitive presence, and computer conferencing in distance education. *American Journal of Distance Education, 15*(1), 7–23.

Garrison, D. R., & Baynton, M. (1987). Beyond independence in distance education: The concept of control. *American Journal of Distance Education, 1*(3), 3–15.

Gibson, W. (1984). *Neuromancer.* New York: Ace Books.

Glahn, C., Specht, M., & Koper, R. (2007). *Smart indicators on learning interactions.* Paper presented at the Second European Conference on Technology-Enhanced Learning, Crete, Greece.

Goffman, E. (1959). *The presentation of self in everyday life.* New York: Anchor.

Goldberg, D., Nichols, D., Oki, B. M., & Terry, D. (1992). Using collaborative filtering to weave an information tapestry. *Communications of the ACM, 35*(2), 61–70.

Golder, S. A., & Huberman, B. A. (2006). The structure of collaborative tagging systems. Journal of Information *Science, 32*(2), 198–208.

Gorham, J. (1988). The relationship between verbal teacher immediacy behaviors and student learning. *Communication Education, 37*, 40–53.

Govani, T., & Pashley, H. (2005). *Student awareness of the privacy implications when using Facebook.* Paper presented at the "Privacy Poster Fair" at the Carnegie Mellon University School of Library and Information Science.

Granovetter, M. (1973). The strength of weak ties: A network theory revisited. American Journal of Sociology, 78, 1360–80.

Gray, K., Annabell, L., & Kennedy, G. (2010). Medical students' use of Facebook to support learning: Insights from four case studies. *Medical teacher, 32*(12), 971–76.

Gregorio, J. (2003). Stigmergy and the world-wide web. *Bitworking.* Retrieved from http://bitworking.org/news/Stigmergy/

Grieco, R., Malandrino, D., Palmieri, G., & Scarano, V. (2007). *Face2face social bookmarking with recommendations: WebQuests in the classrooms.* Paper presented at the 3rd International Conference on Collaborative Computing: Networking, Applications and Worksharing, New York, US.

Gross, R., & Acquisti, A. (2005). Information revelation and privacy in online social networks. *Proceedings of the 2005 ACM Workshop on Privacy in the Electronic Society* (pp.71–80). doi: 1102199.1102214

Group. (n.d.). In *Merriam-Webster's online dictionary.* Retrieved March 5, 2014, from http://www.merriam-webster.com/dictionary/group

Grunwald Associates, LLC. (2007). *Creating & connecting: Research and guidelines on online social and educational networking.* National School Boards Association.

Guilar, J., & Loring, A. (2008). Dialogue and community in online learning: Lessons from Royal Roads University. *The Journal of Distance Education/Revue de l'Éducation à Distance, 22*(3), 19–40.

Gunawardena, C. N., & McIsaac, M. S. (2004). Distance education. In D. H. Jonassen (Ed.), *Handbook of research for educational communications and technology* (2nd ed., pp. 355–96). Mahwah, NJ: LEA.

Gyongyi, Z., Pedersen, J., Koutrika, G., & Garcia-Molina, H. (2008). *Questioning Yahoo! answers.* Paper presented at the WWW2008, Beijing, China.

Harzing, A. W. (2010). Publish or Perish. Melbourne, Australia: Tarma Software Research.

Hase, S., & Kenyon, C. (2000). From andragogy to heutagogy. *Ulti-BASE In-Site,* December. Retrieved from http://pandora.nla.gov.au/nph-wb/20010220130000/http://ultibase.rmit.edu.au/Articles/dec00/hase2.htm

Hase, S., & Kenyon, C. (2007). Heutagogy: A child of complexity theory. *Complicity: An International Journal of Complexity & Education, 4*(1), 111–17.

Heckman, R., & Annabi, H. (2005). A content analytic comparison of learning processes in online and face-to-face case study discussions. *Journal of Computer-Mediated Communication, 10*(2). Retrieved from http://onlinelibrary.wiley.com/doi/10.1111/j.1083-6101.2005.tb00244.x/full

Herder, E., & Kärger, P. (2008). *Hybrid personalization for recommendations.* Paper presented at the 16th Workshop on Adaptivity and User Modeling in Interactive System, ABIS 2008, Würzburg, Germany.

Herrington, J., Oliver, R., & Reeves, T. (2003). Patterns of engagement in authentic online learning environments. *Australian Journal of Educational Technology, 19*(1), 59–71.

Heylighen, F. (2007). Why is open access development so successful? Stigmergic organization and the economics of information. In B. Lutterbeck, M. Bärwolff & R. A. Gehring (Eds.), *Open Source Jahrbuch 2007*, (pp. 165–180). Berlin: Lehmanns Media.

Higgins, E. T. (1987). Self-discrepancy: A theory relating self and affect. *Psychological Review, 94*(3), 319–340. doi: 10.1037/0033-295X.94.3.319

Hillier, B. (1996). *Space is the machine: A configurational theory of architecture*. Cambridge: Cambridge University Press.

Hofstadter, D. R. (2001). Analogy as the core of cognition. In D. Gentner, K.J. Holyoak, & B. N. Kokinov (Eds.), *The analogical mind: Perspectives from cognitive science* (pp. 499–538). Cambridge, MA: MIT Press.

Hofstede, G. (2001). *Culture's consequences: Comparing values, behaviors, institutions, and organizations across nations* (2nd ed.). Thousand Oaks, CA: Sage Publications.

Holmberg, B. (1986). A discipline of distance education. *Journal of Distance Education, 1*(1) 25–40. Retrieved from http://www.jofde.ca/index.php/jde/article/view/306/200

Horn, J. (2008). Human research and complexity theory. *Educational Philosophy and Theory, 40*(1), 130–43.

Huang, T.-C., Huang, Y.-M., & Cheng, S.-C. (2008). Automatic and interactive e-learning auxiliary material generation utilizing particle swarm optimization. *Expert Systems with Applications, 35*(4), 2113–122. doi: 10.1016/j.eswa.2007.09.039

Huberman, B. A., & Kaminsky, M. (1996). *Beehive: A System for Cooperative Filtering and Sharing of Information* (technical report). Xerox PARC.

Hummel, H. G. K., Van Den Berg, B., Berlanga, A. J., Drachsler, H., Janssen, J., Nadolski, R., & Koper, R. (2007). Combining social-based and information-based approaches for personalised recommendation on sequencing learning activities. *International Journal of Learning Technology, 3*(2), 152–68.

Hutchins, E., & Lintern, G. (1995). *Cognition in the wild*. Cambridge, MA: MIT press.

Illich, I. (1971). *Deschooling society*. New York: Harper & Row.

International Telecommunication Union. (2012). Measuring the information society. Retrieved from https://www.itu.int/en/Pages/default.aspx

Internet World Stats. (2012). Internet users in the world: Distribution by world regions – 2012 Q2. Retrieved from http://www.internetworldstats.com/stats.htm

Ireland, T. (2007). Situating connectivism. Retrieved from http://design.test.olt.ubc.ca/Situating_Connectivism

Jacobs, J. (1961). *The death and life of great American cities*. London, UK: Pimlico.

Jadhav, L. (1999). *South-Asian immigrants—Living in two cultures*. Retrieved from http://files.eric.ed.gov/fulltext/ED431337.pdf

James, W. (2000). What pragmatism means. In J. Stuhr (Ed.), *Pragmatism and classical American philosophy* (Vol. 2, pp. 193–202). Oxford: Oxford University Press.

Jamison, J. (2012, February 18). Beyond Facebook: The rise of interest-based social networks [Web log post]. *Techcrunch*. Retrieved from http://techcrunch.com/2012/02/18/beyond-facebook-the-rise-of-interest-based-social-networks/

Janis, I. (1972). *Victims of groupthink*. Boston: Houghton Mifflin.

Jensen, E. (2008). *Brain-based learning: The new paradigm of teaching*. Thousand Oaks, CA: Corwin Press.

Jeong, A. (2003). The sequential analysis of group interaction and critical thinking in online threaded discussions. *American Journal of Distance Education, 17*(1), 25–43.

Jian, H. (2008). Community collaborative filtering for E-learning. *2008 International Conference on Computer and Electrical Engineering, 0*, 593–597.

Joachims, T., Granka, L., Pan, B., Hembrooke, H., & Gay, G. (2005). *Accurately interpreting clickthrough data as implicit Feedback*. Paper presented at the SIGIR '05, Salvador, Brazil. Retrieved from http://www.cs.cornell.edu/People/tj/publications/joachims_etal_05a.pdf

Johnson, D., & Johnson, T. (1994). *Learning together and alone: Cooperative, competitive, and individualistic learning*. Toronto, ON: Allyn and Bacon.

Johnson, S. (2006). *Everything bad is good for you: How today's popular culture is actually making us smarter*. New York: Riverhead Books.

Johnson, S. (2010). *Where good ideas come from: the natural history of innovation* (Kindle ed.). New York: Penguin.

Johnson, S. (2012). *Future perfect: The case for progress in a networked age* (Kindle ed.). New York: Riverhead.

Jonassen, D. (2002). Learning to solve problems online. In C. Vrasidas & G. Glass (Eds.), *Distance education and distributed learning* (pp. 58–75). Greenwich, CO: Information Age Publishing.

Kaminski, D., & Geisler, C. (2012). Survival analysis of faculty retention in science and engineering by gender. *Science, 335*(6070), 864–66. doi: 10.1126/science.1214844

Kanuka, H., & Anderson, T. (1999). Using constructivism in technology-mediated learning: Constructing order out of the chaos in the literature. *Radical Pedagogy, 2*(1). Retrieved from http://auspace.athabascau.ca/bitstream/2149/728/1/Using%20Constructivism%20in%20Technology-Mediated%20Learning_%20_br_Constructing%20Order.pdf

Karampiperis, P., & Sampson, D. (2004). *Adaptive instructional planning using ontologies*. Paper presented at the ICALT 2004, Joensuu, Finland.

Kauffman, S. (1995). *At home in the universe: The search for laws of complexity*. London: Oxford University Press.

Kauffman, S. (2000). *Investigations* (Kindle ed.). New York: Oxford University Press.

Kauffman, S. (2008). *Reinventing the sacred: A new view of science, reason and religion*. Philadelphia, PA: Basic Books.

Kawachi, P. (2009). Ethics in interactions in distance education. In U. Demiray, & R. Sharma (Eds.), *Ethical practices and implications in distance learning* (pp. 24–34). Hershey, PA: IGI Global.

Kay, A. (1996). Revealing the elephant: The use and misuse of computers in education. *The Educom Review, 31*(4), 22–28.

Kay, J., & Kummerfeld, B. (2006). *Scrutability, user control and privacy for distributed personalization*. Paper presented at the CHI 2006 Workshop on Privacy-Enhanced Personalization, Montréal, Canada.

Kearsley, G., & Schneiderman, B. (1998). Engagement theory. *Educational Technology*, *42*(5), 67–86. Retrieved from http://home.sprynet.com/~gkearsley/engage.htm

Kelly, K. (2007). Scan this book! In S. Levy (Ed.), *The best of technology writing* (pp. 69–93). Ann Arbor, MI: University of Michigan Press.

Kelly, K. (2010). *What technology wants* (Kindle ed.). New York: Viking.

Kilfoil, M., Xing, W., & Ghorbani, A. (2005, May). *ARAS: Adaptive recommender for academic scheduling.* Paper presented at the Communication Networks and Services Research Conference, 2005, Halifax, Nova Scotia.

Kim, Y., Sohn, D., & Choi, S. M. (2011). Cultural difference in motivations for using social network sites: A comparative study of American and Korean college students. *Computers in Human Behavior*, *27*(1), 365–72.

Kittur, A., Pendleton, B., & Kraut, R. E. (2009). *Herding the cats.* New York: ACM. Retrieved from http://www.wikisym.org/ws2009/Proceedings/p107-kittur.pdf

Kleinberg, J. M. (1999). Authoritative sources in a hyperlinked environment. *Journal of the ACM 46*(5), 604-632. doi: 10.1145/324133/324140

Kleinberg, J. M. (2007). Cascading behavior in networks: Algorithmic and economic issues. In N. Nisan, T. Roughgarden, E. Tardos, & V. Vazirani (Eds.), *Algorithmic game theory* (pp. 613-632). New York: Cambridge University Press.

Knight, B. G., & Schiff, N. (2007). *Momentum and social learning in presidential primaries.* Providence, RI: Brown University/National Bureau of Economic Research.

Koetsier, J. (2013). How Google searches 30 trillion web pages, 100 billion times a month. *VentureBeat.* Retrieved from http://venturebeat.com/2013/03/01/how-google-searches-30-trillion-web-pages-100-billion-times-a-month/

Kohn, A. (1999). *Punished by rewards: The trouble with gold stars, incentive plans, A's, praise, and other bribes* (Kindle ed.). Boston: Houghton Mifflin.

Kop, R. (2011). The challenges to connectivist learning on open online networks: Learning experiences during a massive open online course. Connectivism: Design and Delivery of Social Networked Learning [Special Issue]. *The International Review of Research in Open and Distance Learning*, *12*(3). Retrieved from http://www.irrodl.org/index.php/irrodl/article/view/882

Kop, R., & Hill, A. (2008). Connectivism: Learning theory of the future or vestige of the past? *International Review of Research in Open and Distance Learning*, *9*(3).

Koper, R., Rusman, E. & Sloep, P. (2005). Effective learning networks. *Lifelong Learning in Europe*, *9*, 18-27.

Koper, R. & Specht, M. (2006). Ten-competence: Life-long competence development and learning. In M. Sicilia (Ed.), *Competences in organizational e-learning* (pp.230-247). Hershey, PA: Information Science Publishing.

Kort, B., Reilly, B., & Williams, N. (2002). *Experiences with civility and the role of a social contract in virtual communities.* Paper presented at the AAAI Fall Symposium 2002, North Falmouth, MA. Retrieved from http://web.media.mit.edu/~bkort/AAAI/kort-reilly-williams-aaai02.doc

Kosko, B. (1994). *Fuzzy thinking.* London: HarperCollins.

Krach, S., Blumel, I., Marjoram, D., Lataster, T., Krabbendam, L., Weber, J., . . . Kircher,
T. (2009). Are women better mindreaders? Sex differences in neural correlates of
mentalizing detected with functional MRI. *BMC Neuroscience, 10*(9). Retrieved from
http://www.biomedcentral.com/1471-2202/10/9

Kreijns, K., Kirschner, P., & Jochems, W. (2003). Identifying the pitfalls for social interaction
in computer-supported collaborative learning environments: a review of the research.
Computers in Human Behavior, 19(3), 335–53.

Kuh, G. D. (2001). Assessing what really matters to student learning: Inside the National
Survey of Student Engagement. *Change, 33*(3), 10–17.

Kurhila, J., Miettinen, M., Nokelainen, P., & Tirri, H. (2002). *Use of social navigation features in
collaborative e-learning.* Paper presented at the AACE E-Learn Conference 2002, Montreal,
Canada.

Kurzweil, R. (1990). *The age of the intelligent machine.* Cambridge, MA: MIT Press.

Lakoff, G. (1987). *Women, fire and dangerous things* (Kindle ed.). Chicago: University of
Chicago Press.

Langton, C. G. (1990). Computation at the edge of chaos: Phase transitions and emergent
computation. *Physica D: Nonlinear Phenomena, 42*(1–3), 12–37. doi: 10.1016/0167-
2789(90)90064-v.

Laroche, L., Nicol, C., & Mayer-Smith, J. (2007). New venues for science teacher education:
self-organizational pedagogy on the edge of chaos. *Complicity: An International Journal of
Complexity and Education, 4*(1). Retrieved from http://ejournals.library.ualberta.ca/index.
php/complicity/article/view/8761

Latour, B. (1987). *Science in action: How to follow scientists and engineers through society.*
Cambridge, MA: Harvard University Press.

Latour, B. (2005). *Reassembling the social: an introduction to actor-network theory* (Kindle ed.).
New York: Oxford University Press.

Lave, J., & Wenger, E. (1991). *Situated learning: Legitimate peripheral participation.* Cambridge:
University of Cambridge Press.

Law, J. (1992). Notes on the theory of the actor network: Ordering, strategy and
heterogeneity. *Systems Practice, 5*, 379–93.

Lee, H. (2005). Behavioral strategies for dealing with flaming in an online forum. *Sociological
Quarterly, 46*(2), 385–403.

Levin, A. (2004). Social software: What's new. [Web log post]. *Many 2 Many.* Retrieved from
http://many.corante.com/archives/2004/10/18/social_software_whats_new.php

Levinger, B. (1996). *Critical transitions: Human capacity development across the lifespan.* Newton,
MA: Educational Development Center.

LinkedIn. (2014). *About LinkedIn.* Retrieved from http://press.linkedin.com/about

Lipman, M. (1991). *Thinking in education.* Cambridge: Cambridge University Press.

Livingstone, D. W. (2000). *Exploring the icebergs of adult learning: Findings of the first Canadian
survey of informal learning practices.* The Research Network for New Approaches to
Lifelong Learning. Working Paper, #10. Retrieved from https://tspace.library.utoronto.
ca/retrieve/4451

Lorenz, E.N. (1963). Deterministic nonperiodic flow. *Journal of the Atmospheric Sciences, 20*, 130–141.

Lowe, W. (2000). Transactional distance theory as a foundation for developing innovative and reactive instruction. *Educational Technology & Society, 3*(1), 1–3.

Mackness, J., Mak, S. F. J., & Wiliams, R. (2010). *The ideals and reality of participating in a MOOC.* Paper presented at the 7th International Conference on Networked Learning, Aalborg, Denmark. Retrieved from http://www.lancs.ac.uk/fss/organisations/netlc/past/nlc2010/abstracts/Mackness.html

Malone, T., Laubacher, R., & Dellarocas, C. (2009). *Harnessing crowds: Mapping the genome of collective intelligence.* MIT Sloan School Working Paper 4732-09. Retrieved from http://18.7.29.232/bitstream/handle/1721.1/66259/SSRN-id1381502.pdf

Margolis, E. (2001). *The hidden curriculum of higher education.* London: Routledge.

Margolis, E., & Romero, M. (1998). "The department is very male, very white, very old, and very conservative": The functioning of the hidden curriculum in graduate sociology departments. *Harvard Educational Review, 68*(1), 1–32.

Marsick, V., & Watkins, K. (2001). Informal and incidental learning. *New Directions for Adult and Continuing Education, 89*, 25–34.

Mayer, R. (2004). Should there be a three-strikes rule against pure discovery learning? The case for guided methods of instruction. *American Psychologist, 59*(1), 14–19.

McCabe, D. L., & Trevino, L. K. (1996). What we know about cheating in college: Longitudinal trends and recent developments. *Change, 28*(1), 28–33.

McCarthy, H., Miller, P., & Skidmore, P. (2004). Introduction. In H. McCarthy, P. Miller, & P. Skidmore (Eds.), *Who governs in an interconnected world?* (pp. 11–21). London: Demos.

McCormick, N., & McCormick, J. (1992). Computer friends and foes: Content of undergraduates' electronic mail. *Computers in Human Behavior, 8*, 379–405.

McCormick, T. H., Salganick, M. J., & Zheng, T. (2010). How many people do you know?: Efficiently estimating personal network size. *Journal of the American Statistical Association, 105*(489), 59–70. doi: 10.1198/jasa.2009.ap08518

McLuhan, M. (1994). *Understanding media: The extensions of man.* Cambridge, MA: MIT Press.

Mehrabian, A. (1969). Some referents and measures of nonverbal behavior. *Behavioral Research Methods and Instruments, 1*(6), 205–07.

Mejias, U. (2005). A nomad's guide to learning and social software. Nov. 1, 2005. [Web log post]. Retrieved from http://blog.ulisesmejias.com/2005/11/01/a-nomads-guide-to-learning-and-social-software/

Merton, R. K. (1968). The Matthew effect in science: The reward and communication systems of science are considered. *Science, 159*(3810), 56–63.

Metcalfe, B. (1995). Metcalfe's Law: A network becomes more valuable as it reaches more users. *Infoworld, 17*(40), 53–54.

Michlmayr, E., Graf, S., Siberski, W., & Nejdl, W. (2005). *A case study on emergent semantics in communities.* Paper presented at the Proceedings of the Workshop on Social Network Analysis, International Semantic Web Conference (ISWC), Galway, Ireland.

Milgram, S. (1967). The small-world problem. *Psychology Today, 1*(1), 61–67.

Miller, P. (2010). *Smart swarm.* London: Collins.

Moore, M. G. (1993). Theory of transactional distance. In D. Keegan (Ed.), *Theoretical principles of distance education* (pp. 23–38). London: Routledge.

Moreland, R. L., & Levine, J. M. (1982). Socialization in small groups: Temporal changes in individual-group relations. *Advances in Experimental Social Psychology, 15*, 137–92.

Nardi, B. A., Schiano, D., & Gumbrecht, G. (2004). *Blogging as social activity, or, would you let 900 million people read your diary?* Paper presented at the Proceedings of the 2004 ACM conference on Computer supported cooperative work, Chicago, IL.

Nardi, B. A., Whittaker, S., & Schwarz, H. (2002). NetWORKers and their activity in intensional networks. *Computer Supported Cooperative Work (CSCW), 11*(1), 205–42.

Nemoto, K., Gloor, P., & Laubacher, R. (2011). *Social capital increases efficiency of collaboration among Wikipedia editors.* Paper presented at the Proceedings of the 22nd ACM conference on Hypertext and Hypermedia, Eindhoven, Netherlands.

Norman, D. A. (1993). *Things that make us smart: Defending human attributes in the age of the machine.* Cambridge, MA: Perseus Publishing.

Norton, A. (1909). *Readings in the history of education: Medieval universities.* Cambridge, MA: Harvard University Press.

O'Brien, T. (2010, January 10). Facebook's Mark Zuckerberg claims privacy is dead. [Web log post]. Retrieved from http://www.switched.com/2010/01/11/facebooks-mark-zuckerberg-claims-privacy-is-dead/

Oblinger, D. G., & Hawkins, B. L. (2006). IT myths. *EducausE review, 500.*

Okita, S. Y., Bailenson, J., & Schwartz, D. L. (2007). *The mere belief of social interaction improves learning.* Paper presented at the Twenty-ninth Meeting of the Cognitive Science Society, Nashville, TN.

Oliver, B. (2008). Commencing undergraduates' self-efficacy and ability in finding academic resources: Are they improving?. *Studies in Learning, Evaluation, Innovation and Development, 5*, 1–8.

Page, L., Brin, S., Motwani, R., & Winograd, T. (1999). *The PageRank citation ranking: Bringing order to the web.* Stanford, CA: Stanford InfoLab.

Page, S. E. (2008). *The difference: How the power of diversity creates better groups, firms, schools, and societies* (New ed.; Kindle ed.). Princeton, NJ: Princeton University Press.

Page, S. E. (2011). *Diversity and complexity.* Princeton, NJ: Princeton University Press.

Palen, L., & Dourish, P. (2003). *Unpacking privacy for a networked world.* Proceedings of the SIGCHI Conference on Human Factors in Computing Systems, ACM, New York, 129–36.

Palloff, R., & Pratt, K. (2005). *Online learning communities revisited.* Paper presented at the 21st Annual Conference on Distance Teaching and Learning, Madison, WI. Retrieved from http://www.uwex.edu/disted/conference/Resource_library/proceedings/05_1801.pdf

Pan, B., Hembrooke, H., Joachims, T., Lorigo, L., Gay, G., & Granka, L. (2007). In Google we trust: Users' decisions on rank, position, and relevance. *Journal of Computer-Mediated Communication, 12*(3), 801–23. doi: 10.1111/j.1083-6101.2007.00351.x

Panitz, T. (1997). The case for student centered instruction via collaborative learning paradigms. [Web log post]. Retrieved from http://home.capecod.net/~tpanitz/tedsarticles/coopbenefits.htm

Pariser, E. (2011). The filter bubble: What the Internet is hiding from you (Kindle ed.). New York: Penguin.

Pask, G. (1976). *Conversation theory: Applications in education and epistemology.* Amsterdam: Elsevier.

Paulsen, M. F. (2003). *Online education and learning management systems: Global e-learning in a Scandinavian perspective.* Oslo: NKI Forlaget.

Pedersen, S., & Macafee, C. (2007). Gender differences in British blogging. *Journal of Computer-Mediated Communication, 12*(4), 1472–1492.

Petrič, G. (2006). Conceptualizing and measuring the social uses of the Internet: The case of personal web sites. *The Information Society, 22*(5), 291–301.

Pfuetze, P. (1954). *The social self.* New York: Bookman.

Piaget, J. (1952). *The origins of intelligence in children.* New York: Basic Books.

Piaget, J. (1970). *Structuralism.* New York: Basic Books.

Piatt, K. (2009). Using alternate reality games to support first year induction with ELGG. *Campus-Wide Information Systems, 26*(4), 313–22.

Pick, T. (2012, 24 July). 72 fascinating social media marketing facts and statistics for 2012 [Web log post]. Retrieved from http://www.jeffbullas.com/2012/07/24/72-fascinating-social-media-marketing-facts-and-statistics-for-2012/

Piezon, S., & Ferree, W. (2008). Perceptions of social loafing in online learning groups. *The International Review of Research in Open and Distance Learning, 9*(2). Retrieved from http://www.irrodl.org/index.php/irrodl/article/view/484/1034

Plato. (1993). *Symposium and Phaedrus.* (B. Jowett, trans.). New York: Dover Publications.

Platt, P., & Willard, A. (1998, May). *The ramblers guide to virtual environments.* Paper presented at the 3D Interface for the Information Worker IEE Colloquium, (Digest No. 1998/437).

Polanyi, M. (1966). *The tacit dimension.* London: Routledge.

Popkewitz, T. S. (1998). Dewey, Vygotsky, and the social administration of the individual: Constructivist pedagogy as systems of ideas in historical spaces. *American Educational Research Journal, 35*, 535–570.

Porter, J. (2008). *Designing for the social web.* Berkeley, CA: New Riders.

Poscente, K. R., & Fahy, P. J. (2003). Investigating triggers in CMC text transcripts. *The International Review of Research in Open and Distance Learning, 4*(2). Retrieved from http://www.irrodl.org/index.php/irrodl/article/view/141/221

Potgieter, F., Basson, R., Roeloffse, J., Steyn, H., Steyn, P., & Steyn, N. (2006). *Towards a philosophy of mLearning: A (South) African perspective.* Paper presented at the mLearn 2006 Conference, Banff, Canada.

Pushpa, M. (2012). ACO in e-Learning: Towards an adaptive learning path. *International Journal on Computer Science and Engineering, 4*(3), 458–62.

Radosevich, D., Salomon, R. & Kahn, P. (2008). Using student response systems to increase motivation, learning, and knowledge retention. *Innovate: Journal of Online Education, 5*(1).

Rafaeli, S., Raban, D. R., & Ravid, G. (2007). Knowledge sharing market. *International Journal of Knowledge and Learning, 3*(1), 1–11.

Rainie, L., & Wellman, B. (2012). *Networked* (Kindle ed.). Cambridge, MA: MIT Press.

Ranganathan, S. R. (2006). *Colon classification* (6th ed.). Delhi, India: ESS Publications.

Renner, R. A. (2009). Ebooks–costs and benefits to academic and research libraries. *Springer. com*. Retrieved from http://www.izdot.com/hive_media/app/webroot/img/publication/sample/publication-174-.pdf

Resnick, P. (2001). Beyond bowling together: Sociotechnical capital. In J. Carroll (Ed.), *Human-computer interaction in the new millennium* (pp. 647–72). New York: Addison-Wesley.

Revans, R. (1982). *The origins and growth of action learning.* London: Chartwell-Bratt.

Richards, G., Hatala, M., & Donkers, P. (2006). Campus Canada records of learning: Secure validation of competence assertions. *Proceedings of International Workshop in Learning Networks for Lifelong Competence Development.* Retrieved from http://dspace. learningnetworks.org

Richardson, J., & Newby, T. (2006). The role of students' cognitive engagement in online learning. *American Journal of Distance Education, 20*(1), 23–37.

Richardson, W. (2006). The new face of learning. *Edutopia, 2*(7). Retrieved http://www. innovationlabs.com/newhighschool/2006/reading%20materials/newfaceoflearning.pdf

Ridgeway, C. L. (1983). *The dynamics of small groups.* New York: St. Martin's Press.

Ridley, M. (2010). *The rational optimist: How prosperity evolves.* London, UK: HarperCollins e-books.

Riedl, M. O., & Amant, R. S. (2003). *Social navigation: Modeling, simulation, and experimentation.* Paper presented at the 2nd International Joint Conference on Autonomous Agents and Multi Agent Systems, Melbourne, Australia.

Roberts, S. J. (1983). Oppressed group behavior: Implications for nursing. *ANS Adv Nurs Sci, 5*, 21–30.

Romero, J., & Machado, P. (2008). *The art of artificial evolution: A handbook on evolutionary art and music.* New York: Springer.

Rose, M. (2004). Comparing productive online dialogue in two group styles: Cooperative and collaborative. *American Journal of Distance Education, 18*(2), 73–88.

Rourke, L., & Anderson, T. (2002). Exploring social presence in computer conferencing. *Journal of Interactive Learning Research, 13*(3), 259–275.

Ru, Z., Guo, J., & Xu, W. (2008). Improving expertise recommender systems by odds ratio. In H. Li, T. Liu, W-Y. Ma, T. Sakai, K-F. Wong, & G. Zhou (Eds.), *Information Retrieval Technology* (Vol. 4993, pp. 1–9). Berlin / Heidelberg: Springer.

Russell, T. L. (2001). *No significant difference phenomenon.* New York: International Distance Education Certification Centre.

Russell, T. L. (2010). No significant difference. [Web log post]. Retrieved from http://www. nosignificantdifference.org/

Ryberg, T., Dirckinck-Holmfeld, L., & Jones, C. (2010). Catering to the needs of the "digital natives" or educating the "Net Generation". In M.Lee & C.McLoughlin (Eds.) *Web 2.0-based e-learning: Applying social informatics for tertiary teaching* (pp. 301–318). Hershey, PA: IGI Global.

Saba, F., & Shearer, R. L. (1994). Verifying key theoretical concepts in a dynamic model of distance education. *The American Journal of Distance Education, 8*(1), 36–59.

Salganik, M. J., Dobbs, P. S., & Watts, D. J. (2006). Experimental study of inequality and unpredictability in an artificial cultural market. *Science, 311*(5762), 854–56.

Salmon, G. (1993). *Distributed cognitions: Psychological and educational considerations*. Cambridge: Cambridge University Press.

Salmon, G. (2000). *E-moderating: The key to teaching and learning online*. London: Kogan Page.

Salmon, G., & Perkins, D. N. (1998). Individual and social aspects of learning. *Review of Research in Education, 23*, 1–24.

Sandberg, A. (2003). We, Borg: Speculations on hive minds as a posthuman state. Retrieved from http://www.aleph.se/Trans/Global/Posthumanity/WeBorg.html

Sandefur, R., & Laumann, E. (1988). A paradigm for social capital. *Rationality and Society, 10*(4), 481–501.

Sanders, R. H., & Dunn, J. M. (2010). The Bologna Accord: A model of cooperation and coordination. *Quest, 62*(1), 92–105.

Schlager, M., & Fusco, J. (2004). Teacher professional development, technology, and communities of practice: Are we putting the cart before the horse? In S. A. Barab, R. Kling, & J. Gray (Eds.), *Designing for virtual communities in the service of learning* (pp. 120–153). New York: Cambridge University Press.

Schrage, M. (2003). Flaming ideas. *Technology Review, 106* (2), 23.

Schwartz, B. (2004). *The paradox of choice: Why less is more*. New York: HarperCollins.

Segaran, T. (2007). *Programming collective intelligence* (Kindle ed.). Sebastopol, CA: O'Reilly.

Semet, Y., Lutton, E., & Collet, P. (2003). *Ant colony optimisation for e-learning: Observing the emergence of pedagogic suggestions*. Paper presented at the IEEE SIS 2003, Indianapolis, IN.

Severance, C. (2012). Teaching the world: Daphne Koller and Coursera. *Computer, 45*(8), 8–9.

Shah, R., & Sandvig, C. (2005). Software defaults as de facto regulation: The case of wireless APs. *TPRC 2005*. Retrieved from http://papers.ssrn.com/sol3/papers.cfm?abstract_id=2120272

Shirky, C. (2003). A group is its own worst enemy [Web log post]. Retrieved from http://www.shirky.com/writings/group_enemy.html

Shirky, C. (2008). *Here comes everybody: The power of organizing without organizations*. New York: Penguin Press.

Shulman, L. (2002). Making differences: A table of learning. *Change Magazine, 34*(6), 36–44.

Siemens, G. (2005). Connectivism: A learning theory for the digital age. *International Journal of Instructional Technology and Distance Learning, 2*(1), 3–10.

Siemens, G. (2006). *Knowing knowledge*. Lulu.com.

Siemens, G. (2012, July 25). MOOCs are really a platform [Web log post]. Retrieved from http://www.elearnspace.org/blog/2012/07/25/moocs-are-really-a-platform/

Singh, S., & Dron, J. (2002). Networking: a study in planning and developing cross-cultural collaboration. *ALT-J, 10*(2), 29–37.

Skinner, B. F. (1974). *About behaviorism*. New York: Vintage Books.

Sloep, P., Kester, L., Brouns, F., Van Rosmalen, P., De Vries, F., De Croock, M., & Koper, R. (2007). Ad hoc transient communities to enhance social interaction and spread tutor responsibilities. *IASTED International Conference Web-Based Education, 2*, 548–554.

Smirnova, E., & Balog, K. (2011). A user-oriented model for expert finding advances in information retrieval. In P. Clough, C. Foley, C. Gurrin, G. Jones, W. Kraaij, H. Lee, &

V. Mudoch (Eds.), *Advances in Informational Retrieval* (Vol. 6611, pp. 580–92). Berlin / Heidelberg: Springer.

Smith, A., & Lias, A. (2005). Identity theft and e-fraud as critical CRM concerns. *International Journal of Enterprise Information Systems*, 1(2), 17–36.

Smith, J. D. (2001). Group development: A review of the literature learning together and a commentary on future research directions. *Group Facilitation*, 31(3), 14–45.

Somenarain, L., Akkaraju, S., & Gharbaran, R. (2010). Student perceptions and learning outcomes in asynchronous and synchronous online learning environments in a biology course. *Journal of Online Learning and Teaching*, 6(2).

Spiro, R. J., Coulson, R., Feltovich, P., & Anderson, D. K. (1988). Cognitive flexibility: advanced knowledge acquisition ill-structured domains. In V. Patel (Ed.), *Proceedings of the 10th Annual Conference of the Cognitive Science Society*. Hillsdale, NJ: Erlbaum.

Springer, L., Stanne, M., & Donovan, S. (1999). Effects of small-group learning on undergraduates in science, mathematics, engineering and technology: A meta-analysis. *Review of Educational Research*, 16(1), 21–51.

Sproull, L., & Kiesler, S. (1986). Reducing social context cues: Electronic mail in organizational communication. *Management Science*, 32(11), 1492–1513.

Stanier, S. (2010). Community@Brighton: The development of an institutional shared learning environment. In J. O'Donoghue, *Technology-supported environments for personalized learning: Methods and case studies* (pp. 50–73). Hershey: IGI Global.

Strater, K., & Richter, H. (2007, July). Examining privacy and disclosure in a social networking community. In *Proceedings of the 3rd symposium on usable privacy and security* (pp. 157–158). ACM.

Stein, D. S., Wanstreet, C. E., Calvin, J., Overtoom, C., & Wheaton, J. E. (2005). Bridging the transactional distance gap in online learning environments. *American Journal of Distance Education*, 19(2), 105–19.

Strayer, J. F. (2007). The effects of the classroom flip on the learning environment: A comparison of learning activity in a traditional classroom and a flip classroom that used an intelligent tutoring system (Doctoral dissertation). Ohio State University, US.

Statisticbrain. (2014a). Facebook statistics. Retrieved from http://www.statisticbrain.com/facebook-statistics/

Statisticbrain. (2014b). Networking statistics. Retrieved from http://www.statisticbrain.com/social-networking-statistics/

Surowiecki, J. (2004). *The wisdom of crowds*. London: Little, Brown.

Sutton, J., Harris, C., Keil, P., & Barnier, A. (2010). The psychology of memory, extended cognition, and socially distributed remembering. *Phenomenology and the Cognitive Sciences*, 9(4), 521–60. doi: 10.1007/s11097-010-9182-y

Swan, K. R., Ice, P., Shea, P., Cleveland-Innes, M., Diaz, S., Garrison, R. (2008). Researching online communities of inquiry: New CoI survey instrument. *Proceedings of World Conference on Educational Multimedia, Hypermedia and Telecommunications*, 5812–5820.

Taleb, N. (2007). *The black swan: The impact of the highly improbable*. New York: Random House.

Talja, S. (2002). Information sharing in academic communities: Types and levels of collaboration in information seeking and use. *New Review of Information Behavioural Research, 3*, 143–159.

Tattersall, C., van den Berg, B., van Es, R., Janssen, J., Manderveld, J., & Koper, R. (2004). *Swarm-based adaptation: Wayfinding support for lifelong learners.* Paper presented at the Adaptive Hypermedia and Adaptive Web-Based Systems Third International Conference, Eindhoven, The Netherlands.

Terveen, L., Hill, W., Amento, B., McDonald, D., & Creter, J. (1997). PHOAKS: A system for sharing recommendations. *Communications of the ACM, 40*(3), 59–62.

Thompson, T. L. (2011). Work-learning in informal online communities: evolving spaces. *Information Technology & People, 24*(2), 184–96.

Tinto, V. (1975). Dropout from higher education: A theoretical synthesis of recent research. *Review of Educational Research, 45*(1), 89–125.

Tough, A. (1979). *The adult learning projects* (2nd ed.). Toronto, ON: Ontario Institute for Studies in Education.

Townsend, A. M., DeMarie, S. M., & Hendrickson, A. R. (1998). Virtual teams: Technology and the workplace of the future. *The Academy of Management Executive, 12*(3), 17–29.

Triandis, H. C. (2004). The many dimensions of culture—Academic commentary. *The Academy of Management Executive, 18*(1), 88–93.

Tuckman, B. W., & Jensen, M. A. C. (1977). Stages of small-group development revisited. *Group & Organization Management, 2*(4), 419–27.

Turchin, V., & Joslyn, C. (1989). *The cybernetic manifesto.* Principia Cybernetica Web. http://pespmc1.vub.ac.be/MANIFESTO.html

Turkle, S. (2011). *Alone together.* New York: Basic Books.

Turner, M., & Pratkanis, A. (1998). Twenty-five years of groupthink theory and research. *Organizational Behavior and Human Decision Processes, 73*(2–3), 105–15.

Usher, E. & Pajares, F. (2008). Sources of self-efficacy in school: Critical review of the literature and future directions. *Review of Educational Research, 78*(4), 751–796.

Vaill, P. (1996). *Learning as a way of being: Strategies for survival in a world of permanent white water.* San Francisco: Jossey-Bass.

Van de Ven, A. D., Delbecq, A., Koenig, R. (1976). Determinants of coordination modes within organizations. *American Sociological Review, 41*(2), 322–38.

van den Berg, B., van Es, R., Tattersall, C., Janssen, J., Manderveld, J., Brouns, F., . . . Koper, R. (2005, September). *Swarm-based sequencing recommendations in e-learning.* Paper presented at the Intelligent Systems Design and Applications, Wroclaw, Poland.

Vander Wal, T. (2007). Folksonomy [Web log post]. Retrieved from http://vanderwal.net/folksonomy.html

van Gelderen, E. (2010). *An introduction to the grammar of English* (Rev. ed.). Philadelphia, PA: John Benjamins Publishing Company.

Vasalou, A., Joinson, A. N., & Courvoisier, D. (2010). Cultural differences, experience with social networks and the nature of "true commitment" in Facebook. *International Journal of Human-Computer Studies, 68*(10), 719–28.

Vassileva, J. (2008). Toward social learning environments. *IEEE Transactions on Learning Technologies, 1*(4), 199–214.

von Hippel, E. (2005). Democratizing innovation: The evolving phenomenon of user innovation. *Journal für Betriebswirtschaft, 55*(1), 63–78. doi: 10.1007/s11301-004-0002-8

Voss, J. (2005). *Measuring Wikipedia.* Paper presented at the Conference of the International Society for Scientometrics and Informetrics.

Vygotsky, L.S. (1978). *Mind and Society: The development of higher psychological processes.* Cambridge, MA: Harvard University Press.

Walther, J. B. (1994). Anticipated ongoing interaction versus channel effects on relational communication in computer-mediated interaction. *Human Communication Research, 20,* 473–502.

Walther, J. B. (1996). Computer mediated communication: Impersonal, interpersonal, and hyperpersonal interaction. *Communication Research, 23*(1), 3–43.

Warnick, B. R. (2008). *Imitation and education: A philosophical inquiry into learning by example.* New York: SUNY Press.

Waterfield, B. (2012, December 7). Text messages direct to your contact lens. *The Daily Telegraph.* Retrieved from http://www.telegraph.co.uk/technology/news/9729403/Text-messages-direct-to-your-contact-lens.html

Watts, D. (2003). *Six degrees: The science of a connected age.* New York: Norton.

Wearsocial. (2014). WhatsApp hits billion daily messages. Retrieved from http://wearesocial.net/blog/2014/03/whatsapp-hits-billion-daily-messages

Wei, R., & Lo, V.-H. (2006). Staying connected while on the move. *New Media & Society, 8*(1), 53–72. doi: 10.1177/1461444806059870

Weiss, R. P. (2000). Brain-based learning. *Alexandria-American Society for Training and Development, 54*(7), 20–24.

Wellman, B., Boase, J., & Chen, W. (2002). The networked nature of community: Online and offline. *IT & Society, 1*(1). Retrieved from http://homes.chass.utoronto.ca/~wellman/publications/networkednature/vol01-1-A10-Wellman-Boase-Chen.PDF

Wenger, E. (1998). *Communities of practice: Learning, meaning and identity.* New York: Cambridge University Press.

Wenger, E., Trayner, B., & Laat, M. d. (2011). *Promoting and assessing value creation in communities and networks: A conceptual framework.* Heerlen, Netherlands: Ruud de Moor Centrum, Open Universiteit of the Netherlands.

Wexelblat, A., & Maes, P. (1999, May). *Footprints: History-rich tools for information foraging.* Paper presented at the CHI '99 Conference on Human factors in Computing Systems, Pittsburgh, PA.

Wikimedia. (2014). Wikipedia statistics. Retrieved from: http://stats.wikimedia.org/EN/Sitemap.htm, 2014

Wilson, B., Ludwig-Hardman, S., Thornam, C., & Dunlap, J. (2004). Bounded community: Designing and facilitating learning communities in formal courses. International Review of Research on Open and Distance Learning, 5(3). Retrieved from http://www.irrodl.org/index.php/irrodl/article/view/204/286

Wilson, E. O. (2012). *The social conquest of earth* (Kindle ed.). New York: Liveright Pub. Corporation.

Wilson, S., Liber, O., Johnson, M., Beauvoir, P., Sharples, P., & Milligan, C. (2007). Personal learning environments: Challenging the dominant design of educational systems. *Journal of e-Learning and Knowledge Society, 3*(2), 27–38.

Winner, L. (1997). Resisting technoglobalism's assault on higher education. In M. Moll (Ed.), *Tech high: Globalization and the future of Canadian education.* Ottawa, ON: Canadian Centre for Policy Alternatives. Fernwood Publishing.

Wittgenstein, L. (1965). *Philosophical investigations.* (G.E.M. Ancombe, Trans.). New York: Macmillan.

Wöhner, T., Köhler, S., & Peters, R. (2011). *Automatic reputation assessment in Wikipedia.* ICIS Conference Shanghai. Retrieved from http://aisel.aisnet.org/icis2011/proceedings/onlinecommunity/5/

Wong, L.-H., & Looi, C.-K. (2010). Swarm intelligence: New techniques for adaptive systems to provide learning support. *Interactive Learning Environments, 20*(1), 19–40. doi: 10.1080/10494821003714681

Yang, Y. J., & Wu, C. (2009). An attribute-based ant colony system for adaptive learning object recommendation. *Expert Systems Application, 36*(2), 3034–47. doi: 10.1016/j.eswa.2008.01.066

Yeats, W. B. (1956). *The collected poems of W. B. Yeats.* New York: Macmillan.

Young, J. R. (2010). High-tech cheating abounds and professors bear some blame. *Chronicle of Higher Education* (March), 28.

Yu, Z. (2009). *Wiki-enabled emergent knowledge processes through acceleration of stigmergic collaboration* (Master of Philosophy Dissertation). City University of Hong Kong, Hong Kong.

Zacker.org. (2014). Higher-ed LMS market penetration: Moodle vs. Blackboard+WebCT vs. Sakai. Retrieved from zacker.org/higher-ed-lms-market-penetration-moodle-vs-blackboard-vs-sakai

Zaslow, J. (2002, November 26). If TiVo thinks you are gay, here's how to set it straight. *Wall Street Journal.*

Zhang, A. (2003). *Transactional distance in web-based college learning environments: Towards measurement and theory construction* (Doctoral dissertation). Virginia Commonwealth University, Richmond, Virginia.

INDEX